T&T Clark Religion and the University Series

Series editors:

Gavin D'Costa
Mervyn Davies
Peter Hampson

Volume 2

Christianity and the Disciplines
The Transformation of the University

Religion and the University Series

The *Religion and the University Series* is concerned with the revitalization of Christian culture through the reform of the University and more widely with the revitalization of religious culture through University education. The series aims to demonstrate a creative and imaginative role for the Christian theological perspective within the university setting. Contributions to this series are welcome and prospective editors and authors can gain further information at http://continuumbooks.com/series/detail.aspx?SeriesId=2220.

Christianity and the Disciplines is the second volume in the series. The first volume was concerned to demonstrate positively the creative relationship between philosophy and theology; this second one seeks to facilitate a critical and positive relationship between Christianity and the wide variety of intellectual disciplines. Subsequent volumes will broaden and deepen these discussions.

The common assumptions driving the first two volumes are: (a) theology operates within an ecclesial context, being accountable to the community of faith within the rigours of reason informed by faith, and stimulated and informed through contact with the sources of belief and lived experience of it; (b) philosophy operates with a limited autonomy accountable to the community of faith as well as the wider professional guild of philosophers; (c) philosophy is the handmaiden to theology and together they form a bridge to relate to the other sciences and disciplines; (d) that the many disciplines have been shaped by the university culture within which they have developed and sometimes, not always, their presuppositions, methods and focus of enquiry can be inimical to the Christian faith; (e) Christians working in the secular academy or within a Christian university within these disciplines have the task of uncovering these issues, when appropriate, and showing the positive and creative relationship these disciplines have with the Christian vision; (f) the idea of a Christian university should be viewed positively.

Oliver Crisp is Professor of Systematic Theology at Fuller Theological Seminary, Pasadena and formerly Reader in Theology at the University of Bristol.

Gavin D'Costa is Professor of Catholic Theology at the University of Bristol. He is also adviser to Committees of the Church of England and the Roman Catholic Church on Theology and Other Faiths.

Mervyn Davies is Scholar in Residence at Sarum College, Salisbury and honorary Senior Lecturer in Theology at the University of Bristol.

Peter Hampson is Visiting Fellow at Blackfriars Hall, Oxford, Emeritus Professor of Psychology at the University of the West of England and Adjunct Honorary Professor of Psychology at the National University of Ireland, Maynooth.

Christianity and the Disciplines

The Transformation of the University

Edited by

Oliver D. Crisp
Gavin D'Costa
Mervyn Davies
and
Peter Hampson

Foreword by

Most Revd and Rt Hon. Rowan Williams
(Archbishop of Canterbury)

B L O O M S B U R Y

LONDON · NEW DELHI · NEW YORK · SYDNEY

Bloomsbury T&T Clark
An imprint of Bloomsbury Publishing Plc

50 Bedford Square   1385 Broadway
London   New York
WC1B 3DP   NY 10018
UK   USA

www.bloomsbury.com

Bloomsbury is a registered trade mark of Bloomsbury Publishing Plc

First published 2012
Paperback edition first published 2014

British Library Cataloguing-in-Publication Data
A catalogue record for this book is available from the British Library.

ISBN: HB: 978-0-567-04045-9
PB: 978-0-567-57111-3

Library of Congress Cataloging-in-Publication Data
A catalogue record for this book is available from the Library of Congress.

Typeset by Newgen Imaging Systems Pvt Ltd, Chennai, India
Printed and bound in Great Britain

Contents

Foreword

Rowan Williams

If theology is about the truth, it has to be engaged – intensely, riskily, care-fully – with all the ways in which human beings in general talk about truth and believe they discover and cope with it. Thomas Aquinas, in response to the well-intentioned but disastrous idea that 'religious' truth belonged to a differ-ent order from other truth claims, insisted that there were not several different kinds of truth but ultimately one. But equally, he and the tradition he represents reject the two obvious mistakes that can arise in the wake of this. We cannot say that theology simply supplies 'truths' that are lacking in other disciplines in the sense of giving supplementary information; and we cannot proceed on the assumption that the way in which truth claims are arrived at in other discourses can be borrowed and expected to work in theology. In other words, theology has to think about what its claims to truthfulness mean, and it has to have at least some purchase on the question of what it is simply to think and to know.

Because theology is not based on a set of revealed propositions (which is not the same as saying that it can manage without propositional content), it can slip into a sentimental and impressionistic mode at times, focusing on the edifying effect of certain ways of talking and taking refuge in an appeal to metaphor or the 'poetic' in ways that are both dated and muddled. Any useful discussion of metaphor, as recent decades have abundantly shown, demands some hard think-ing about language and reference. And any working poet would be surprised to be told that their work was absolved from precision or from the inexorable dif-ficulty of truth-telling. If theology is indeed to be a participant worth listening to in the conversation of the academy, it needs – perhaps not to have a theory of language and reference – but certainly to be able to display what it thinks about thought and knowing.

And it will do this as it always has when it is serious – by grappling with what is being said more widely about these things. As the historical essays in volume 1 demonstrate, this sometimes means that theologians become both embroiled in unwinnable arguments (unwinnable because no one defines their terms properly) and seduced by what look like decisive and compelling models. But without false starts no progress is made: it is almost always the interesting mistake that really generates fresh mental energy. There is no honest avoiding of these risks. And here in this the second volume of this collection, we are helped to see how a wide variety of 'sense-making' practices and discourses can be involved with theology in the work of finding sustainable, defensible ways of talking about humanity that do not leave out what is awkward or settle for what works in the small scale and short term. As has often been said, theology is bound to be an anthropology – and if it is, it is immediately bound up with other anthropologies, discussing, affirming, contesting and, so theology would claim, always enlarging. What theology constantly looks to is a way of characterizing what is human that makes it clear that there is no adequate 'humanism' without reference to God, and, more specifically, to the Second Adam.

These essays, then, make the ambitious presupposition that theology cannot escape ontology of some sort, and so has to do the work that is so comprehensively and clearly set out here. And in a university world where what counts as knowing, what counts as sustainable truth claims and, ultimately, what counts as 'humanistic' are all issues surrounded by some confusion at the moment, theology's contribution to the conversation is not trivial. The humanities sorely need defences against functionalist barbarity – and so, for that matter, do most of the sciences. And what happens to these questions in the university is significant for what happens to them in our culture overall. Academic questions are not – as it were – purely academic questions.

Theology has the opportunity of saying essential and properly awkward things in current debates about scholarship and learning. These essays are an impressively comprehensive resource as we seek to make the best use of such an opportunity.

Archbishop Rowan Williams

Notes on Contributors

Lucy Beckett taught English, Latin and History for 20 years at Ampleforth Abbey and College. Her books include *In the Light of Christ: Writings in the Western Tradition* (Ignatius Press, 2006), a study of more than 30 writers from Plato to Czeslaw Milosz in relation to Christian truth and the history of Christianity and *A Postcard from the Volcano*, a novel set in Weimar, Germany (Ignatius Press, 2009), shortlisted for the Dayton Literary Peace Prize 2010. She has lectured widely, including at Notre Dame University, and regularly reviews for the *Times Literary Supplement*.

William Cavanaugh is Senior Research Professor in the Center for World Catholicism and Intercultural Theology at DePaul University. His latest books are *Migrations of the Holy* (Eerdmans, 2011) and *The Myth of Religious Violence* (Oxford, 2009). His books have been translated into French, Spanish and Polish. His areas of specialization are political theology, economic ethics and ecclesiology.

Fernando Cervantes is Reader in History at the University of Bristol. He is the author of *The Devil in the New World* (Yale, 1994) and has published widely on the intellectual and religious history of early modern Spain and Spanish America. He has held fellowships at the Institute for Advanced Study, Princeton, the Centre for Medieval and Renaissance Studies, UCLA and the Liguria Study Centre for the Arts and the Humanities, Bogliasco, Italy. In the spring quarter of 2009 he held the Tipton Distinguished Visiting Chair at the University of California, Santa Barbara.

Oliver Crisp (editor) is Professor of Systematic Theology at Fuller Theological Seminary, Pasadena, USA, formerly Reader in Theology at the University of Bristol, UK. He has taught at the University of St Andrews and Regent College, Vancouver, BC, and held two research fellowships in the United States. He is author or co-editor of *Jonathan Edwards: Philosophical Theologian* with Paul Helm (Ashgate, 2003), *Jonathan Edwards and the Metaphysics of Sin* (Ashgate, 2005), *Divinity and Humanity: The Incarnation Reconsidered* (Cambridge, 2007), *An American Augustinian: Sin and Salvation in the Dogmatic Theology* *of William G. T. Shedd* (Paternoster and Wipf & Stock, 2007) and *Analytic Theology: New Essays in the Philosophy of Theology,* edited with Michael Rea (Oxford, 2009).

Mervyn Davies (editor and contributor) is Scholar in Residence at Sarum College, Salisbury, where he lectures on Christian Spirituality and is Programme Leader for the master's programme in Christian Approaches to Leadership. He is also an honorary Senior Lecturer in Theology at the University of Bristol supervising postgraduate students in Newman studies. He has organized and contributed to numerous conferences in the United Kingdom on Newman especially aimed at the wider public. He also works nationally with Anglican, Methodist and Catholic organizations on ecumenical, theological and organizational approaches to Christian Leadership. He was formerly Director of Studies at Wesley College, Bristol, and for 11 years Principal of a Sixth Form College. His recent books include editing *A Thankful Heart and a Discerning Mind* (2010) and (co-authored) *Leadership for a People of Hope* (Continuum, 2011).

Gavin D'Costa (editor) is Professor of Catholic Theology, University of Bristol. He advises the Church of England and Roman Catholic Committees on Other Faiths on theology and other faiths, and also the Pontifical Council for Other Faiths, Vatican City. In 1998 he was visiting Professor at the Gregorian University, Rome. His publications include: co-written, *Only One Way? Three Christian Responses on the Uniqueness of Christ in a Religiously Plural World* (SCM, 2011); *Christianity and World Religions, Disputed Questions in the Theology of Religions* (Blackwell, 2009); *Theology and the Public Square: Church, University and Nation* (Blackwell, 2005); *The Meeting of Religions and the Trinity* (Orbis Books, 2000).

Celia Deane-Drummond is Professor in Theology at the University of Notre Dame, IN, USA. Previously she held a Chair in Theology and the Biological Sciences at the University of Chester, UK. In May 2011 she was elected Chair of EFSRE. In 2009 she was seconded to CAFOD. Her recent books include *ReOrdering Nature* (Continuum, 2003), *The Ethics of Nature* (Wiley-Blackwell, 2004), *Ecotheology* (DLT, 2008), *Christ and Evolution* (Fortress, 2009), editor *Creaturely Theology* (SCM Press, 2009), *Seeds of Hope* (CAFOD, 2010), editor *Religion and Ecology in the Public Sphere* (Continuum, 2011), editor *Rising to Life* (CAFOD, 2011).

Richard Finn OP is a Dominican Friar and Fellow of Blackfriars Hall, Oxford. He is a member of the Theology and Classics Faculties of Oxford University. He is the author of *Almsgiving in the Later Roman Empire* (Oxford University Press, 2006) and *Asceticism in the Graeco-Roman World* (Cambridge University Press, 2009). He served as Regent of Blackfriars Hall, Oxford, from 2004 until Easter 2012.

Peter Hampson (editor and contributor) is a Visiting Fellow at Blackfriars Hall, Oxford. He was formerly Professor of Psychology at the University of the West of England, Bristol. His publications include (with Peter Morris) *Imagery and Consciousness* (Academic Press, 1983), *Understanding Cognition* (Blackwell, 1996) and co-edited (with David Marks and John Richardson) *Imagery: Current Developments* (Routledge, 1990). His current research interests include theology–psychology dialogue, the rationality, assumptions and fideistic bases of different intellectual traditions, and religion, theology and interdisciplinarity in contemporary higher education.

John Harper is RSCM Research Professor of Christian Music and Liturgy at Bangor University, where he directs an International Centre for Sacred Music Studies, and is Emeritus Director, The Royal School of Church Music. He is the author of *The Forms and Orders of Western Liturgy* (1992) and executive editor of the monastic hymnal, *Hymns for Prayer and Praise (1996, 2011)*, and *Music for Common Worship (2000–07)*; from 2009 to 2012 he has led the research project *The Experience of Worship in Late Medieval Cathedral and Parish Church*. During the 1970s he directed the music at St Chad's Cathedral, Birmingham; in the 1980s he was Fellow, Organist and Tutor of Magdalen College, Oxford.

Michael Heller is Professor at the Philosophical Faculty of the Pontifical University of John Paul II in Cracow. He is a member of the Pontifical Academy of the Sciences in Rome, and an adjoint member of the Vatican Astronomical Observatory (*Specola Vaticana*). He is a laureate of the Templeton Prize and founder of the Copernicus Center for Interdisciplinary Studies. His scientific interests cover the fields of relativistic physics, especially relativistic cosmology, mathematical methods in physics, history and philosophy of science, and relations between science and theology. He has authored several books and many research papers, and is also a member of many international societies.

Robin Kirkpatrick is Professor Emeritus of Italian and English Literatures at the University of Cambridge. He has written numerous books on Dante's work including *Dante's Paradiso and the Limitations of Modern Criticism* (Cambridge University Press, 2010) and on the relationship between Italian and English literature in the Renaissance, such as *English and Italian Literature from Dante to Shakespeare: A Study of Source, Analogue and Divergence* (Longman, 1995) and *The Renaissance (Arts Culture and Society in the Western World)* (Longman, 2001). He is a poet. His translation of Dante's *Commedia*, published by Penguin, has been on the shelves in various editions since 2006.

Alister McGrath is Professor of Theology, Ministry, and Education at King's College London, and head of its Centre for Theology, Religion and Culture. He was formerly Professor of Historical Theology at Oxford University. After his undergraduate degree in Chemistry, McGrath gained an Oxford doctorate for his work in molecular biophysics. Many of his recent publications focus on the relation of theology and the biological sciences, especially his *Darwinism and the Divine: Evolutionary Thought and Natural Theology* (Blackwell, 2011).

Vittorio Montemaggi is Assistant Professor of Religion and Literature in the Department of Romance Languages and Literatures at the University of Notre Dame, where he is also Concurrent Assistant Professor in the Department of Theology and Fellow of the Nanovic Institute for European Studies. His publications include *Dante's 'Commedia': Theology as Poetry* (University of Notre Dame Press, 2010), co-edited with Matthew Treherne.

John Polkinghorne worked for 25 years as a theoretical particle physicist before becoming an ordained Anglican priest. He is Fellow of the Royal Society, a laureate of the Templeton Prize and former President of Queens' College, Cambridge. His many books on science and religion include *Belief in God in an Age of Science* (Yale, 1998), *The God of Hope and the End of the World* (SPCK/Yale, 2002), *Exploring Reality* (SPCK/Yale, 2005) and *Science and Theology in Quest of Truth* (SPCK/Yale, 2011).

Nicholas Rengger is Professor of Political Theory and International Relations at St Andrews University, and Global Ethics Fellow at the Carnegie Council for Ethics and International Affairs, New York. He has published in many areas of political philosophy, intellectual history, international relations and philosophical theology. His most recent book is *Evaluating Global Orders* (Cambridge University Press, 2011) and he has just finished *State of War? Teleocratic Politics, the Just War and the Uncivil Condition in International Relations* and *Dealing in Darkness*, a collection of his essays on Political Theory and International Relations.

Julian Rivers is Professor of Jurisprudence at the University of Bristol. His research interests lie mainly in the area of legal and constitutional theory, with particular interests in legal reasoning and the relationship between law and religion, in which areas he has published widely. He translated (from German) Robert Alexy's *Theory of Constitutional Rights* (Oxford University Press, 2002) and also published *The Law of Organized Religions: Between Establishment and Secularism* (Oxford University Press, 2010). He is a member of the Editorial Advisory Board of the *Ecclesiastical Law Journal*, and Editor-in-Chief of the *Oxford Journal of Law* and Religion.

Steven J. Sandage is Professor of Marriage and Family Studies at Bethel University in St Paul, MN, and a Licensed Psychologist in practice with Arden Woods Psychological Services in New Brighton, MN, USA. He is co-author of three books, *To Forgive Is Human, The Faces of Forgiveness: Searching for Wholeness and Salvation* and *Transforming Spirituality: Integrating Theology and Psychology*. His current research interests include the psychology of forgiveness and spirituality, intercultural psychology, couples and family therapy, intercultural development, the integration of psychology and theology and suicide.

Andrew Sloane is Lecturer in Old Testament and Christian Thought at Morling College, Sydney (Australian College of Theology). Andrew initially trained as a doctor, before turning to theology. His research interests include philosophy and ethics and Old Testament interpretation. He is author of *On Being a Christian in the Academy: Nicholas Wolterstorff and the Practice of Christian Scholarship* (Paternoster, 2003), *At Home in a Strange Land: Using the Old Testament in Christian Ethics* (Hendrickson, 2008) and editor of *Tamar's Tears: Evangelical Engagements with Feminist Old Testament Hermeneutics* (Pickwick, 2012).

James Sweeney CP is Senior Lecturer in Pastoral Theology at Heythrop College, University of London and director of the Heythrop Institute: Religion & Society. His specializes in the sociology of religion. He is co-editor of *Keeping Faith in Practice: Aspects of Catholic Pastoral Theology* (SCM, 2010) and co-author of *Talking about God in Practice: Theological Action Research and Practical Theology* (SCM, 2010).

Introduction

THEOLOGY AND THE DISCIPLINES:
BUILDING A 'CHRISTIAN CULTURE'

THE EDITORS

I

In the first volume we explored the question of different philosophies becoming different types of handmaiden to theology. We tried to show this in a historical context so one could notice that even philosophies that are often associated as being explicitly hostile to Christianity, such as Marxism and postmodernism, could become helpful to Christian theologians to articulate the truth of the Gospel. These encounters are ongoing engagements and the results are yet to be fully assessed. This is true of Plato and Aristotle, but in a different way from newer philosophies such as those of Marx and Derrida. One remarkable facet of these differing interactions between theology and philosophy are those special moments when the truth of the gospel illuminates philosophy and even questions some forms of philosophy, while at the same time the majesty of philosophy can provide conceptual tools to develop something that theology wishes to say – as Aquinas discovered with Aristotle. There is no simple and single pattern underlying the relationship between these two disciplines, although the essayists in volume one had the underlying conviction that philosophy is important to the business of theology, even when theology might be severely critical of and criticized by philosophy. But the basic argument of volume one was that theology needs philosophy to flourish – and philosophy best flourishes in this handmaiden role.

In this second volume we take the second step implicit in the engagement of theology and philosophy: how then does theology relate to the other non-theological disciplines? That is a question asked equally in the classroom of church-run schools, universities and seminaries. But it is also a question asked by the Christian who might be an economist in the World Bank or who works in the pharmacy and has to dispense abortifacient or the Christian who works in the research laboratories of a large chemical company. Much hinges upon this relationship for so many people, not least non-Christians who sometimes lovingly cherish Christian schools and send their children there (as happened to the elites in colonial India and many a Muslim in the United Kingdom today). At the same time there are many Christians and non-Christians who totally oppose such educational institutions arguing they are pre-modern and that education should be a single process with a neutral methodology at best, or have a state ideology at worse, for all persons, whatever their religious belief.

These 'secularizing' views may well find roots in a Christian intuition within the history of its educational institutions – and within Christian theology in the late medieval period. In one sense there is a chasm between theology and the non-theological disciplines for theology's proper object is 'God', who is utterly other than creation and upon whom creation is dependent. The intellectual disciplines all have their own created subject matter that is peculiar to their beloved 'objects' of study, be it the training of musicians with the history of music, or the focus on the biological world peculiar to the waters that covered the earth – marine biologists. This gulf between the created and uncreated order has meant that for large periods of history theology as an academic discipline was done in careful isolation from other disciplines and these other disciplines, as in the University of Paris, were forbidden to trespass upon the subject matter of theology: God. Some argue that the secularization of the disciplines ironically began with these assumption embedded in the University of Paris. There are many such contested sites which are 'blamed' for theology's own self-secularization and isolation which include Duns Scotus and the emergence of nominalism.

The emergence of the modern research university in Berlin in the nineteenth century began to transform the shape of the sacred canopy that had until then hung over many European universities. Of course, there was never a single conception of the university at any time in history, although this claim will be severely tested in the face of the current near-global economic recession. But Berlin did bring into play a model that was replicated in many countries and implicit in Berlin was the fragmentation of the disciplines precisely because they were now united under a new secular canopy emphasizing research: specialization, the employment of tools and methodologies that should be scientific, and the fetishization of the importance of knowledge for its own sake. Berlin was exported to the United States and other parts of Europe which in turn exported it along with European imperial powers setting up universities throughout the empire.

Two effects of this long, slow, complex historical process are particularly important for this volume of essays, although the entire historiography of the universities has only just begun. First, it meant that scholars in biology or literature or economics became specialists just as theologians did. The disciplinary boundary lines were girded with steel. It meant that conversation across the disciplines became more difficult and less possible as the teacher in the research universities had to embody the image of the successful specialist. Second, this process further eroded the possibility of a Christian culture, minimally understood as a Christian attempt to articulate thoughts and practices about economics, politics, history, biology and so on. Despite this disciplinary fragmentation, leading intellectuals from non-theological disciplines felt increasingly comfortable speaking across the disciplines to argue the falsity of Christianity, even though their subject matter might be technically thought as being unable to address this question. But it requires skilful theologians, philosophers and specialists in that particular area (physics, biology and so on) to rebuff such critiques. This anti-Christian intellectual ethos which exists in variously sized pockets echoes some of the earlier speaking across disciplinary boundaries when theologians told scientists they must be wrong because theologians knew best. The 'battle' between 'religion and the sciences' at the level of serious scholarship is thankfully on the verge of becoming stale. In the popular mind the story still has many different narrations and is sadly too often portrayed as a conflict and war that can only have one winner.

But the chasm between theology and the disciplines was also a gulf crossed by theology itself in the doctrine of the incarnation. If Christianity has partial responsibility for this fragmentation of vision, it is also the only hope for the restoration of a united vision. The incarnation meant that the entire created world was the arena of redemption and the whole person was involved: the biological, the economic, the artistic, the literary, the political and so on. The doctrine of the incarnation meant that theology was also concerned with the shape of the created order. There were constant periods in the history of all denominational forms of Christianity that evinced an interest in 'Christian culture', developing a sense that all our knowing had to be underpinned by love, awe and worship, not just by instrumental control over the created world, which all too often included control and reduction of the human. Christian universities that might have been the bulwark of such a culture sometimes became the places of the 'dying of the light', rather than its bright shining.

This volume takes its place between multifaceted ideas of a Christian culture and a Christian university and in one sense can also be read independently of those constructs. It simply tries to encourage a conversation that is absolutely essential for the future of Christianity and its intellectual standing in culture between theology and the disciplines. The best way to do this was to get Christian intellectuals who were established in a natural, social or human science to reflect on their practices, on their positioning within institutions, and on their sense of how their research might be shaped if their Christian convictions were allowed to operate alongside and with their professional disciplines. We wanted to ask two questions. Methodologically, what shifts might occur in your subject and the study of your subject if Christianity were taken as true.

Substantively, what transformations might be seen in your subject area if the truth of Christianity were to penetrate those like yourselves who study and engage with the subject.

We believe this is one of the first works to consider seriously the different types of sciences, which we have grouped into three, and run this questions across the entire spectrum. There have been studies that have examined the arts, the social sciences and the natural sciences, but we have tried to muster the entire symphonic range knowing that babble could easily ensue. Our writers are actually united by shared assumptions which produce a harmony of the disciplines that is truly a musical feast. In this collection we can glimpse the exciting and complex task of generating and enacting a 'Christian culture', minimally, a society where the Christian churches are places of worship and praise to the one true God and thus taking God's world with utter seriousness in each one of its many dimensions. A Christian school or university might be just one facet of this task, but that raises difficult questions about the nature of the university. Many of our contributors come from outside 'Christian universities' and many are unhampered in their research when operating within secular universities, so matters are inevitably and deeply complex. But in the long run, Christian schools and universities are the way in which churches take responsibility for the process of education so that knowledge, wonder, love and service may once more be united. That they have been related in ghastly and faulty ways does not mean that there is no challenge to face, no task to be undertaken, no generation of minds to train in a different mould from how the world views the world. This volume is a small step forward in a long conversation that is urgently required.

II

In Chapter 1, Mervyn Davies helps set the scene for the remainder of the volume by examining how Newman's educational ideal offers some real challenges as well as possibilities for contemporary theory and practice in higher education. Following Newman, he argues that higher education becomes impoverished if it denies or neglects the importance of the creative link between Christianity and other disciplines – a link which can enable dialogue and collaboration in the search for truth. Second, he explores Newman's contention that faith perspectives are essential for the integrity of higher education itself; otherwise it runs the risk of being based on principles which diminish a full understanding of knowledge and our humanity. Newman believed that the contribution that Christianity could make was not only essential for true education to flourish, but also for the health of society as a whole. Newman's own time, as ours today, was heavily influenced by a detrimental utilitarian outlook, and with great prescience he foresaw the marginalization of faith perspectives in the twentieth and twenty-first centuries. Davies argues that the consequences of this impoverishment for higher education means that there is an urgent need for higher education reform in which not only faith traditions and theological exploration play their rightful and vital part, but the full range of disciplines co-operate in truth seeking as well. Ways in which the various disciplines can engage with the challenge of faith and develop in the process are then explored in the remaining 16 chapters, beginning with the natural and life sciences.

Writing on mathematics (Chapter 2), Michael Heller reflects on Einstein's declaration that science does nothing but decipher the mind of God. He argues that this can be understood as a continuation of the time honoured book of nature metaphor. Heller focusses on the scientific reconstruction of the world as a blueprint of creation and considers the following. (a) Its rationality, revealed most clearly in the fact that the structure of the world is best disclosed with the help of mathematics, the most rational creation of the human mind. (b) Its self-contained character, consisting in the fact that all chains of explanatory inferences lie entirely within the world's structure. It is this property of the world's structure that results in the full methodological autonomy of the hard sciences. (c) Its dynamic character, allowing us to conclude that the act of creation is a dynamic act itself, and that the temporal character of the world is an imprint of the very nature of this act. (d) Its subtle sensitivity to the interplay of law-like and contingent elements. The laws of nature are essential aspects of the mathematical structure of the world, but they cannot operate without the intervention of some randomness present in their initial or boundary conditions. Even the most chancy or random events are well integrated into the blueprint of the universe.

The idea that the deep intelligibility and wonderful order of the universe can be understood as signs of the mind of God behind creation is then further developed in Chapter 3 on physics. John Polkinghorne maintains that the 'fine-tuning' of the laws of nature necessary for a world with carbon-based life can be seen as signs of divine purpose. He also points out that issues of causality and temporality, though constrained by science, require for their settlement acts of metaphysical decision. It is not yet fully understood, for example, how the clear and reliable world of everyday experience emerges from its cloudy and fitful quantum substrate. The likelihood that the universe will eventually end in decay is a prediction that encourages theology to look beyond cosmic death to belief in the ultimate faithfulness of the creator. Polkinghorne reminds us that the physical world as revealed by quantum physics can be very surprising, so the physicist does not think that the shape of rationality can be determined a priori, but only by recourse to belief motivated by actual experience.

Neither Heller nor Polkinghorne assume that the basic methods of mathematics or physics will change as a result of their discipline's dialogue with

Christianity. Instead they explain how such a dialogue provides meaning and metaphysical depth. In other words, as far as the hard sciences are concerned, Christianity contextualizes maths and physics by owning them as truth seeking endeavours which reveal the basic intelligibility of creation.

The emergence of life introduces higher order issues for the scientist, philosopher and theologian. Alister McGrath (Chapter 4) outlines the origins of biology as a distinct university discipline, noting the significant impact of 'natural theology' as a catalyst for this development. In the late eighteenth and early nineteenth centuries, studying the ordering and beauty of the living world was seen as religiously important, leading to a growing interest in the study of biology. Understanding this background allows for a better appreciation of the impact of Darwinism upon both biology and Christian theology, which is explored in some detail in this essay. In particular, McGrath's essay examines how many contemporary academic debates about issues in biology have clear religious dimensions – such as the question of whether evolution can be considered to be 'teleological'. This chapter provides a good foundation for understanding why evolutionary theory has proved to be so problematic, both religiously and ideologically.

Celia Deane-Drummond next considers the broad sweep of the environmental sciences in Chapter 5, arguing that they are multidisciplinary even within their own realm as science. She points out that the particular relevance of environmental sciences to wider considerations to do with the human condition has become increasingly obvious. These range from local contested issues through to highly volatile global economic and political standpoints. She suggests that the theological voice is relevant in public debates about human practices, including broad questions about human relationships with the earth and each other. It is in this sense therefore, as well as in the sense of belief in the worth of the natural world as creation, that Christian theology has a stake in environmental concerns, for it impinges on crucial questions about justice and what justice might mean in global contexts. Deane-Drummond argues for a strong Christian voice in such debates, and for working towards building trust and accountability across the social sphere, including the way the sciences are practiced. In theological language, faith and moral responsibility alongside particular virtues of practical wisdom become highly relevant to contested debates. Deane-Drummond maintains that environmental scientists who are also Christians have a special obligation and responsibility to use their talents for the wider good of the human and ecological community.

Andrew Sloane assesses areas of critical interaction between Christian faith and medicine understood as an intellectual discipline and a professional practice in Chapter 6. Noting that the discipline operates within both 'Western' and 'non-Western' contexts, he outlines and critiques how it has attempted to address the issues raised on non-religious principles and articulates a Christian alternative from a broadly neo-Calvinist perspective. Sloane suggests that illness is a problem not only because it adversely affects people but because it interferes with their ability to function in relationships. Medicine as a social practice (or profession) is thus an inherently moral enterprise which exists in and for a given community, aiming, as far as is practicable, to return people to proper functioning in their relationships and as persons. This Christian vision enables us to discern what health care ought (and ought not) to be provided for members of a community, and to reshape medicine as a moral practice. The importance of a Christian perspective emerges since this provides a coherent way of thinking about human flourishing.

Moving from the biological to the human and social sciences introduces wider issues of human freedom, intentionality and purpose. These are of intrinsic relevance to the subject matter of these disciplines, as well as raising pressing questions about grace and God's providence. James Sweeney evaluates theology's relationship with sociology and their underlying assumptions – assumptions which are more than items of theory and derive from praxis. Sweeney reminds us that in theology the fundamental assumption, arising from living religious traditions, is that God is real; from this all else proceeds. In sociology there is a fundamental assumption that human social conduct is ordered rather than simply random, and therefore explicable. This too derives from life: it is how people usually perceive themselves. These assumptions manifest different underlying ontologies – explicitly in theology (an ontology of grace) and implicitly in sociology (an ontology as some form of social constructivism). Sociology, in relating to religious ontology (the 'truth claims'), is necessarily constrained – except when it makes an ideological commitment to atheism – to be 'methodologically agnostic'. But by having to leave the realm of grace an open possibility, sociology is limited in declaring any final view about the human and social world. If there *is* more to what the eye can see, what the eye can see is in some measure deficient. This asymmetry of theology and sociology characterizes the interdisciplinary relationship between them.

Some of these issues are taken up in different ways in Chapters 8 and 9 on aspects of psychology and its therapies. Peter Hampson reviews existing approaches to psychology–theology dialogue and connects these with classic views on the connections between Christianity and culture. Closely resembling Sweeney's theological approach, Hampson also focuses on the issue of grace and raises the question as to how God might be understood to make a (psychological) difference while acknowledging that God is not another univocal cause among causes. He argues that a participatory ontology offers the architectonic theological framework needed to contextualize psychology properly. While in general terms this will leave existing methods of psychology unchanged,

Hampson notes that research questions and foci could well alter and raises the possibility that existing methods can be supplemented by drawing on tradition based thinking, and the model of a reflective, prayerful scientist.

From a more practice based perspective, Steven Sandage, in Chapter 9, then concentrates on a relational approach to the integration of Christian theology and psychotherapy training. Although grounded differently, his chapter complements Hampson's in terms of its practical application as opposed to its theoretical concerns, and its specific engagement with therapy as opposed to the discipline of psychology as a whole. Sandage offers relational models of: (a) spirituality, (b) integration of theology and social science, (c) hermeneutics, (d) alterity and diversity and (e) virtue as important domains for integrative psychotherapy training. Differentiation of self is summarized as a key construct for integrating relational spirituality and human development. The integrative relevance of sociocultural contexts and empirical research are also emphasized. Recent research on the virtue of forgiveness is used to illustrate the value of a relational approach to theological and psychological integration. Finally Sandage considers useful practical applications of a relational model of training.

Law, politics and economics can be taught as social sciences which study humans engaging with complex cultural practices. They raise issues similar to those of the human sciences but also introduce their own domain specific questions.

A theology of legal education is different from a theology of law, maintains Julian Rivers in Chapter 10. Rivers starts by reviewing six historic paradigms of legal education. The recent rise of 'Christian Legal Studies' is best seen as only one newcomer in the postmodern multiplicity of subject matters and methodologies. In searching for an appropriate theological framework, he rejects the familiar natural law–legal positivism debate. Instead, Christian legal education should be located in a dialectic between 'fallen law' and 'redeemed law' which allows full scope for the historical contingencies of the law. His chapter concludes that the Christian Law School is not the most appropriate institutional location for this type of education. Rather, the Christian legal scholar should be seeking to develop supplementary materials and contexts alongside the 'secular' law school.

Nicholas Rengger then explains, in Chapter 11, that despite the rupture between political science and international relations and Christian theology that has dominated the fields for much of the post-war period, there are clear signs that this rupture is now being healed. Influential political theorists and scholars of international relations are taking theology seriously – and vice versa – and important avenues of work are being opened up. His essay examines three key areas of debate between theology and politics: the historical debate over the theological origins of modern political thought, the debate over the character of the secular and the debate on the possibilities of seeing politics anew through theological lenses. He assesses the arguments offered in these contexts by thinkers such as John Paul II, Benedict XVI, Michael Allen Gillespie, Jean Bethke Elshtain, Oliver O'Donovan, Charles Taylor, John Milbank and Stanley Hauerwas. Rengger argues that while all these areas of work contain great insights, particular aspects of the character of global change also bring some serious questions that the 'new political theologians' have yet to fully consider and which might point in a new and challenging direction for their work.

The way we think about economics raises interesting issues of human nature and motivation as well as institutional and educational policy. In Chapter 12, William Cavanaugh explores the ways in which economics as a discipline is described and the work such descriptions do in situating economics within a faith-based university. He examines three different images Christian economists use to describe economics: economics as science, economics as ethics and economics as theology. Cavanaugh argues that only by examining the theology implicit in economies and economics can a fully satisfying science of economics emerge. Only this version of the science can comfortably accommodate the fact that all economics supposes a particular articulation of what ultimate reality is like. Debate between 'orthodox' and 'heterodox' economists, Cavanaugh suggests, can reveal the true theological basis of economics.

Chapters 13–17 approach the human condition and its relation with God through its artistic and cultural products, represented here by literature, history, classics, and music. Robin Kirkpatrick and Vittorio Montemaggi are already confident that vigorous connections have by now been established in the academy between theological and literary study. They examine the ways in which both theology and literature may best be able not merely to tolerate but also to promote imaginative ambiguity. Their argument concentrates on two particular texts, Shakespeare's Macbeth and the Ugolino episode of Dante's Inferno, where theological issues are seen to reveal themselves once the reader's eye is directed to tensions lying beneath the lexical surface. Their essay is a 'worked example' of how theology can be creatively and skilfully used in literary criticism.

Lucy Beckett is more circumspect about the state of English Literature teaching in higher education as a whole. She gives a critical account of the short history of English Literature as a degree subject. After the 1860s English replaced Latin and Greek as the basis of 'the humanities', secularism came to prevail among the educated, and it was hoped that 'culture', in particular 'poetry', might replace Christianity as that which gives meaning to life. Beckett claims that Arnold's project was given deceptive rigour by I. A. Richards and the massively influential F. R. Leavis. The collapse of the project since the 1960s, into a beliefless free-for-all in which value judgement was discredited, revealed its fundamental flaw: the regarding of literature as absolute and Christian (and all) truth as relative. Enthusiasm for literary theory and the disintegrative effect of a wide range of unconnected specialisms further confused the discipline. For Beckett, hope for the future must lie in the encouragement of those sure of the value of good writing to grasp what these words mean and what they entail since such meanings are ultimately grounded in God's truth, beauty and goodness.

History proper is the topic of Fernando Cervantes' chapter. In a philosophical climate that assumes the universe to be explicable in mechanistic terms, the role of the historian should logically be the mere accumulation of facts without giving any heed to their wider significance. Yet historians rarely behave like this; whether they like it or not, their ideal of knowledge is not rational analysis but imaginative vision. It is now generally taken for granted, for example, that even when we analyse the world theoretically we cannot help being agents in that world; this means that our representation of reality is intrinsically grounded in the way we deal with things. With these considerations in mind, Cervantes aims to demonstrate the importance of a philosophical understanding of historical knowledge that does not lose sight of its theological underpinnings. After all, he maintains, it was Christianity that first showed that time is lineal, not cyclical, and that there is an intelligible meaning to the development of events in time.

Richard Finn examines the historical relationship between the academic disciplines of theology and classics in anglophone scholarship over recent centuries, especially in Oxford and Cambridge, to observe how theology has partially fragmented into a series of sub-specialities organized around critical questions posed by the Enlightenment, while classics has largely grown in coherence as a study in culture across a broadly defined period. Nonetheless, classics in the field of Early Christian Studies in particular can benefit from insights derived from theology, which challenges the apparent closure of classics from wider educational concerns and goals. A fuller engagement of the two disciplines invites the classicist to integrate their understanding of the Ancient World within a larger philosophical, ethical and theological formation.

Taking as its starting point Aidan Kavanagh's thesis that liturgy is already primary theology, John Harper sets out to examine the relationship between the theological academy and the practice of liturgy, especially liturgy with music, in our last chapter. The exceptional tradition of choral services in British cathedrals and university college chapels offers unique opportunities for practice-led research not only in universities with college chapel choirs but through partnership between cathedrals and neighbouring universities. Harper's chapter outlines some of the possibilities and opportunities of placing theology within a practice-led research context. Using research into late medieval liturgy as an example, it explores the potential for better understanding of the relationship of liturgy, music, space, artefacts and religious experience, as well as related theological insights, and the potential for comparable work in other periods, including the present. Such research can also connect with other recent initiatives in the relationship of theology and music.

Whichever way we look across the academy then, from mathematics to medicine to music, from environmental sciences to economics, from physics to psychology to politics, from law to literature, from biology to history or from sociology to classics there are already lively interconnecting debates taking place between apparently distinct secular disciplines, Christianity and Christian theology. The common and sometimes contrasting themes raised by these debates some of which, arguably, could develop and cross-fertilize better within more supportive institutional contexts, include the intelligibility of creation, purpose, grace, human flourishing, truth seeking, coherence and convergence of explanation, participation and representation, imagination and culture to name but a few. The power of Christian faith to serve as a genuine and trustworthy, powerful metanarrative for all this soon becomes apparent.

We believe we have been privileged to assemble an impressive set of chapters whose arguments will continue to reinforce and nourish each other in the future. We are especially grateful to our distinguished contributors for their enthusiastic involvement. We hope that the reader is as excited as we are that dialogue between Christianity and the disciplines is well and truly happening and that they may themselves be motivated to contribute to some of these ongoing debates.

Chapter 1

Newman's Challenge to the Contemporary University

Mervyn Davies

(Sarum College, Salisbury)

It is fair to say that Newman's educational writings represent to both the critics and defenders of the twenty-first century university the most complete ideal of the nature of a university that has yet been penned for 'Newman identified many of the central issues regarding the functions of a university on any occasion and gave lasting literary form to an argument that still mesmerises scholars'.[1] That said, we should not underestimate the importance of Wilhelm von Humboldt who developed the principle of free and universal education for all. It was his idea of combining both teaching and research in one institution that guided him in establishing the University of Berlin in 1810. The structures he created became the model for the modern university in most Western countries from the 1870s. While there are some parts of Newman's and von Humboldt's thinking that may seem antithetical, Boulton and Lucas rightly see their ideas as complementary and foundational in most respects.[2]

As MacIntyre noted, however, Newman's philosophical view is now simply incompatible with what contemporary higher education is about and for which it has been funded.[3] However, it is precisely this contention that has received the most attention being based, it is argued, on 'flawed premises' by which universities are closely linked to the production of economic growth and hence to government directed targets that could leave them as universities only in name. Von Humboldt argued strongly against this trend and here Newman agreed.[4] The primacy of the economic link is clearly made in the 2010 Report *Securing a Sustainable Future for Higher Education* which explored the options for the funding of higher education[5] and reinforced still further in the government White Paper *Higher Education: Students at the Heart of the System* (June 2011).[6] This view is about as far removed from Newman's as could be imagined.

As Culler observed, for Newman a good society is secured by forming good people to belong to it which is done by presenting to them an ideal of what it means to be fully human in contrast to those who avoid the difficulty of this task by treating society and its members as primarily material producers and consumers and who look to nothing more elevating than promoting this as their aim.[7] Lord Browne's Report attracted similar criticism from contemporary commentators for whom government policy is a fundamental redefinition of higher education in which the only social value to be pursued is an economic one. Arguably, the logic of such a position is that only the applied sciences should continue to receive public finance as being directly economically benefi- cial. 'Browne is contending that we should no longer think of higher education as the provision of the public good, articulated through educational judgment and largely financed by public funds . . . Instead we should think of it as a lightly regulated market in which consumer demand, in the form of student choice, is sovereign in determining what is offered by service providers (i.e. universities).'[8]

Newman's contemporary, Richard Simpson, wrote that 'Newman gives us colossal fragments, but he does not usually construct a finished edifice'.[9] This is true of his educational writings which in consequence are not always entirely consistent with one another. Although *The Idea of a University* comes near- est to a 'finished edifice', Tillman rightly reminds the reader that it needs to be taken alongside *The Rise and Progress of Universities* and the *Benedictine Essays* which arguably are of equal importance in balancing the view of the *Idea* and give a more rounded account of his position.[10] The evidence of what Newman actually did in Dublin is also important in *My Campaign in Ireland*.[11] Neglecting this has led to problems of interpretation.

For example, in her Introduction to the Millennium Edition of *Rise and Progress of Universities and Benedictine Essays*, Tillman argued that it is quite wrong to conclude by relying simply on the 'Dublin Discourses' that Newman had no interest in research.[12] *Atlantis,* the university periodical that he started, was to be the organ for professors to publish their research which he saw as a duty.[13] The conclusion that Newman 'took it for granted that research was for institutions other than universities' is therefore not an accurate reading of his position or practice. Tillman points out that Newman set up faculties such as the Medical School and the Irish Archaeological Department, which he maintained 'have their value intrinsically whether students are present or not'. Nevertheless, he distinguishes, in the Preface to the *Idea*, between academies and universi- ties because to 'discover' and to 'teach' are different functions, not necessarily found in the same person, yet which need each other as parts to a whole and hence are not to be done in isolation or at the expense of the other. Indeed sys- tem and organization are always to be subordinated to the personal influence of the tutor and the taught. Without this, any academic institution is like an 'Arctic Winter': 'it will create an icebound, petrified, cast-iron university and nothing else'.[14] A purely economic view thus makes casualties of them: teach- ing becomes merely preparation for a particular career, research the creature of whatever funding source will pay for it and its commercial agenda; the lack of personal influence will impoverish learning. Here Newman's university and collegiate principles serve to balance each other. Newman, however, regarded publication of research findings as an obligation to society as well as to the very *integrity* of a university as he understood it, which he stressed in his University Rules and Regulations (1856).

Culler maintains that what Newman did in practice 'came far closer to the modern conception of a university, with its professional schools, its specialized research, and its program of service to the community at large than did either of the English Universities which he took as his model'.[15] Indeed the deficiencies in both teaching and research at Oxford in Newman's time had been of particular concern to him, as was the lack of pastoral care of students. His aim in Dublin was to bring these different functions together in a coherent and effective manner, underpinned by a common *philosophy* and value system which is committed to the communal nature of the search for truth, the human perfection of the individual and the benefit of the common good, a balanced triumvirate in equipoise.

The nineteenth century was a tumultuous period of change which saw the emergence of an organized educational system from a relatively inchoate one of the 1800s. There was a crucial stage of transition between 1850 and 1870 when the state made significant interventions to 'examine and report on all levels of education, from the ancient universities (Oxford and Cambridge) to the elementary schools for the masses'.[16] No less than five Royal Commissions examined all levels of education which led to legislation that largely established the system that we have today although there have been subsequent significant revisions. Newman, as a founder of a school as well as a university, was well aware of these developments as of course was his disciple Matthew Arnold, whose work *Culture and Anarchy* shared many of Newman's concerns although not all of his conclusions,[17] a view also of many contemporary commentators.[18]

Newman and Arnold are most at one when considering what cultivation of the mind means and in their opposition to the increasingly powerful utilitarian philosophy put forward by men such as Lord Henry Brougham, Sydney Smith and the *Edinburgh Review*, who argued that the classical education, which was then prevalent, should be replaced by 'useful' knowledge leading to a trade or profession. It was a direct consequence of a view which did not allow the spectrum of disciplines to influence the student or to interact and dialogue with one another.[19]

One development of this position was to exclude theology as an academic discipline which the newly founded University of London had done. Newman laid some of the responsibility for this on forms of religion which simply regarded faith as a sentiment like patriotism and not something concerned with truth,[20] but he also blamed the increasingly secular and utilitarian age. For him, students needed to have some grasp of the whole of the field of knowledge not just its parts, or at least to be aware that there is a 'whole' and that no one discipline exhausts what can be said about reality. Newman here argued as much against any shallow general acquaintance with the field of knowledge 'enfeebling the mind by a profusion of subjects' as he did against narrow specializing which deforms it, advocating a process which 'is the preparation for knowledge' and its acquisition in a manner which developed what he called 'intellectual eyes'.[21] The true researcher, as much as the undergraduate student, needs therefore to be genuinely educated.

Newman drew a parallel with 'health' in relation to the body and 'virtue' in relation to the moral nature of a person. Newman clearly had in mind here not just 'health' as the absence of disease but as the well-being of the body, which is not the same as being skilled at a particular physical activity. The equivalent of this in the intellectual sphere is 'perfection' by which he means 'culture of the intellect'.[22] That which brings this about is Liberal Education. What should be taught is what will tend to bring about 'mental culture'.[23]

This is useful but in a very different sense from what Locke meant and there-fore raises a different set of questions as to what should be taught. Just as you can look after the body with a 'simple view as to its general health' so the mind can be cultivated and exercised in order to bring about its intellectual perfec-tion. If learning a physical skill is not the same as being in a general state of health, likewise learning a particular vocational skill or trade or specialism is not the same as having a well-educated mind.

The development of health and the development of an educated mind are, in Newman's view, prior to the development of skills in any particular role and, moreover, assist in the fulfilment of whatever activity people engage in. To be liberally educated thus brings enormous benefits to whatever calling a person follows. This is why Newman with Coleridge and Arnold conceived of education as that which is 'the harmonious development of those qualities and faculties that characterize our humanity'.[24] Newman explains why this is important:

> General culture of the mind is the best aid to professional and scientific study; and the man who has learned to think and to reason and to compare and to discriminate and to analyze, who has refined his taste and formed his judgment and sharpened his mental vision, will not indeed at once be a lawyer, or a pleader, or an orator, or a statesman, or a physician, or a good landlord, or a man of business, or a soldier, or an engineer, or a chemist, or a geologist, or an antiquarian, but he will be placed in that state of intellect in which he can take up any one of the sciences or callings I have referred to, or any other for which he has a taste or special talent, with an ease, a grace, a versatility and a success, to which another is stranger.[25]

Newman went on to argue that to have developed an educated mind is not only useful, that is beneficial, but is a duty that is owed to society because it develops people of judgement who bring a range of qualities to any profession over and above the skills required to do it. He was at pains to deny any suggestion that he disparaged courses that led to the professions but argued that society needed educated people for its health. Newman called this the 'formation of the citizen' which is the function of a university. He amplified this by saying that 'if a practical end is to be assigned to a University course, I say it is that of training good members of society', and adds: 'It aims at raising the intellectual tone of society, at cultivating the public mind, at purifying the national taste, at applying true principles to popular aspirations, at giving enlargement and sobriety to the ideas of the age, at facilitating the exercise of political power, and refining the intercourse of private life.'[26]

How will this come about? Newman responded: 'It is education which gives a man a clear and conscious view of his own opinions and judgments, a truth in developing them, an eloquence in expressing them and a force in urging them. It teaches him to see things as they are, to go right to the point, to disentangle a skein of thought, to detect what is sophistical and to discard what is irrelevant.'[27]

Newman's quarrel with Locke was not just that he would exclude from serious consideration anything that 'does not teach us some temporal calling' but that he was engaged in a kind of educational and cultural reductionism which is bad for society as a whole. What we would now call the Arts and the Humanities therefore become particularly vulnerable from a utilitarian view or when commercial interests are at stake.[28]

In *Culture and Anarchy*, Arnold captured much of what Newman was saying when he spoke of 'culture being a pursuit of our total perfection by means of getting to know, on all the matters which most concern us, the best which has been thought and said in the world; and through this knowledge, turning a stream of fresh and free thought upon our stock notions and habits'.[29]

To fail to do this will mean that no one learns from history, or questions established practice or corrects mistakes leading to mechanically repetitive and often disastrous behaviour. MacIntyre illustrates this point further by putting forward the view that 'a surprising number of the major disorders of the latter part of the twentieth century and of the first decade of the twenty first century have been brought about by distinguished graduates of some of the most distinguished universities'.[30]

Whether this claim is true or not, Newman's contention was that a utilitarian model of education *by its very nature* abdicated any role in character forming of students that society so badly needs for its well-being.

Newman's view of the university is the antithesis of the position also cri-tiqued by Boulton and Lucas that recent 'statements of government ministers, officials, funding agencies and research councils' put forward the view that the function of universities is to provide 'direct in-out benefits for society's economic prosperity'. The assertion is made that 'there is a high correlation between pros-perity, social contentment and university research' and thus it can be concluded that 'universities have a primary duty' to engage in this socially useful activity in exchange for taxpayers' support and to be 'dynamos of growth' and 'generators of wealth creation'.[31]

To make this the primary aim of a university and not to subordinate it to some higher one, as Newman did, is to make wealth creation the ultimate moral good. The history of the first decade of the twenty-first century should make us wary of doing that. Liberal Education is therefore one of the bastions of defence against human folly and should be pursued as an intrinsic good in its own right for 'a university that moulds itself only to present demands is not listening to its historians'.[32]

The section on 'Education' in Boulton and Lucas' paper comes very near to what Newman advocated with its emphasis on the training of the mind and the critical faculties as *primary* ends. Like Newman they argue against the direction of students towards courses that are perceived as bringing the 'greatest material benefit' to them or society, advocating instead allowing them the choice of 'stud-ies that speak to a student's enthusiasms' as a more effective way of achieving the educational aim of a university.

How is this to be achieved? Newman was clear about the task when he said that 'enlargement' consists in 'an energetic and simultaneous action' upon and towards new ideas. It also consists in the 'formative capacity' of reducing these to order, digesting what we have learnt into what we have previously received and our 'mental centre'. Ideas must also be compared one with another and con-nected with each other. A great intellect is one which 'takes a connected view of old and new, past and present, far and near, and which has an insight into the influence of all these on one another; without which there is no whole, no centre. It possesses the knowledge not only of things, but also of their mutual and true relations; knowledge not merely considered as acquirement, but as philosophy'.[33]

For true enlargement to take place there must be an analytical, distributive and harmonizing process. Simply being well-read, or having a great memory or being learned in a particular field or possessing a great deal of information, is not the same as culture of the mind. Nor is it the same as people having seen much of the world and travelled widely or played a conspicuous role in it, recounting what they have experienced only as 'so many phenomena'.[34] 'That only is true enlargement of mind which is the power of viewing many things at once as one whole, or referring them severally to their true place in the universal system, of understanding their respective values, and determining their mutual dependence.'[35]

Why is this so important? Some people, he suggested, become so obsessed with one object or topic that they exaggerate its importance and make it the measure of all else whereas other people become so confused that they lose their way in the mass of ideas that have been presented to them, and an intellect which has been:

> Disciplined to the perfection its powers, which knows, and thinks while it knows, which has learned to leaven the dense mass of facts and events with the elastic force of reason, such an intellect cannot be partial, cannot be exclusive, cannot be impetuous, cannot be at a loss, cannot but be patient, collected and majestically calm, because it discerns the end in every beginning, the origin in every end, the law in every interruption, the limit in every delay; because it ever knows where it stands, and how its path lies from one point to another.[36]

True enlargement of mind, which comes about by thought and reason exercised upon knowledge, has therefore a kind of moral as well as intellectual character about it. It is not the same as being virtuous or religious but it has something of those aspects about it, nonetheless.[37] Newman continues: 'It is almost prophetic from its knowledge of history; it is almost heart-searching from its knowledge of human nature; it has almost supernatural charity from its freedom from littleness and prejudice.' How this is prepared for in the education of the young, Newman sets out in Part II of the *Idea* in his discussion on 'Elementary Studies' (chapter IV).

Newman was insistent that a university exists to teach universal knowledge.[38] Indeed its purpose is to ensure that 'all knowledge whatever, is taken into account in a University'. His philosophical position is that all knowledge is connected and that the different disciplines are concerned with parts of the whole that we call reality.[39] He did not conceive of the term 'universal' as something quantitative but as an awareness of the unity and integrity of knowledge to which the parts contribute. He refers to this as the 'circle' of knowledge in which each part balances, informs and corrects the others because it is not discrete but helps to form the whole. To enable this to happen requires a discipline which maps the interrelationships. This is done in two ways: the first by the university, following Aristotle, adopting the overarching philosophical principle of the circle of knowledge (with theology as encompassing God *and* the nature of reality as an essential component in understanding the nature of knowledge). All branches of study must be seen to form a 'whole or a system' and not as 'isolated and independent of one another' because they 'run into each other, and complete each other'.[40]

The second way is provided by the fact that a university exists to bring people together from all parts. 'Accordingly, in its simple and rudimental form, it is a school of knowledge of every kind, consisting of teachers and learners from every quarter.'[41] It follows that a university is 'in its essence a place for the communication and circulation of thought, by means of personal intercourse'. This he called 'mutual education' which is 'one of the great and incessant occupations of human society'.[42]

Crucial to this is the role of the great teacher in the university for 'its great instrument, or rather organ, has ever been that which nature prescribes in all education, the personal presence of a teacher', who is the 'living voice, the breathing from, the expressive countenance' of truth. It is the possibility of this encounter of student and teacher that makes a university a reality. Newman had much to say in his writings about personal influence, the role of the tutor and the place of learning in a community context and the necessity of this in a university.[43] He distinguished between the university and the college as represented in the roles of the professor and the tutor. The professor may deliver the lectures of genius and stimulation, but it is the tutor who should guide the students in their reading, discipline and habits of study, bringing together personal and intellectual development.[44] Newman was talking here of young men of 16 or so within the context of a Catholic institution but the principle remains the same: the importance of guidance and direction of students' studies and the provision of the conditions for real learning, which the rapid proliferation of higher education institutions in recent decades has arguably yet to take sufficiently seriously.

Newman also envisaged the different disciplines to be in dialogue and conversation with each other rather than in competition, so that a university that is worthy of the name forms an ethos that encourages such collaboration and mutual exploration.[45] It is also essential to Newman's idea that no area of knowledge is excluded on utilitarian or secular grounds. If that happens, there is imbalance because each of the disciplines treats of reality under different aspects. To deliberately neglect or omit one is a form of reductionism and to be less of a learning institution that is 'philosophically constructed'.[46] He recognized, however, that it may not always be practicable for one institution to be able to do this and that the ideal may only be achievable by some sort of collaboration and a philosophical sense of the unity of knowledge conveyed by teaching.

What is even more serious is that the utilitarian and consumerist ethic that he saw as prevalent in society even in the early nineteenth century, lowers and denigrates our view of all that makes us truly human and this is the critical issue.[47] While Newman was clear that only the Christian Gospel can regenerate the heart, the university stands as a beacon, 'a seat of wisdom, a light of the world', and therefore can be said to have a kind of prophetic role. For this he was adamant that a university needed the freedom in which 'the intellect may safely range and speculate', 'where inquiry is pushed forward, and discoveries verified and perfected, and rashness rendered innocuous and error exposed by the collision of mind with mind, and knowledge with knowledge'.[48]

The exclusion of theology from the university then is especially serious. Newman was emphatic in claiming that not only is theology a branch of knowledge but that it enters into every other discipline. For Newman, theology is what we can know about God put into a system and as such is different from the kind of formation to be found in a seminary or theological college which is orientated towards practice.[49] He regarded clergy training as 'an art or a business making use of Theology' which is different from the liberal pursuit of theology – an important distinction given the relatively late development of theological colleges in the formation of Church of England clergy and the place of seminaries in Roman Catholicism.

In the *Idea* he includes under the heading of theology both philosophical or natural theology and the *credenda* of Revelation but maintained that its study is that of a strict deductive science comparable to geometry with the existence of God as a given, a problematic position in a secular context. In other writings, however, he also sees it as 'inductive and synthetic', which underlines the importance of not seeing his work in isolation.[50] Theology deals with a complementary question to the physicist who contemplates the nature of the universe and tells us about it. He would have endorsed the view of John Polkinghorne that science and religion are intellectual cousins under the skin: 'They are both part of the great human endeavour to *understand*.'[51]

Theology holds the ring for all knowledge which otherwise has a tendency to fragment or become distorted. It is the 'highest indeed, and widest' of the sciences, a 'first among equals' as Ker argues.[52] Newman could then argue that balance will only be maintained if each discipline is true to its integrity and does not make claims that go beyond it, such as 'that religion is not a science, and that in religion scepticism is the only philosophy' which happens when an empirical methodology usurps the territory and methodology of a different discipline.[53] On the contrary, theology has a role of 'completing and correcting' other sciences'.[54]

At the beginning of the *Idea* Newman argued that a university that excludes the study of theology is either really saying it is something that is devoid of intellectual content or that an important branch of knowledge has been omitted in which case it is incorrect to call such a place a university. [55]In consequence, it will prevent the inclusive intake to a university that Newman envisaged and also inhibit those dialogues and conversations which are of a university's essence.

He gave further examples of the potential limitation of universal knowledge by which different disciplines can be excluded by the adoption of a particular prejudice: ethics, history, metaphysics and physics, for example are all potential casualties of a partial view. We might want to note the fate of philosophy of education that has become the victim of centrally imposed government policies which make it 'unnecessary', as a contemporary example.

All this implies that certain kinds of questioning and investigation which may be key to what it means to be human are in danger when the principle of universal knowledge and its role in the pursuit of truth is abandoned. The formative experience of students also becomes impoverished. Theology benefits from the profusion of disciplines that surrounds it, stimulating its enquiry and providing reference points for fruitful dialogue in a common pursuit.[56] Newman himself exemplified this by using many images and ideas drawn from science, mathematics, music, literature and classical learning in many of his theological writings. Newman's first article 'On the Study of Mathematics', illustrates this point and was published in the twentieth volume of *The Christian Observer* arguing that 'no science perhaps is more adapted to confirm our belief in the truth of Christianity than that of mathematics, when cultivated with a proper disposition of mind' (i.e. because feelings or prejudices are excluded). His own study of geology left him unruffled and open to the idea of evolution well before it became an issue of contention.

Newman attributed the cause of this malaise not just to the secular world where the pursuit of wealth was fast becoming the ultimate good, but claimed also that certain parts of Protestant Europe had contributed to it by maintaining that '[r]eligion consists, not in knowledge, but in feeling or sentiment' thereby abandoning the idea that faith is an intellectual act with knowledge as its object. Pietism is singled out as one example, eighteenth-century Evangelicalism another. Thus religion is based 'not on argument', but on 'taste and sentiment'.[57] Newman goes on to illustrate the problem in the wider compass of education as a whole by citing the Minutes of the Council on Education for the years 1848–50 where he found that one of Her Majesty's Inspectors of Schools had firmly placed 'Religious and Moral Education' under the heading of 'the Inculcation of Sentiment' in the curriculum of schools with poetry and music, which do not have a measurable economic value.

Where such a view prevails, Newman had observed, it is impossible to argue for any position for theology in a university or much dialogue between the disciplines and religion. The consumerist approach to modern universities, we might note today, only makes the problem worse for, increasingly, their funding comes from sources which have very specific agendas and prescriptive expectations of outcomes. The study of religion in the twenty-first century is likely to become a casualty of this but also many other humanities disciplines, for the same reason: they have become increasingly marginalized in current policy about university education to be knocked down like dominoes in a fuse. The discussion thus comes back to what theology can be in a contemporary university at the mercy of such pressures.[58] Despite this, several contemporary writers have noted that Newman 'does little to defend his claim that theology is knowledge' when arguing for its inclusion in a university but his view of theology is in the same tradition as Aquinas.[59]

Newman's reply was to appeal to its potential to provide a forum in which 'it is pledged to admit, without fear, without prejudice, without compromise, all comers, if they come in the name of truth', and theology is concerned with ultimate truth. A university that is true to itself acts as kind of umpire, 'a high protecting power of all knowledge and science', impartial to all disciplines.[60] Has the contemporary university abandoned this, reflecting perhaps the *mores* of society? Newman's philosophical position thus covers not only the *nature* of a university but also the *manner* in which it should conduct its teaching and research.

The Church, Newman argued, must take some responsibility for the state of affairs in which it finds itself. He observed in a public lecture in the School of Medicine in Dublin that he detected an element of suspicion amongst the 'educated and half-educated portions of the community', of a certain contempt of theology by those who are not 'over-religious' and an undervaluing and prejudice against the discoveries of science by some fundamentalist religious minds who do not really understand what theology is. This leads to needless antagonism on both sides, and to the caricatures of religion which are a feature of the twenty-first century critics.[61]

It is important to note that Newman claimed to be making a philosophical case for his concept of a university which, *in itself*, does not imply a relationship to the Christian Church nor does it depend on it. Nevertheless, he argued that the university needs the Church for its *integrity*. By this he meant its wholeness, health, well-being and perfection, its *bene esse*. In the *Historical Sketches*, Newman showed the immense benefit the development of learning has received from Christianity historically, not least through the great religious orders. In Newman's eyes, Christianity brought not only the Gospel but civilization to peoples in many parts of the world and with it an elevated, rounded view of humanity and reality.[62]

The prevailing philosophy of the day, to which so much of education was becoming in thrall, does the opposite, he argued. The more aspects or constituents of universal knowledge are marginalized, the lower becomes our estimation of all that contributes to the formation of a human being. There is something countercultural about an institution which stands against this trend and which refuses to give an inflated accolade of objectivity to some disciplines by denying value to others, on the basis of a flawed philosophy. The Church has, by and large, been a good patron of the disciplines and all that expresses the human spirit. In that sense it can be regarded as a kind of trustee or guarantor that the university remains faithful to its nature. Is this a future role for faith communities?

Newman, however, envisaged a situation in which theology is not just the 'objective', detached *study* of religion, but a *pursuit* in the tradition of 'faith seeking understanding'; not a secularized form of theology or merely religious studies. Gavin D'Costa is right in pointing out the link not only between theology and faith, but also between theology and prayer.[63] St Anselm's *Proslogion* begins with the monk on his knees in prayer, a fact usually neglected by commentators in their interpretation of this difficult work. It is the hostility to this understanding of theology and of faith in the public square that is now a restriction of academic freedom.

What kind of freedom of inquiry and discussion is then possible? On the one hand Newman was insistent that theology has to fight its own corner with the other disciplines in the university and hence theology can often be a noisy and argumentative process,[64] but he also recognized that the Church might have a legitimate interest where core matters of faith are concerned.[65] This is not the same as governance by the Church which should seek to preserve the university's independence, but what defence is there if the Church should exceed its powers? Newman addressed this issue in some of his other writings[66] but also turned the argument the other way round by suggesting that the Church needed universities as one of the means of developing an educated laity who can play their full part in the Church and the world, which was integral to his ecclesiology and sense of mission.[67]

It can be argued, rightly, that we live in a different world than Newman which does not share many of his assumptions, but it was one in which many of the features of the modern and postmodern world were emerging about which he was remarkably prescient,[68] not least the threat from utilitarianism to any discipline especially to those belonging to the arts and humanities.

Newman also saw the problem of the right relationship of faith and reason as a key issue in his time, devoting many of his writings to this theme. His writings on education complement this, for people need to be taught to use their reason well for the good of the whole and here universities have a crucial role.

Benedict XVI picked this up in his lecture to public figures in Westminster Hall in September 2010:

> This 'corrective' role of religion vis-à-vis reason is not always welcomed, though, partly because distorted forms of religion, such as sectarianism and fundamentalism, can be seen to create serious social problems

themselves. And in their turn, these distortions of religion arise when insufficient attention is given to the purifying and structuring role of reason within religion. It is a two-way process. Without the corrective supplied by religion, though, reason too can fall prey to distortions, as when it is manipulated by ideology, or applied in a partial way that fails to take full account of the dignity of the human person.[69]

He then called for a serious and in-depth dialogue between faith and reason in all their forms for the 'good of civilization'.

Providing a forum for this must surely be at the very heart of what it means to be a university and, given the problems faced in the twenty-first century, one of its essential tasks. In a university the different disciplines can contribute to the circle of knowledge through dialogue, conversation and collaboration. For this it needs genuine academic freedom for the pursuit of truth but it also requires commitment that the overarching philosophy that Newman advocated be made real in both teaching and research.

How realistic is this? Adrian Hastings in his seminal work *A History of English Christianity 1920–1990* sums up the changing position of faith in society which provides a parallel:

> Seen in retrospect the 1950s seem almost like a golden age of King Solomon, the sixties an era of moral prophecy of a fairly Pelagian sort. The period in which we have arrived is quite other, an age of apocalyptic, of doom watch, in which the tragedies of an anguished world become just too many to cope with, yet in which there is the strongest feeling that there may still be worse to come.[70]

He identified three responses to this view: the first is to simply despair of any ultimate meaning in the world or in history and argued that many Christians in the 1980s in effect adopted this position. The second is retreat into a privately religious, sacral sphere, abandoning the struggle for the secular state as irremediably corrupt and this, too, he says has been attractive to many. The last position, which few seem prepared to adopt, is that of Augustine in *The City of God*: to take the long view of the ultimate redeemability of things, despite all apparent evidence to the contrary.

Hastings' first two positions are different ways of abandoning the argument. In a time of economic recession and a prevailing view about which there can only be severe reservations, the Augustinian option is the only one if true learning, like faith, is to flourish. Faith communities, especially the Christian Church have a crucial role to play here: as critical friends, as enablers of conversations, as creative and imaginative partners, as providers of alternative models for the exploration of meaning. As Boulton and Lucas remind us: 'It is the totality of the university enterprise that is important, as the only place where that totality of ourselves and our world is brought together, and which makes it the strongest provider of the rational explanation and meaning that societies need.'[71] Newman would have agreed.

Notes

1 Sheldon Rothblatt (1997), *The Modern University and Its Discontents, the Fate of Newman's Legacies in Britain and America* (Cambridge: Cambridge University Press), p. xii.

2 Geoffrey Boulton and Colin Lucas (2008), 'What Are Universities For?' *League of Research Universities Paper*, September 2008, Introduction.

3 Alasdair MacIntyre (2009), 'The Very Idea of a University: Aristotle, Newman and Us', *The British Journal of Educational Studies*, December 2009.

4 Boulton and Lucas (2008), 'What Are Universities For?' paras 14 and 18.

5 *Securing a Sustainable Future for Higher Education – An Independent Review of Higher Education Funding and Student Finance*, October 2010, especially paras 1.1–1.3.

6 'In particular, we want schools and students to understand which GCSE and A-Level choices lead to which degree courses (and ultimately which careers, and what those careers pay)', para. 2.19. 'The relationship between universities and colleges, students and employers is crucial to ensuring that students experience the higher education they want while studying and leave their course equipped to embark on a rewarding career', para 3.47.

7 Dwight A. Culler (1955), *The Imperial Intellect* (New Haven: Yale University Press).

8 Stefan Collini (2010), 'Browne's Gamble', *London Review of Books*, 32(21): pp. 23–25, 4 November 2010. I am grateful to Professor Peter Hampson of the University of the West of England who drew my attention to this article. Retrieved on 31 October 2011 from www.lrb.co.uk/v32/n21/stefan-collini/brownes-gamble.

9 Editor of *The Rambler* in 1858, cited in Thomas J. Norris (2010), *Cardinal Newman for Today* (Dublin: The Columbia Press), p. 62.

10 John Henry Newman (2001), *Rise and Progress of Universities and Benedictine Essays* (Gracewing: University of Notre Dame Press). The two should surely inform each other, as John Paul II argued in his 'Apostolical Constitution on Catholic Universities', Ex Corde, para. 7. Nevertheless, Newman is clear that teaching is the primary function of universities. See Collini's concern about the effects of the RAE exercises on teaching in 'Browne's Gamble'.

11 *My Campaign in Ireland*, ed. W. Neville (1896 privately printed). Cf. Culler, *The Imperial Intellect*, especially notes 36 and 37 to chapter 11. Culler also argued that Newman anticipated the modern university in more ways than are usually recognized, Culler, *The Imperial Intellect*, p. 226.

12 Introduction, p. lxx.

13 Ibid., pp. lxx–lxxiv. See N. Lash, 'Wisdom, Understanding and the Catholic University', *Louvain Studies*, 33: pp. 295–6 who maintains that Newman's *Idea*

'had no place for, or interest in research', a position that only holds if the Idea is treated in isolation.

14 *Historical Sketches* (1893), Vol. III, p. 77.
15 Culler, *The Imperial Intellect*, p. 226.
16 See Brian Simon (new ed. 1999), *Education and the Social Order* 1940–1990 (London: Lawrence and Wishart), p. 23f.
17 See Raymond Williams (1961), *Culture and Society 1780–1950* (London: Penguin), Part I, chapter 6: 'J. H. Newman and Matthew Arnold', in which he claims that Newman in the Idea 'is virtually announcing the task which Arnold was about to undertake in Culture and Anarchy', p. 120.
18 Cf. Boulton and Lucas, 'What Are Universities For?' passim.
19 *The Idea of a University*, Discourse III, pp. 58ff. Unless stated otherwise, all references to Newman's works are to the uniform edition.
20 *Idea*, Discourse II, pp. 19–23, 25–29. Along with poetry, music and art.
21 *Idea*, Discourse VI, p. 144.
22 *Idea*, Discourse VII, p. 162.
23 Ibid.
24 S. T. Coleridge, *On the Constitution of Church and State*, p. v.
25 *Idea*, Discourse VII, p. 166.
26 Ibid., pp. 177–8.
27 Ibid., p. 178.
28 The suspicion of all areas of study which employ eloquence and imagery goes back at least to Hobbes and Bentham for whom poetry was a form of 'mis-representation', see Coulson's (1970) important discussion in *Newman and the Common Tradition* (Oxford: Clarendon Press), pp. 6–8.
29 J. Wilson (ed.) (1971), *Culture and Anarchy* (Dover: Cambridge), p. 11.
30 'The Very Idea of a University', pp. 17–18.
31 Boulton and Lucas, 'What Are Universities For?' para 16, p. 6 and para. 18, p. 6.
32 Ibid., para. 23, p. 7 and para. 30, p. 9.
33 *Idea*, Discourse VI, p. 134.
34 Ibid., p. 135.
35 Ibid., p. 137.
36 Ibid., p. 139.
37 Cf. James Arthur and Guy Nicholls (2007), *John Henry Newman* in Vol. 8 of the Continuum Library of Educational Thought, series ed. Richard Bailey (London: Continuum), pp. 129ff.
38 *Idea*, Discourse II, p. 20.
39 *Idea*, Discourse II, p. 20f.
40 *Idea*, Discourse IX, p. 214.
41 *Historical Sketches*, Vol. III, p. 6.
42 Ibid.
43 *Historical Sketches*, Vol. III, chapter 6, passim. Newman was highly critical of this lack when he became a tutor at Oriel. See Henry Tristram (ed.) (1956), *Autobiographical Writings* (London and New York: Sheed and Ward), p. 88.
44 *Historical Sketches*, Vol. III, pp. 77–8.
45 That Newman tried to model this can be seen by studying the bridge-building lectures and essays in Part II of the Idea entitled 'University Subjects'.
46 *Idea*, Discourse II, p. 21.

47 *Parochial and Plain Sermons*, Vol. VI, pp. 219–20 and many other passages. For example: 'To settle down in a satisfied way in the world as they find it, to sit down in the "mire and dirt" of their natural state, to immerse themselves and be absorbed in the unhealthy marsh which is under them. They tend to become part of the world, and be sucked in by it, and (as it were) changed into it; and to lose all aspirations and thoughts, whether good or bad after anything higher than what they are.'
48 *Historical Sketches*, Vol. III, chapter 2, 'What Is a University', p. 16.
49 *Idea*, Discourse V, p. 108.
50 *Idea*, 'Christianity and Physical Science', p. 434. Newman maintained that it should not be problematic for a Christian foundation; T. Merrigan (1991), *Clear Heads and Holy Hearts*, Louvain Theological and Pastoral Monographs No 7. (Louvain: Eeerdmans,Peters Press); see Merrigan's important discussion of Newman's 'theological style' and its interpretations, op. cit, pp. 142–8.
51 J. Polkinghorne (1994), *Quarks, Chaos & Christianity* (London: SPCK), pp. 11–12.
52 *Idea*, 'University Subjects' VI, p. 427; cf. Ian Ker (1988), *John Henry Newman* (Oxford: Oxford University Press), p. 392.
53 Ibid., p. 448.
54 *Idea*, Discourse III, p. 63.
55 *Idea*, Discourse II, p. 21.
56 'On the study of Mathematics' in *Christian Observer*, Vol XX, Boston 1822, pp. 293–5.
57 Ibid., pp. 28–31.
58 Cf. Gavin D'Costa (2005), *Theology in the Public Square* (Oxford: Blackwell). He speaks of a kind of 'Babylonian Captivity' of theology in the Modern University especially as found in the United Kingdom and the United States.
59 See Gerard Loughlin's discussion in 'Theology in the University' in Ian Ker and Terrence Merrigan (2009), *The Cambridge Companion to John Henry Newman* (Cambridge: Cambridge University Press), p. 229.
60 *Idea*, University Subjects VII, pp. 458–9.
61 *Idea*, Part II, chapter 8, p. 457.
62 *Idea*, Introductory, pp. 12ff.
63 D'Costa, *Theology in the Public Square*, chapter 4, passim.
64 *Apologia*, p. 252.
65 *Idea*, Discourse I, Introductory, p. 10.
66 See *Via Media* and *On Consulting the Faithful in Matters of Doctrine*, especially Newman's metaphor of the Three Offices of Christ. The importance of balance between them in the Church is relevant here in exploring the place and scope of theological enquiry.
67 *Lectures on the Present Position of Catholics*, 1851, pp. 388–91.
68 Cf. the famous biglietto speech of 1877 in *My Campaign in Ireland*, pp. 393–400.
69 Benedict XVI Address, Westminster Hall, 18 September 2010, retrieved from www.vatican.va/holy_father/benedict_xvi/speeches/2010/september/documents/hf_ben-xvi_spe_20100917_societa-civile_en.html.
70 A. Hastings (1991), *A History of English Christianity 1920–1990* (3rd ed.) (London and Philadelphia: Trinity Press International), p. 660.
71 'What Are Universities For?' para. 61.

PART 1

NATURAL AND LIFE SCIENCES

Chapter 2

MATHEMATICS: BREAKING THE CODE OF CREATION

MICHAEL HELLER
(Pontifical University of John Paul II, Cracow)

I *The Book of Nature*

The metaphor of the Book of Nature goes back to the age of the Church Fathers, especially Origen and St Augustine. While Origen made a comparison between 'the written laws of the states' and the 'ultimate law of nature which probably comes from God',[1] St Augustine proposed 'to consider the whole of creation, regarding God as its author, by reading so to speak in the great book of nature'.[2] Olaf Pedersen explains that the context of this quotation shows that it was used by St Augustine against the Manicheans to argue that the created world is good because God is its creator.[3] St Augustine speaks also about nature as a mirror or *speculum*. Both these metaphors (book and mirror) were alive in the later history. In a mirror we see a reflected image, in a book we read what the author wants to tell us. An image in the mirror is to be passively contemplated, whereas ideas from a book are read with some effort at comprehension. This is why the creators of modern science preferred the book metaphor. Galileo stressed that the book of nature cannot be understood 'unless one knows the characters in which it is written', that is unless one knows mathematics. The following passage from Galileo's *Assayer* is often quoted in this regard: 'Philosophy is written in a great book which is constantly held open before our eyes—that is the universe—but it cannot be grasped unless one knows the characters in which it is written. . . . These characters are triangles, circles and other geometric figures, without the aid of which man cannot grasp a word of the language, and without which one would simply wander vainly in a dark labyrinth'.[4]

However, the book of nature soon started to surprise researchers with its apparent loopholes and blank pages. Strangely enough, both scientists and theologians exhibited a strong tendency to fill in these gaps in the current knowledge with the 'hypothesis of God'. This was true not only in the early period of modern science but happens today as well when, for instance, some thinkers try to identify the Big Bang singularity, a typical example of a gap in our knowledge, as a creative act of God. This is clearly against the spirit of the book of nature metaphor. We can speculate about the author's thoughts only from what we read and understand and not from a book's blank pages. In this sense, Einstein's saying that science does nothing but deciphers the Mind of God can be understood as a continuation and deepening of the time honored book of nature metaphor. Following this way of thinking, I will, in the rest of the essay, contemplate the structure of the world as reconstructed by the sciences and theologically interpreted as a blueprint of creation. The synopsis that follows elucidates the main lines of the idea.

In section II, I consider select aspects of the Christian concept of creation. In my view, the metaphysical objective of the creation doctrine is to justify the world's existence and its rationality (in fact, these are but two sides of the same coin). In this respect the key biblical text concerning the doctrine of creation is the Prologue to the Fourth Gospel.

The rationality of the world is best visible in the method of physics. Mathematics is a formal science of structure ('a morphology of structures'); in physics, some of these structures are interpreted as structures of the world. The unprecedented effectiveness of this method lies in the agreement of theoretical predictions with the results of experiments and observations. This kind of rationality reflects, to some extent, the rationality of the act of creation. This is considered in section III.

In section IV, I further develop this line of reasoning. Any mathematical structure consists of a network of logical inferences. These inferences, when interpreted in physical theories as dependencies between phenomena, fulfill an explanatory role, and some of them can be interpreted as causal dependencies. The postulate that the network of these dependencies should be self-contained is a cornerstone of the scientific method. This means that the explanatory or causal chains of dependencies should not go beyond the universe itself, that is the universe must be explained in terms of the universe itself. This is why the so-called God of the gaps arguments always remain in conflict with the 'spirit of science'. God should not be sought where explanatory or causal chains reach their end (where our knowledge fails) but in His entire work of creation.

Two aspects of the 'blueprint of the universe' deserve our special attention: probabilistic and temporal. I deal with them in sections V and VI.

In section V, I argue that the so-called chancy or random events fit well into this blueprint. Moreover, without them the system of physical laws would not function. Therefore, chancy or random events are not a 'foreign body' in the work of creation but rather part of its vital elements. In section VI, I turn to the issue of time. Analyses related to both macroscopic entropy and gravitational entropy, together with the fact that the universe has a unique global history (what is an exception rather than the rule in the set of all theoretically possible universes), lead to the conclusion that time is not an ontological precondition of creation, but rather an 'imprint' impressed on the created world. This is in conformity with the traditional doctrine of God's atemporality, but when considered from the perspective of the creaturely word, reveals a dynamical aspect of creation.

II Creation and the Mind of God

Any serious attempt to look for the author of the book of nature bring us to considerations focused around the issue of creation. Although the basics of this issue were already present in the Old Testament, its full elaboration was the result of a synthesis of Christian thought with Greek philosophy. I think that the cornerstone of this synthesis was laid down in the Prologue to St John's Gospel. The term *logos* was a technical term in Greek philosophy. For Heraclitus, *logos* was a principle of knowledge and order in the cosmos, for Aristotle the synonym of a rational discourse and for the Stoics the divine principle animating the world (a sort of a rational soul of the world). It was Philo of Alexandria who transferred the concept of *logos* from Greek philosophy to Jewish thought. In his view, God is totally transcendent, and the only way to have access to God is through ratio and knowledge, that is through the *Logos* of God.

There are strong reasons to believe that the author of the Fourth Gospel built upon the Jewish and Greek traditions but regarded them from a radically new perspective. In his vision, *Logos* is not an 'emissary' of God, as in Philo's view, but God Himself ('and the Logos was with God, and the Logos was God', Jn 1.1), and not an abstract principle of world's rationality, as with the Stoics and Plato, but the One who is the Rational Creator of all beings ('all things were made by him; and without him was not any thing made that was made', Jn 1.3). This is why *the Logos made flesh* (Jn 1.14) was so shocking for both Jews and the Greeks.

I think that the beginning of the Fourth Gospel constitutes the most fundamental biblical text as far as the Christian theology (and philosophy) of creation is concerned. The struggling of generations of Christian (and not only Christian) thinkers to cope with the creation problem could be regarded as an attempt to penetrate the overwhelming vision of St John.

Putting aside the dramatic theological content of the creation doctrine (especially its relation to Incarnation), let us focus on its metaphysical aspect (although metaphysics and theology are strongly interwoven here). It was Leibniz who expressed it in the most concise form when, in his *Principles of Nature and Grace Based on Reason*, he asked: 'Why is there something rather than nothing?' And after posing this question he immediately added: 'After all, nothing is simpler and easier than something.'[5] An infinite gap between nothing and something is at the core of the doctrine of creation. It is not the beginning of the cosmic history that counts here (it is relegated to the rank of a secondary issue), but rather the very justification of the existence of anything that is.

There is another question, similar in its weight to the Leibniz question. It was emphatically formulated by Einstein: 'Why is the universe comprehensible?' and Einstein hastened to add: 'This is the mystery we shall never comprehend.'[6] The fact that this question was formulated by Einstein is especially telling. Einstein, more convincingly than anybody else, has demonstrated that the world's comprehensibility is of a mathematical character. For him to comprehend the world meant to know 'the Mind of God', the mind He had in His planning the universe. Galileo's mathematical language of the book of nature is for Einstein a kind of programme or blueprint according to which the world is functioning. In this context, Einstein's idea of the mind of God is not far from the Greek concept of *logos* as the principle of the world's rationality, and it can be almost automatically accommodated to the Christian philosophy of creation. A direct implication of this approach is that in planning the universe God was thinking in a mathematical-like way. By saying this we are back to Leibniz's penetrating insights; in the margin of a text entitled *Dialogus* he wrote: 'When God calculates and thinks things through, the world is made.'[7] For God to plan is to execute the plan, and, if planning is mathematical, the effect must be like a mathematical structure.

We thus have two equally vital and equally overwhelming questions: first, 'Why is there something rather than nothing?' and second, 'Why is the universe comprehensible?' In my view, they are not two separate questions, but rather two expressions of the same concern – the concern of the roots of being.[8] Irrationality excludes from existence. Existence presupposes rationality. The roots of rationality are the same as the roots of existence.

III Blueprint of the Universe

The mystery of creation is thus the mystery of rationality and this mystery most clearly reveals itself in the fact that the structure of the universe is best disclosed with the help of mathematics, the most rational creation of the human mind. In this perspective, mathematics is not only a language in which *we describe* the world, but also a tool with the help of which we penetrate the deep layers of its architecture.

There are several philosophies of mathematics dealing with the question 'what is mathematics about?' Unless we go deeper into the technical layers of this question, almost everybody agrees that mathematics is a science of structures. It is interesting to note that Saunders Mac Lane, one of the founders of the mathematical theory of categories, initially expressed the view that this theory will be able to provide the foundations for all of mathematics (to a better extent than does the theory of sets). However, when this expectation did not materialize, he changed his opinion and started to believe that although the category theory does not actually provide foundations of mathematics, it has a 'foundational significance' since it shows why mathematics has no foundations. It organizes the whole of mathematics into one big 'structure of structures' in which everything is related with everything, and nothing could be regarded as more basic than the rest of the whole.[9]

This 'mathematical structuralism' is well grounded in mathematical practice. In pure mathematics one works with abstract structures and relations between structures; in applied mathematics one tries to identify some of these structures as the structures of the physical world and deduce from them conclusions that could be compared with the results of measurements.

It is an 'ontological surprise' that this sketched strategy works so wonderfully. This 'unreasonable effectiveness of mathematics' is often employed as an argument on behalf of the realist standpoint in the philosophy of physics. John Worrall writes emphatically: 'It would be a miracle, a coincidence on a near cosmic scale, if a theory made as many correct empirical predictions as, say, the general theory of relativity or the photon theory of light *without* what that theory says about the fundamental structure of the universe being correct or "essentially" or "basically" correct.'[10] I do not want to enter here into a long lasting discussion concerning realist or instrumentalist interpretation of physics; I would only argue that the 'rationality of creation' is wonderfully reflected in the following scheme: mathematics is a 'morphology of structures'[11] and when some parts or aspects of this morphology are used to disclose the intimate working of nature (i.e. when they are interpreted as structures of the physical world), they lead to an unprecedented success both as far as empirical predictions and technical applications are concerned.[12] The message we can read from this analysis is that the rationality of mathematics and its effectiveness in the physical world tells us something about the rationality of creation.

There are three participating aspects in this striking strategy: mathematics, the physical world and the human mind that creates (or discovers?) mathematics and applies it to the world. This shows that the human mind is not an alien in the rationality of creation but rather its pivotal element. Although the rationality transcends the human mind, the latter plays an active part in this subtle strategy.

IV *The Causal Power of Mathematics*

A tacit assumption implicit in the scientific method asserts that the mathematical 'structure of structures', as implemented in the physical world, is self-contained. To understand what this means, let us go a step further in our analysis of the scientific method. Any mathematical structure used by a physical theory is in fact a net of logical inferences which are interpreted as dependencies between certain physical magnitudes. The theory gains credibility if at least some of these dependencies are empirically verified. However, in order to make the net of inferences transparent and, so to speak, prepare it for confrontation with empirical data, they must be computationally developed, that is abstract structures must, with the help of computations, be translated into concrete formulae able to provide numerical outputs. In this way, the structure of a physical theory is not a static entity; its various elements interact with each other. Exactly in this interaction consists an explanatory function of physical theories. A physical phenomenon is explained if it is placed within the network of dependencies and, in this manner, its interaction with the rest of the structure is displayed.

Some of these explanatory dependencies are often interpreted as causal relations. Hume's critique of causality is well-known and, with many variations, almost commonly accepted among philosophers. It asserts that since all our knowledge comes from experience, we can only know the temporal succession of phenomena but not causal relations between them. We can only know that *B post A* and not that *B propter A*. However, such a naïve empiricism cannot be accepted any longer in the context of the sciences. If there exists a correspondence between mathematical structures of physical theories and the structure of the world then at least some inferences within mathematical structures correspond to some 'inferences' (dependencies) within the physical world. Such dependencies can be interpreted as causal dependencies. And they are not reduced to temporal successions. Many of them display a truly dynamical nexus between phenomena. This is also valid as far as classical physics is concerned. In Hume's time, physicists were too busy conducting research with the help of the newly invented method to pay enough attention to the method itself. Today we know that no direct contact, or even immediate temporal succession, is strictly necessary for causal interactions. It is enough to think about entanglement phenomena in quantum mechanics here: a rich class of effects in which measurement results of some physical magnitudes, such as the spin of particles, are correlated with each other even if no physical signal can travel between them.

Let us consider an example showing 'causal dependencies' between phenomena. A reaction is known in nuclear physics in which a neutron decays into a proton and emits an electron and an antineutrino. The theory of weak nuclear reactions teaches us that in this reaction a down quark, a constituent of the neutron, transforms into an up quark and emits a boson W^-, which in turn decays into an electron and an antineutrino. This chain of processes is deduced from the theory of weak nuclear interactions. But is this only a *description* of what is going on? There are particles that behave in a certain way, and does it just happen that there is a mathematical structure that correctly describes what such particles 'are doing'? First of all, in physics there are no 'material particles' that would be independent of a theoretical structure. Particles, such as neutrons, protons, quarks and so on, are only 'places' in a mathematical structure interpreted as a structure of the world. The nature of these particles is entirely determined by this structure, and it is this structure that also determines the behaviour of particles.

Philosophers often claim that 'abstract structures', such as mathematical structures, or 'abstract objects' are causally powerless.[13] This could be true as far as pure mathematics is concerned, but does not hold good with regard to the mathematical structures physics employs to investigate the physical world.

In every physical theory, in every explanation of a single phenomenon, a totalitarian tendency of scientific method is latent. If the totality is meaningless, why should this part or aspect of it be explainable? This is why it is not only the network of dependencies within a single theory that is relevant for our consideration. Some chains of explanatory (or causal) dependencies go beyond single theories and are extended to inter-theory relations. There are not only individual phenomena here but rather the entire universe that is to be explained. And here we finally come to the postulate demanding that the method of science should be self-contained. This means that explanatory dependencies, forming the 'structure of structures' of the universe, should nowhere go beyond the universe itself. The universe must be explained in terms of itself. Whether such a 'total explanation' will ever be achieved is another problem, but as long as science lasts this postulate will always remain a cornerstone of scientific method.[14]

For this reason all so-called God of the gaps examples of reasoning, arguing on behalf of God's existence from unexplained phenomena in nature, are doomed to be against the 'spirit of science'; this is why God cannot be understood in a way similar to the ways in which we understand other causes acting in the world and in our everyday life. God is not a cause prior to or above all other causes (even in an analogous sense). When God 'calculates and thinks things through', all explanatory and causal dependencies come into being. They are not independent realities merely controlled by God; they are elements of His thinking and His calculations. A metaphoric language is better here than any pretense of strict reasoning.

V *Chance and Necessity*

In many theology-like discussions chance is regarded as a rival of God. For instance, supporters of the so-called intelligent design doctrine tend to minimize the role of chance in biological evolution in order to leave a place for God's purposeful action in the world. In fact, it cannot be denied that in the structure of the universe there is a subtle interplay of law-like and contingent elements. The laws of nature are essential aspects of the mathematical structure of the world, but they cannot operate without some involvement of some degree of randomness present, mainly in their initial or boundary conditions. How can this be translated into our idea of 'God calculating the universe'? And what exactly does 'chance' or 'casual event' mean in this context? We speak about chance if we are confronted with an event which happens in spite of the fact that its (a priori) probability is small. This small probability is somewhat related to our feeling of unexpectedness which is usually associated with casual events. Since the term 'small' is rather undetermined we must connect a chancy event with a probability that is less than one. By doing this, we find ourselves within the context of the probability calculus.

Probability calculus (or more technically, theory of probabilistic measure) is a beautiful and well-developed branch of mathematics. From the formal point of view it does not differ from other mathematical theories. Deduction from premises to conclusions proceeds in exactly in the same way as in the rest of mathematics. The conclusion that something will happen with probability 1/10 is as certain as is the result of a well-determined mathematical operation. A certain indeterminacy or a degree of uncertainty of the outcome does not come from the formal side of mathematics but from our interpretation. Roughly speaking, there are two major approaches to interpreting probability: subjective (or epistemic) interpretation sees the source of probability in our ignorance of some events while objective interpretation regards probability as a measure of an indeterminacy that is really present in the world. Sometimes it is difficult to decide whether a given probabilistic account is due to our ignorance or to indeterminacy inherent in the process itself. Some 'mixed cases' are possible. It often happens that a law of physics, expressed in the form of a differential equation, is strictly deterministic, but its initial conditions are, from the point of view of the law itself, purely contingent. Think, for example, of a stone thrown by John. Its trajectory is deterministically determined by the Newtonian law of motion, but its initial conditions (starting point and starting velocity) are left for John's fantasy. However, without the initial conditions, be they chosen by John or by some other physical processes, the law would remain inactive. This is a typical situation; laws of nature could not operate without a certain admixture of chancy events.

The blueprint of the universe consists of the network of mathematical structures interpreted as laws of physics. In this network some places are left that must be filled in by chancy events, without which the entire system would be ineffective. The chancy events are not 'irrational gaps' in the otherwise highly rational system. They are modeled by a mathematical theory of probabilistic measures (probability theory) and are not 'less mathematical' than the rest of the structure.

Thus, random or chance events are not an anomaly in creation but instead are some of its essential and most crucial aspects. In God's 'thinking things through' probabilistic calculations are as important as the rest of mathematics.

VI *Time and Dynamics*

I would finally like to emphasize another important characteristic of the 'work of creation' – its temporal or dynamical aspect. Even from the physical point of view time is problematic, in the sense that it generates many difficult problems. On the one hand, it seems, through the second law of thermodynamics, to impose a severe constraint on physical processes; on the other hand, the theory of general relativity provides strong reasons to believe that the existence of global time in the universe is something that, in general, should not be expected. Let us first focus on the relativistic context.

In general relativity the decomposition of space–time into space and time separately depends on the choice of coordinate system and, in general, it is not possible to choose coordinates in such a way that time could cover the entire space–time manifold. Therefore, in such a general case, there is no single global time extending from minus infinity to plus infinity or from the beginning of the cosmic history to its end. In the general case, the history of the universe dissolves into many 'local histories'. Stephen Hawking's theorem states the conditions that must be satisfied in the universe for it to admit a global time.[15] Evidently, our universe (or at least this part of it that we control with our observations) belongs to this particular subset of universes which satisfy these conditions.[16] In fact, we have been able to reconstruct our cosmic history starting from the Big Bang.

Why is our universe so special? This is a difficult question. The question becomes even more difficult if we turn to the second law of thermodynamics. As it is well known, it is this law that determines the 'time arrow'. A physical magnitude called entropy measures the degree of order present in a given system, according to the rule: greater order, smaller entropy. Increase of entropy (increase of disorder) determines the arrow of time, which flows from smaller entropy to greater entropy.[17] This is a 'natural' direction of time since entropy is a statistical magnitude and greater entropy is more probable than smaller entropy. It follows that 'in the beginning' (in the Big Bang) the entropy was minimal, and consequently the state of the universe highly improbable. Why?

This 'why' signals only the first and easier part of the problem. It was Roger Penrose who noticed that besides the usual thermodynamical entropy we must also take into account entropy connected with gravitational field (gravitational entropy). This measures the degree of 'clumpiness' of gravity. In Einstein's theory, gravity is related to the space–time curvature: a uniform gravitational field corresponds to smooth or even space–time; a clumpy gravitational field (e.g. due to black holes of complicated structures) corresponds to highly uneven space–time. Penrose argues that in the Big Bang the gravitational entropy of the universe was minute, and in the final state of the universe it will be enormous. Moreover, this difference is by many, many orders of magnitude bigger that the one due to the usual thermodynamical entropy.[18] This implies that the initial state of the universe had to be very, very special. Why? Penrose has developed a very subtle hypothesis to answer this question,[19] but it is abstract and remains debatable.

The above considerations are just a sample of the results and hypotheses based on present physical theories which suggest that time is not a priori with respect to the universe and its laws, a sort of an ontological necessity, but rather a part or an aspect of a blueprint according to which the universe functions. We should also remember that present physical theories are only approximations of what physicists call fundamental physical theory, and journalists call a final theory or theory of everything. Such a theory is expected to unify general relativity and quantum physics (into a quantum gravity theory) possibly together with the theory of unified physical forces (i.e. gravitational, electromagnetic and weak and strong nuclear forces). Today we have only some candidates for such a theory; the best known among them are: superstring theory together with its newer version called M-theory, loop quantum gravity, quantum dynamical triangulation and the family of proposals based on non-commutative geometry and quantum groups. Some of these theories claim that the final theory should be 'background independent', that is physical processes reconstructed by this theory should require no background, such as space–time, to develop. According to the background independence postulate, neither space nor time (at least in their present form) exist on the fundamental level; they emerge only when physics goes beyond this level.[20]

Based on the view presented above, we are entitled to infer that the act of creation is not a temporal act. Time is an imprint on the work of creation, the result of the act of creation and not its ontological precondition. This is in conformity with the traditional doctrine of God's atemporality, going back to the Church Fathers (especially St Augustine) and medieval philosophy (especially

St Thomas Aquinas). However, a temporal imprint is an important character-istic of the creaturely world. In physical theories, time serves to parameterize dynamical processes, but the true dynamics cannot be reduced to the fact that a process is developing in time. In mathematical equations used to model a dynamic system there is something substantially more than temporal succes-sion of states: the present state of the system is the result determined (although possibly only in a probabilistic sense) by the preceding state of the system, and it itself determines what will follow it. There are strong reasons to believe that it is this dynamical nexus that belongs to the essence of dynamical systems, and that terms, such as precedent and following, need not be understood in a temporal sense. Analogously, we could claim that although the act of creation is not temporal, it is *par excellence* dynamic. According to the traditional doctrine (St Thomas), the act of creation consists in a continual dependence of the cre-ated world in its existence on God. This traditional doctrine needs to be supple-mented by the remark that this dependence in existence should be understood in an eminently dynamic sense. When viewed by the human mind, immersed in the flowing time, such dynamics are perceived as a 'continual creation'; not only in the sense of 'sustaining in existence', but in the truly dynamic sense: The evolu-tion of the universe and of all its subsystems (the evolution of life included) is creation in the making.

VII Summary

The metaphor of the Book of Nature goes back to Origen and St Augustine. The latter speaks also about nature as a mirror or *speculum*. Both these metaphors were alive in the later development of the tradition. In a mirror we see a reflected image, in a book we read what the author has written. This is why the creators of modern science preferred to adopt the book metaphor. Galileo emphasized that the book is incomprehensible unless one knows mathematics. But the book of nature soon revealed blank pages which scientists and theologians tended to fill with 'the God hypothesis'. This still happens nowadays when some thinkers try to interpret a modern knowledge gap, the Big Bang singularity, as a creative act of God. But the character of a book's author is to be intuited from what is written in it, not from its blank pages. Hence, Einstein's claim that science does nothing but decipher the mind of God continues and deepens the Book meta-phor; it does not use God to cover explanatory gaps. Building on this, I viewed the world's structure, as reconstructed by the natural sciences and interpreted theologically, as creation's blueprint. I focused on the following aspects of this blueprint: First, its rationality, which most clearly reveals itself in the fact that the structure of the world is best disclosed with the help of mathematics, the most rational creation of the human mind. Second, its self-contained character, consisting in the fact that all chains of explanatory inferences must lie entirely within the world's structure. It is this property of the world's structure that results in the full methodological autonomy of the sciences. Third, its subtle sensitivity to the interplay of law-like and casual elements. The laws of nature are essential aspects of the mathematical structure of the world, but they cannot operate without the intervention of some randomness present in their initial or boundary conditions. Even the most chancy or random events are well composed into the blueprint of the universe. Fourth its temporal and dynamic character, allowing us to conclude that the act of creation is not a temporal act, but rather an imprint on the work of creation; not an ontological precondition of creation, but rather its result. However, from the perspective of the human mind, immersed in time, creation reveals its truly dynamic side: not only as 'sustaining in existence', but also as 'becoming in the making'.

Notes

1   Origen, *Contra Celsum*, 5, 37.
2   St Augustine, *Contra Faustum*, 32, 20.
3   O. Pedersen (2007), *The Two Books* (Vatican City State: Vatican Observatory Foundation), chapter 3.
4   D. Dubarle (1967), 'Galileo's Methodology', in E. McMullin (ed.), *Galileo, Man of Science* (New York and London: Basic Books), pp. 295–314; quotation from p. 300.
5   English translation by Jonathan Bennett, retrieved from www.earlymoderntexts.com/pdf/leibphg.pdf.
6   See A. Einstein (1978), 'Physics and Reality', in *Ideas and Opinions* (New York: Dell), pp. 283–315.
7   In C. I. Gerhardt (ed.), *Die philosophischen Schriften von G. W. Leibniz*, Vol. VII, Halle, 1846–1863, pp. 190–3.
8   For more see chapters 18 and 21 of my book, M. Heller (2009), *Ultimate Explanations of the Universe* (Berlin and Heidelberg: Springer).
9   S. Mac Lane, 'The Protean Character of Mathematics', in J. Echeverra and A. Ibarra (eds), *The Space of Mathematics* (New York: De Gruyer), pp. 3–12.
10   J. Worrall (1989), 'Structural Realism. The Best of Both Worlds', *Dialectica* 43: pp. 97–124.
11   E. Landry, 'Category Theory: The Language of Mathematics', retrieved from www.scistud.umkc.edn/psa98/papers/.
12   For more see my paper, M. Heller (2006), 'Discovering the World Structure as a Goal of Physics', in *Paths of Discovery* (Vatican City: The Pontifical Academy of Sciences); *Acta*, 18: pp. 154–67.
13   Michael Dummet presents such a standpoint in the following way: 'It is a common complaint about abstract objects that, since they have no causal powers, they cannot explain anything, and that the world would appear just the same to us if they

did not exist.' M. Dummett (2002), 'What Is Mathematics About?' in D. Jacquette (ed.), *Philosophy of Mathematics. An Anthology* (Oxford: Blackwell), pp. 19–29; quotation from p. 22.

14 See my book, M. Heller (2009), *Ultimate Explanations of the Universe* (Berlin and Heidelberg: Springer).

15 See S. W. Hawking and G. F. R. Ellis (1973), *The Large Scale Structure of Space-Time* (Cambridge: Cambridge University Press), pp. 198–201 (Proposition 6.4.9).

16 This has nothing in common with a highly disputable idea on the existence of 'parallel universes' (the so-called multiverse hypothesis). The 'subset of universes' is here a synonym of a subset of solutions to Einstein's equations of the gravitational field. Each solution is regarded as a theoretically possible universe of its own.

17 Entropy can remain constant only for reversible processes.

18 For more see R. Penrose (1989), *The Emperor's New Mind* (New York and Oxford: Oxford University Press), chapter 7; R. Penrose (2004), *The Road to Reality* (London: Jonathan Cape), chapter 27.

19 See R. Penrose (2010), *Cycles of Time* (London: Bodley Head).

20 See, for instance, my article, M. Heller (2002), 'Time of the Universe', in G. F. R. Ellis (eds), *The Far-Future of the Universe* (Cambridge: Cambridge University Press), pp. 53–64.

Chapter 3

CHRISTIANITY AND PHYSICS

JOHN POLKINGHORNE

(Emeritus, Queens' College, University of Cambridge)

Research in physics is hard work. Like all worthwhile activities, it includes a degree of wearisome routine which has to be endured. In addition, there are occasional experiences of frustration, as the good ideas of the morning look less persuasive in the cold light of the afternoon. Yet many people of high academic talent are content to devote their lives to physics. They do so, I believe, because they desire to understand the physical world as deeply as possible. Physicists, consciously or unconsciously, are realists, believing that what they come to know is telling them what the physical world is actually like. Physics has been remarkably successful in this quest for understanding, whether its concern has been with the properties of subatomic matter, cosmic history, or complex phenomena on a scale in-between.

This great success of physics has been enabled by the modesty of its ambition. It seeks only to ask the single fundamental question – What are the processes by which things happen? – and it brackets out other fundamental questions, such as whether there is meaning or purpose present in what is happening. The dimension of reality that physics investigates is limited, for it confines itself to the realm of the impersonal, where there is power to manipulate and repeat phenomena at will, thereby affording the subject its great secret weapon of experimental verification. (Even an observational science like cosmology, whose phenomena cannot be repeated, depends greatly upon the experimental sciences for gaining its understanding.) In consequence of this concentrated focus, the history of physics frequently displays the eventual attainment of a universally agreed understanding of the nature of some specific physical regime. Physics has proved capable of furnishing reliable maps of the physical world as that world is found to operate on specific scales. Yet the achievements of physics are never final and complete, for exploring phenomena on a different scale (higher energy, smaller distance) may reveal new and totally unexpected properties. No map can give an exhaustive account of the actual terrain. The classical mechanics of

Isaac Newton had to give way to quantum mechanics for processes on the scale of atoms or smaller, just as Newton's theory of gravity had eventually to give way to Einstein's theory of general relativity. Newtonian gravitational theory is accurate enough to enable sending a space explorer to Mars, but it is inadequate to the discussion of the strong gravitational fields surrounding a black hole.

Despite these considerable successes in specific regimes, there remain some unsolved problems for physics concerning relationships between different regimes. The most celebrated of these issues is the measurement problem in quantum theory (for an introduction to quantum physics, see, for example, Polkinghorne 2002a). Measurements on quantum entities will often not yield a uniquely determinate outcome, repeated every time, but very precise predictions can be made for the probabilities of obtaining different results on different occasions. Yet there is no universally agreed and satisfactory account of how a particular result emerges on a particular occasion. This is an example of the fact that it is not fully understood how the apparently clear and reliable macroscopic world of classical physics, in which measurements take place, arises from its cloudy and fitful microscopic quantum substrate. The fact of the matter is that physics' understanding, though often impressive, is also distinctly patchy. A related example is provided by attempts to formulate what one may call quantum chaology. Chaos theory is a feature of classical physics which was only clearly recognized in the middle of the twentieth century. It shows that there are many classical systems which are so exquisitely sensitive to the finest detail of their circumstances that their future behaviour soon becomes effectively unpredictable. It turns out that the level of relevant detail quickly comes to fall below the limit of quantum uncertainty and so there is strong motivation to seek to integrate the two theories. However, they are incompatible, for quantum theory has an intrinsic scale set by Planck's constant, which gives a meaning to 'large' or 'small', while chaos theory is fractal (the same all the way down) and it is scale free.

A second limitation on the current power of physics is provided by the recognition that there are fundamental issues about the nature of reality that are constrained by physics but not totally determined by it. An important example is the nature of causality. Quantum physics is unquestionably probabilistic, but this fact might arise either from an intrinsic epistemological ignorance of all the factors which together actually determine precisely what will happen, or from the ontological existence of an irreducible degree of physical indeterminism. Heisenberg's uncertainty principle states that for a quantum entity one cannot simultaneously know its position (where it is) and its momentum (how it is moving). Heisenberg derived this result from an epistemological analysis of what can be measured. However, Niels Bohr, and most physicists following him, have interpreted this fact, not simply as necessary ignorance but as an ontological signal of actual indeterminism. Yet, in the 1950s, David Bohm showed that there is an alternative interpretation of quantum theory, fully deterministic in its character, which produces the same probability predictions as the Copenhagen interpretation (Bohm and Hiley 1993). For Bohm, the uncertainty principle is simply an epistemological principle of unavoidable ignorance, rather than an ontological principle of intrinsic indeterminism. Because of the empirical equivalence of these two interpretations, the choice between them has to be made on metaphysical grounds. Most physicists side with Bohr against Bohm because they judge the latter's interpretation, clever and instructive though it is, to be too contrived in its character to be metaphysically pleasing. The existence of these two empirically equivalent interpretations makes it clear that the nature of causality is not settled by considerations of physics alone. The subject, properly evaluated, cannot claim to have established the causal closure of the world on its own terms, based exclusively on the exchange of energy between constituents. Other causal principles may also be at work. Metaphysical conclusions about causality can properly be influenced by considerations from outside of physics, such as those deriving from anthropology or theology. It is possible to take with absolute seriousness all that an honest physics can tell us and not conclude that there is no scope for the exercise of agency, either human or providential (Polkinghorne 2005, pp. 7–37).

A similar state of affairs relates to the true nature of temporality (Polkinghorne 2005, pp. 113–26). Relativity theory intimately relates time and space together, but careful analysis shows that this does not inevitably imply, as some have claimed, that the true reality is the whole space–time continuum (the so-called block universe), with the human impression of a moving present simply being a trick of psychological perspective. Reaching a conclusion about the nature of temporality, while constrained by physics, requires also an act of metaphysical decision in which extra-scientific consideration can again properly play a part in choosing between the block universe and a world of unfolding becoming.

Acknowledging these limitations does not, however, imply that within its properly defined domain of competence, physics is not able to reach reliable conclusions. We have very good reason to believe that truly scientific questions can be expected to receive scientific answers, even if sometimes those answers are hard to find, as current problems in integrating quantum theory and general relativity illustrate. As a result, physics remains methodologically naturalistic, not looking outside itself to solve its own legitimate problems. However, the self-limited character of physical enquiry, in relation to the questions it asks and the kind of encounter with reality that it considers, means that this *methodological* strategy offers no warrant for a *metaphysical* assertion of the truth of reductive physicalism.

Many questions of great significance lie beyond the self-limited power of physics to answer. Some of these are meta-questions, which arise out of scientific experience but are not themselves scientific in character, so that responding to them takes us beyond the domain of physics itself. Perhaps the most important of these meta-questions is one that simply asks, 'Why is deep science possible at all?' Of course, we may expect that evolution will have shaped the human brain in such a way that we can make sense of the everyday world in which we have to survive. It is quite another matter, however, that human beings are also able to understand the subatomic world of quantum physics, remote from direct impact upon us and requiring for its understanding counterintuitive modes of thought. This ability surely cannot be thought of as just an incredibly lucky spin-off from survival necessity. The fact is that the universe has proved to be astonishingly transparent to rational enquiry. And the mystery is deeper than that, for it is mathematics – that seemingly most abstract of subjects – which furnishes the key to unlock these cosmic secrets. It is an actual technique of discovery in fundamental physics to seek theories whose mathematical expression is in terms of 'beautiful equations'. (Mathematical beauty is something that mathematicians can recognize and agree about. It involves qualities such as economy and elegance and the property of being 'deep', that is extensive consequences are found to flow from a seemingly simple starting point.) This quest for mathematical beauty is no act of aesthetic indulgence on the part of the theoretical physicists, for time and again in the 300-year history of modern science, it has been found that it is only these mathematically beautiful theories which are the ones that, by their long-term fruitfulness of explanation, persuade us that they are truly describing aspects of physical reality. A distinguished nuclear physicist, Eugene Wigner, once asked 'Why is mathematics so unreasonably effective?' How is it that the reason within (the mathematical thoughts of our minds) and the reason without (the deep order of the physical world) match each other so perfectly? Cosmic intelligibility is a profound fact about the universe and it would surely be intolerably intellectually lazy to treat it simply as a happy accident. Physicists are glad to exploit the opportunities that this fact offers, and to enjoy the experience of wonder at the marvelous order thus disclosed, but speaking as physicists they are unable to explain this remarkable property of the universe. Asking 'Why is science possible?' puts a highly significant issue onto the agenda of enquiry. A meta-question of this kind is too profound a matter for it to be reasonable to expect it to receive an answer of such an indisputable character that only the stupid could disagree. Different thinkers may approach the issue in different ways, but I believe the most persuasive and intellectually satisfying answer to this meta-question is provided by theology.

The rational transparency of the cosmos which makes science possible and the rational beauty of the cosmos which affords the scientist the reward of wonder for the toil involved in research speak of a world that is shot through with signs of mind. Christian theology indeed sees the Mind of the Creator behind the marvelous order of creation. It asserts that the universe is intelligible precisely because it is a divine creation and human beings are, to use an old and powerful phrase, made in the image of their Creator. For the Christian, the ability to do science is one aspect of the *imago Dei*.

There is a second meta-question that arises from physics, 'Why is the universe so special?' Scientists do not, on the whole, much like things to be special. They prefer the general. Our natural expectation was that the cosmos would be just a common specimen of what a universe might be like. However, as physicists have come to understand many of the processes which, over 13.7 billion years, have turned an initial, almost uniform ball of energy into the home of saints and scientists, they have come to realize that the potentiality for this astonishing fertility was built into the physical fabric of the world from the start. The laws of nature which operate in this world (laws which science itself does not explain, but simply accepts as the given basis of its explanation of detailed happenings) had to take a very precise, finely tuned form if the eventual evolution of carbon-based life were to be possible anywhere in the universe (Barrow and Tipler 1986; Holder 2004). Many considerations lead to this unexpected conclusion, which has been given the not altogether appropriate title of the Anthropic Principle. (Of course, it does not relate to the specificity of homo sapiens, but to the possibility of carbon-based life in general; 'The Carbon Principle' would have been a better choice, but it is now too late to change.) One example will have to suffice. The most vital chemical element in living beings is carbon, since its properties permit the formation of the long chain-molecules which are the biochemical basis of life. However, the very early universe made only the two simplest chemical elements, hydrogen and helium. The only place where carbon has subsequently been made is in the stellar nuclear furnaces that came into being when the first stars condensed, many millions of years later in cosmic history. The process by which this happens is both beautiful and delicate. Carbon can form by the fusion of three helium nuclei, but for entities as small as nuclei this cannot happen all at once: it has to take place through the intermediate state in which two helium nuclei have fused to form beryllium. Unfortunately, the state of beryllium made in this way is highly unstable and so would not last long enough for a third nucleus to get attached in a straightforward way. The process is only possible because there happens to be a very large enhancement effect (a resonance) occurring at just the right energy to make the process of attachment go anomalously fast. If the laws of nuclear physics had been even a little different from what they actually are, either there would be no resonance at all, or it would be at the wrong energy. Many other fine-tunings of this kind are required if life is to be a possibility and, remarkably, despite the different character of the phenomena to which they relate, they are all consistent with each other.

All physicists agree about the scientific fact of the specificity of a universe capable of evolving carbon-based life. Disagreements arise over what meta-scientific significance might be attributed to this fact. If the universe were not fine-tuned, then, of course, we would not be here to think about it, but, once again, it does not seem intellectually satisfying to treat this remarkable property as simply a happy accident. Christian theology can interpret fine-tuning as the Creator's gift of an inbuilt fertile potentiality to creation. Those who wish to resist the threat of theism are driven to the expedient of hypothesizing the existence of the multiverse, a vast, possibly infinite, portfolio of different universes, all separate from each other and all unobservable by us. The fine-tuning of our universe is then held to be just a matter of chance, a kind of winning ticket in a gigantic multiversal lottery. Although there are some highly speculative theories which might support the existence of many other universes, the multiverse is essentially a metaphysical explanation, just as the universe understood as a creation is a metaphysical explanation. However, the concept of the cosmos as creation receives collateral support from other considerations, such as cosmic intelligibility, of a kind which seems lacking for the multiverse. There is a cumulative case for theistic belief. Moreover, even an infinity of worlds would not of itself guarantee the existence of one which had the properties necessary for the generation of life. After all, there are an infinite number of even integers, but none of them have the property of oddness.

The appeals to cosmic intelligibility and cosmic fine-tuning which we have been considering as supporting belief in the existence of a Creator represent a revived and revised form of natural theology, the enquiry which seeks to learn something of God from general experience rather than by appeal to specific acts of divine revelatory disclosure. However this modern version is different in its character from the old-style natural theology of people like William Paley and the authors of the Bridgewater Treatises. The arguments of these latter thinkers were based on appealing to the aptness of living beings to life in their environment, seen as being the result of the acts of a divine Designer. This argument lost its force in 1859 with the publication of Charles Darwin's *On the Origin of Species*, showing how the process of natural selection, sifting and preserving small difference between successive generations, could, over long periods of time, result in consequences which had the appearance of design without requiring the direct intervention of a Designer. With the benefit of hindsight we can see that those early apologists were making a mistake about the true relationship between science and theology. The role of the former is to gain understanding of the character of the processes of nature (including such matters as the processes by which a functionally effective complex system like the mammalian eye could develop), and it does not need assistance from theology in this task. I have already said that scientific questions can be expected to receive scientific answers. The role of Christian theology is not to try to do science's work for it, but to set scientific discoveries in a wider and deeper context of intelligibility, in the manner that we sought to do in the discussion of cosmic intelligibility and fine-tuning. The true relationship between science and theology is complementary rather than adversarial. They are friends and not foes in the great human quest for truthful understanding.

Physicists are often impressed by the wonderful order of the universe and this can lead them to embrace a kind of cosmic religiosity, even if they do not adhere to a religious faith tradition. Einstein once said that in making his great discoveries he felt like a child in the presence of the Elders. He liked to speak of 'the Old One', but at most he thought of God as an impersonal principle of cosmic order and he was emphatic that he did not believe in a personal God. The fact is that natural theology pursued in the style that we have been considering can offer significant insight, but it is limited in the kind of evidence that it considers and so it can only offer a correspondingly limited picture of the divine nature. At best, a rather 'thin' concept of God emerges, such as the idea of 'the Great Mathematician' or 'the Cosmic Architect'. On its own this is as consistent with the spectatorial God of deism as it is with the providentially active God of Christianity. Many questions are left unaddressed – such as whether God has an individual care for individual creatures – and their answering depends upon taking seriously the testimony associated with more personal forms of encounter with divine reality. This latter enquiry is one about which physics has nothing to say.

Cosmology has often been seen as a branch of physics possessing particular significance for Christian theology because of its scientific account of the history of the universe. While this is certainly of interest, it is important to recognize that the principal concern of the doctrine of creation is with why things exist, rather than how things began. The fundamental question it addresses is not 'Who lit the blue touch paper of the big bang?' but 'Why is there something rather than nothing?' God is as much the Creator today, holding the universe in being by the divine will, as God was 13.7 billion years ago. In consequence, even if highly speculative theories about the origin of the Big Bang – such as the idea that it arose from a fluctuation in a prior quantum ur-vacuum – were to prove to be correct, they are not of special significance for theology. Recently Stephen Hawking (2010) appealed to an idea of this kind (based on M-theory, a poorly understood generalization of string theory), saying that it showed there was no need for a divine Creator. This claim is simply a category mistake. M-theory is not self-explanatory, as if its existence were an inevitable fact. If indeed our universe did start in this way, the M-theory that enabled it to do so was itself an expression of the sustaining divine will of the Creator, like any other physical fact.

Of genuine concern to theology, however, is how the universe is expected to end (Polkinghorne 2002b). Every story that physics has to tell ends eventually in decay and futility. Not only do persons die on a time scale of tens of years, but the universe itself will die on a timescale of very many billions of years, most probably by continuing to expand, thus becoming increasingly colder and more dilute until all carbon-based life will have disappeared from everywhere within it. From the point of view of physics, these gloomy prognostications arise from the operation of the second law of thermodynamics. It states that entropy (the measure of disorder) will always increase in any closed system. This is because there are overwhelmingly more ways of being disorderly than there are of being orderly, so it is statistically certain that the waters of chaos will rise inexorably. This picture of the inevitability of future futility might seem to put a question mark over the Christian claim that the universe is a meaningful creation. The distinguished physicist and staunch atheist Steven Weinberg once said that the more he understood the universe, the more it seemed pointless to him (Weinberg 1977, p. 149).

There is certainly no natural expectation, of a kind that physics might express, of there being a destiny beyond death, either for individual persons or for the universe itself. But science has only one story to tell, the 'horizontal' story of the unfolding of present process. Christian theology has a different story to tell, the 'vertical' story of God's faithfulness. This was the point that Jesus made in his argument with the Sadducees about whether there is a human destiny beyond death (Mk 12.18–27), in which he said that the God of Abraham, Isaac and Jacob is 'God not of the dead, but of the living'. The faithful God did not abandon the patriarchs at their death as if they were broken pots to be discarded. Christian theology has never denied the reality of death, but it believes that it is not the ultimate reality, for the last word lies with God and not with mortality. The Christian hope is expressed in terms of death and resurrection, the belief that this present old creation will eventually be transformed by God into the new creation, a process that Christians believe has already begun in the seminal event of the resurrection of Christ. These are matters on which physics is powerless to speak, either for or against, except perhaps in one small respect. If the new creation is indeed to be a world in which 'death will be no more, mourning and crying and pain will be no more' (Rev. 21.4), its 'matter' will have to be different from the matter of this world. Paul recognized this when he wrote, 'flesh and blood cannot inherit the kingdom of God, nor does the perishable inherit the imperishable' (1 Cor. 15.50). To a physicist it does not seem incoherent to believe that God could bring into being a new kind of 'matter', so endowed with strong self-organizing principles that it is not subject to the thermodynamic drift to decay that characterizes the matter of this world.

Some general lessons about the search for understanding can be learnt from physics and then find an application elsewhere in the human quest for truth, including in Christian theology (cf. Polkinghorne 2007, 2009). Physicists have found that reality is often surprising, proving to have properties beyond human powers to have anticipated. Commenting in 1928 on the discoveries of his physicist colleagues, the biologist J. B. S. Haldane said they had shown that the universe was not only queerer than we had thought, but queerer than we could have thought without the nudge of nature pushing thought in a wholly unexpected direction. Paul Dirac made it clear that the counterintuitive character of quantum physics derived from the foundational assumption of the superposition principle. This states that there are quantum states which combine together (superposition in a well-defined mathematical sense) possibilities that commonsense would say are immiscible. The electron can be in a state in which it is simultaneously both 'here' and 'there'. This is a middle term of a kind undreamed of by Aristotle, whose logic was based on the law of the excluded middle, requiring that either A (here) or not-A (there) were exclusively the case. In consequence, a new kind of quantum logic applies in the subatomic quantum world. It is also the superposition principle which explains how the trick of wave/particle duality is possible. In a Newtonian world, there can only be states with a definite number of particles present (look and count them). In the quantum world, however, there can be states with an *indefinite* number of particles, formed by the superposition of states with definite numbers of particles. It is these states which turn out to have wave-like properties.

Another counterintuitive property of quantum physics is quantum entanglement. Albert Einstein, who by his discussion in 1905 of the photoelectric effect had been one of the grandfathers of quantum physics, came later to hate his grandchild. Einstein could only conceive of physical reality in terms of precise and unproblematic objectivity and so he deeply disliked and distrusted the cloudy unpredictabilities of conventional quantum physics. Consequently, he was always looking for some way to show that quantum theory was unsatisfactory and incomplete. In the mid-1930s, in collaboration with two young colleagues, he felt that he had found it. Einstein pointed out the quantum theory predicted that once two quantum entities, such as two photons, had interacted with each other, they could become so mutually entangled as effectively to form a single system, with the consequence that acting on one of them would induce an instantaneous change in the other, however far apart they had separated since the interaction had taken place. Einstein felt that this was so 'spooky' an idea that it showed there was something wrong in quantum thinking. However, many years after Einstein's death, clever experiments in the 1980s showed that this entangled quantum property of non-locality (togetherness in separation) is indeed a property of nature. Once again the physical world had proved queerer than we could have thought.

The often surprising character of physics, so strikingly illustrated by quantum theory, means that the instinctive question for a physicist to ask about a proposal, whether within physics or beyond it, is not 'Is it reasonable?' as if we thought we knew beforehand the shape that rationality had to take. No one in 1899 would have considered wave/particle duality to be reasonable, and in fact any competent philosopher would have been willing to 'prove' its impossibility. Nevertheless, this is how light actually behaves. Consequently the instinctive question for the physicist to ask is 'What makes you think that might be the case?' On the one hand this is an open question, not seeking to lay down beforehand the acceptable character that an answer must take, but on the other hand it is demanding, for a strange proposal will not be accepted unless motivating evidence is presented in its support. I like to call this approach 'bottom-up thinking', seeking to proceed from experience to the attainment of understanding, in contrast to a top–down approach, attempting to start from clear and certain general ideas before descending to the consideration of particulars. The trouble with the latter approach is that its general ideas have often turned out in the end to be neither clear nor certain.

There is no universal form that rationality has to take. Thinking has to be allowed to be shaped by the nature of what is being thought about. Quantum logic has to be recognized as operating in the quantum world. Similarly, there is no universal epistemology. The quantum world can be known only in its cloudy uncertainty and an attempt to attain Newtonian clarity is condemned to fail.

These lessons from physics have an obvious cousinly relevance to Christian theology in its search for truthful understanding. The two natures of Christ, human and divine, represent a duality deeper and yet more mysterious than wave/particle duality in physics. Yet I believe that the concept of this theological duality, affirmed at Chalcedon, arose from wrestling with the facts of Christian experience, recorded in the New Testament and confirmed in the continuing life of the Church, which forced believers to use language both human and divine in giving an adequate account of their encounter with their risen Lord, and not from some form of ungrounded metaphysical speculation.

Many physicists are both wistful and wary about religion. They are wistful because they can see that physics by itself does not explain everything and they would like a broader and deeper understanding than it can offer on its own. Religion offers such a wider view, but they are wary because they fear it does so on unacceptable terms. Their mistaken view of faith is that it involves the acceptance of strange beliefs treated simply as non-negotiable assertions by some unquestionable authority and, naturally, they do not wish to commit intellectual suicide. Believing physicists will want to try to show their colleagues that there are motivations for their Christian beliefs, which deserve serious consideration. The leap of faith is not into the dark, but into the light.

Finally, there are aspects of the physical world which, without forming the basis for an apologetic argument in defence of theistic belief in the manner of natural theology, are nevertheless illuminatingly consonant with such a belief. In considering them, the flow of argument is not from nature to God but from belief in God to a deeper understanding of nature. Such an approach can be called a 'theology of nature'. An example would be the striking degree of relationality that physics has discovered to be present in the universe. The interrelatedness of space, time and matter in general relativity would be one case, but the most striking example is quantum entanglement. Even the subatomic world cannot adequately be treated atomistically. It seems that nature fights back against a crass reductionism. Christian theology, with its Trinitarian concept of the one true God, believes that relationality is deeply imbedded in the Godhead itself, in the eternal exchange of love between the three divine Persons, and so it is not surprised to find this palely reflected in the character of creation. Of course, no one would claim that quantum entanglement implied the doctrine of the Trinity, but it is certainly consonant with it.

We should take absolutely seriously all that physics can tell us about the nature of the physical world, recognizing honestly both the insights that it has to offer and also the limitations on the kind understanding that it can attain which are imposed by its self-defined mode of enquiry. Doing so will not prove a threat to Christian belief, but it will lead to enhanced respect for the wonder of creation. Those seeking to serve the God of truth have no need to fear the discoveries of science, but they should welcome truth from whatever source it may come. By no means all truth comes from physics, but some does and Christian theology should accept it with gratitude.

Bibliography

Barrow, J. and Tipler, F. (1986), *The Anthropic Cosmological Principle*. (Oxford: Oxford University Press).

Bohm, D. and Hiley, B. J. (1993), *The Undivided Universe* (London: Routledge).

Hawking, S. W. (2010), *The Grand Design* (London: Bantam Press).

Holder, R. D. (2004), *God. the Multiverse and Everything* (Aldershot: Ashgate).

Polkinghorne, J. C. (2002a), *Quantum Theory: A Very Short Introduction* (Oxford: Oxford University Press).

Polkinghorne, J. C. (2002b), *The God of Hope and the End of the World* (London: SPCK; New Haven: Yale University Press).

Polkinghorne, J. C. (2005), *Exploring Reality* (London: SPCK; New Haven: Yale University Press).

Polkinghorne, J. C. (2007), *Quantum Physics and Theology* (London: SPCK; New Haven: Yale University Press).

Polkinghorne, J. C. (2009), *Theology in the Context of Science* (London: SPCK; New Haven: Yale University Press).

Weinberg, S. (1977), *The First Three Minutes* (London: Andre Deutsch).

Chapter 4

Biology in a Christian University

Alister E. McGrath

(King's College, University of London)

Humanity has been intrigued by the natural world since the dawn of civilization. How are we to make sense of the world of living creatures, and their patterns of behaviour? How are we to account for its complexity? Anticipations of many modern scientific disciplines – such as biology and zoology – can be seen in the classical era, especially in the writings of Aristotle. There can be no doubt that the study of plants and animals should be integral to the work of a university. But what of a Christian university? How does this discipline find its place in a broader vision of the Christian mind?

I The Origins of the Academic Discipline of Biology

The serious scientific study of the biological world is generally regarded as having begun in the seventeenth century, and was unquestionably catalyzed by religious motives and concerns. The invention of the microscope allowed the fine details of the structure of biological organisms to be investigated more closely, and opened up new ways of thinking about nature – and its divine creator. In his *Principles and Duties of Natural Religion* (published posthumously in 1675), John Wilkins (1614–72) emphasized the beauty and complexity of both the physical and biological realms, and praises technological advances – such as the telescope and microscope – which allowed these to be more fully appreciated.

Yet the aesthetic appreciation of nature was only one aspect of the Christian engagement with nature in the later seventeenth century. The biological world, it was realized, was charged with apologetic potential, in an age when atheism and scepticism started becoming culturally significant. An awareness of the beauty of the biological world gradually gave way to a growing belief that the complexity of both plant and animal life could be interpreted persuasively as evidence of divine design. Although this idea is hinted at in earlier works, it started becoming increasingly significant through works such as John Ray's *Wisdom of God Manifested in the Works of the Creation* (1691). Here we see the emergence of a theme which resonates throughout the natural sciences, seen from a Christian perspective – that the beauty of nature is a tangible if imperfect witness to the greater beauty of God.

One of the most significant developments that shaped the emergence of biology as an academic discipline was due to the eighteenth-century Swedish naturalist Carl von Linné (1707–8), more generally known by the Latinized form of his name, Linnaeus. Linnaeus lectured in botany at the University of Uppsala from 1730, and introduced the scientific classification of biological species. Linnaeus' detailed classification of species conveyed the impression to many of his readers that nature was fixed from the moment of its origination. This fitted in well with a traditional and popular reading of the Genesis creation accounts, and suggested that the botanical world of today more or less corresponded to that established in creation. Each species could be regarded as having been created separately and distinctly by God, and endowed with its fixed characteristics.

In the late eighteenth century, such assumptions led to a growing interest in 'natural history' for religious reasons. Following the lead of John Ray, many believed that the wisdom and glory of God could be discerned, albeit indirectly, through the study of the biological world. Where Newton and others had encouraged the study of astronomy as a means of reinforcing Christian faith in the seventeenth century, the later eighteenth century came to see the study of plants and animals as more effective means of reinforcing belief in a creator God, and defending Christianity against its sceptical critics.

The high water mark of this trend is widely seen as lying in William Paley's *Natural Theology; or Evidences of the Existence and Attributes of the Deity, Collected from the Appearances of Nature* (1802), which documented and emphasized the complexity and beauty of the plant and animal world, and interpreted this as evidence of 'contrivance' – that is to say design and construction. Paley (1743–1805) was not an academic scientist. At the time of writing, Paley was Archdeacon of Carlisle, a senior ecclesiastical position, rather than an academic scientist. The category of the 'gentleman naturalist' was well-established at this time, and is perhaps best known through Gilbert White's *Natural History and Antiquities of Selborne* (1789). Like Paley, White was a clergyman with a deep interest in the natural world, which led him to make close observations of plants and animals in their natural habitats. His diary for the period 1783–4 remains one of the best historical sources for the dramatic climatic impacts of the extended volcanic eruptions in Iceland which are thought to have killed six million people across Europe.

Paley compared God to one of the mechanical geniuses of the Industrial Revolution. God had directly created the world in all its intricacy and complexity, just as a skilled engineer might design and construct a watch or a telescope. Paley accepted the viewpoint of his age – namely that God had constructed (or 'contrived') the world in its finished form, as we now know it. Paley argued that the present organization of the world, both physical and biological, could be seen as a compelling witness to the wisdom of a creator god.

Paley's *Natural Theology* had a profound influence on popular English religious thought in the first half of the nineteenth century, and impacted significantly on the academic culture of the early nineteenth century. For example, Oxford University established a large natural history collection, which was assembled in the Museum of Natural History in 1836, arranged along lines suggested by the chapters of Paley's *Natural Theology*. The idea was to lay out examples of the natural world, particularly its plants and animals, in such a way as to exhibit the 'wisdom of God'.

Paley was deeply impressed by Newton's discovery of the regularity of nature, which allowed the universe to be thought of as a complex mechanism, operating according to regular and understandable principles. Nature consists of a series of biological structures which are to be thought of as being 'contrived' – that is constructed with a clear purpose in mind. Paley used his famous analogy of the watch on a heath to emphasize that contrivance necessarily presupposed a designer and constructor. 'Every indication of contrivance, every manifestation of design, which existed in the watch, exists in the works of nature'. Indeed, Paley argues, the difference is that nature shows an even greater degree of contrivance than the watch. Paley is at his best when he deals with the description of mechanical systems within nature, such as the immensely complex structure of the human eye and heart. Yet Paley's argument depended on a static worldview, and simply could not cope with the dynamic understanding of the natural world underlying Darwinism – to which we now turn.

II *The Advent of Darwinism*

Biology was still not fully integrated into the academic world of the mid-nineteenth century. Although some of its aspects were covered in the curriculum of medical schools, the emergence of schools or faculties of biology was still – with a few local exceptions – some distance away. It should therefore not be the cause for great surprise that one of the most significant biological discovereries of the Victorian age should be due to a 'gentleman scientist', outside the British academic establishment.

The publication of Charles Darwin's *Origin of Species* (1859) is rightly regarded as a landmark in nineteenth-century science. On 27 December 1831, HMS *Beagle* set out from the southern English port of Plymouth on a voyage that lasted almost 5 years. Its mission was to complete a survey of the southern coasts of South America, and afterwards to circumnavigate the globe. The small ship's naturalist was Charles Darwin (1809–82). During the voyage, Darwin noted some aspects of the plant and animal life of South America, particularly the Galapagos Islands and Tierra del Fuego, that seemed to him to require explanation, yet which were not satisfactorily accounted for by existing theories.

One popular account of the origin of species, widely supported by the religious and academic establishment of the early nineteenth century, held that God had somehow created everything more or less as we now see it. Darwin knew of Paley's views, and initially found them persuasive. However, his observations on the *Beagle* raised some questions. On his return, Darwin set out to develop a more satisfying explanation based on his own observations and those of others. Although Darwin appears to have hit on the basic idea of evolution through natural selection by 1842, he was not ready to publish. Such a radical theory would require massive observational evidence to be marshalled in its support.

Four features of the natural world seemed to Darwin to require particularly close attention, in the light of problems and shortcomings with existing explanations.

1. The forms of certain living creatures seemed to be adapted to their specific needs. Paley's theory proposed that these creatures were individually designed by God with those needs in mind. Darwin increasingly regarded this as a clumsy explanation.
2. Some species were known to have died out altogether – to have become extinct. This fact had been known before Darwin, and was often explained on the basis of 'catastrophe' theories, such as a 'universal flood', as suggested by the biblical account of Noah.
3. Darwin's research voyage on the *Beagle* had persuaded him of the uneven geographical distribution of life forms throughout the world. In particular, Darwin was impressed by the peculiarities of island populations.
4. Many creatures possess 'rudimentary structures', which have no apparent or predictable function – such as the nipples of male mammals, the rudiments of a pelvis and hind limbs in snakes and wings on many flightless birds. How might these be explained on the basis of Paley's theory, which stressed the importance of the individual design of species? Why should God design redundancies?

These aspects of the natural order could all be explained on the basis of Paley's theory. Yet the explanations offered seemed more than a little cumbersome and strained. What was originally a relatively neat and elegant theory began to crumble under the weight of accumulated difficulties and tensions. There had to be a better explanation. Darwin offered a wealth of evidence in support of the idea of biological evolution, and proposed a mechanism by which it might work – *natural selection.*

The *Origin of Species* sets out with great care why the idea of natural selection is the best mechanism to explain how the evolution of species took place, and how it is to be understood. The key point is that natural selection is proposed as nature's analogue to the process of artificial selection in stockbreeding. Darwin was familiar with these issues, especially as they related to the breeding of pigeons. The first chapter of the *Origin of Species* therefore considers 'variation under domestication' – that is the way in which domestic plants and animals are bred by agriculturists. Darwin notes how selective breeding allows farmers to create animals or plants with particularly desirable traits. Variations develop in successive generations through this process of breeding, and these can be exploited to bring about inherited characteristics which are regarded as being of particular value by the breeder. In the second chapter, Darwin introduces the key notions of the 'struggle for survival' and natural selection to account for what may be observed in both the fossil records and the present natural world.

Darwin then argues that this process of domestic selection or artificial selection offers a model for a mechanism for what happens in nature. 'Variation under domestication' is presented as an analogue of 'variation under nature'. A process of natural selection is argued to occur within the natural order which is analogous to a well-known process, familiar to English stockbreeders and horticulturalists: 'As man can produce and certainly has produced a great result by his methodical and unconscious means of selection, what may not nature effect?'

In the end, Darwin's theory had many weaknesses and loose ends. For example, it required that speciation should take place; yet the evidence for this was conspicuously absent. Darwin himself devoted a large section of *The Origin of Species* to detailing difficulties with his theory, noting in particular the 'imperfection of the geological record', which gave little indication of the existence of intermediate species, and the 'extreme perfection and complication' of certain individual organs, such as the eye. Nevertheless, he was convinced that these were difficulties which could be tolerated on account of the clear explanatory superiority of his approach. Yet even though Darwin did not believe that he had adequately dealt with all the problems which required resolution, he was confident that his explanation was nevertheless the best available. He merely needed to persuade everyone else that this was the case.

Popular accounts of the reception of Darwin's ideas in England often focus on the meeting of the British Association at the Museum of Natural History at Oxford on 30 June 1860. The British Association had always seen one of its most significant objectives as being to popularize science, drawing on both university professors and 'gentlemen scientists' to advance its agendas. As Darwin's *Origin of Species* had been published the previous year, it was natural that it should be a subject of discussion at the 1860 meeting. Darwin himself had been invited to speak, but was in ill health and was unable to attend the meeting in person. According to the popular legend, Samuel Wilberforce, Bishop of Oxford, attempted to pour scorn on the theory of evolution by suggesting that it implied that humans were recently descended from monkeys. He was then duly rebuked by T. H. Huxley, who turned the tables on him, showing him up to be an ignorant and arrogant cleric.

The truth of the matter was that Wilberforce had written an extensive review of the *Origin of Species*, pointing out some serious weaknesses. Darwin regarded this review as significant, and modified his discussion at several points in response to Wilberforce's criticisms. The review shows no trace of 'ecclesiastical obscurantism'. Nevertheless, by 1900 the legend was firmly established, and went some way towards reinforcing the conflict or warfare model of the interaction of science and religion.

Since Darwin's time, there have been many developments which have led to modification and development of his ideas. These include the clarification of the mechanism of inheritance of acquired traits by Gregor Mendel (1822–84), the discovery of the gene by Thomas Hunt Morgan in 1926 and the clarification of the critical role of DNA in the transmission of genetic data, particularly through the establishment of its double helix structure by James Watson and Francis Crick. On the basis of their research, Crick proposed what he called the 'Central Dogma' of a neo-Darwinian view of evolution – namely that DNA replicates, acting as a template for RNA, which in turn acts as a template for proteins. The long and complex DNA molecule contains the genetic information necessary for transmission encoded using the four nucleotide bases: adenine (A), guanine (G), thymine (T) and cytosine (C) arranged in sequences of base pairs.

Today, the term 'Darwinism' is generally used to mean the general approach to biological evolution set out in Darwin's canonical works, as developed and extended through clarification of the molecular basis of inheritance. It forms the basis of all modern discussions of the relation of biology and religious belief, and frames academic debates about the mutual relation of science and religion. This leads us to consider the role of Christian universities in shaping and influencing such discussions.

III Christian Universities and Debates about Biology

Debate about the mutual interaction of Darwinism and Christian thought have proceeded since the 1870s, at both popular and academic levels. One of the most significant responses to Darwin, mingling scientific appreciation and religious evaluation, was due to Asa Gray (1810–88), Professor of Natural History at Harvard University. In recent years, however, academic discussion of Darwinism has tended to focus on a number of issues, all of which are clearly relevant to the vision of a Christian university. The following are of particular importance, and will be considered in the remainder of this chapter. Each delineates an area of discussion which is entirely appropriate to a Christian scholarly community, particularly when the interaction of theology with other disciplines is encouraged and affirmed.

1. Is Darwinism to be considered as a provisional scientific theory, or a normative vision of reality?
2. What Christian theological framework is best adapted to engage contemporary understandings of biological evolution?
3. Does Darwinism entail normative judgements about the origins of ethical or religious beliefs?
4. Does Darwinism eliminate any notion of design or purpose within nature, whether this is understood religiously or otherwise?

These are clearly debates in which a (real or theoretical) Christian university can offer an important interdisciplinary context, informed by a Christian intellectual framework, for the exploration and development of such questions.

IV Darwinism: Scientific Theory or Ideology?

One of the most remarkable developments of the last few years has been the appearance of a number of high-profile populist books offering a critique of religion based on a presumed intellectual link between developments in biology, especially evolutionary biology, and atheism. Two of these, both published in 2006, are of particular interest: Daniel Dennett's *Breaking the Spell* and Richard Dawkins' *The God Delusion*. Both these works reflect a conviction that Darwin's theory of evolution – as developed in the light of Mendelian genetics and our understanding of the place of DNA in the transmission of inherited information – is more than just a scientific theory, on the same epistemological level as other such theories. It is a worldview, a total account of reality. Darwinism, Dawkins suggests, is a 'universal and timeless' principle, capable of being applied throughout the universe. In comparison, rival worldviews such as Marxism are to be seen as 'parochial and ephemeral'.

Where most evolutionary biologists would argue that Darwinism offers a *description* of reality, Dawkins presents it as an *explanation* of things. Darwinism is a worldview, a *grand récit*, a meta-narrative – a totalizing framework, by which the great questions of life are to be evaluated and answered. For this reason, we should not be surprised to learn that Dawkins' account of things has provoked a response from postmodern writers, for whom any meta-narrative – whether Marxist, Freudian or Darwinian – is to be resisted as a matter of principle. Similarly, Daniel Dennett's *Darwin's Dangerous Idea* sets out to show 'why Darwin's idea is so powerful, and why it promises – not threatens – to put our most cherished visions of life on a new foundation'. Darwinism, for Dennett, is a 'universal acid' that erodes outdated, superfluous metaphysical notions, from the idea of God downwards. Darwinism, he asserts, achieves a correlation of 'the realm of life, meaning, and purpose with the realm of space and time, cause and effect, mechanism and physical law'. The Darwinian world is devoid of purpose and transcendence, in that all can and should be explained by the 'standard scientific epistemology and metaphysics'. The Darwinian worldview demystifies and unifies our experience of the world, and places it on more secure foundations.

This transition from Darwinism, considered as a provisional scientific theory applying to one aspect of reality, to Darwinism, considered as a universal worldview – 'reductionism incarnate' (Dennett) – encounters some serious difficulties. One is the obvious point that all scientific theories are to be regarded as provisional, open to correction – and possibly even requiring to be abandoned – in the light of accumulating observational evidence and advancing theoretical understanding. Dawkins is aware of this problem, and is quite explicit about its consequences.

> Darwin may be triumphant at the end of the twentieth century, but we must acknowledge the possibility that new facts may come to light which will force our successors of the twenty-first century to abandon Darwinism or modify it beyond recognition. (Dawkins 2003, p. 81)

The religious and metaphysical implications of this will be obvious. Yet Dawkins seems reluctant to incorporate this appropriate note of caution in his bold statements about the triumph of Darwinism as a worldview. This is clearly an issue which requires further discussion, not least because of its interdisciplinary implications. The Christian University is clearly a suitable context for such explorations and reflections.

V Theological Frameworks and Evolutionary Theory

The debate over how evolution is to be accommodated theologically has become intensely polarized, with two theories gaining at least some degree of support.

In the first place, there is a form of metaphysical naturalism – often linked to the notion of Darwinism as a worldview – which holds that evolutionary theory eliminates any conceptual space for God. This approach, found in the writings of both Dawkins and Dennett, affirms the intrinsically atheist implications of evolutionary theory.

At the other end of the ideological spectrum, 'creationism' and 'Intelligent Design' hold that a specifically Christian approach to the biological world entails either the explicit rejection of the notion of biological evolution, or its severe restriction.

Young Earth Creationism holds that the earth was created in its basic form between 6,000 and 10,000 years ago; Old Earth Creationism, however, has no particular difficulty with the vast age of the world, and argues that the young earth approach requires modification in certain respects. For example, the Hebrew word *yom* (day) may need to be interpreted as an 'indefinite time participle' (not unlike the English word while), signifying an indeterminate period of time which is given specificity by its context. In other words, the word day in the Genesis creation accounts is to be interpreted as a long period of time, not a specific period of 24 hours. Intelligent Design, a movement which has gained considerable influence in the United States in recent years, argues that standard Darwinism runs into significant explanatory difficulties, which can only be adequately resolved through the intentional divine creation of individual species.

Interestingly, what unites both ends of this spectrum of possibilities is the belief that the acceptance of the notion of biological evolution entails atheism. Yet such approaches ignore the rich and extensive Christian engagement with the interpretation of Scripture, particularly the book of Genesis, dating from the patristic age. One of the major contributions that a Christian university might make to the debate over the relation of evolution and creation is to advert to this. To illustrate this point, we may consider the views of Augustine of Hippo (354–430) on the question of creation, drawing on his *Literal Meaning of Genesis,* written between 401 and 415.

One of the most important ideas developed in this work is that God's instantaneous action of creation *ex nihilo* is not to be understood as being limited to the primordial act of origination, but extends to include both the origination of the world and its subsequent development. Augustine understands this process of development in terms of the unfolding of 'seminal reasons' (*rationes seminales* or *rationes causales*) embedded within the created order in God's act of creation. God created the world complete with a series of dormant multiple potencies, which were to be actualized in the future through divine providence.

Where some might think of creation in terms of God's insertion of new kinds of plants and animals readymade, as it were, into an already existing world, Augustine rejects this as inconsistent with the overall witness of Scripture. Rather,

God must be thought of as creating in that very first moment the potencies for all the kinds of living things that would come later, including humanity.

Certain principles of order were embedded within the creation, which developed as appropriate at later stages. The idea was not original to Augustine, in that earlier Christian writers had noted how the first Genesis creation narrative spoke of the earth and the waters 'bringing forth' living creatures, and had drawn the conclusion that this pointed to God endowing the natural order with a capacity to generate living things. There are thus two 'moments' in creation, corresponding to a primary act of origination, and a continuing process of providential guidance. While conceding that there is a natural tendency to think of creation as a past event, he insists that God must be recognized to be working even now, in the present, sustaining and directing the unfolding of the 'generations that he laid up in creation when it was first established'.

Augustine argues that this does not mean that God created the world incomplete or imperfect, in that 'what God originally established in causes, he subsequently fulfilled in effects'. The world was created with an inbuilt potentiality to become what God intended it to be over time, which was bestowed in the primordial act of origination. It is not difficult to see how Augustine's theological framework can be correlated with some recent approaches to systems biology – such as Stuart Kauffman's argument that sufficiently complex networks of chemical reactions will necessarily self-organize into autocatalytic cycles, which can be regarded as the precursors of life. The types of self-organization exhibited by such networks can therefore be seen as an essential factor in evolution, complementing the Darwinian process of natural selection.

It can be seen that this theological framework offers an important way of accommodating and framing biological theories of evolution. There are defensible and viable theological alternatives to evolutionary naturalism on the one hand, and to various forms of creationism on the other. The rich historical resources of Christian theology can thus be brought to bear on this important biological and cultural question. The theologically rich notion of creation does not actually entail either Creationism or Intelligent Design. A Christian university offers an intellectual environment which allows a creative and potentially very productive dialogue between theology and biology, allowing for their mutual enrichment.

VI *Darwinism, Values and Beliefs*

A final debate of importance concerns the implications of evolutionary theory for significant human ideas, including ethical values and religious beliefs. Darwin himself suggested that ethics resulted from essentially biological pressures, although he did not develop these ideas. Herbert Spencer (1820–1903) developed Darwin's ideas into what is often known as 'social Darwinism'. Spencer elevated observations about the biological world (such as the struggle for existence, natural selection and the alleged 'survival of the fittest') into prescriptions for human moral conduct. Spencer suggested, for example, that the weak ought not to be helped to survive, in that 'to aid the bad in multiplying, is, in effect, the same as maliciously providing for our descendants a multitude of enemies'. Spencer's philosophy gained a significant popular following, particularly in North America in the nineteenth century, but declined significantly in the twentieth century. Julian Huxley (1887–1975) tried to breathe new life into evolutionary ethics, but faced widespread criticism for failing to acknowledge that he was simply projecting his own moral values onto the history of humanity. His moral naturalism, it was argued, assumed precisely the moral vision he pretended to discover.

More recently, writers such as E. O. Wilson have argued that ethics arises from biological necessity, and can be explained on the basis of humanity's biological and social evolution. In his *Sociobiology: The New Synthesis* (1975), Wilson defined sociobiology as 'the systematic study of the biological basis of all social behavior'. Ethics, following this understanding, evolved under the pressure of natural selection. Sociability, altruism, cooperation, mutual aid and so on are all explicable in terms of the biological roots of human social behaviour. Moral conduct aided the long-term survival of the morally inclined species of humans. According to Wilson, the prevalence of egoistic individuals will make a community vulnerable and ultimately lead to the extinction of the whole group. Sociobiology and evolutionary psychology frequently make an appeal to human evolutionary history in accounting for the physiological and behavioural traits of an organism – such as altruism – as evolutionary adaptations. Sociobiologists tend to see cultural evolution as being very closely controlled by biological evolution, and cultural traits as being selected on account primarily of their biological functionality.

These ideas have provoked fierce debates, which remain unresolved. For example, is it not reasonable to suggest that human beings have moved beyond their original biological roots and transcended their evolutionary origins? If so, surely they would be able to formulate goals in the pursuit of goodness, beauty and truth that have nothing to do directly with personal survival, and which may at times even militate against it? And how can one move from 'is' to 'ought'? In other words, how can the observation of biological behaviour act as the basis for ethics?

The debates over whether evolution explains human morality remain significant, and have been extended to the question of whether an evolutionary explanation can be offered for religious belief. The main biological question here is whether belief in God can be explained persuasively in purely naturalist terms as an evolutionary outcome. It is important to appreciate that a functional athe-ism is as much the presupposition as the conclusion of such approaches, which have a tendency to logical circularity. Four possible lines of argument might be considered.

1. Religious beliefs have no adaptive functions, so that their presence and success in human populations is to be explained by other means.
2. Religious beliefs can be considered as byproducts of more fundamental and essentially adaptive features of human cognition.
3. Religious beliefs are to be considered as adaptations which play a positive role in enabling humanity to deal with environmental complexity.
4. Religious beliefs are essentially cultural adaptations that co-evolve and interact with natural adaptations.

The difficulty faced by all these theories is that it is still unclear whether religious belief is to be regarded as adaptive or not. While some writers have assumed that there is no obvious adaptive function to religious belief, the evidence for this is far from secure. While a case can be made for religion being interpreted in adaptationist terms, any such conclusion must be regarded as insecure, resting on less than reliable evidential foundations.

VII Does Evolution Have a Purpose?

Finally, we must consider whether a Darwinian universe is devoid of goal and purpose. This is a complex question, in that 'purpose' is not strictly an empirical notion, it is something that is inferred, not something that is observed. Dawkins holds that an arbitrary and purposeless biosphere is an intrinsic aspect of evolu-tionary theory: the universe is characterized by an absence of purpose and goals. One may speak of 'apparent design', but this is merely an imaginative construc-tion of the human mind. Any purpose, design or goal we attribute to nature is invented, not discerned.

Yet this is not how Darwin's early leading interpreters saw things. T. H. Huxley ridiculed those who interpreted Darwin in this manner. Huxley was quite clear that traditional approaches to teleology – such as that adopted by Willliam Paley – faced a formidable challenge from Darwin's account of evolu-tion. Yet the theory of evolution, he argues, bears witness to a 'wider teleology', rooted in the deeper structure of the universe. Certain approaches to teleol-ogy had been discredited by Darwin, Huxley argued. And in their place, a new understanding of the notion arose, grounded in the capacity of the universe to produce life. The strong resonance with contemporary reflections on a 'fine-tuned' universe can hardly be overlooked.

No less significantly, the core dogma of the absence of goals in evolutionary biology has been challenged. For example, the biologist Francisco J. Ayala has defended the use of teleological language in biological explanation. The adaptations of organisms can be considered to be explained teleologically when their existence can be accounted for in terms of their contribution to the reproductive fitness of the population. Such adaptations – such as organs, homeostatic mechanisms or patterns of behaviour – are observed to have had a beneficial impact on the survival or reproductive capacities of organisms, which can be considered as the phenomenological goal towards which they tend.

Others have pointed to the significance of the phenomenon of evolutionary convergence for the question of purpose and goals in nature. The Cambridge biologist Simon Conway Morris, for example, argues that the evolutionary process seems to navigate its way to a small number of apparently predetermined solutions. For Conway Morris, 'convergent evolution' – which he defines as 'the recurrent tendency of biological organization to arrive at the same solution to a particular need' – points to the tendency of the evolutionary process to converge on a relatively small number of possible outcomes. 'The evolutionary routes are many, but the destinations are limited.'

For Conway Morris, 'life has a peculiar propensity to "navigate" to rather precise solutions in response to adaptive challenges'. 'Islands of stability' exist in the midst of an essentially inhospitable ocean of maladaptivity; the evolutionary search engine finds its way to these islands, not on account of its purposeful questing, but because of the inevitability of the points of termination. One could speak of 'Darwin's compass', in that evolution appears to find its way to a relatively small number of outcomes.

This is clearly an important debate, with obvious metaphysical implications, which still has some considerable way to go.

VIII *Conclusion*

The complexity and importance of discussions about biological evolution, human identity and human beliefs is of such importance that it is essential to establish an informed forum within which they can be discussed and explored. Modern biology is beginning to rediscover the notion of teleology, and explore its possible implications. Might evolution be much more directed as a process than might hitherto have been realized? Might we begin to speak of islands of stability (Conway Morris) in biological space? This important discussion requires a community which is both biologically and theologically informed – a relative rarity in today's world. Yet the vision is worth pursuing, not least on account of the intellectual enrichment that it offers. If such an intellectual community does not presently exist, then it must most certainly be invented.

Bibliography

Allen, David Elliston (1994), *The Naturalist in Britain: A Social History* (Princeton, NJ: Princeton University Press).

Ayala, Francisco J. (1970), "Teleological Explanations in Evolutionary Biology,' *Philosophy of Science*, 37: pp. 1–15.

Benson, Keith R. (1988), "From Museum Research to Laboratory Research: The Transformation of Natural History into Academic Biology', in R. Rainger, K. R. Benson and J. Maienschein (eds), *The American Development of Biology* (Philadelphia: University of Pennsylvania Press), pp. 49–83.

Boyd, Robert and Richerson, Peter J. (1985), *Culture and the Evolutionary Process* (Chicago: University of Chicago Press).

Braddock, Matthew C. (2009), 'Evolutionary Psychology's Moral Implications'. *Biology and Philosophy*, 24: pp. 531–40.

Conway Morris, Simon (2003), *Life's Solution: Inevitable Humans in a Lonely Universe* (Cambridge: Cambridge University Press).

Cornell, John F. (1986), 'Newton of the Grassblade? Darwin and the Problem of Organic Teleology', *Isis* 77: pp. 405–21.

Corsi, Pietro (2005), 'Before Darwin: Transformist Concepts in European Natural History', *Journal of the History of Biology*, 38: pp. 67–83.

Cunningham, Conor (2010), *Darwin's Pious Idea: Why the Ultra-Darwinists and Creationists Both Get It Wrong* (Grand Rapids, MI: Eerdmans).

Dawkins, Richard (1986), *The Blind Watchmaker: Why the Evidence of Evolution Reveals a Universe without Design* (New York: W. W. Norton).

Dawkins, Richard (2003), *A Devil's Chaplain* (New York: Houghton Mifflin).

Dawkins, Richard (2006), *The God Delusion* (Boston: Houghton Mifflin).

Dennen, J. van der, Smillie, David and Wilson, Daniel R. (eds) (1999), *The Darwinian Heritage and Sociobiology* (Westport, CT: Praeger).

Dennett, Daniel C. (1995), *Darwin's Dangerous Idea: Evolution and the Meaning of Life* (New York: Simon & Schuster).

Dennett, Daniel C. (2006), *Breaking the Spell: Religion as a Natural Phenomenon* (New York: Viking).

Dietrich, Michael R. (1998), 'Paradox and Persuasion: Negotiating the Place of Molecular Evolution within Evolutionary Biology', *Journal of the History of Biology*, 31: pp. 85–111.

Kaufman, Stuart (1995), *At Home in the Universe: The Search for Laws of Complexity* (Harmondsworth: Penguin, 1995).

Knuuttila, Simo (2001), 'Time and Creation in Augustine', in Eleonore Stump and Norman Kretzmann (eds), *The Cambridge Companion to Augustine* (Cambridge: Cambridge University Press), pp. 103–15.

Kim, Yoon Kyung (2006), *Augustine's Changing Interpretations of Genesis 1–3: From De Genesi contra Manichaeos to De Genesi ad litteram* (Lewiston, NY: Edwin Mellen Press).

Lucas, John R. (1979), 'Wilberforce and Huxley: A Legendary Encounter', *Historical Journal*, 22: 313–30.

Mayr, Ernst (2004), *What Makes Biology Unique? Considerations on the Autonomy of a Scientific Discipline* (Cambridge: Cambridge University Press).

McGrath, Alister E. (2004), *Dawkins' God: Genes, Memes and the Meaning of Life* (Oxford: Blackwell).

McGrath, Alister E. (2011), *Darwinism and the Divine: Evolutionary Thought and Natural Theology* (Oxford: Wiley-Blackwell).

Midgley, Mary (2002), *Evolution as a Religion: Strange Hopes and Stranger Fears*, 2nd edn (London: Routledge).

Moore, James R. (1979), *The Post-Darwinian Controversies: A Study of the Protestant Struggle to Come to Terms with Darwin in Great Britain and America, 1870–1900* (Cambridge: Cambridge University Press).

Numbers, Ronald L. (1992), *The Creationists: The Evolution of Scientific Creationism* (New York: Knopf).

O'Hear, Anthony (1997), *Beyond Evolution: Human Nature and the Limits of Evolutionary Explanation* (Oxford: Clarendon Press).

Pennock, Robert T. (2001), *Intelligent Design Creationism and Its Critics: Philosophical, Theological, and Scientific Perspectives* (Cambridge, MA: MIT Press).

Shennan, Stephen (2002), *Genes, Memes and Human History: Darwinian Archaeology and Cultural Evolution* (London: Thames & Hudson).

Wilson, David Sloan (2002), *Darwin's Cathedral: Evolution, Religion, and the Nature of Society* (Chicago: University of Chicago Press).

Wilson, David Sloan and Wilson, Edward O. (2007), 'Rethinking the Theoretical Foundation of Sociobiology', *Quarterly Review of Biology*, 82: pp. 327–48.

Wilson, Edward O. (1975), *Sociobiology: The New Synthesis* (Cambridge, MA: Harvard University Press).

Zeitz, Lisa M. (1994), 'Natural Theology, Rhetoric, and Revolution: John Ray's *Wisdom of God*, 1691–1704', *Eighteenth Century Life*, 18: pp. 120–33.

Chapter 5

THEOLOGY AND ENVIRONMENTAL SCIENCES

CELIA DEANE-DRUMMOND
(University of Notre Dame)

I The Spectrum of Environmental Sciences

Environmental sciences, perhaps more than any other of the natural sciences, includes within its scope a number of sub-disciplines, ranging from soil science and microbiology through to ecology, geology, geography, chemistry and physics. The focus – as the name implies – is on using these different scientific disciplines as tools in order to probe more fully scientific knowledge about the environmental context in which human life is situated and the impact of human activity on the natural environment. An area of environmental science that has come under increasing attention in recent years is that of climate change. However, I suggest that perhaps the *core* discipline within this loosely assembled group is the science of *ecology*, particularly because ecology by definition is about interrelationships between living things that the environmental scientist tries to understand. Ecology has also been dubbed a 'subversive' science, in that it is concerned more with interrelationships between living things rather than presuming a methodological reductionism characteristic of many of the other experimental natural sciences. Nonetheless, the extent of its subversion is relative in that different subdivisions within ecological science itself may use reductionist methods in so far as they are reliant on the particular tools and methodologies of chemistry, physics and mathematics, though generally the end in view is a practical one concerned with understanding interrelationships between systems and living things, rather than one that is aiming to understand observations at, for example, the molecular or atomic level. In environmental science, interrelationships are viewed on an even wider scale compared with ecological science, and may include geological and physical or chemical factors as well as particular concerns about public health issues. This makes its remit far wider than that of ecology proper, even though the terms environmental science and ecology are often used interchangeably. It is therefore impossible to define with any clarity the philosophical basis for the environmental sciences, except in so far as they are energized by pragmatic concerns regarding human impacts on and interrelationships in the natural world.

Nonetheless, it is highly instructive to explore ecology briefly as a sub-discipline, since the philosophy of ecology has undergone a considerable paradigm shift in the last 90 years, and many of those who are engaging with ecology from other disciplinary perspectives in the humanities have not recognized either that this shift has occurred or its importance, with one or two exceptions.[1] Gaining a basic understanding of this new perspective on ecology is important, since how human beings respond to changes in the environment that become public currency or those that are experienced directly will depend on preconceived views about the natural world. Ecology in its original formulation viewed ecological systems as essentially closed, self-regulating, free of disturbance and independent of human influences. The idea of 'wild' nature untouched by human interference captured the imagination of pioneers in environmental ethics.[2] As research progressed, ecosystem boundaries came to be viewed as being far more fluid than previously thought, so that the prospect of self-regulation seemed unlikely, and at best in any one case there seems to be an equilibrium state rather than a persistent equilibrium. This leads to the view that ecological systems are in a state of flux, are open to external as well as internal influences, are subject to a multiplicity of complex control systems and are open to human disturbance.

The cultural idea of a 'balance of nature' still persists in the public imagination and in many works of philosophy, ethics and theology and may make it harder to accept the accumulating evidence for the actual impacts that humans are having on ecological systems. Significantly, where the idea of stability exists, it may also lead either to less awareness of the possible impacts of human beings on climate change, or a fearful hostility towards any change as undermining some previously conceived stable ecological state. In addition, it may make it harder to accept that human interference is justified even in a limited way, through schemes of environmental restoration, for example, that attempt to restore ecological functioning to a site that has been severely degraded by human activity.[3] This raises important questions about what kind of restoration is desirable, that is precisely *which* ecological system is to be protected given the complex history of living systems in relation to human beings. More explicit interference in living systems by humans through deliberate genetic modification and biotechnology using plants and other animals is also likely to have environmental implications, though the precise extent of these cannot be predicted in advance.[4] Of course, the *scale* at which changes are measured may give the superficial appearance of stability, in that if the time scale is short, then changes are not detected, or if the measurements are on a large enough scale, then the system may appear stable. The idea that human beings inhabit a relatively stable ecological home that is now perceived to be under threat is also a prevalent myth in much religious reflection on the topic of ecology and environment.[5] If theology and philosophy are to contribute to considerations about the environmental sciences, then their practitioners need to be aware that the disciplines themselves integral to that science are changing in their perspectives. They must recognize that their responses to those sciences need to be informed by awareness of the current scientific consensus, without necessarily taking direct ethical currency from those outlooks. A fear of ethical naturalism, understood as an attempt to derive ethical norms from observations of the natural world, is no excuse for theologians or ethicists to be in ignorance about or refusal to engage in dialogue with the basic insights of the relevant sciences.

II Cross-Disciplinary Issues

Environmental sciences are not just complex in that they embed a range of other natural sciences, they are also cheek by jowl with the human sciences as well, including sociology, law, politics and economics. The necessity for strong environmental laws, especially in those nations dependent on industrialized and oil-driven economies, means that environmental policy is built into the framework of governance in the Western world. 'Human ecology' was a term coined originally by social scientists, but Pope John Paul II also adopts this term when discussing the moral imperative of environmental concern.[6] This is significant, as his emphasis on human ecology marks not simply a turn to nature as distinct from culture, but the specific responsibility of human beings in relationship with different facets of the natural world. The political, legal and social aspects of environmental science mean that cultural questions concerned with religion are relevant in mapping out public aspects of environmental practice. Hence, theological discussion has a contribution to make not just in dialogue with the scientific practice, but how it is implemented in different social, political and cultural contexts. Theology becomes *public theology*, and it could be seen as a task of a Christian university to contribute to such a voice in public debates.

Peter Scott has argued that we live in a *camera obscura* world, that we are living in a situation where we are failing to recognize our fundamental ecological dependency as human beings, and because what we see is upside down, we choose to ignore the challenge that such ecological dependency raises.[7] Importantly, however, he believes that such a distorted vision is especially true for city dwellers living in the northern hemisphere and as such considerations about the natural world become squeezed out of the agenda in politics; so that following the financial crash environmental questions have become marginalized. Importantly, Scott envisages the public sphere to be *procedurally*, rather than programmatically, secular; in the first instance religious traditions can be included in the conversation, while in the second case religious views are excluded as irrelevant, a matter of course.[8] Scott goes further in suggesting that religious traditions contribute to those traditions that make up the public sphere in such a way that they are constitutive of it, rather than externally related to it. In Europe and North America, for example, the religious tradition that has most dominated the development of the public sphere is Christianity. A Christian university would therefore be expected to make an active contribution to this public realm in contested disputes about environmental problems and concerns. The secular foundation of many historical universities may disguise the Christian tradition that is latent in their cultural history in a manner that has some resonance with the positive place that religious traditions may play in procedural secularism in the public realm as outlined by Scott. This opens up a place for religious traditions at the table in the public sphere in contested issues about the environment and as a corollary, a Christian university amidst those that are avowedly secular. Such conversations are of importance if human beings are going to come to an adequate appreciation of the foundational importance of ecology for human existence.

In addition to political concerns, it is worth mentioning the significance of economic and social concerns in dealing with environmental challenges. How far and to what extent environmental questions should become associated with economic cost raises enormous philosophical issues about the appropriateness of economic labels for matters of intrinsic value, where education and the environment could be seen to share common ground.[9] German economist Hans Diefenbacher concludes that placing an economic value on some aspects of environmental loss is meaningless, such as loss of a whole country, through global sea rise for example. Further, those calculations that suggest how much it might cost to act might be misunderstood if the costs were used to forecast the economic alternative of inaction. In a development context where there are severe climate challenges facing the most vulnerable sections of the human community, the global challenge shifts again, for in this case any proposal for sustainability understood in terms of environmental as well as social accountability means that economic prosperity has to be reconceived so that it is no longer centred on growth.[10]

III A Case Study in Environmental Science: Climate Change

Climate science *qua* science is not in a position to make absolute predictions, and this presents a difficulty when translating scientific ideas into policy making. However, the evidence for changes in the recent past are agreed even by sceptics, and the weight of evidence is in favour of the view that the changes in climate will continue to impact severely on sea levels, water availability, food distribution, health, biodiversity loss and economics.[11] Although the scientific community was in agreement about the results of the work of the Intergovernmental Panel on Climate Change (IPCC), doubts sown in the media undermined public confidence in these conclusions. The IPCC attempted to respond to this pressure by creating a style of presentation in its work that was suitable for policy makers, and other non-specialists. Uncertainty, for example, is part of scientific methodology, but policy makers might have concluded that expressing levels of uncertainty meant there was little confidence in the outcome. In order to get around this difficulty, terms such as 'virtually certain' were used in the IPCC summary documentation for policy makers, including the view that the bulk of the carbon dioxide increase and associated global warming were anthropogenic, that is caused by human activity. In those parts of the world where climate change has rather less impact, it is relatively easy to be in a state of denial about the importance of human activity in climate change, an issue that I will return to again later.

Once we recognize that the problem exists, it then becomes part of the much *wider* remit of environmental degradation, loss of resources and biodiversity loss as a result of human activity recognized for at least the last half century. The difficulty in this case, as in some other environmental problems and issues, such as habitat loss, is that human activity is indirect, so that there is no conscious awareness of degradation. The impact is indirect, mediated through an increase in carbon footprint, and as a result it is difficult for individuals to recognize a sense of responsibility. I suggest that one of the responsibilities of theologians is to remind or even shock their listeners that what we are witnessing in the observations of the environmental sciences in terms of biodiversity loss, habitat destruction and climate change is that relationships are breaking down on all levels. We might even choose to name this a new category of sin. While liberation theologians have, in the past, with due cause, spoken of *structural sin* as that which impacts on the political sphere, the kind of activity that is relevant in the case of environmental devastation including climate change encompasses *both* individual and structural sin. Furthermore, in so far as its impacts are often mediated through natural disasters of one sort or another it includes what traditional philosophy has termed 'natural evil' as well. I suggest, therefore, that we need to come up with a new terminology appropriate for this kind of activity, where the human link to the events are disguised, and name it *anthropogenic evil*, that is evils brought about by human activities at the broadest level. I also think it appropriate to name this *anthropogenic sin*, in so far as it reflects a breakdown of relationships in a manner that is dishonouring to God as Creator of all that is.[12] One of the difficulties, of course, is working out precisely what contribution human beings are making to events that would happen anyway, but the increase in frequency of severe climate events is more likely than not to be connected with human activity in terms of carbon and other greenhouse gas emissions. Climate scientists have termed this anthropogenic impact. Of course, the level and extent of sin or evil will vary, but it leads to both environmental injustice and ecological injustice. The corollary of this is, that having recognized such injustice, we not only confess our guilt, but also find ways to seek ameliorating the situation through a constructive approach to the issues at all levels, be they local and practical or political and economic.

I am defining environmental injustice as the uneven and disproportionate impact of climate change on the poorest communities of the world, leading to death, homelessness or a permanent refugee status. It is relatively easy to extend traditional categories of social justice to such situations. Of course, eventually the impact will be so extreme that most human populations will be threatened in one way or another, but for the time being this is not yet the case. More radical is the possibility of ecological justice. I suggest that this category is relevant not just in terms of species extinction, which can be categorized in the language used by Marilyn Adams as a horrendous evil, but also the lack of flourishing of non-human creatures and stable habitat that results from distortions in climate.[13] Ecologists can help us decide which species might be able to tolerate impacts of climate change or indirect impacts on habitat more than others, but the irreversible loss of many species through loss of habitat is, I suggest, one of the most devastating effects of climate change.

Of course, we might need to ask ourselves what we mean by ecological justice, since traditional writers have commonly excluded the non-human and future generations in moral categories as those that cannot have responsibilities. However, along with many other secular sociologists, such as Andrew Dobson, I would argue for the importance of considering all creatures as worthy recipients of justice, even if it might be debatable as to the extent to which they can also be agents of justice.[14] Much the same argument applies to future generations of humans and other creatures. In addition, the advantage of justice language is that it allows us to consider the levels of just working, between people, in constitutive justice, between a state and individuals, in distributive justice, and between the individual and a state in what might be termed, to use classic characterization, legal, general or contributive justice.

The difficulty, of course, is that where there are mutually competing claims as recipients of justice, which or who should take priority in such decisions and what version of justice should we use? In such a context we cannot avoid applying practical wisdom to such cases, where the judgement of prudence will inform who and what takes priority in any given context. Climate change also includes, of course, international justice in so far as any one state or nation acting alone will not be able to ameliorate the impacts of climate change. The classic notion is also complicated today by the fact that many multinational companies have even greater economic powers compared with some nation states, yet in legal terms are treated as individuals. For theologians, justice has a theological dimension in so far as acting justly is one of the vocations of the Christian community, reflecting an understanding of a God who acts justly and has special care for the poor and vulnerable in society. Working out what justice requires is one of the most challenging aspects of social theory, as it depends on given notions of whether, for example, justice should be a procedural approach, or directed to more substantive notions of the common good, as in natural law theory for example. The former has tended to dominate in liberal Western societies, under the influence of John Rawls, but a case can be made for alternatives that attempt at least to provide an outline of what basic goods might entail for human and non-human communities of creatures. Martha Nussbaum has attempted to do this in her more recent work, *Frontiers of Justice*.[15]

I suggest that philosophical understanding of justice in terms of principles to be enacted is not sufficient for the witness of the Christian community. Instead, I believe that greater attention needs to be paid to justice as a *virtue* to be nurtured and developed in communities of shared faith. The demands of principled justice provide only the baldest of outlines of what needs to be done; justice as virtue anticipates a greater degree of commitment to action, in so far it is not just about what I am doing, but who I am *becoming* in showing forth and demonstrating just acts. Furthermore, such a view is helpful, for as Aquinas has reminded us forcefully, justice is the second of the cardinal virtues, the first being prudence, or practical wisdom. In the context of climate change, practical wisdom or prudence is as necessary to enable appropriate action as justice, one cannot be considered without the other. Moreover, it is important to point out that, like justice, prudence has a political as well as an individual dimension. In addition, just as charity is integral to wisdom, and the means through which wisdom can flourish, it is an essential ingredient of justice making. This is one reason why a virtue approach to justice is necessary as well as more principled approaches, for it reminds us of the importance of a holistic approach to other virtues, for it is doubtful that any single approach to such complex problem solving will be sufficient.

IV *Building Trust and Accountability*

Justice making is not the only area in which theology may offer a distinctive approach to complexities thrown up by the environmental sciences, beyond the Western focus on contractual or procedural versions of social justice making. The gift of theology to the natural sciences in general concerns its experience with what might be termed multidisciplinarity, of which the Roman Catholic theologian Karl Rahner was only too well aware. Karl Rahner believed that scientific specialization made it impossible to achieve a comprehensive view of reality, which he terms a 'gnoseological concupiscence'. Of course, the environmental sciences perhaps suffer less from this form of arrogance, but its particular pragmatic specialism may give a distorted view about the particular merits of a reliance on the science alone in order to frame political and public decision-making. The heavy reliance on science was one feature of the United Nations Conference of Parties global discussion on climate change in Copenhagen in 2009.[16] Theology's focus on transcendence at its best reminds all sciences of their subjectivity, replacing what Rahner believed was an individual science's tendency to monopolize other sciences and its failure to listen to other approaches.[17] In my experience the failure to listen to other approaches and the tendency to monopolize may be found just as readily among theologians, though the over-confidence in science expressed in various forms of scientism bolstered by public support may be diminishing. In other words theology presents a rationality of knowing that reminds scientists of their responsibility as *citizens* as well as scientists. This is crucial for environmental sciences that intersect with economic, political and policy decision-making. Both theology and in this case environmental sciences perform a vital task for the other, in that they both keep their respective knowledge in proportion. Or, one might say, a reminder to stay humble. While ignorance in one's own field or specialism may lead to the same sense of humility, which I understand to mean an accurate assessment of one's capacities and limits, rather than self-depreciation, an interdisciplinary conversation brings this to the foreground in a particularly sharp way. In my experience, ironically, perhaps, those who wish to keep their subject domain 'pure' of other disciplinary questions and values may *devalue* such interdisciplinary conversations. This means that where there is a choice involved in, for example, the particular direction of research where a number of possibilities present themselves, then there may be *theological reasons* why one course may seem more appropriate than others.

Theology not only has something to offer, as suggested earlier it *also* needs to recognize the significance and place of scientific knowledge, so theology is to be crafted in cognisanze of the main tenets of particular sciences and in genuine dialogue with those sciences. This is, perhaps, the benefit of a university informed by Christian values, for the dialogue becomes facilitated through a mutual respectful recognition of the other as a valid scholarly conversation partner. This is distinct from the more problematic notion of ideologically *driven* research where the ideology sets the agenda for the kind of questions that can be asked in either science or theology, though how far any scientist or theologian is entirely free from particular commitments is open to question. A core theological value from the perspective of Roman Catholic theology that is relevant in discerning between different scientifically justifiable courses of action is orientation towards the common good. This is distinctive from secular philosophical approaches to social goals where commonly even the *idea* of the common good is eschewed in favour of a thin procedural version of what justice requires. In my own view not only does that good need to be sought, in addition it needs to include the widest possible scope of human life and other forms of life in all their diversity. In this thick version of the common good, it encompasses the knowledge and insights offered by the concrete investigations of the environmental sciences alongside the affirmation of the goodness of the natural order from a theological perspective. Ethical questions come to the surface where there are conflicts of goods, or where it is not clear what the common good might entail.

Scientists who are familiar with professional issues in ethics, such as those in environmental sciences, more often than not use case studies where ethical dilemmas are involved. But the model for resolving tricky decision-making is loaded towards cost/benefit analysis that reflects an underlying consequentialist approach to ethics.[18] This might be thinned out still further to mean compliance with legal restrictions. Theological reflection presents alternatives to this approach in that while the orientation to the common good shows that in one sense consequences are important, it is a much richer sense of purpose compared with that thinly represented in terms of economic (rather than social) benefits. Further, this is only one facet of what ethical discernment might entail. There are other viable ethical alternatives, including, for example, deontological (principled) approaches to ethics, and virtue ethics. Principled approaches in Roman Catholic traditions are most heavily represented by natural law traditions that set a particular framework for ethical decision-making, though so far this has focused more specifically on human subjects rather than environmental questions. The relatively recent massive growth in nanotechnologies is, perhaps, a good example of the blurring of science and technology as traditionally defined as representing theory and practice. Like genetically modified organisms (GMOs) the main ethical issues involved seem to be associated with impacts on human health and the environment. However, perhaps surprisingly, so far this does not seem to have become a pressing issue for public discussion, at least in the UK context. In the most recent encyclical *Caritas in Veritate*, for example, Pope Benedict XVI challenges the massive growth in technological possibilities. The seeming liberating capacities of new technologies for human life need to be tempered, so that 'human freedom is authentic only when it responds to the fascination of technology with decisions that are the fruit of moral responsibility'.[19]

But what might that moral responsibility for scientists entail? This is where, it seems to me, lies the possibility for theological ethicists to make a further contribution – secular approaches to ethics leave out religious issues. But in considering the complex relationship between science and society it makes little sense to omit religion. It is *religious issues* that are uppermost in the minds of many of those concerned about different ethical issues in science, especially bioethics. It is all the more pressing because in recent years public trust in science seems to be dwindling. Climate science is a particularly good example of this: following leaked emails from the University of East Anglia research facility, a series of media reports collectively known as 'Climategate' entered the public sphere. There seems to have been a significant drop in public support of science after this incident, even though the scientists themselves were later exonerated. According to Charles Kennel, fellow of the California Council of Science and Technology (CCST), a public opinion poll from the Pew Research Center, tracking trust in science, recorded a steep 25-point drop in the 3-month period following the COP-15 Conference. In October 2010, at the pre-council and council meeting of the CCST, which aims specifically to link up the discoveries of science with state and federal policy making in an informed manner, the issue of trust and accountability in science was the main focus of discussion.[20] One particularly pressing issue was potential conflicts of interest when commercial companies were funding research.[21] There seems to be a double problem emerging: first the lack of trust in science by the public, and secondly, the lack of accountability by some scientists, serving to erode that trust still further. But if public trust in science collapses, support for scientific research and technology will begin to be undermined.[22]

Trust in theological language is better translated as *faith* and accountability as *moral responsibility*. For scientists to be in a position to address ethical issues in their research from their own faith perspective in the public domain, I suggest that they need to become *trilingual*, not just bilingual, a term coined in discussions of public theology. By this I mean that the approach to ethics used must make sense in the scientific, public and religious spheres. One way to open up the possible contribution of religion in science is to expose scientists to the way theology is used in the public sphere. That way, scientists, who are also religious, can begin to have the confidence that the language they are using will make sense in secular culture, as well as within the religious communities in which they are embedded. Of course, internal debates within the Roman Catholic or Christian communities may allow scientists to engage in a deeper way with theological traditions.

The German philosopher Jürgen Habermas allows for the possibility of religion as well as science entering public debate in his recent admission that modern societies are failing in their task. He identifies contemporary 'trends towards a breakdown in solidarity in different sectors of society' that seem to be a mirror image of the rise in the imperatives of the market.[23] He diagnoses the need for a reformed global order, but considers that the political will for such a shift is profoundly missing.[24] This point is particularly significant in the context of international political negotiations around climate change that have tended to rely on IPCC reports grounded in scientific discourse. Habermas' philosophy is indebted to Kant, and, unlike some other continental philosophers, he refuses to 'give up' on reason. But reason, if tempered by solidarity in its broadest global sense, takes on a different shape.

V *Christian Practical Wisdom and the Environmental Sciences*

The shape of that reasoning, and one to which I have returned again and again in thinking through practical issues of ethics in a science context, is that of *practical wisdom* or prudence. Practical wisdom or prudence in the classic tradition of medieval theologian Thomas Aquinas is one of the intellectual virtues of practical reason. It entails deliberation, judgement and action, all of which are relevant to ethical facets of scientific practice. In the deliberative phase of prudence, a sense of history or *memoria* is in juxtaposition with present knowledge, or *circumspection* and anticipation of the future, or *foresight*. Along with these elements we find those familiar to scientific research, namely insight and reason, though reason in the classic tradition had a broader meaning compared with that following the Enlightenment.[25] But perhaps equality relevant is the facet of *docilitas*, or teachability, for this capacity is essential for those engaged in complex decisions that require insights from a variety of perspectives.

Environmental ethical dilemmas that I have suggested above require cross-disciplinary conversation to illustrate this difficulty, especially as they relate to global perspectives. During my time on secondment with the Catholic Fund for Overseas Development where I worked specifically on the theological issues connected with sustainability, I became much more aware of the difficulties in translating theological concepts into terms that make sense at the policy and political level. This also applies to scientific concepts, so that translating different aspects of scientific uncertainty in areas such as climate change into terms that make sense to policy makers is extremely difficult. The facet of classical practical wisdom known as *solertia*, or the ability to act well in the face of the unexpected is vitally needed given the high stakes involved in such discussions. In the Thomistic tradition, practical wisdom also works alongside the other cardinal moral virtues of justice, temperance and fortitude. All three are relevant in the context of debates about climate change. I am not suggesting that only scientists dealing with issues such as climate change have the responsibility to express these virtues, but rather all involved need to consider *how* they can become exemplars of such virtues. I have also become interested more recently in the context of climate science debates in considering what it means to express a collective conscience.[26] By this I am retrieving an idea originally put forward by sociologist Emile Durkheim, but not in the same manner, in that I am critical, as are many other social scientists, of his insistence on the facticity of what he terms 'social facts'. However, the idea of collective conscience is, I suggest, a useful heuristic tool in order to mobilize both the Christian community and communities at larger scales to think about responsible collective action alongside action by individuals.

The particular role of the environmental scientist could be viewed as a specific example of the more general proposition offered by Pope John Paul II in his address to the Pontifical Academy of Sciences, where he claimed: '*Truth, freedom and responsibility are connected in the experience of the scientist.*'[27] He also made a similar point a few years later in claiming: 'Scientists, precisely because they "know more," are called to "serve more." Since the freedom they enjoy in research gives them access to specialized knowledge, they have the responsibility of using that knowledge wisely for the benefit of the entire human family.'[28] Those who are environmental scientists working in a Christian university have a particular obligation to understand their scientific research in vocational terms as service to humanity at large. How far such a vocation is realistic as an address to all environmental scientists in all contexts is a moot point, but in this case the scientist who is also a Christian can provide a witness to his/her faith by the way they wish to interpret and develop their science, and the questions that they ask, as well as through more traditional practices of Christian discipleship.

Notes

1   See David M. Lodge and Christopher Hamlin (eds) (2006), *Religion and the New Ecology* (Notre Dame: University of Notre Dame Press).

2   See C. Deane-Drummond (2004), *The Ethics of Nature* (Oxford: Blackwells/Wiley), pp. 29–38.

3   The topic of environmental restoration is beyond the scope of this chapter, but it is an area that has exercised the attention of environmental philosophers such as Eric Katz, who has argued consistently against such a view, and that any human attempt to restore nature is a deception and that nature properly speaking is independent of human interference. See E. Katz (1993), 'Artifacts and Functions: A Note on the Value of Nature', *Environmental Values*, 2: pp. 223–32. While he could be challenged philosophically on the basis of whether his sharp division between the 'natural' and the 'artefact' is tenable, from the perspective of contemporary ecological science his view does not make much sense either, since no 'natural' systems are 'pure' or free from human interference in the way he assumes to be the case.

4   For further discussion of this topic, see C. Deane-Drummond (1997), *Theology and Biotechnology* (London: Cassell); C. Deane-Drummond (2008), *Ecotheology* (London: DLT).

5   Ernst Conradie discusses this tendency among ecotheologians at length in his book on anthropology from an ecological perspective. See E. Conradie (2005), *An Ecological Christian Anthropology: At Home on Earth?* (Ashgate: Basingstoke).

6   Pope John Paul II, *Centesimus Annus*, 1991, §38. I provide a fuller discussion of the concept of human ecology in Pope John Paul II and other related matters in C. Deane-Drummond, 'Joining in the Dance: Catholic Social Teaching and Ecology', *New Blackfriars*, 93: 1044, March 2012, pp. 193–212.

7   Peter Scott (2011), 'Right Out of Time? Politics and Nature in a Postnatural Condition', in C. Deane-Drummond and H. Bedford-Strohm (eds), *Religion and Ecology in the Public Sphere* (London: Continuum), pp. 57–75.

8   Scott (pp. 59–60) takes the contrast between programmatic and procedural secularism from Rowan Williams (2008), 'Secularism, Faith and Freedom', in G. Ward and M. Hoelzl (eds), *The New Visibility of Religion* (London: Continuum), pp. 45–56.

9   For a discussion on assigning an economic value to environmental issues see H. Diefenbacher (2011), 'Climate Change and the (Economic) Value of Nature –The Role of Economic Thinking in the Public Sphere', in Deane-Drummond and Bedford-Strohm, *Religion and Ecology*, pp. 77–88.

10 Disputes in this matter became rife at the thirteenth global summit on climate change, see C. Deane-Drummond (2011), 'Public Theology as Contested Ground: Arguments for Climate Justice', in Deane-Drummond and Bedford-Strohm, *Religion and Ecology*, pp. 189–209. For an explicit discussion of an economic alternative see Timothy Jackson (2009), *Prosperity Without Growth: Economics for a Finite Planet* (London: Earthscan).

11 How far these changes are approaching what is known as a 'tipping point' of irreversible damage is under discussion. Many prominent authors, including those writing from an ethical perspective informed by theology, such as Michael Northcott, take the view that global climate is close to the tipping point. See M. Northcott (2008), *A Moral Climate: The Ethics of Global Warming* (London: DLT).

12 See C. Deane-Drummond (2008), *Ecotheology* (London: DLT).

13 Marilyn McCord Adams (1999), *Horrendous Evils and the Goodness of God* (Ithaca: Cornell University Press).

14 A. Dobson (1998), *Justice and the Environment: Conceptions of Environmental Sustainability and Dimensions of Social Justice* (Oxford: Oxford University Press).

15 There is insufficient space to discuss this in any detail, but I have compared Nussbaum's capability approach with a contractual approach in relation to different models for theological ethics in C. Deane-Drummond (2011), 'Deep Incarnation and Eco-Justice as Theodrama', in S. Bergmann and Heather Eaton (eds), *Ecological Awareness: Exploring Religion, Ethics and Aesthetics* (Berlin: Lit Verlag), pp. 193–206. See also, M. Nussbaum (2006), *Frontiers of Justice* (Cambridge: Harvard University Press, Belknap). Her stress in this book was on other animals and the environment as a context for human activity, rather than consideration of climate change or environmental issues as such.

16 Deane-Drummond, 'Public Theology as Contested Ground'.

17 K. Rahner (1997), *Theological Investigations*, Vol. 13, trans. D. Bourke (London: DLT), p. 95. See also C. Deane-Drummond, *Theology and Biotechnology: Implications for a New Science* (London: Geoffrey Chapman).

18 This is just as true in decisions about controversial areas such as GMOs as other environmental issues; see C. Deane-Drummond and B. Szerszynski (2003), *ReOrdering Nature: Theology, Society and the New Genetics* (London: Continuum).

19 Pope Benedict XVI (2009), *Caritas in Veritate* (London: Catholic Truth Society), §7.

20 I was invited to this meeting at the Beckman Conference Center, National Academies of Sciences and Engineering in Irvine (USA) on 18 October 2010. Dr Marchant from the University of Arizona, Law Faculty, who specializes in legal issues relating to environmental concern is co-organizing a conference with the Royal Society in Cambridge (UK) in July 2012 on threats to the university and science.

21 Professor Beth Bernside raised this issue at the CCST meeting from her perspective as former Provost of Research at the University of California, Berkeley.

22 While the issue of public trust in different facets of science could be analysed through social science research, mapping the meaning of trust in its fullest sense goes beyond tracing that trust to the release of oxytocin in the brain. I am not criticizing this research as such, but the way the conclusions reached by that research *may* lead to reductive ways of thinking about what trust entails. Correlation between oxytocin and a number of different neurological affective capacities, such as trust, gratitude and so on, demonstrates the *biological* correlates for trust, rather than amounts to proof that trust is satisfactorily characterized by neurological explanations, or that oxytocin is the only bio-molecule involved in this process. Paul Zak from the Center for Neuroeconomics Studies at Claremont Graduate University discussed the scientific aspects of trust at the CCCT Council Meeting on 19 October 2010.

23 J. Habermas (2010), 'A Reply', in J. Habermas et al., *An Awareness of What Is Missing: Faith and Reason in a Post-Secular Age*, trans. Ciaran Cronin (Cambridge: Polity Press), p. 73 (full ref. pp. 72–83).

24 Habermas, 'A Reply', p. 74.

25 A full discussion of this aspect is outside the scope of this chapter, but Jean Porter has written authoritatively on this aspect in J. Porter (2005), *Nature and Reason: A Thomistic Theory of Natural Law* (Grand Rapids: Eerdmans).

26 As presented to the annual conference on Theology and Climate Change for the Society for the Study of Christian Ethics, and C. Deane-Drummond (2011), 'A Case for Collective Conscience: Climategate, COP-15, and Climate Justice', *Studies in Christian Ethics*, February 2011.

27 Pope John Paul II, *Address to the Pontifical Academy of Sciences*, 13 November 2000, retrieved from www.vatican.va/holy_father/john_paul_ii/speeches/2000/oct-dec/documents/hf_jp-ii_spe_20001113_plenary-acad-science_en.html.

28 Pope John Paul II, *Address to the Pontifical Academy of Sciences*, 11 November 2002.

Chapter 6

CHRISTIANITY AND THE TRANSFORMATION OF MEDICINE

ANDREW SLOANE

(Morling College, Sydney)

I Introduction

The care of the sick has a long and cherished tradition in Christianity. From the distinctive practices of the early Christian communities and their care for abandoned children and plague victims through to the contemporary hospital system, Christian faith has nourished and informed costly engagement with human suffering.[1] It has also prompted careful reflection on the nature of medicine, its connection to Christian understandings of God and our calling and the roles it plays in human community.[2] My task in this piece is to continue that conversation, paying particular attention to where medicine finds itself in the early twenty-first century and the challenges that brings to Christian understanding of medicine and its role in the academy. I will begin by outlining my understanding of the current contexts in which medicine operates, leading to a brief discussion of ways that the discipline has sought to address the issues which medicine faces. I will then present a Christian understanding of medicine as both a scholarly and a social practice, articulating the philosophical-theological framework which informs this perspective. This understanding will seek to flesh out features of medicine as an inherently moral practice, one informed by a Christian social vision and shaped by key theological commitments. I will close with some reflections on two matters: access to health care, and the implications of a Christian vision of medicine for the ethos of medical education.[3]

II The Context(s) of Medicine in the Early Twenty-First Century

Medicine operates in diverse contexts: roughly, in a 'Western' context of infinite 'want' and the associated reduction of a profession to a product to be consumed; in a 'developing' context of infinite need and the associated vulnerability to exploitation and deprivation. Let me tell the stories of two young women to illustrate and articulate this difference. One, whom I shall call Mara, is dying in an ICU in a major hospital in Australia. The other, whom I shall call Naomi, is dying at home in rural Angola. Mara is 19, and has Acute Myeloblastic Leukaemia. She was diagnosed a year ago, but has been non-compliant with her treatment regimen. She was admitted to hospital 1 week ago with an acute relapse, with septicaemia, circulatory collapse, acute renal failure and acute respiratory failure. On admission to the ICU, her condition was acknowledged to be irreversible; nonetheless, because she is young, she has been aggressively treated in ICU with artificial ventilation, circulatory support and peritoneal dialysis. After eight days of treatment, she is experiencing multiple organ failure which is unresponsive to treatment. The ICU team is attempting to persuade her family to take her off the ventilator and cease circulatory support with the knowledge that she will die soon thereafter. Naomi is 19 and has end-stage AIDS. She was infected with HIV 4 years ago after being raped by her uncle (he knew he was infected but believed that unprotected sex with a virgin would 'clean him' of 'slim disease', the local name for HIV and AIDS). She has had sporadic antiretroviral therapy, but her poverty, the fragile post-war Angolan economy and lack of basic infrastructure means that she has had no reliable access to the drugs (despite international successes in 'universal access' to free antiretroviral therapy), or to adequate nutritional support. She is emaciated, has multiple skin lesions and persistent diarrhoea and now has fulminant, multi-drug resistant tuberculosis (and no access to the appropriate anti-TB therapy). She cannot afford to go to hospital, which is chronically under-resourced and overtaxed, and is being cared for by her mother while she dies. This is the world in which we live, and of which a Christian approach to medicine must be cognizant.

A number of things emerge from these stories. First, the social and economic contexts in which medicine is practised variously enable and constrain possibilities of health care; indeed, those social and economic contexts are the most significant determiners of levels of health and illness for the members of those communities. This suggests that health care is not primarily about improving the health of the community, but about providing care to vulnerable people. Second, paradoxically, both the over- and under-supply of medical services can compromise this care. It is clear how the under-supply of medical services compromises the care of needy people: while I could catalogue instances, I think Naomi's story makes this plain. But so can the over-supply of medical services. Many of the most frequently discussed issues in both bioethics and the philosophy of medicine relate to end-of-life decisions; frequently those discussions revolve around the withdrawal or withholding of life-prolonging therapy when that is seen as 'futile'.[4] Such questions arise in situations of 'medical plenty' when treatments are applied because they are available not because they are likely to be of benefit for the patient, with the result that the person and her needs are lost in a forest of technological possibilities, and biomedicine replaces caring for a dying person.[5] Again, I could catalogue instances, but I think Mara's story illustrates this well enough.[6] Third, and perhaps most obviously, huge disparities exist in the level of health care available to people in different communities (and, for that matter, different sectors of the same communities—especially in, say, the US health care 'system'). These disparities are themselves a great challenge facing both medical ethics and the vision and practice of medicine from a Christian perspective. How have those who practise or philosophically analyse medicine responded to these challenges?

III Medicine's Responses to These Challenges

The biomedical model has dominated views of medicine since the late twentieth century. It views health and disease primarily in terms of biological functioning and, allied with advances in medical technology and analytical tools such as evidence-based medicine, has resulted in obvious improvements in medicine as a technical practice.[7] However, this grafting of the Baconian view of science and technology as power or control onto the tradition of Hippocratic beneficence has created significant issues for medicine as a practice.[8] This has become particularly evident in the clash between proliferating medical technologies of increasing complexity and expense and the limitations of health care budgets even in the 'developed' world. From this perspective, the only legitimate constraint on treatment options is whether it is likely to benefit this particular patient's biological functioning, without reference to broader concerns of the nature of medicine and justice. Indeed, in such a view, caring for a patient as a person has become problematic, with the healing value of the physician–patient relationship being factored out of analysis of the efficacy of treatment, and the importance of caring for those who cannot be cured being 'problematized'.[9] Legitimate criticism of medical paternalism in consort with 'thin' understandings of personal autonomy and the rampant consumerism of late capitalism have complicated this, eroding the notion of medicine as a *profession* (an inherently moral enterprise involving the exercise of both the patient's and the physician's agency), reducing doctors to service providers. Medicine becomes a biomedical consumer product aiming at 'health' (cure) and the eclipse of suffering and personal limitation (enhancement). As such, it becomes an idolatrous enterprise, embodying (often literally) the false values of 'developed' nations, offering 'tech-fixes' for personal and social 'problems'.[10] And so the personal and relational nature of medicine and the clinical encounter are lost and broader personal and social issues ignored, while health care costs and inequalities both increase.

One response is to turn to social utility as the criterion by which medicine and medical care are justified.[11] While various costs and benefits are factored into different utilitarian analyses, these approaches suffer from common problems: not only do patient interests become subordinated to social concerns, but they fail to account for medicine as a distinctive practice.[12] Alternatives such as Beauchamp and Childress's attempt to develop a 'theory-neutral' principlist approach to medical ethics,[13] or Jensen's proposal of a particularist, communitarian theory of medicine are equally inadequate:[14] the first, because it results in a 'thin', procedural approach to medical ethics and fails to consider what medicine is as a social practice; the second because it does not allow for moral critique of the values of the particular communities that generate priorities in health care, leaving intact the commodification of health care as a consumer product.[15] Neither addresses the fundamental moral nature of medicine or its location in broader issues of social vision and normative perspectives on human beings and the human community.

IV *Christian Responses to These Challenges*

More effective responses have come from Christian philosophers and theologians of medicine. Hauerwas criticizes modern medicine for its failure to operate out of a coherent story of humanity and human community, and calls on the Church to furnish communities of moral agency, grounded in the lived practices of the Church, which can nourish an alternative medical practice.[16] Furthermore, he reminds us of the centrality of suffering and vulnerability to the human condition and that, whatever else it might be, medicine is a response to that vulnerability, rather than a technique to gain mastery over the human condition.[17] Verhey, taking a similar line, has called on Christians to remember and articulate their story in the context of medicine, noting the many ways that it both informs and challenges medicine as it is currently practised.[18] Meilaender has shown the 'thinness' of the moral vision that underlies most discussions of medical ethics and bioethics, with the result that bioethics (and medicine informed by it) has lost both the 'soul' and the 'body'; more adequate reflections on health care need to be informed by a (Christian) 'worldview'.[19] This need not lead us to conclude that a Christian vision results in radically incommensurable medical practices,[20] as Pellegrino and Thomasma illustrate.

Drawing on both the Thomistic tradition and phenomenological approaches to medicine, Pellegrino and Thomasma argue for a philosophy of medicine that is derived internally from the defining features of medicine as a social practice, in contradistinction to biomedical and other reductionist models.[21] While Pellegrino's alternative analysis rests on a flawed demarcationist understanding of medicine,[22] there are, nonetheless, certain phenomena which are central to or paradigmatic of medicine. For Pellegrino, medicine is an inherently moral enterprise whose fundamental features arise out of the exposure of human vulnerability in the experience of illness and the response to it in the healing relationship of physician and patient. The power differential inherent in this experience means not only that medicine cannot be reduced to a commodity to be freely traded in the market, but that it bears moral freight. The physician's power – both of knowledge and skill and the freedom to use them – meets the patient's need with the goal of caring for a needy person and, where possible, returning them to autonomy. Properly understood this autonomy is not that of late modern capitalism's myth of the unconstrained pursuit of whatsoever goals an individual may choose, but the freedom to live within the constraints of the human condition as an agent. Furthermore, such care is incumbent on all human communities. Rooted in the Hippocratic tradition and its developments in medieval and modern medicine, this helping and healing relationship allows for the appropriate care of those who cannot be cured – and the refusal to pro-vide futile 'curative' treatment to them – and for that to be done in a context that values the *relationship* between physician and patient for both its intrinsic and its instrumental value.[23]

Clearly, Pellegrino wants philosophy of medicine to emerge from medicine as a practice, especially (the phenomenology of) the clinical relationship. While he sees the need for a Christian vision to inform the practice of medicine, espe-cially in a biotechnological world which leaves us 'abandoned to a plethora of means and a poverty of ends',[24] this is largely overlaid on an understanding of medicine that he sees as emerging by way of reflection on its phenomenology as a social practice.[25] While there is some truth in this claim, it relies on a particular understanding of medicine as a practice, even the primacy of the healing rela-tionship, which is derived from or coheres with, a bigger vision of human life. This is not peculiar to *Christian* theorists: all understandings of disciplines such as medicine are informed by and are expressions of a particular belief system.[26] This brings me to a Christian philosophical-theological framework for medicine which provides the necessary context for understanding medicine and its role in human life.

V A Philosophical-Theological Framework for the Christian Practice of Medicine

A neo-Calvinist approach to scholarship adopts an epistemology that is both person- and situation-specific and critical-realist in contrast to both the supposed value-neutrality of modernist scholarship with its quest for rational consensus and the relativism or radical pluralism frequently associated with what is often called 'postmodernism'. Nicholas Wolterstorff encourages Christians to engage in scholarship in such a way that the central beliefs entailed in Christian faith critically inform the practice of scholarship, and the vision of *shalom* central to the biblical story informs the projects in which they engage.[27] That is, Christian faith functions internally in a Christian's scholarly practice as a control in the devising and appraising of theories and in shaping heuristic decision making. While such a view recognizes the inherent plurality of scholarship necessitated by the different presuppositions that inform different intellectual traditions, it does not require that a Christian's scholarship be *different* from that developed by their non-Christian counterparts, merely *faithful* to their Christian commitments. A truly *Christian* understanding of medicine, while acknowledging the paradigmatic features of the discipline and practice of health care, is framed in a broader Christian vision of the world, human community and the nature of human existence grounded in the biblical narrative.[28]

There are key 'moments' in the grand-narrative of God's relationship with the cosmos and its creatures that inform a Christian view of medicine.[29] This story of the creation of *shalom,* its distortion by sin, God's work of restoration of *shalom* in history culminating in the incarnation, ministry, death and resurrection of Jesus and its consummation in a new heavens and earth, is both our story as Christians and our call as followers of Jesus.[30] It is the context for our life in the world, including the practice of medicine: 'that is the context for medicine: in the alleviation of the bitter consequences of the Fall; in staying the hand of death, for a season; in anticipating the final resurrection of the body'.[31] As creatures who are intrinsically finite and who live in a world which is now frequently hostile, we are both inherently vulnerable and gifted with inestimable dignity. As such, illness both reminds us of that inherent vulnerability and calls forth our compassion and care turning to those who are ill in loving relationships, rather than abandoning them in the isolation that suffering generates.[32] But it also reminds us of our own limitations and that of our care: for such vulnerability is inherent in the human condition and cannot be transcended; such weakness will persist until the final transformation of all things, a goal that can only be attained following the cruciform path of our Lord.[33] There is no escaping vulnerability or death, just as there is no escaping the call to action that the vulnerability of others and the threat of a (reasonably) avoidable death mediate, as we see in the healings of Jesus.

Furthermore, medical research, both in the fundaments of biomedical sciences and in clinical practice, is justified and compelled by this story.[34] By virtue of our creation in the image of God, we are entrusted under God with the task of understanding and shaping the world in which we live: as creatures we are both subjects who seek to understand, and objects of our own study.

Furthermore, the brokenness of the world and of human existence compels us to understand it and seek to devise ways to ameliorate its effects on our fellow creatures. Both this research and the care it enriches ought to have a particular concern for the weak and the vulnerable: not only are they the special object of God's concern, it is that vulnerability that evokes the care that shapes and justifies the very existence of medicine (something that Christians involved in medical research ought to bear in mind). Thus, medicine is a practice of enquiry that seeks to understand the world (including human beings) and a social practice that seeks to change it so as to care for vulnerable people and better enable human flourishing.

VI Medicine as an Inherently Moral Enterprise and a Christian View of Society

This vision also reshapes medical practice (and so education), so as to encourage the effective moral agency of both professionals and patients.[35] The power differential intrinsic to the doctor–patient relationship itself generates a moral call, for in a Christian view of the world, power and privilege generate a corresponding responsibility to serve (Mt. 20.25–28).[36] Illness, injury or handicap are problems because they adversely affect people and interfere with their ability to function in relationships, exposing their vulnerability and diminishing their flourishing.[37] Medicine as a social practice (or profession), in turn, exists in and for a given community and aims to care for people in their weakness and vulnerability, deal with the disruption caused by disease processes, injury or deformity and return people to proper functioning in their relationships and as persons, as far as this is practicable. This both justifies the existence of medicine and establishes its goal. While fighting disease or improving a community's health are important, they are *means* (or the appropriate goals of other practices) rather than the *ends* of medicine.[38] Medicine's *telos* is to provide care for vulnerable people and, where this is possible and as far as this is practicable, to remove impediments to human flourishing, restoring people to proper personal and relational functioning. Such a perspective both enhances the moral character of medicine as a practice and enables us to resist the 'technological imperatives' which can overwhelm personal concerns for the sake of technical possibilities.

This enables us, in turn, to discern what health care ought to be provided for the members of a community, and to question the appropriateness of some uses of medicine. Practically (and philosophically), we need to distinguish between caring and curing: the first is always the concern of medicine, the second sometimes. Theologically, we need to distinguish between medicine as an idolatrous attempt to wrest mastery over the human condition and delude ourselves that we can transcend our creaturely limits, and our responsibility to humbly care for the vulnerable in response to the realities of human frailty.[39] Victory over death is God's gift in the Gospel, one we will receive in the eschaton, not medicine's gift that we can claim here and now.[40] As we know from the Gospel, overcoming weakness is not the only form that response to vulnerability takes, for our God is the one who uses the weak to shame the strong, and whose power is most clearly manifest in our weakness (1 Cor. 1.26–31; 2 Cor. 12.7–10). This, allied with the realization that the Gospel proclaims only an eschatological victory over death, and one which necessarily passes through suffering and death rather than bypassing them, reminds us both of the limits of health care and of the responsibility to care for people in their weakness and suffering, doing what we can in shared humanity to care for them in their incurable suffering or dying.[41]

VII A First Application: Access to Health Care

As we turn to issues of access to health care, we need to realize that medicine exists in and for a given community and is both individual and corporate: individual, inasmuch as the very essence of the clinical relationship is a person in need going to another person so that need can be met; corporate, inasmuch as the existence of the institutions, and the ability of medical professionals to engage in such a clinical relationship arises out of, and is funded by, a community's commitment to meet the health needs of those who comprise it. In relation to the latter, the vision of *shalom* generates 'sustenance rights', to goods which society has an obligation to provide, such as food, water, housing, education, basic health care and so on.[42] These are rights, because they are necessary for functioning in community, and without them people are unable to function meaningfully in relationships and pursue the ends for which they were created.[43] Beyond these sustenance rights that societies are obliged to meet, society may choose to offer us other services, which go beyond meeting those basic needs. When applied to medicine this gives rise to two interlocking criteria: health care services are justified if (1) they are components of basic health care to which everyone is entitled as a 'sustenance right' *or* (2) their provision offers reasonable hope of return to a reasonable level of relational functioning, and will not impinge on the provision of sustenance rights to others. These criteria mean we should always provide those basic health services which, within a given community, can be justified as sustenance rights, and provide just and equitable access to other resources.[44] It also means we should refrain from mere enhancement, as it fails to meet these criteria and ignores the inherent morality of medicine as a practice.[45]

Determining exactly which services can be included legitimately within the scope of 'basic health care' is a complex and situation-specific task, but a good case can be made for including those services which 'cluster' around community health and good quality GP services, because such services are required if the relational dysfunction occasioned by illness is to be effectively overcome.[46] Other services (such as critical and tertiary levels health care) should not be included in our sustenance rights, but seen as extra services that society offers to those in need (health care 'mercies') which are to be judged on a 'relational cost–benefit analysis'.[47] We need to realize that '[n]o system, however ingeniously devised, can gratify all wants, tamp down all worries, or remove the mark of mortality from our frame'.[48]

This, of course, has significant implications for a global perspective on medicine and the inequalities in the distribution of health and health care services, as can perhaps be best seen by returning to the cases with which I began. Mara's care, it seems to me, is frankly inappropriate and ethically unjustified. While it is appropriate to initiate a trial of a particular treatment to see whether it might have effect,[49] in this case, Mara was clearly dying. The appropriate response is to care for her (and her family) while she dies, rather than using sophisticated 'curative' therapy when that is acknowledged to be futile. Such treatment both medicalizes her dying, alienating her and her family from her dying body, and is an unjust use of limited resources. It seems not only to cohere with an unacceptable notion of medicine as a consumer product, but to verge on being an idolatrous and self-deceiving attempt to overwhelm human vulnerability rather than care for one who suffers because of it.[50]

Naomi's case is equally clear, and equally unacceptable. Here we see the inevitable enmeshing of medicine in a broader social context, so that the instability and poverty of the nation as a whole adversely impact on the community structures and functioning, undermining the very possibility of a sustainable level of basic health care. Of course, dealing with these underlying social issues would not only establish the conditions in which an appropriate level of health care could be provided, it would itself be a major factor in improving the overall health of the community.[51] This involves not just significant changes in the domestic circumstances and policies of countries such as Angola, but a significant contribution from other, wealthier countries, including assistance in providing a decent basic level of health care. One effect of adopting this vision of medicine is to challenge physicians (and physicians in training) with their responsibilities as global (medical) citizens: we need to expand our horizons beyond those of our own countries and our possible career paths, to include the greater suffering and vulnerability of those in 'developing' countries. This does not mean that we must all become medical missionaries or volunteers for *Medicins Sans Frontier*: but some of us should, perhaps a great many more than are currently involved.

VIII Conclusion: A Christian Vision of Medicine and the Ethos of a Medical School

Let me conclude by summing up my argument, and reflecting on what it might mean for the shape of medical education from a Christian point of view. The diverse contexts in which medicine operates, contexts of oversupply and commodification, and undersupply and injustice, require an effective response, one that is best provided in a Christian vision of medicine in the context of human community. This enables us to see medicine as primarily providing care to vulnerable people and, in light of that, seeking to help people return to a reasonable level of relational functioning either by way of 'healing' their illness or enabling them to cope with it. It is an inherently moral enterprise, which, as well as entailing appropriate research into human vulnerability and its treatment, requires the shaping of moral agents. It also enables us to understand the value and limitations of medical care and consider the appropriate levels of its provision in the various contexts in which we find ourselves.

In applying this to medical education, I want to consider not curriculum design or pedagogical strategies, but *ethos*.[52] Issues of values, social vision and so on should be written into the whole of the curriculum rather than having them quarantined in particular subjects on ethics or philosophy of medicine;[53] it certainly needs to go beyond a narrow focus on legal and bioethical issues.[54] By analogy with theological education, perhaps medical education should have three main 'competencies' that it seeks to foster: acquisition of the knowledge base required to be a good clinician (such as the basics of medical science and an understanding of human vulnerability and the workings of interpersonal relationships); acquisition of the skill base required to be a good clinician (such as the basics of personal engagement with suffering and vulnerable people, history taking, physical examination, the appropriate use of investigations and so on); the shaping of persons as moral agents and spiritual beings who might be the kind of people who are able to care for those who are ill and who understand their role in the human community. This last might be achieved through a kind of 'moral apprenticeship': just as we identify people who are exemplars of the knowledge and skills required for good medical practice and equip them for the task of training their medical successors as clinicians, so we ought, perhaps, to identify people who are exemplars of the moral excellences required for effective helping and healing and equip them for the task of shaping their professional successors as moral agents. And just as clinical training requires the enlisting of a range of people and institutions, such as research facilities, universities and teaching hospitals, so this shaping of moral agency might enlist institutions such as the Church, along with individuals who are 'experts' in 'Christian practice'.[55]

So might the Christian moral vision, and the institutions that seek to live by it, bring about the transformation of medicine, and its practitioners.[56]

Notes

1 See, for instance, Allen Verhey (2003), *Reading the Bible in the Strange World of Medicine* (Grand Rapids: Eerdmans), pp. 1–13.

2 See, for instance, Paul Ramsey (2002), *The Patient as Person: Explorations in Medical Ethics*, 2nd edn (New Haven: Yale University Press); H. Tristram Englehardt, Jr. and Fabrice Jotterand (eds) (2008), *The Philosophy of Medicine Reborn: A Pellegrino Reader* (Notre Dame: UNDP); Stanley Hauerwas (1986), *Suffering Presence: Theological Reflections on Medicine, the Mentally Handicapped, and the Church* (Edinburgh: T&T Clark); Stephen E. Lammers and Allen Verhey (eds) (1998), *On Moral Medicine: Theological Perspectives in Medical Ethics*, 2nd edn (Grand Rapids: Eerdmans).

3 Please note: my focus in this piece is on a Christian philosophical theology of medicine, rather than the narrower issues of bioethics that occupy most Christian discussions. Edmund D. Pellegrino (2008), 'What the Philosophy of Medicine *Is*', in H. Tristram Englehardt Jr and F. Jotterand (eds), *The Philosophy of Medicine Reborn: A Pellegrino Reader* (Notre Dame: UNDP), pp. 23–48, draws a helpful distinction between philosophy *and* medicine, philosophy *in* medicine and philosophy *of* medicine.

4 See, e.g. Eric Chwang (2009), 'Futility Clarified', *Journal of Law, Medicine & Ethics* 37: pp. 487–95.

5 On caring when there is no reasonable possibility of 'cure', see Ramsey, *The Patient as Person*, pp. 113–64.

6 See also 'Contexts for Medical Ethics and the Challenges of Religious Voices: Reports of the Working Groups', in A. Verhey (ed.) (1996), *Religion & Medical Ethics: Looking Back, Looking Forward* (Grand Rapids: Eerdmans), pp. 120–9; Robin Attfield (1990), 'The Global Distribution of Health Care Resources', *Journal of Medical Ethics* 16: pp. 153–6; Fran Baum (2008), *The New Public Health*, 3rd edn (South Melbourne: Oxford University Press), esp. pp. 227–45; Ann Pederson (2006), 'Feminist Perspectives in Medicine and Bioethics', in P. Clayton and Z. Simpson (eds), *The Oxford Handbook of Religion and Science* (Oxford: Oxford University Press), pp. 836–49.

7 Miles Little (2003), '"Better than Numbers . . .": A Gentle Critique of Evidence-Based Medicine', in I. Kerridge et al. (eds), *Restoring Humane Values to Medicine: A Miles Little Reader* (Sydney: Desert Pea), pp. 103–29.

8 Allen Verhey (2000), 'The Spirit, Globalization, and the Future of Medicine', *Southwestern Journal of Theology* 42: pp. 79–105; Verhey, *Reading the Bible*, pp. 68–98.

9 See Kay S. Toombs (1995), 'Chronic Illness and the Goals of Medicine', *Second Opinion* 21: pp. 11–19.

10 For the notion of 'technique', see Jacques Ellul (1964), *The Technological Society* (New York: Knopf); *What I Believe* (Grand Rapids: Eerdmans, 1989); for medicine

and idolatry, see Joel Shuman and Brian Volck (2006), *Reclaiming the Body: Christians and the Faithful Use of Modern Medicine* (Grand Rapids: Brazos).

11   See, e.g. Nicholas Rescher (2006), 'The Allocation of Exotic Medical Lifesaving Therapy', in H. Kuhse and P. Singer (eds), *Bioethics: An Anthology* (Oxford: Blackwell), pp. 410–20; Paul T. Menzel, 'Rescuing Lives: Can't We Count?' in Kuhse and Singer, *Bioethics: An Anthology*, pp. 407–9.

12   John F. Kilner (1995), 'Rationing and Health Care Reform', in J. F. Kilner et al. (eds), *Bioethics and the Future of Medicine: A Christian Appraisal* (Carlisle: Paternoster), pp. 290–301; Ruud H. J. ter Meulen (2008), 'The Lost Voice: How Libertarianism and Consumerism Obliterate the Need for a Relational Ethics in the National Health Care Service", *Christian Bioethics* 14: pp. 78–94.

13   Tom L. Beauchamp and James F. Childress (1994), *Principles of Biomedical Ethics*, 4th edn (Oxford: Oxford University Press), pp. 3–119, 326–94.

14   Uffe Juul Jensen (1987), *Practice and Progress* (Oxford: Blackwell); cf. Max Charlesworth (1993), *Bioethics in a Liberal Society* (Cambridge: Cambridge University Press), pp. 107–59.

15   Alasdair MacIntyre (1987), *Whose Justice? Which Rationality?* London: Duckworth; Gilbert Meilaender (1995), *Body, Soul, and Bioethics* (Notre Dame: UNDP), pp. 1–36; Edmund D. Pellegrino and David C. Thomasma (1997), *Helping and Healing: Religious Commitment in Health Care* (Washington: Georgetown University Press), pp. 1–83, 126–61.

16   Hauerwas, *Suffering Presence*, esp. pp. 1–17, 23–62.

17   Stanley Hauerwas (1990), *Naming the Silences: God, Medicine, and the Problem of Suffering* (Grand Rapids: Eerdmans).

18   Verhey, 'The Spirit, Globalization, and the Future of Medicine', pp. 79–105; Allen D. Verhey (2001), 'The Practices of Piety and the Practice of Medicine: Prayer, Scripture, and Medical Ethics', in *Seeking Understanding: The Stob Lectures, 1986–1998* (Grand Rapids: Eerdmans), pp. 191–250; Verhey, *Reading the Bible*, pp. 1–67, 359–93.

19   Meilaender, *Body, Soul, and Bioethics*, pp. 1–59; Gilbert Meilaender (1996), *Bioethics: A Primer for Christians* (Grand Rapids: Eerdmans), pp. 1–10.

20   As does H. Tristram Englehardt (2000), 'Bioethics at the End of the Millennium: Fashioning Health Care Policy in the Absence of a Moral Consensus', in S. Wear et al. (eds), *Ethical Issues in Health Care on the Frontiers of the Twenty-First Century* (Dordrecht: Kluwer), pp. 1–16.

21   Pellegrino and Thomasma, *Helping and Healing*, pp. 1–12, 26–38; Pellegrino, 'What the Philosophy of Medicine *Is*', pp. 37–41; Edmund D. Pellegrino, 'Philosophy of Medicine: Should It Be Teleologically or Socially Constructed?' in *The Philosophy of Medicine Reborn*, pp. 49–61; 'The Internal Morality of Clinical Medicine: A Paradigm for the Ethics of the Helping and Healing Professions', in *The Philosophy of Medicine Reborn*, pp. 62–84; 'Medicine Today: Its Identity, Its Role, and the Role of Physicians', in *The Philosophy of Medicine Reborn*, pp. 127–46.

22   Pellegrino, 'Medicine Today', pp. 135; for problems with demarcationist views of science, see Andrew Sloane (2003), *On Being a Christian in the Academy: Nicholas Wolterstorff and the Practice of Christian Scholarship* (Carlisle: Paternoster), esp. pp. 11–73, 127–8.

23   Pellegrino and Thomasma, *Helping and Healing*, pp. 13–66; Edmund D. Pellegrino, 'Humanistic Basis of Professional Ethics', in *The Philosophy of Medicine Reborn*,

pp. 87–100; 'The Commodification of Medical and Health Care: The Moral Consequences of a Paradigm Shift from a Professional to a Market Ethic', in *The Philosophy of Medicine Reborn*, pp. 101–26; Pellegrino, 'Medicine Today', pp. 140–4; cf. Dónal P. Mathúna (2002), 'Spirituality and Alternative Medicine', in J. F. Kilner et al. (eds), *Cutting-Edge Bioethics: A Christian Exploration of Technologies and Trends* (Grand Rapids: Eerdmans), pp. 116–30; Diann B. Uustal, 'The Ethic and Spirit of Care', in *Cutting-Edge Bioethics*, pp. 142–56; Toombs, 'Chronic Illness and the Goals of Medicine', pp. 11–19; Meulen, 'The Lost Voice', pp. 86–93.

24 Pellegrino and Thomasma, *Helping and Healing*, p. 4.

25 See, for instance, *Helping and Healing*, pp. 13–38, 54–66; cf. pp. 39–53, 67–83; Pellegrino, 'Philosophy of Medicine', pp. 51–2; 'Internal Morality of Medicine', pp. 62–84.

26 Nicholas Wolterstorff (1984), *Reason Within the Bounds of Religion*, 2nd edn (Grand Rapids: Eerdmans); Sloane, *On Being a Christian in the Academy*, esp. pp. 111–254.

27 Nicholas Wolterstorff (1983), *Until Justice and Peace Embrace* (Grand Rapids: Eerdmans); Wolterstorff, *Reason Within the Bounds of Religion*; Sloane, *On Being a Christian in the Academy*.

28 See, e.g. Craig G. Bartholomew and Michael W. Goheen (2004), *The Drama of Scripture: Finding Our Place in the Biblical Story* (Grand Rapids: Baker Academic); Kevin J. Vanhoozer (2005), *The Drama of Doctrine: A Canonical-Linguistic Approach to Christian Theology* (Louisville: Westminster John Knox).

29 See Scott B. Rae and Paul M. Cox (1999), *Bioethics: A Christian Approach in a Pluralistic Age* (Grand Rapids: Eerdmans), pp. 91–127. What follows draws on Hauerwas, *Suffering Presence*, pp. 1–17, 23–62; *Naming the Silences*, esp. pp. 39–99, 101–12, 48–51; Verhey, 'The Spirit, Globalization, and the Future of Medicine', pp. 84–105; 'Piety and Medicine', pp. 191–250; *Reading the Bible*, pp. 1–67, 359–93.

30 Wolterstorff, *Until Justice and Peace Embrace*, pp. 69–72. He sees *shalom* as characterized by relationships of justice, equality and delight.

31 Nigel M. de S. Cameron, 'The Christian Stake in Bioethics: The State of the Question', in Kilner et al., *Bioethics and the Future of Medicine*, pp. 3–13.

32 Karen Lebacqz, 'Alien Dignity: The Legacy of Helmut Thielicke for Bioethics', in *Religion & Medical Ethics*, pp. 44–60; Rae and Cox, *Bioethics*, pp. 128–56. For an excellent general account of the importance of the phenomena of human vulnerability in moral discourse and the formation of moral agents, see Alasdair MacIntyre (1999), *Dependent Rational Animals: Why Human Beings Need the Virtues* (London: Duckworth).

33 Francis Cardinal George, 'The Need for Bioethical Vision', in *Cutting-Edge Bioethics*, pp. 90–100.

34 Robert M. Veatch (1994), 'Research on "Big Ticket" Items: Ethical Implications for Equitable Access', *The Journal of Law, Medicine and Ethics*, 22: pp. 148–51.

35 I retain the language of 'profession' and 'patient', as it reminds us of the vulnerability of the ill, the power inherent in the healing relationship and the attendant responsibility. Patients are vulnerable people in need of the care of moral agents, not clients or customers in a more-or-less powerful position requesting a service from a morally neutral provider.

36 For the notion of moral call, see John Hare (2001), *God's Call: Moral Realism, God's Commands, and Human Autonomy* (Grand Rapids: Eerdmans).

37   Andrew Sloane (1998), 'Painful Justice: An Ethical Perspective on the Allocation of Trauma Services in Australia', *The Australian and New Zealand Journal of Surgery* 68: 760–3. I will use the term 'illness' as a shorthand expression for illness, injury or handicap, recognizing that they are nonetheless distinct phenomena.

38   This means that a philosophy of medicine does not need to first define health before it can define medicine and its goals. See also Roberto Mordacci and Richard Sobel (2004), 'Health: A Comprehensive Concept', in A. L. Caplan et al. (eds), *Health, Disease, and Illness: Concepts in Medicine* (Washington, DC: Georgetown University Press), pp. 104–9; Baum, *The New Public Health*, pp. 3–16.

39   Shuman and Volck, *Reclaiming the Body*, esp. pp. 27–40.

40   'Some Issues and the Future of Theological Reflection: Reports of the Working Groups', in *Religion & Medical Ethics*, pp. 130–41.

41   Rae and Cox, *Bioethics*, pp. 217–52; Verhey, *Reading the Bible*, pp. 99–144.

42   For an articulation and defence of 'sustenance rights', see Wolterstorff, *Until Justice and Peace Embrace*, pp. 73–98; and for its application to health care, Joseph Boyle (1996), 'Catholic Social Justice and Health Care Entitlement', *Christian Bioethics* 2: pp. 280–92.

43   See also Baum, *The New Public Health*, p. 3; People's Health Movement (2001), 'People's Charter for Health'.

44   I will refrain from using the term 'primary health care' because it means very different things in the context of public health and the (medical) health care system. 'Basic health care', by which I mean those services which, roughly speaking, cluster around a good general practice, avoids that confusion. For the relation of basic health care and public health, see Rogers et al. (1999), 'Linking General Practice with Population Health' (Bedford Park, SA: National Information Service of the General Practice Evaluation Program).

45   George, 'The Need for Bioethical Vision', pp. 98–100. It also allows for the exercise of the physician's moral agency in the face of 'consumer' demand, for which see Edmund D. Pellegrino, 'The Physician's Conscience, Conscience Clauses, and Religious Belief: A Catholic Perspective', in *The Philosophy of Medicine Reborn*, pp. 281–306. Most purely *cosmetic* surgery provides a good case in point: it generally deals not with what interferes with proper relational functioning, but with inscribing on our bodies the values of late modern consumerism with its valuing of youth (and corresponding fear of death) and its devaluing of age and wisdom.

46   See Sloane, 'Painful Justice', pp. 761–2.

47   For similar lines of argument, see Clark E. Cochran (2007), 'Health Care Reform: Justice and the Common Good', in J. F. Morris (ed.), *Medicine, Health Care, & Ethics: Catholic Voices* (Washington, DC: Catholic University of America Press), pp. 309–33; Verhey, *Reading the Bible*, pp. 359–93.

48   William F. May (2002), 'The Patient as Person: Beyond Ramsey's Beecher Lectures', in Paul Ramsey (ed.), *The Patient as Person: Explorations in Medical Ethics*, 2nd edn (New Haven: Yale University Press), pp. xxix-xliii.

49   Robert D. Orr (2009), *Medical Ethics and the Faith Factor* (Grand Rapids: Eerdmans), pp. 14–15.

50   Uustal, 'The Ethic and Spirit of Care', pp. 142–56; 'Issues and Theological Reflection', p. 139.

51   For this, see Baum, *The New Public Health*, pp. 227–45, 77. For general issues of poverty and its alleviation and their impact on communities, see www.un.org/

millenniumgoals/; www.micahchallenge.org.au/; www.makepovertyhistory.com.au/ (all accessed on 31 May 2010).

52　For a helpful discussion of curriculum design, see Myles N. Sheehan (2007), 'A Struggle for the Soul of Medicine', *America*, 197(14) (November 5): pp. 9–17.

53　It might be worth considering a 'capping' unit which seeks to have a student incorporate the more diffuse discussions of ethos, etc., through the course into an integrated whole and reflect on what this means for them as morally responsible medical agents in a global context.

54　Such as is evident, in say, Consensus Statement by Teachers of Medical Ethics and Law in UK Medical Schools (1998), 'Teaching Medical Ethics and Law Within Medical Education: A Model for the UK Core Curriculum', *Journal of Medical Ethics* 24: pp. 188–92.

55　For the notion of experts in Christian practices, see William Alston (1991), *Perceiving God: The Epistemology of Religious Experience* (Ithaca, NY: Cornell University Press).

56　I would like to express my thanks and appreciation to a number of people who helped me think through these issues and commented helpfully on earlier drafts: Phill and Di Marshall of Morling College and SIM; Dr James Clarke of Newcastle; Professor Wendy Rogers of Macquarie University; Dr Margaret Wilkins of Morling College; Professor Peter Hampson of the University of West England.

PART 2

HUMAN AND SOCIAL SCIENCES

Chapter 7

THEOLOGY AND SOCIOLOGY

JAMES SWEENEY
(Heythrop College, University of London)

I Introduction

At the meeting of an association dedicated to the scientific study of religion which I attended not so long ago, the president in her welcome address announced the different disciplines represented, all in their various stripes of sociology, anthropology, psychology, history, and so on, and she ended by asking 'have I left anyone out?' 'Yes', I spoke up, 'theology!' Thus is the erstwhile 'Queen of the Sciences' overlooked – even by a religiously sympathetic president, who seemed quite surprised that she had not thought to include theology.

It is easy to be wrong-footed in these circumstances when 'scientific' is allowed to define the scope of academic legitimacy. What is meant by science here is, in fact, empirical methodology, not broader scientific enquiry. But sociology just as much as theology is affected by this narrowed definition; its claim to be scientific, while rightful in itself, cannot compete with that of the natural sciences – 'real' science. Sociology's scientific claims lie closer to those of theology. Theology is the considered, theoretical elaboration, or *science*, of religion and faith – just as sociology is of society: both are fundamentally interpretative sciences.

There are many possible ways of tackling the relationship of sociology and theology: as an instance of the working of reason and faith in human affairs, and their (perhaps) mutually corrective roles; or from the point of view of an interdisciplinary link-up between them, and the epistemological factors implied; or their different ways of framing religion itself; or by examining the actual use that theology makes of sociology and vice versa; or even to see them as mutually exclusive, as in fact many do.[1]

I will proceed by examining first of all the underlying assumptions of theology and sociology, and put forward a view of how the two disciplines stand in relation to each other. In section III, I will discuss the actual forms of engagement between them. But I need to say something about the perspective from which I approach the task. One could try to be an objective arbiter between the two disciplines, but that is an awkward position. The alternative is to take one's stance in one or the other discipline. My approach will be in terms of theology evaluating its engagement with sociology. The other way around is also valid, of course, and is appropriate if personal theological *commitment* is not involved. As will become clear, there are implications for how the issue is handled whichever stance is taken.

It would not be realistic to attempt to cover the whole range of theological traditions and sociological schools and the multiple possibilities of their interconnection. The internal diversifications within sociology and theology – the several different sociological paradigms; the different theological schools and theologies springing from different religions and faith traditions – mean that generalizations about them and their relationship have to be handled with care. In what follows I am thinking of the mainline theological tradition of Western Christianity on the one hand and general sociology on the other, in particular the sociology of religion.

II *Foundations*

a Status Questionis

Where theology and sociology rub against each other is above all in the field of practice. Both, in the end, are practical disciplines in the sense that, however theoretical their formulation, they are ultimately in service of 'real life' issues and identifiable constituencies. Social scientists engage with the various trades of the politician and civil servant, business leaders and financiers, trade unionists and social workers. Theologians engage with bishops and priests and ministers, chaplains and catechists and pastoral workers and the person in the pew. But all is not neat and tidy. These fields overlap; theologians (and bishops) will want to say something to the politician and the industrialist, while the sociologist casts a cold eye on the religious education teacher in the faith school or how the bishop exercises authority.

The distinctions should be kept between religion and theology and society and sociology – the second in both cases being reflection on the first. Sociology is in (critical and constructive) service of socioeconomic-political-cultural life while theology serves the life of faith and the institutions of the religious traditions – again, hopefully, critically and constructively. The sociology of religion takes up an external-outsider stance on religious faith whereas theology is an insider perspective, and practical or pastoral theology relies on the social sciences to analyse issues of religious practice.

The ways that religion and society, and therefore theology and sociology, are implicated in each other are historically and contextually determinate. Care must be taken about the particularity of religious life and practice. Religion has distinctive characteristics in the United States different from those in Europe; more strikingly different again is religion in Latin America, Africa and Asia. How Judeo-Christian religion relates to society differs from Islam, and their approaches are markedly different from the philosophies of the Eastern religions. The implications of the 'secular society' in Britain are different from French *laïcité*; Islamic Turkey's secularism is not the same as Hindu India's.

Theology and sociology both have concern for what occurs in the diverse societal spheres of politics, economics, family and kinship, work, education, and so on; but this is not simply common ground. They both have their own fundamental ways of perceiving human-social reality which derive from their originating assumptions. The City of God grasped in religious faith and the earthly city open to sociological inspection are overlapping perceptions of reality. The basic categories of faith and reason, the sacred and the profane, religion and the secular are conceptualized within sociology and theology according to their own frames of reference; the ideas may overlap but they are not identical.

Dialogue between sociology and theology is undertaken quite regularly, but it tends to get bogged down. There is a historical legacy here. Sociology came into being to explain the changes in society that flowed from the Enlightenment and the rise of science and the Industrial Revolution, changes which were seen precisely as ending the dominance of the religious worldview. As religion came to be considered passé, theology was no longer seen as valid knowledge; its subject matters could be subsumed within philosophy and anthropology and it would give way to a sociological take on reality. Religion's social and world-sustaining forces would in time transfer to a proper scientific base; Comte and Marx had different views of what that involved.

Theology today, however, has taken new heart from the re-emergence of religion in the public square, even to the point of some theologians such as John Milbank mounting a counterattack on sociological ambitions. The expectation of a wholesale and inevitable secularization is now widely recognized as naïve and religion seems set fair to continue in a multiplicity of expressions. In this context, Radical Orthodoxy's critical appraisal of sociology has been of intense, if often skeptical, interest to other theologians.[2] Not many sociologists have taken notice, however, except those who specialize in religion, and only those among them, such as David Martin, who are sympathetic to theology, and they, in fact, mostly react against Milbank's full frontal attack.

These are the latest skirmishes in a long running battle. What is interesting is that the dividing line here is not between sociologists and theologians but between believers across the two academic camps. Previously the forces of modernity and religion were pitted against each other with the heavy artillery of philosophy and theology deployed in passionate debate. While today's science versus religion debate, stoked by the 'new atheists', can be just as passionate, the intellectual standard often disappoints. Although one should not underestimate continuing public scepticism and aversion to religion, the critical questions about religion and society today, and the locus of dispute between theology and sociology, no longer concern belief versus non-belief, but how the perspectives of faith and the secular manage to co-exist.[3] The main battleground now is cultural rather than epistemological or institutional.

There are, nevertheless, deep tensions between sociology and theology. They both have their own inherent fragilities and they face battles about their public credibility. The root and branch critique both of them face arises from the privileging of 'science' as the only real knowledge. For those who portray religion as simple superstition allied to a magical worldview, theology as its *committed* intellectual investigation can be nothing more than gobbledygook; clever and even interesting gobbledygook may be, but gobbledygook nonetheless. It is now common to use 'theological' to denote the obscure and arcane. Sociology too is often dismissed as no more than commonsense dressed up in obfuscating language; or as thinly disguised political ideology, usually left leaning; or as unable to meet scientific standards of generalization and falsifiability. These critiques leave both disciplines vulnerable, so that bringing them together is a fraught exercise.

b Assumptions

One assumption we can leave aside is that religious faith and theology are totally lacking in validity. This is pervasive in the culture today and the default position of many if not most people, and has serious consequences for theology's ability to operate as public knowledge. It is, of course, an *assumption*, for it is impossible to prove the negative that God does not exist. But once it is made, which is a perfectly reasonable thing to do for which reasonable arguments can be adduced, there is nothing more to be said about the relation of sociology and theology other than determining how to cope with the persistence of an illusion.

Theology, however, proceeds on the assumption that God does indeed exist. This assumption, while it is argued for reasonably in apologetics, is more than an element of theory or a preliminary at the basis of a theoretical scheme. The assumption of the existence of God and what follows from it arises from the living traditions of religious faith in which it is embedded; it is a matter of socio-religious praxis rather than just abstract theory.

Sociology too, as structured human enquiry, operates on fundamental assumptions of its own: for example that human social conduct is ordered in some fashion that can be demonstrated rather than being simply random and chance occurrence. This too derives from social praxis for it is how people usually perceive their lives; it is fundamentally the same assumption that the natural sciences make about the intelligibility of the universe, that the universe has regularities, or laws, that can be understood and that it is not simply absurd.

The usual stance in sociology about religion's assumptions and the truth claims that flow from them is agnostic. Of course some social science traditions such as Marxism are openly atheistic and proceed on that basis and treat religion as 'the opium of the people'. In general, however, sociology quite properly disavows any competency to pronounce on whether there is a God or not or whether religious doctrines have any basis in the truth about things; it is committed to methodological agnosticism.[4] Thereafter sociology treats religion and theology as social data to be inspected in the same way as any other data. Whether 'agnostic' is truly agnostic is, of course, debatable since human perception is never neutral nor social science value free. It can even be that atheistic assumptions, deriving from the life praxis of individual sociologists or sociological schools, are smuggled into sociological analysis. The historic theory of secularization has been open to criticism on that basis.

c Ontologies

These theological and sociological assumptions frame social reality in quite different ways and manifest different underlying ontologies. A basic theological starting point for defining the reality of the human, and therefore how faith relates to society, is the doctrine of nature and grace – the understanding of a created order which is graced or penetrated by the active presence of God. The theology of grace has been transformed in recent decades, especially in Roman Catholic circles, in a marked move away from any deist conception of God as has been prevalent in much philosophy of religion and was reflected also in a theology which made a radical disjunction of the realm of grace from that of nature. That theological understanding has given way to an integrated view whereby all reality, and especially humanity, is understood as shot through with the divine presence or grace. This does not mean that grace is one empirical reality alongside other empirical realities, and therefore open to direct inspection, but rather that the 'whole', understood in terms of its ultimate significance, is constituted, and therefore has to be defined, by what lies in a depth or transcendent dimension that is not directly observable.[5]

This notion of grace is at the heart of the ontology or metaphysics which articulates in theological terms what is fundamentally constitutive of the reality of the human and the wider social arena within which human life is carried on. It is an ontology which derives from a religious perception and assumption, not something that can be empirically established. As a view of the world, it arises within a historical religious tradition, and it is kept in function by virtue of the regular continued experience of believers who, in a great variety of ways, live out this worldview and are thereby enabled to find the existential meaning of their lives.

The sociological view of reality, on the other hand, is determined by the fundamental purposes of the discipline and the historical origins from which these are derived. These purposes are, in a word, to explain societal change, and specifically the profound structural changes that culminate in what we know as modernity; sociology is modernity's child. Its prior assumptions about the nature of social reality are a philosophical matter; but as there is no one philosophy or philosophical consensus on which to depend, sociology's reality assumptions are inevitably guided by the historical context in which the dis-cipline emerged and the societal processes and dynamics which it identifies as driving social change. This context was quite specific: the profound cultural and social shift in which the theological portrayal of society as a *given* was rejected and in its place a vision was enshrined of society as *produced* in an ongoing and ever more extensive process of rationalization, the goal of which (most strongly expressed in modernity's early phase) is 'progress'.

The ontology or metaphysics underlying sociology which derive from this history is clearly of a different order from the religious ontology of grace. Its social constructivist view (which is bolstered by evolutionary thinking) recasts the way all social ontologies, including religious ontology, are framed; for (*pace* the fundamentalists) it is no longer possible to see the world-as-is com-ing directly and without intermediate causality from the hand of God. At the same time, being agnostic about any ultimate causality, sociology expounds a resolutely secular vision of the world in which human-social reality is what is observable, what can be described and analysed in the categories of reason. If there is a realm of reality beyond the observable, sociology has no knowledge of it and it cannot enter into the scope and definition of the real as that is framed sociologically.

Sociologists, of course, are real people who may not be at all agnostic or atheist in their personal lives, and who carry out their professional work with care and in tandem with their religious and life commitments. Anyway, most people do not dwell overlong on their ontological assumptions. Nevertheless, the ontologies in the background of sociology and theology have their effect in structuring minds and imaginations. The two ontologies do not simply sit alongside one another. The perceptions of reality as the simply observable and of reality as graced, while not necessarily totally divergent, work differently.

Herein lies the deep tension between a sociological and a theological perspective. The ontology of grace is not simply another step on a continuum beginning with the observable, an optional step, as it were, that the religious believer takes; it is rather a perception that changes everything. And the secular ontology of the observable, since it is constrained to leave the realm of grace as an open possibility, places limits on what sociology can say about the human and social world. If there *is* more than what the eye can see, then what the eye can see is in some measure deficient.

What the eye cannot see is grace. Divine grace is the touch of God on the human, and God is beyond all human knowing and perceiving; but the touch is humanly real. Karl Rahner describes it as 'a dark loving contact' or, following St Bonaventure, a 'spiritual touch'. Grace, although not directly observable, is understood as a dynamic element in human existence and a reality to be appropriated. It can enter conscious awareness in a certain measure, an event that Rahner calls 'transcendence becoming thematic'. Within this perspective all human experience, because it touches on transcendence, is understood as having the capacity to be and become religious experience or experience of grace. This happens when the grace that interpenetrates regular human experience rises to – an always opaque – consciousness, a way of knowing 'as in a glass darkly' (1 Cor. 13.12).

This coming to awareness of grace, however, does not occur in a simple movement of human consciousness itself. What 'graced existence' refers to is a matter of gift. While, in Rahner's perspective, a non-graced humanness does not *in fact* exist, the distinction of nature and grace is necessary to preserve the primordial giftedness of divine grace; grace is always a gift given in divine freedom. The human appropriation of grace, therefore, is a matter of receptivity, a willingness to receive. Appropriation happens in a moment of openness, a moral act, a movement of will and of spirit which itself remains dependent on the grace appropriated; and the religious *knowing* that results – that is to say *belief* – is a different kind of knowing from the simply rational, while not being simply irrational. What is observable here sociologically is the human moral act of believing, and it can be the subject of empirical exploration, although care is needed to respect it in its full intentionality rather than reductively.

d Terms of Engagement

These observations about underlying assumptions and ontologies lead to a conclusion about the relationship between the two disciplines. Given its ontology of reality as the observable and its methodological agnosticism, sociology in any dealings with theology cannot deliver a *final* perspective on social reality. Agnosticism by definition leaves an open question, and a social worldview premised on an open question is somehow incomplete. As one scholar puts it:

> Not knowing how the universe really is organized – not knowing if it is organized at all – the scholar of religion seeks not to establish a position in response to this question but to describe, analyse, and compare the positions taken by others. (McCutcheon 1999, pp. 216–17)[6]

This opens up a certain sociological dystopia, which is closely connected to the demise of the secularization paradigm which has for long been central to the sociology of religion.

The assumption of an inevitable, progressive, wholescale secularization of society is now largely, although not universally, agreed to be a faulty historical reading. In fact, it was (and is) an ideological reading, not a sociological finding nor even a properly sociological theory. While a more moderate secularization thesis can be defended,[7] in its thoroughgoing form it arises from a prior reading of the nature of social reality in which religion is epiphenomenal and without substance of its own; that is to say it reflects an atheist ontology.

The fundamental issue here – about the nature of social reality – is a philosophical and theological matter rather than sociology as such; but the philosophical position taken has a direct bearing on the interpretative tasks of sociology. The prior, non-sociological commitment taken – in favour of an atheistic view of reality or reality as graced – will influence how the issue of faith and the secular and their co-existence is posed and how it is handled both theoretically and in day-to-day practice. The sociology of religion, remaining methodologically agnostic, operates in the tension between these two visions of human social reality. This puts limits on sociology, especially in terms of its predictive capacity, and this is a significant loss since sociology has long asserted an ability not only to decipher historical patterns of change but also to point to social futures, with secularization prominent in the social destiny. In fact, of course, sociologists have never been much noted for an ability to predict social change; the collapse of Communism was almost totally unforeseen within the sociological community, while some within the Church intuited the vulnerability of a system that stripped out human values and left a hollowed-out society. This is a fundamental quandary for sociology: operating within a secular horizon of human social life but unable to justify it as definitive, and not having the capacity to adjudicate in the matter, sociology is left without teleological signposts.

The issue then arises of the parameters within which sociology works and how to situate theology in relation to the whole sociological enterprise. Classical Christian theology has always been open to the resources of reason; the application of reason to matters of faith is central to theology – evident in, for example, the formulation of the Creed. Reason is also acknowledged for its capacity to purify faith and save it from the excesses of fundamentalism and fanaticism.[8] Sociology, then, as the rational exploration of social structure is a legitimate interlocutor of theology, even if historically the exchange has often been difficult. On the other hand, it is less obvious that sociology can acknowledge theology – as distinct from the more neutral discipline of religious studies – as a legitimate dialogue partner.

In the political field, thinkers such as Habermas[9] and Rawls[10] have been willing to admit the validity of a religious contribution to public debate, so long as rational ground rules are respected. They may even see this as useful, recognizing that secular political rationality suffers from a certain value and motivational deficit, and that reason and the secular can be degraded to mere ideology. Reason, in this respect, depends on something more than reason – on some primordial 'human-faith grounding'. Religious traditions and their 'comprehensive views' and characteristic ways of engaging with public issues ought not to be denied public hearing. Indeed, according to Habermas, it is valid to put forward in public debate the religious-faith inspiration of a political view as long as it is communicated in a way that is accessible to, even if not adhered to by, the general public. In the political sphere, then, the religious dimension can be, and often is acknowledged; but the theoretical social science disciplines cannot admit any *intrinsic* need of religion or theology. They cannot draw on the *transcendent* perspective of religious faith in the way that, in the reverse direction, theology draws on reason.

III Engagement

The structure of the religious-secular dialogue, then, is asymmetrical. Whereas faith can and does integrate reason in its operations, reason can at best accommodate but cannot integrate faith. This leads to the question of precisely how theology relates to or incorporates sociology. What kind of interdisciplinary relationship, if any, is possible? Can their individual disciplinary integrity be maintained without collapsing the one into the other? Two contemporary theologians and two sociologists can be used to illustrate the main positions, and how the debate today cuts across sociology and theology more than between them.

a Theology Vis-à-Vis Sociology and Vice Versa

The asymmetry between theology and sociology is taken up by Timothy Radcliffe who makes a daring proposal about their potential for relationship.[11] He distinguishes sociological 'explanation' – the understanding of an event in terms of social dynamics – from theological 'recognition of the event as revelatory of God and his purposes' (p. 166). Theology does not bring any competing, or even complementary, theoretical 'perspective' of its own to a conversation with sociology. Its task is a creative one, not a matter of simply repeating or explicating religious visions of the world, nor aligning them with social scientific accounts, but 'the establishment of an illuminating relationship' between the two.

Theology, says Radcliffe drawing on Cornelius Ernst, is 'an encounter of Church and world in which the meaning of the gospel becomes articulate as an illumination of the world' and in which 'the meaning that men succeed in making of themselves and their experience is transformed to become a disclosure of that meaning of meaning that we call God' (pp. 169–70). He proposes that sociology, as one of the ways of making sense of experience, can be 'a locus for the encounter of gospel and world'. This happens, however, not by 'importing a particular "theological perspective", but rather by the internal transformation of sociology itself' (p. 177). Radcliffe recognizes the internal validity of the sociological enterprise but wants to push further into the realm of belief. Although he does not explain precisely how 'transformation' may come about, when thus transformed or subsumed sociology becomes an inner moment within theology. This might, of course, be seen as a simple theological takeover.

John Milbank is less accommodating and makes a more trenchant critique, particularly of the sociology of religion. His charge is that, as part of the Enlightenment project, sociology usurps the place of theology and becomes itself a kind of theology or 'anti-theology', with at its origins an ontology of violence which underpins the modern nation state. Milbank, seeking to rehabilitate metaphysics as essential for framing the reality of the social, derives from the Christian narrative a socially and politically oriented ontology of peace. He is critical not only of sociology but of liberal theology, which has sought to borrow from elsewhere a fundamental account of society or history, and then to see what theological insights will cohere with it. But it has been shown that no such fundamental account, in the sense of something neutral, rational and universal, is really available. It is theology itself that will have to provide its own account of the final causes at work in human history, on the basis of its own particular and historically specific faith.[12]

In Fergus Kerr's words, 'theology is already social theory, and social theory is already theology'.[13] Milbank warns that if theology does not frame or position the secular, the secular will position it. It is an apposite caution in view of the sociological dystopia analysed above, even if one may not wish to follow Milbank to his more extreme conclusions.

It is hardly surprising that Milbank's views grate on sociologists, especially those with theological interests. For David Martin, Milbank's theological project is an attempt to 'out-narrate' its opponents. Martin takes a more measured view, describing his intellectual purpose as 'to make sense of Christianity, not as a set of propositions but as a repertoire of transforming signs in historic engagement with the deep structures of power and violence'.[14] Such a project criss-crosses the borders of sociology and theology, but Martin is circumspect in the competence he attributes to sociology:

> we enter a conversation with others on the basis of certain criteria of logic, evidence, coherence and comparison . . . putting forward tentative hypotheses which are ordered by controlling paradigms and assumptions. The material of our scientific scrutiny comprises worlds of meaning and symbol and these are part of a narrative of personal motives and social projects that takes unexpected turns . . . (it is) possible to pursue the sociology of religion in a spirit of sympathetic understanding rather than see faith as an alienated delusion destined to disappear in the process of rationalization and the dialectics of history.[15]

Martin's 'conversational' sociology is probing and tentative and he approaches the border with theology not in an agnostic spirit but with open questions.

Kieran Flanagan is a sociologist who pushes further into the theological realm. He gives short shrift to much contemporary theology for reducing sociology to number crunching and failing to appreciate its imaginative and interpretative characteristics, and for the naïve way 'liberal' theology uses sociological materials and methodologies. The crucial point for Flanagan is that sociology commands the ground of culture on which theology operates; neglect of this has led theology (and much official Church teaching) astray. 'It is on the ground of culture, and with an ear to it, that sociology picks up resonances that theologians high on the walls of the city of God do not.'[16] Sociology is not simply to be subsumed within theology, as Milbank would have it, but has the role of critical 'watchman' for the religious to whom theologians should attend.

Flanagan is also critical of sociology for its handling of the realm of the religious. Its task is to analyse the social dynamics of identity and cohesion – which it sees expressed in, for example, civic religion and new age spirituality – and it is also expected to maintain and refurbish these dynamics; but here sociology is irredeemably partial and fatally flawed. In a surprising and non-sociological jump Flanagan avers that only Christianity, and specifically Catholicism, is fit for the task. This leads to an imaginative, theologically infused sociology of religion, a daring articulation of the deep social reality of religion, but it risks importing normative theological judgements directly into sociology, and on the other hand subsuming theology within sociology.

b Theology Engaging with Sociology

These positions (all of religious believers) do not so much pit theology and sociology against one another as relate them quite differently. The point to make is that any interdisciplinary engagement requires a reflexive awareness of a discipline's limits. Theology has to be alert to *how* it is using sociology or, in other words, to the underlying philosophy of social science. The essential theological shift has been the recognition of the practical nature of theology. What Vatican II did for Catholic theology was, as John McDade says, to relocate it 'in the middle of human history and experience'.[17] To deliver on this requires an appropriate methodology.

The basic theological approach here has been reading the signs of the times.[18] This starts with a social analysis of current realities and then, in a further step, 'discerns' them; that is to say theology seeks to explicate these realities in their inner meaning. This is theology's creative move, and sociology in this exercise becomes an inner moment within theology – but without losing anything of its own specificity.

Of course reading the signs of the times is a theological act.[19] It depends upon the prior assumption of the reality of God. Research collaboration between theologian and sociologist in this task is certainly eased if on a personal level they see eye to eye on this. Even so, cooperation between open-minded persons with radically different ontologies is also possible. Findings of the social sciences with an atheistic provenance may also contribute to theological insight – the use of Marxist analysis in some liberation theologies being a (controversial) case in point.

The two disciplines are not competing ways of providing theoretical knowledge. Their epistemological 'raw data' are different. The primordial form of knowing that theology works with is belief, whereas sociology works with our regular, ordinary, 'common sense' knowledge of the world. The task, in both cases, is to systematize and thematize and refine the raw data as theory – sociological and theological. In the case of theological theory – or doctrine – its epistemological status derives from the specific nature of religious belief as a fundamentally moral act which derives from openness to the operation of grace.[20] Sociology, on the other hand, handles reality and articulates truth by its various procedures of objectification and interpretation. Theology has to take such findings seriously in their own right. This goes beyond the traditional idea in Catholic studies of the 'handmaid of theology' (*ancilla theologiae*) – traditionally philosophy – with the implication of it having subsidiary status. Such a way of theorizing the relationship would undervalue the human sciences as distinct academic disciplines and merely instrumentalize them, it would not do justice to the specificity of sociology – nor indeed of theology.[21]

c 'Sites' of Theology in Sociology

What, then, does theology actually do? How does it relate to the reality laid out in the sociological account? One could only satisfactorily answer this question by extensive reference to actual examples of theological enquiry. There is ready cooperation at the technical level, and practical or pastoral theology routinely uses sociological surveys, questionnaires, interview procedures and data analysis to acquire a grasp of social and ecclesial practices. But there is also an epistemological level interchange. Here we can make a brief visit to a couple of standard sociological 'sites'.

'Spirituality' is a much discussed feature of contemporary culture and an obvious place to look for sociological-theological convergence. As an emergent sociological construct spirituality is commonly seen in disjunction from 'religion'. The concept has a long history. It migrated from the world of faith, first into theological obscurity, and then into postmodern culture. The sociology of the shift has been well charted.[22] Attempts to reclaim this ground by religious groups often proceed by conceding that floating free from institutional religion is valid in itself,[23] and that spirituality is rooted in and constituted from personal experience, sometimes communal experience but more typically the 'deep experiences of the self'.[24] The tension here with traditional Christian disciplines such as obedience and embracing the Cross is obvious.

While theology may contest the disjunction from religion, it should be able to see further. It expects to find the presence of grace. Evidence of this would be if the practices of 'spirituality' succeed in engendering receptivity in practitioners, deeper awareness of giftedness, a real movement of will and spirit in an openness that flowers in generous regard of 'the other'. An adequate sociological and psychological account is a pre-requisite here because it could be that actual practices of 'spirituality' camouflage one or the other form of oppression or alienation, quite the opposite of grace. What theology would do would be to encourage the spiritual 'seeker' not to rest in deep experiences but to transcend them in openness to the greater reality. An instance of this came up in research with one person's comment about an 'all-inclusive and non-demanding' Church congregation: 'it's so non-expectational that it's magnetic'.[25] The deep attraction of the Gospel shone through an under-stated proclamation, such that people felt free.

So, sociology can lead into theology, and theological truth be uncovered within a sociological account of spirituality. But theology may be the one providing assistance, with sociological explanation reached via theological insight. The revision of secularization theory might be seen this way. José Casanova's work bears the hallmark of an implicit theological sense clarifying sociological analysis. His subtle disentangling of secularization theory's various strands enables him to argue that religion's public role is not simply undermined in modernity but sustained in a new way. The argument is rigorously analytic, but its persuasiveness is heightened by an unmistakeable theological hinterland which comes out in the insightful way he presents his religious case studies and his theologically attuned historical understanding of the realms of the sacred and the secular.[26]

The same can be noted in Danièle Hervieu-Léger's analysis of secularization. She frames the issue as one of change and continuity in modernity, and explains this in terms of the dynamics of beliefs and believing. Traditional Christian *beliefs* may lose ground but the dynamic of *believing,* in secular as well as religious contexts, is a constant. Modernity both undermines religious believing *and* reconstitutes it, but now within a more diverse field of believing. Her effort at this point to pin down the specific form of religious believing takes on an unmistakeable, even if unacknowledged, theological character. She comes to a definition from research into apocalyptic communities living an alternative lifestyle; they were driven to reclaim older traditions such as monasticism for the purpose of self-legitimation; they laid claim to some ancient line, a 'cloud of witnesses', to validate their lifestyle. On this basis, Hervieu-Léger defines religion as a 'chain of memory'; this is the specificity of religious believing among the diversity of modern forms of believing.[27]

There is, however, something arbitrary here: religious groups are not unique in conserving memory. Trade unions, army regiments, university colleges all derive legitimacy from historical events and long standing traditions. It is not clear *sociologically* why this is the specific character of religious believing, but it is very apt *theologically.* The central act of Christian worship derives from what has been handed down, 'what I received from the Lord . . . do this in memory of me' (I Cor. 11.23–24). *Anamnesis* is at the heart of Christian life and theology.[28]

IV Conclusion

This chapter has concentrated on theology evaluating its relationship with sociology. It would, of course, be illuminating to have a parallel discussion of sociology considering its relation to theology. The chapter has laid out foundational features of theology and sociology, the assumptions on which they operate and underlying ontologies. The argument is that sociology, having to be agnostic on religious truth, finds itself located in the tension between underlying atheist/secular ontology and the ontology of grace. The asymmetry between them is such that while theology can adopt the critical resources of reason on which sociology relies, sociology may be alert to but is unable to adopt the perspectives of religious faith. This sets intrinsic limits to sociology and limits in its dealings with theology. Nevertheless, there is an essential contribution of sociology to enable theology to be an effective practical discipline. Conversely, theology can bring enlightenment to sociology.[29]

Notes

1   Sociology's interest not just in religion but in theology is foundational. Max Weber's work is a classic example, Max Weber (1930), *The Protestant Ethic and the Spirit of Capitalism* (London: Allen & Unwin); as is the work of his friend the theologian Ernst Troeltsch, see Ernst Troeltsch (1931), *The Social Teaching of the Christian Churches* (London: Allen & Unwin).

2   John Milbank, Catherine Pickstock and Graham Ward (1999), *Radical Orthodoxy: A New Theology* (London: Routledge).

3   Charles Taylor (2007), *A Secular Age* (Cambridge, MA: Belknap Press of Harvard University Press).

4   Peter Berger originally called it 'methodological atheism'; see Peter Berger (1967), *The Sacred Canopy* (Garden City, NY: Doubleday); also Douglas V. Porpora (2006), 'Methodological Atheism, Methodological Agnosticism and Religious Experience', *Journal for the Theory of Social Behaviour*, 36(1): pp. 57–75.

5   Karl Rahner (1975), 'Supernatural Existential', in Karl Rahner (ed.) and J. Cumming (exec. ed.), *Encyclopedia of Theology: A Concise Sacramentum Mundi* (London: Burns & Oates); Philip Endean (2004), *Karl Rahner and Ignatian Spirituality* (Oxford: Oxford University Press), pp. 46–8 and 233–4.

6   Russell McCutcheon (ed.) (1999), *The Insider/Outsider Problem in the Study of Religion* (London and New York: Cassell).

7   José Casanova (1994), *Public Religions in the Modern World* (Chicago: University of Chicago Press).

8   This was the theme of Pope Benedict's speech in Westminster Hall, 17 September 2010.

9   Jürgen Habermas (2005), 'Pre-Political Foundations of the Democratic Constitutional State?' in Jürgen Habermas and Joseph Ratzinger (eds), *The Dialectics of Secularization: On Reason and Religion* (San Francisco: Ignatius Press), pp. 19–52.

10 John Rawls (2009), *A Brief Inquiry into the Meaning of Sin and Faith: With 'On My Religion'*, ed. Thomas Nagel (Cambridge, MA: Harvard University Press); see also Joshua Cohen and Thomas Nagel, 'John Rawls: On My Religion. How Rawls's Political Philosophy Was Influenced by His Religion', *Times Literary Supplement*, 18 March 2009.

11 Timothy Radcliffe (2004), 'Relativizing the Relativizers: A Theologian's Assessment of the Role of Sociological Explanation of Religious Phenomena and Theology Today', in D. Martin, J. O. Mills and W. S. F. Pickering (eds), *Sociology and Theology: Alliance and Conflict* (Leiden: Brill), pp. 165–77. Originally published in 1980, this is still one of the best discussions of the topic.

12 John Milbank (1990), *Religion and Social Theory: Beyond Secular Reason* (Oxford: Blackwell), p. 382.

13   Fergus Kerr (1992), 'Simplicity Itself: Milbank's Thesis', *New Blackfriars*, 73 (June 1992): pp. 306–10.
14   Martin Martin (2001), 'Personal Reflections', in R. K. Fenn (ed.), *The Blackwell Companion to Sociology of Religion* (Oxford: Blackwell), pp. 23–38, 23.
15   David Martin (2005), *Towards a Revised Theory of Secularization* (Aldershot: Ashgate), p. 25.
16   Kieran Flanagan (2007), *Sociology in Theology: Reflexivity and Belief* (London: Palgrave Macmillan), p. 31.
17   John McDade (1991), 'Catholic Theology in the Post-Conciliar Period', in A. Hastings (ed.), *Modern Catholicism* (London: SPCK), p. 423.
18   Michael Kirwan (2010), 'Reading the Signs of the Times', in James Sweeney, Gemma Simmonds and David Lonsdale (eds), *Keeping Faith in Practice: Aspects of Catholic Pastoral Theology* (London: SCM), pp. 49–63.
19   Henri-Jérôme Gagey (2010), 'Pastoral Theology as a Theological Project', in James Sweeney with Gemma Simmonds and David Lonsdale (eds), *Keeping Faith in Practice: Aspects of Catholic Pastoral Theology* (London: SCM), pp. 80–98.
20   For a full discussion of this see George Lindbeck (1984), *The Nature of Doctrine: Religion and Theology in a Post-Liberal Age* (London: SPCK).
21   On interdisciplinary challenges, see Louis-Marie Chauvet (2010), 'When the Theologian Turns Anthropologist', in James Sweeney with Gemma Simmonds and David Lonsdale (eds), *Keeping Faith in Practice: Aspects of Catholic Pastoral Theology* (London: SCM), pp. 148–62.
22   Guiseppe Giordan (2007), 'Spirituality: From a Religious Concept to a Sociological Theory', in Kieran Flanagan and Peter C. Jupp (eds), *A Sociology of Spirituality* (Aldershot: Ashgate), pp. 161–80.
23   Droogers, André Droogers (2007), 'Beyond Secularisation and Sacralisation: Lessons from Study of the Dutch Case', in Kieran Flanagan and Peter C. Jupp (eds), *A Sociology of Spirituality* (Aldershot: Ashgate), pp. 81–100.
24   Paul Heelas, Linda Woodhead, et al. (2005), *The Spiritual Revolution; Why Religion Is Giving Way to Spirituality* (Oxford: Blackwell).
25   Helen Cameron, Deborah Bhatti, Catherine Duce, James Sweeney and Clare Watkins (2010), *Talking About God in Practice: Theological Action Research and Practical Theology* (London: SCM), p. 115.
26   José Casanova (1994), *Public Religions in the Modern World* (Chicago: University of Chicago Press).
27   Danièle Hervieu-Léger (2000), *Religion as a Chain of Memory* (Cambridge: Polity Press).
28   On defining religion in religious studies using Hervieu-Léger's thesis see James L. Cox, 'Religion without God: Methodological Agnosticism and the Future of Religious Studies', The Hibbert Lecture, Herriot-Watt University, 2003, available at www.thehibberttrust.org.uk/lectures.htm.
29   For a discussion of this in relation to anthropology, see Deborah Bhatti (2011), *The Rite of Christian Initiation of Adults and Liminal Experience: A Theological Anthropological Interpretation*, unpublished PhD thesis, Heythrop College, University of London.

Chapter 8

Theology and Psychology

Peter Hampson
(Blackfriars Hall, Oxford)

Secular psychologists can be forgiven for their professional disinterest in the existence of God. After all, even theologians with impeccably orthodox credentials have suggested that God makes no especial difference to how things are! Theologian Herbert McCabe used to claim, for example, that God makes no *particular* difference but instead makes *all* the difference, since any 'god' who engages in a particular way, as an efficient cause among other causes, cannot be the God of orthodox Christianity, the creator of all that is.[1] Hence the issue of God's involvement need not affect our particular descriptions of how things work. Human behaviour, experience and mental life are reliably as they are, irrespective of whether or not humans are created; accounts of psychological functioning can thus bracket the God question. Supporters of this view can with some legitimacy argue that *methodological* naturalism can be assumed as a pragmatic research strategy without any further philosophical implications, reductive or otherwise.[2] Even those practitioners of psychology sympathetic to religion need not concern themselves with fundamental metaphysical questions, at least not when engaged in their science. The assumption of methodological naturalism does not imply a commitment to a comprehensive ontological naturalism.[3]

At one level this is probably a sensible way to proceed.[4] Surely what we might call the heartlands of academic psychology, its scientific study of cognitive, developmental and social processes, the nature of personality and individual variation, abnormal psychology, neuropsychology and so on, can be approached without concern as to whether God created its subject matter or not? Psychology is a biological and a social science after all. Are not sciences obligated to approach their discipline with naturalistic methods?

Yes, at one level, psychology has its own methods and autonomous sphere of activity, but here is the first rub. Aspiring to a 'true' or even approximately true description of human behaviour, experience, and mental life using psychology alone or in interaction with recognized 'cognate' disciplines, presupposes that psychology's existing practices, methods, concepts, suppositions and findings can be guaranteed to deliver that truth.[5] It further suggests that psychology is in good standing as an intellectual tradition, situated in the right place in the academic family. But there are two pitfalls here. First, such an avowedly, if soft, naturalist stance begs the question of the genealogy of psychology's concepts and theories. Even if it is recognized that such concepts are not ahistorical in the strictest sense, it tacitly implies that their history, and, we might add, their coherence and validity, can be explicated without serious reference to theology. Second, it further implies that all epistemic crises as arise from time to time within psychology can be solved or eased either with the resources of psychology alone, or maybe with help from its nearest neighbours, biology, sociology, cultural studies or secular philosophy perhaps, but not from theology.[6] Yet neither implication need follow. Psychological concepts often have long histories, stretching back into theology, and history often illuminates the present. Although it is an intellectual tradition with its own intrinsic standards of rationality, psychology can still accept assistance from potentially 'rival' traditions, such as theology, tricky issues of commensurability and translatability notwithstanding.[7]

And here is a second rub. Suppose that the Christian tradition is correct in believing that humans are not simply gifted with existence and participation in being, but, as sentient, rational and desiring creatures, that they are also invited into friendship and communion with God. Suppose, that is, that Aquinas is right and that there are two orders of gift, the *effectus naturae* and the *effectus gratiae*.[8] Are not gifts usually perceived, received and, we hope, appreciated? I write 'usually' since their recognition and reception with gratitude is likely to be affected by individual factors. If so, not only does their significance as gift have general psychological relevance, even a perceived gift would have such, but it shifts, ontologically speaking, from being a meaning*less* illusion to a meaning*ful* reality. Human experience thus construed, even so simple an experience as saying 'yes' with gratitude to life, cannot be *merely* a psychological phenomenon, explicable *fully* in an ontologically naturalist way divorced from wider metaphysical considerations. It thrives on richer ontological air.[9]

Orthodox Christian theology can supply this richer atmosphere. It invites psychology to consider that people are diachronically, synchronically, materially and spiritually situated in what we might dub a 'participatory theophany' or 'the ecology of God',[10] from whom all meaning derives. And, just as we might assume aviation psychologists to understand a little about aerodynamics and the principles of efficient flight, so we might expect psychologists, especially but not only those concerned with religion, morality or spiritually meaningful actions, to appreciate at least something of what we might call *theo*-dynamics and the principles of a flourishing life.

Suppose, further, that the Christ event is historically pivotal, not simply in relation to linear, salvation history, but also, or as a consequence, because He shows us once and for all the fullest possibilities of the human condition.[11] The celebrated §22 of the Vatican document *Gaudium et Spes*,[12] makes this abundantly clear:

> The truth is that only in the mystery of the incarnate Word does the mystery of man take on light. For Adam, the first man, was a figure of Him Who was to come, namely Christ the Lord. Christ, the final Adam, by the revelation of the mystery of the Father and His love, fully reveals man to man himself and makes his supreme calling clear . . . He Who is 'the image of the invisible God' (Col. 1.15), is Himself the perfect man. To the sons of Adam He restores the divine likeness which had been disfigured from the first sin onward. Since human nature as He assumed it was not annulled, by that very fact it has been raised up to a divine dignity in our respect too. For by His incarnation the Son of God has united Himself in some fashion with every man.

Might this not be of some *psychological* significance, and might not a theological account of that event prove helpful for psychology?

So, while reference to God is not strictly necessary for psychology, it does not follow that engagement with *theology* is of no help at all, nor that theology is poorly equipped to help psychology complete its project. This chapter explores how academic (scientific) psychology would benefit from such a principled engagement. It considers how psychology could change in its assumptions, emphases and philosophical underpinnings as well extending its range of topics and, controversially, some of its methods, by interacting with theology and how this would alter how the discipline is taught and researched. As it happens, there are already examples which are yielding benefits of cultural dialogue between Christianity and psychology, and interdisciplinary interactions between psychology and theology. Given the current state of the field, there is merit in such a plurality of approaches, but there is scope too for a deeper, ultimately 'transdisciplinary' engagement governed by orthodox Christian theology. I take the latter to include a broadly Catholic emphasis on the interdependence of faith and reason and a rejection of the concept of 'pure nature'.[13]

Before considering how theology and psychology are now reconnecting, it is worth remembering that complex genealogical relationships between the two disciplines are easily obscured by focussing on the synchronic. Psychology is a child of modern philosophy; its prehistory is therefore the history of philosophy. Yet philosophy in turn has a long involvement with and eventual separation from theology. Why should this matter for psychology? According to

Milbank: 'Modern philosophy . . . has no autonomous ability to assess the conditions of its own genesis.'[14] By which he means autonomous independently from theology. Hence, we can infer that psychology has no autonomous ability to assess the conditions of *its* own genesis either, but now such an assessment must also include the transmitted effects of the splitting of philosophy from theology and the consequent cultural divorce of faith from reason. This is part of a bigger story, of intellectual history and its deviations, which complements Taylor's magisterial discussion of the rise of secularity.[15] If modern philosophy is marked by the outcome of earlier theological controversies[16] then psychology is likely to bear similar though maybe less obvious signs of its troubled past. The sins of the theological fathers shall be visited on the psychological sons.

Its theological patrimony aside, psychology's philosophical parentage is easy to chart.[17] Several influential approaches and methods in psychology emerged from and are still underpinned by post-Cartesian philosophy, which is not to imply that all psychological theorizing is dualistic, far from it, simply that its philosophical parentage is both recent and arguably limited. The once hegemonic behaviourism rested on empirical foundations from Locke and Hume. Its more liberal methodological variant, cognitive psychology, relies as much if not more on Kantian themes, as does Piagetian developmental psychology. Both cognitive psychology and behaviourism owe a debt to associationism. The psychophysics of Fechner and Wundt can be traced back to its Leibnizian psychophysical parallelist roots. Although positivist methodologies support much of experimental psychology, the influence of the later Wittgenstein is evident in the emergence of discursive and qualitative methods used widely (and especially) in European social psychology. None of these influences and putative biases might matter unduly were it not for the fact that these philosophical traditions, arguably anyway, generally privilege epistemology over ontology, reflect the outcome of a post-Scotist, nominalist univocity, tend to split fact from value and faith from reason, embody a notion of reason as ratiocination and faith as sentiment, thereby separating subjectivity from objectivity and leave a godless subject gazing out on an inert world.[18] Other traditions pre-dating Descartes[19] or less powerful post-Kantian voices[20] have had less influence and recent systematic and philosophical theology has had virtually none.

Against this, it could be argued that psychology possesses sufficient resources of its own to repair itself in time – just as analytical philosophy managed to extricate itself from too stifling a positivism during the last century[21] – were it not that a (modernist) culture of forgetting afflicts modern psychology to such an extent that its practitioners are often blissfully unaware of the longer history of their theoretical constructs. Thus, there is little grasp of how some psychological concepts have become bowdlerized or intellectually degraded over time,[22] how certain concepts and deep assumptions now taken for granted and seen as 'obvious' in psychology reflect contested theological turns only now being recovered and fully understood,[23] or that useful concepts have been lost along the way.[24] More worryingly still, there is little shared understanding that seemingly irreconcilable 'splits' in the discipline, of which the major one is probably the disconnection of 'scientific' from 'hermeneutic' approaches, might have been avoided, or at least attenuated, had the discipline not been anchored philosophically in the way that it is,[25] nor been wedded so closely to the ideal of science as 'Newtonian' rather than to a more humane and teleological Aristotelian enterprise.[26] The situation is further compounded by the fact that too few theologians are aware of the complex nature of modern psychology. Many theologians, it seems, still equate psychology with the psychodynamic tradition, assume that its primary concerns are with therapy and are unaware of its contemporary breadth, scope and characteristic methods. Nor are they fully appraised of its many positive achievements; lacking the ability to speak both languages, they are unable to advise it appropriately.[27]

Later on I shall put more flesh on these bones. First two clarifications are in order. In suggesting that psychology suffers from various crises, biases and conceptual confusions I am not denying that it remains an impressive cultural achievement which has often greatly benefitted humanity. Current understanding of rehabilitation strategies for the brain injured, the ergonomic principles for designing aircraft cockpits, the analysis of the processes in reading, or the management of chronic pain, to choose but four arbitrary examples, is due in no small part to psychology. Such advances have undoubtedly made human lives more hopeful, safe, fulfilling and less of an ordeal. Second, none of the preceding should be taken to imply that there have been no specific connections between Christian *religion* and psychology; the psychology of religion, pastoral theology and psychology in the service of the Church in the broader sense are all ways in which this has fruitfully occurred. There have also been serious attempts recently to explore 'the value of psychology in general for Christians and the issues and problems in psychological study and counseling practice for people of faith.'[28] In their edited essay collection, Johnson and Jones outlined four important approaches whose labels are now routinely used in US Christian Psychology circles: integrationist; levels-of-explanation; Christian psychology; Biblical Counselling. Each approach has its distinctive strengths, but they have typically emerged either from evangelical settings in which Bible based Christianity predominates, or from liberal Protestant contexts, and so their explicit use of philosophical theology, at least of a systematic, orthodox variety, has been somewhat underplayed. The practical focus of a great deal of this work has also been counselling and therapy rather than academic psychology more generally.[29]

There is however a wider debate and we can now identify three emerging approaches in the theology-psychology dialogue in the United States and United Kingdom which somewhat predictably resemble classic encounters between Christianity and culture.[30] So, integrationist,[31] or liberal-compatibilist positions[32] tend, on the whole, to leave unchallenged the basic principles of psychology, but are optimistic both as to the prospects for enriching the content of psychology through a fuller engagement with 'Christian' topics, and for theology and psychology to co-operate in the reconstruction of theological anthropology.[33] 'Christian Psychology' proper, on the other hand, is more assertive and positions Christianity as over and against secular culture. Eric Johnson, an especially strong champion of this approach, has made creative use of Reformed Epistemology as part of a re-engineered philosophy of science for psychology,[34] as well as tirelessly leading and inspiring the Christian psychology movement as a whole. Here is a movement, wary of aspects of secular psychology's biases, which stands strong as an evangelical witness. It has been criticized, however, for risking the isolation of its Christianized psychology. From a more liberal perspective Worthington writes: 'It is Christian psychology's non-scientific methods and the frank incorporation of the existence of truly non-naturalistic phenomena and beings that would ghettoize Johnson's Christian psychology within the discipline of psychological science.'[35] A Catholic equivalent based on a magisterial approach to theology has also been proposed.[36]

Given the current state of theology-psychology dialogue it is probably unwise to decide definitively between integrationism and Christian psychology. They overlap considerably and debates between them are generally conducted in a productive, ecumenical and charitable spirit. Together with the third approach, which I shall outline shortly, it may be more sensible to think of all the three in terms of overlapping circles or as the corners of a triangle bounding a share space, rather than completely independent conflicting positions. Nevertheless, and risking some general comparisons, both liberal-integrationism and Christian psychology tend to be 'post-Kantian' in their assumption that faith and reason are separate categories, with Christianity representing the former and psychology, the child of enlightenment philosophy, the latter. Differences arise largely in their confidence that this gap can be bridged. Integrationism being the more optimistic of the two appears to have greater trust in secular reason and empirical psychology's methods. The two approaches are both epistemologically focussed, varied as to their Christology, and generally somewhat univocal in their (often tacit) ontology.

The third potential engagement of theology with psychology entails a different relationship between faith and reason, theology and philosophy. Reflecting the depth of the orthodox, Christian tradition in a philosophically and theologically sophisticated way, it embeds psychology within a robust theological architectonic so as to identify and potentially heal some of psychology's epistemic crises. Trans-disciplinary in its outlook it gives psychology its own space, but suggests that a more comprehensive understanding of human nature will require a reconstructed discipline transcending current disciplinary boundaries and assumptions of the human sciences. It neither subsumes a Christianized psychology to the current culture of secularity, thereby privileging reason of sorts over faith, nor unduly ghettoizes it through Christian assertion, whether reductively fundamentalist or dogmatic, thereby privileging faith of sorts over reason. In terms outlined by H. R. Niebuhr,[37] it avoids the extremes of the Christ of culture and the Christ against culture positions opting instead for some version of Christ over or transcending culture.

Such a third way is sorely needed. Its relevant theological resources already exist, but their application to psychology is still in its infancy. But what is its essence? It is the application to psychology of the findings and developments of the broad, *ressourcement* tradition in Catholic theological scholarship especially but not exclusively as recently represented by the High Anglican Radical Orthodoxy (RO) project, or more generally, what has been recently termed 'romantic orthodoxy'.[38] Labels can easily be divisive. Terms such as 'Catholic', 'radical orthodoxy' or even 'Thomistic' can be seen as triumphalist banners of an in-group, or as ill-mannered attempts to claim the uplands of orthodoxy against all comers. That said, the RO movement and its fellow travellers have focussed attention on many issues pertinent to interdisciplinary debates. Hence, I simply use the label RO here for expository convenience as a prototypical example of a sort of third engagement, while thinking more generally of the broad family of theologically orthodox Catholic approaches.[39]

RO uses the vast resources of the theologically orthodox Christian tradition, including early and late mediaeval sources, to critique secularity and late modernity.[40] It begins by recovering the doctrine of participation of all existence, being, and to this we can add thinking, feeling and acting in God. This non-dualist reading of Plato, developed and Christianized by Augustine, Proclus, Aquinas and others, stands opposed to a two world ontology divided into an inert or grace-less nature and a supernatural realm. It implies that there is no such thing as 'pure nature', autonomous from God, but that all is gifted to share in God's life, though to varying degrees and kinds. Rejecting simple dualisms, RO neither collapses into pantheism, nor is subsumed into panentheism, nor retreats into deism. Instead God is radically different from but utterly intimate with creation, which asymmetrically depends for its existence on the divine.

God's radical difference from creation, the fact that He is not a being among beings nor an efficient cause among causes but one transcending being and cause, means that all talk of God is unavoidably analogical, rather than univocal. In one of its more controversial moves, RO asserts that being itself is 'on loan' analogically. We share being as gift, living not autonomously from God but in utter dependence on Him.[41] Because, too, God escapes capture by human concepts and language, and at the heart of the Christian mystery is the union without mixture of the infinite, necessary, divine, with the finite, contingent, created, not only is all religious language analogical but it acknowledges through paradox and the 'coincidence of opposites'[42] possible signs of deeper Christian truth. There is thus a deep apophasis and 'learned ignorance'[43] at the heart of the Christian faith.

Orthodox metaphysics have methodological consequences in debates with psychology. In line with mainstream Catholic thinking, RO views the relation between faith and reason as interpenetrative and mutually implicative, not as separate. All human reasoning, scientific as well as theological, is grounded on some sort of belief or pre-reflexive assent and is not reducible to ratiocination but involves imagination, metaphor and analogy. Nor is faith the blind acceptance of strange propositions but is itself reliant on reasoning. In this respect RO is simply true to traditional, pre-modern as well as more recent restatements of the Christian tradition.[44] Second, the close relationship between faith and reason forbids the segregation of theology from philosophy.[45] Theology is certainly not just faith expressed in fancy language and philosophy cannot or should not be detached from its metaphysical aspects. Ultimately, however, theology and 'sacred doctrine' are seen as being at a higher level of participation than philosophy, so philosophy becomes variously the handmaiden of or even part of theology.[46] Faith, however, is primary in the sense that before theologizing there is pre-reflexive, loving assent.[47] Religious knowing is situated, personal and communal. It begins in awe and is grounded in doxology and liturgy.[48] Third, RO insists on explicating the genealogy of ideas; concepts have histories. In itself this statement is not novel, but it has important implications for theological engagement with psychology.

What might the application of an RO approach to psychology look like? For a start, psychology is immediately placed in a different interdisciplinary environment and invited to become a truly trans-disciplinary science. Psychology and theology are hierarchically ordered in different degrees of participation, but both are equally subordinate to divine *scientia*, the mind of God. This simple act of repositioning recruits psychology, like philosophy, into the role of handmaid to theology. I am aware that such an act of disciplinary 'one-upmanship' will be seen as contentious by many. That aside, here is a relationship with a history since work done by theology already alters the context in which psychology conducts some of its labours. For instance, RO's embrace of a participatory ontology and consequent challenge to Scotist univocity[49] entails a rejection of various other dualisms which, for better or for worse, may have become part of psychology's stock in trade, including the modern disjunction between so-called subjectivity and objectivity. An immediate question for psychology is, obviously, whether this particular tool has outlived its usefulness. If it answers in the affirmative it must consider the consequences of dispensing with such an 'obvious' dichotomy. And these consequences are not trivial. They challenge the inevitability of a representational account of mind at the heart of cognitive psychology, the seemingly unbridgeable chasm between first person, hermeneutic and scientific methods, and the privileging of the nominal and possible over the real or actual in scientific and everyday understanding.

Engagement with RO would also encourage openness to new methods, and sources of data. At the very least, psychology would be urged to attend more to the genealogy of its concepts, opening up some for reanalysis, such as habit or relationality, re-admitting or repristinating ones whose meaning has become lost or occluded such as the will, passions or desire, and qualifying or questioning the validity of others such as ego strength or self-esteem. More radically still, orthodox theology suggests there is scope in psychology for prayer and reflection. 'What an outrageous claim!' the secular cry goes up! But there are already well-argued suggestions that this could be appropriate for interdisciplinary work in general,[50] here we are merely suggesting the same for theology's relationship with psychology. This is not to suggest that prayer is some sort of naïve, petitionary alternative to standard disciplinary methods – quite the reverse in fact – but it does remind us that our thinking and our experiencing as well as our being are utterly dependent on God. Its disavowals notwithstanding, psychology makes abundant if covert appeals to the introspective plausibility of many of its arguments and relies on 'phenomenological presuppositions'[51] when doing so; explicitly grounding such pre-theoretical reflections and discernments in the Trinitarian life can only make them more open, honest and ultimately comprehensible. Effective models for this type of engagement already exist in theology of course, as the witness of Augustine, Anselm, Aquinas, Cusa and others abundantly shows.

I have already alluded to RO's general challenge to representational, or 'mediational'[52] theories of mind. This has other consequences. By situating people in a participatory ontology, orthodox theology encourages psychology to take a new look at some forgotten or neglected issues. The co-constitution of mind and reality, Aquinas's *adequatio*, means that not only might psychological powers be in a process of actualization toward their goals, but also reach their perfection in them.[53] Suddenly, an analogical exploration of 'movement', teleology and form are back on the agenda, and long suppressed topics such as will-as-desire, passions, habit as 'non-identical repetition', and ontological deepening brought back into play, as the sole and unquestioned allegiance of psychology to post-Enlightenment philosophy is challenged by more classical sources.

New topics are then opened up for psychology to examine. Admittedly this is already happening as a result of liberal and more evangelical approaches to dialogue. Think of important work on virtues such as forgiveness, or the defence of altruism for example. But a fuller dialogue with the wealth of the orthodox tradition would make available a rich historical approach to psychological thought based on the reflections of acknowledged spiritual masters, reflections which cannot be reduced to 'mere' psychologizing or simple 'autobiography'.[54]

For most of its development, psychology has offered a de-contextualized largely ahistorical account of its phenomena. Releasing this constraint would open up the discipline. Cultural psychology has begun this by situating beliefs and affects in sociocultural contexts, a truly theologized psychology would add the full diachronic sophistication that is sorely needed.[55] A good example of the sort of data requiring such a nuanced treatment was offered recently by Mgr Roderick Strange in a talk on Newman.[56] Newman's conversion from the Anglican communion to Rome was not without psychological cost. He moved, rapidly, from a state of intellectual dissatisfaction yet full and emotionally affirming engagement with the cut and thrust of the issues of the day, to a condition which while more intellectually satisfying was, quite frankly, emotionally unsupportive and cold. With the benefit of hindsight we can see that he battled on for some time with fortitude in a state we would now characterize as depression or learned helplessness. Yet a purely individual psychological account here is clearly insufficient. On cultural and religious grounds Newman's conversion was part of his longer journey from low church Evangelicalism, through High Anglicanism to Roman Catholicism. As this progressed, Newman's religious knowing developed from a relatively simple sense of God's presence to a more paradoxical and complex sense of the light and the dark of God's presence and absence, mirroring the difference between the denominational beginnings and end of his journey. At the very least, an account of Newman's 'depression' needs to take into account this life-shaping cultural-religious narrative. But in a wider theological framework it is possible to see Newman's spiritual growth over this period as one in which he genuinely becomes closer to God through acceptance of tribulation and a growing sense of God's complex yet faithful involvement with the world. God is to found in all moods and none, in all things, seen and unseen. As some of us in discussion later agreed, this theological gloss bears an intriguing resemblance to aspects of the classical mystical ascent. But without this gloss, understanding Newman too easily collapses back to a cultural narrative, or to abnormal, individual psychology.

Perhaps, however, the greatest challenge of RO's engagement with psychology is the issue of the normative and the perfect raised by Christology. As §22 of *Gaudium et Spes* asserts, 'only in the mystery of the incarnate Word does the mystery of man *(sic)* take on light'. This is a strong statement. Rather than simply establishing central tendencies or norms of behaviour, areas such as moral psychology receptive to the idea would be encouraged to consider the actuality of the human condition at its best, not merely its potentialities or its baselines. A radical Christological perspective thus reverses the normal explanatory sequence. Its actualities define both the possibilities and perfections of humanity. The fact too that, as *imago Dei*, personhood is ultimately a *mystery*, even if not completely unintelligible, indicates that an apophatic dimension characterizes our knowledge of persons as well as our knowledge of God. Here, though, is a dimension which bridges the epistemic gap between subjectivity and objectivity, through participation in and analogy with divine knowing, while at the same time reminding psychology of its explanatory limits.

Much, however, would be left untouched, and, in this sense at least, 'normal' psychology is granted its autonomous sphere of activity. Certainly, one option for psychology would be to acknowledge more fully its limitations and simply retreat into a limited, scientific account of certain facets of human nature, resisting both scientistic fantasies and metaphysical extension.[57] This is a route clearly open to areas of cognitive neuroscience. But, if psychology's spirit of intellectual adventure is such that it wishes to 'explain' further such issues as meaning, purpose, intention or even relationality, it must accept that its explanations cannot be hegemonic, it will require help from other disciplines, especially theology, and it will need to reflect on whether psychology is a science in its entirety or a discipline which is tasked with straddling the problematic divide between the sciences and humanities, or at least, as we have seen, between science and hermeneutics.

Defending the legitimate autonomy of psychology, at whatever level, should not rule out psychology's availability as a helpmate for theology. Theology too can receive guidance and instruction from psychology. For instance more detailed theoretical accounts can be brought to bear on clearly related accounts, proposed independently by theology. So, for example, dual process models of social judgement, or Iain McGilchrist's recent creative work on the cultural implication of hemispheric differences,[58] can usefully be brought into dialogue with accounts of religious knowing such as Newman's account of real and nominal apprehension and assent. Adult autonomy at one level does not preclude relationality and interdependence at another. In practice, though, the practical, curricular and pedagogic relationships that obtain between psychology and theology will most likely depend as much on the nature of the teaching institution as on the particular model of theology-psychology partnership in play. Institutional aims, purposes and theological assumptions bring additional and appropriate constraints to bear. Thus, it is entirely appropriate for a Catholic *graduate* psychological school such as the Institute for the Psychological Sciences in Washington, DC, to apply Catholic teachings directly to clinical practice within a curriculum which combines a study of philosophical and theological sources with empirically sound therapeutic techniques, or for the 'IGNIS', *Akademie für Christliche Psychologie* to 'demonstrate the healing and helping presence of God both in the theoretical and practical aspects of psychology and (to) live and pass on the Gospel of Jesus Christ in this field' and to do much the same from a more Protestant evangelical perspective.[59] Equally, Fuller Theological Seminary does excellent work not least with its annual 'integration' symposium. Similarly the broad coverage of psychology of religion and psychology and religion by the Cambridge University 'Psychology and Religion Research Group' accommodates various approaches to theology-psychology interactions in its attempts to construct a scientifically well-informed, shared, theological anthropology.

But what we do not appear to have yet, at the time of writing, is a mainstream university or college setting in which the wider discipline of psychology, not simply therapy, is framed by orthodox theology from first degree level onwards, and which views theology as operating at a higher level of participation and therefore superordinate to psychology – with theology now not simply at the centre of the disciplinary circle[60] but higher up the hill. Psychology programmes, routinely and rightly, have courses in the biological *bases* of mind, emotion and behaviour, why not also the theological *ultimacy* of consciousness, desire and action, programmes informed but not determined solely by psychology nor naively situated by theology? Courses on Christian anthropology variously attempt this, but they are often taken in seminaries which, as a mirror image the secular department of psychology lacking theology, frequently lack the full expertise and resources of psychology.

Such an institution would expect undergraduates studying psychology without exception to have reasonable familiarity with theology and philosophy. Its methods would be innovative, its pedagogy prayerful, its setting most probably ecclesial. We are a long way from realizing this in 'mainstream' psychology degrees *ab initio*. Still, current developments are encouraging. After all, once there was no secular,[61] and once there was no psychology separate from theology. In God's good time this might be true again. For God does make all the difference when all is said and done!

Notes

1   H. McCabe (1987), *God Matters* (London and New York: Mowbray), pp. 2–9. See also P. J. Hampson, (2005), 'Beyond Unity, Integration and Experience: Cultural Psychology and Mediaeval Mysticism', *New Blackfriars*, 86(1006): pp. 622–41, for further discussion.

2   C. Cunningham (2010), *Darwin's Pious Idea* (Cambridge, UK: Eeerdmans), espe-
    cially pp. 265–9, for a critical discussion.
3   C. Southgate, C. Deane-Drummond, P. Murray, M. Negus, L. Osborn, M. Poole,
    J. Stewart and F. Watts (1999), *God, Humanity and the Cosmos: A Textbook in
    Science and Religion* (Edinburgh: T&T Clark), for a discussion of this distinction,
    pp. 162–3.
4   Ignoring the psychology of religion or moral psychology which inevitably entail
    some reference to God or to the 'good', even if subsequently to treat them as
    fictions.
5   Setting aside the commonplace that all any science offers is inevitably provisional.
6   This is another version of what Cunningham calls the 'no theology mantra',
    Cunningham, *Darwin's Pious Idea*, p. 333.
7   For a general discussion of translatability and commensurability between traditions
    see A. MacIntyre (1988), *Whose Justice? Which Rationality* (London: Duckworth),
    especially pp. 349–88, and for a useful summary, L. Bretherton (2006), *Hospitality
    as Holiness: Christian Witness Amid Moral Diversity* (London: Ashgate), pp. 9–33.
    However, see J. Milbank (1990), *Theology and Social Theory: Beyond Secular
    Reason* (Oxford: Blackwell), pp. 326–79, for an alternative, rhetorical as opposed
    to dialectical, account of the rationality of traditions. (I am grateful to Dr Johannes
    Hoff for reminding me of the importance of this.)
8   St Thomas Aquinas, *Summa Theologiae*, 1a, 1.8. ad1. For a nuanced reading which
    avoids the trap of positing either a *natura pura* or of reducing grace to a single order
    of participation, see R. te Velde (2006), *Aquinas on God: The 'Divine Science' of the
    Summa Theologiae* (Farnham: Ashgate), pp. 147–69. See also Sweeney, Chapter 7,
    this volume, for a further useful discussion of grace.
9   Extending Cunningham's claims, I am suggesting that for psychology as well as
    biology, 'both epistemology and ontology meet', *Darwin's Pious Idea*, p. 174.
10 Not solely in the sense of ecological theology, with its concern for stewardship of
    the world, but in the sense that we live in the cosmos, an ontological ecosystem radi-
    cally dependent on God.
11 A. Riches (forthcoming), *Christ: The End of Humanism* (Grand Rapids: Eerdmans).
12 Pope Paul VI (1965), *The Pastoral Constitution of the Church in the Modern World:
    Gaudium et Spes*, retrieved on 2 February 2011 from www.vatican.va/archive/
    hist_councils/ii_vatican_council/documents/vat-ii_cons_19651207_gaudium-
    et-spes_en.html.
13 The variety of orthodoxy exemplified here it is perhaps best captured by what
    Milbank has dubbed 'romantic orthodoxy', J. Milbank (2010), 'Romantic and
    Classical Orthodoxy', *Modern Theology* 26(1): pp. 26–38.
14 R. Shortt (2009), 'Radical Orthodoxy: A Conversation', in J. Milbank and S. Oliver
    (eds), *The Radical Orthodoxy Reader* (London: Routledge), pp. 35–6.
15 C. Taylor (2007), *A Secular Age* (Cambridge: Harvard University Press, Belknap).
    Following Taylor I am assuming that the 'desacralization' story is insufficient
    to account for the rise of secularity. As Oliver argues, its rise 'involves the
    replacement of a certain view of God and creation with a different view which
    still makes theological claims . . . The problem is that this "mock-theology"
    or "pseudo-theology" is bad theology'. S. Oliver (2009), 'Introducing Radical
    Orthodoxy: From Participation to Late Modernity', in Milbank and Oliver, *The
    Radical Orthodoxy Reader*, p. 6.

16   O. Crisp, M. Davies, G. D'Costa and P. Hampson (eds) (2011), *Theology and Philosophy: Faith and Reason* (London: Continuum).

17   Although not always made clear to its students.

18   J. Milbank (2009). 'The Grandeur of Reason and the Perversity of Rationalism: Radical Orthodoxy's First Decade', in Milbank and Oliver, *The Radical Orthodoxy Reader*, pp. 367–404, especially pp. 379–86.

19   Ibid., pp. 384–7.

20   Ibid., p. 386. See also F. Schleiermacher (1995), *Dialectic, or the Art of Doing Philosophy: A Study Edition of the 1811 Notes* (trans., Terrence N. Tice) (Atlanta, GA: Scholars Press), for a relatively underexplored, 'non-Hegelian' philosophical route out of Kant, potentially helpful for healing psychology's split of 'science' from 'hermeneutics'.

21   For example, W. V. O. Quine, (1951), 'Two Dogmas of Empiricism', *The Philosophical Review*, 60: pp. 20–43.

22   See, for example, T. Dixon (2003), *From Passions to Emotions: The Creation of a Secular Psychological Category* (Cambridge: Cambridge University Press).

23   An example would be the highly influential representational theory of mind and its dependence on the turn to univocity. See C. Pickstock (2005), 'Duns Scotus: His Historical and Contemporary Significance', *Modern Theology* 21(4): pp. 543–74, reprinted in Milbank and Oliver, *The Radical Orthodoxy Reader*, pp. 116–46, see especially pp. 118–19.

24   For example the will as desire, the passions and *habitus*.

25   See note 20 in this chapter.

26   See also B. Flyvbjerg (2001), *Making Social Science Matter: Why Social Inquiry Fails and How It Can Succeed Again* (Cambridge: Cambridge University Press); S. Toulmin, (2001). *Return to Reason* (Cambridge, MA: Harvard University Press).

27   MacIntyre, *Whose Justice*, pp. 370–88, on issues of 'translation' between traditions.

28   E. L. Johnson and S. L. Jones (2000), *Psychology and Christianity: Four Views* (Downers Grove, IL: IVP Academic).

29   See also Chapter 9, in this volume, by S. J. Sandage.

30   H. R. Niebuhr (1951), *Christ and Culture* (New York: Harper and Row). See also J. Milbank, S. Oliver, Z. Lehmann and P. J. Hampson (forthcoming), 'Radical Orthodoxy and Christian Psychology: I Theological Underpinnings', Interview with John Milbank and Simon Oliver, *Edification, Transdisciplinary Journal of the Society of Christian Psychology*.

31   See, for example, N. Murphy (2005), 'Philosophical Resources for Integration', and 'Theological Resources for Integration', in A. Dueck and C. Lee (eds), *Why Psychology Needs Theology: A Radical-Reformation Perspective* (Grand Rapid: Eerdmans), pp. 2–52. (I include levels of explanation and emergentist approaches, which often tend toward process theology, as varieties of liberal-integrationism here. I do not consider biblical counselling further in this essay on the grounds that it makes little contact with philosophical theology.)

32   F. Watts (2002), *Theology and Psychology* (London: Ashgate). Watts argues that psychology and theology should remain distinct but seen as offering 'complementary perspectives on reality'. He rejects 'the idea that psychology is a subordinate discipline' (p. 8).

33   F. L. Shults and S. Sandage (2006), *Transforming Spirituality: Integrating Psychology and Theology* (Grand Rapids: Baker Academic).

34   E. Johnson (2007), 'Towards a Philosophy of Science for Christian Psychology', *Edification: Journal of the Society for Christian Psychology*, 1(1): pp. 5–20.

35   E. Worthington (2007), 'A Bridge too Far: Response to "Towards a Philosophy of Science for Christian Psychology" by Eric L. Johnson', *Edification: Journal of the Society for Christian Psychology*, 1(1): pp. 37–9. Sandage, personal communication, also doubts Christian psychology's power to influence wider psychology and considers it possibly naïve in failing to question theological and hermeneutical assumptions and the influence of cultural contexts.

36   E. C. Brugger (2009), 'Psychology and Christian Anthropology', *Edification: Journal of the Society for Christian Psychology*, 3(1): pp. 5–18.

37   See note 30, in this chapter.

38   See note 13, in this chapter.

39   Overall, Catholicism has been highly receptive to science but, until recently, seems to have been more suspicious of psychology than its sister denominations having had less exposure to it. For complex historical, socio-cultural, economic and intellectual reasons, Catholics were somewhat under-represented in the early days of the now culturally dominant Anglo-American psychology; its founding fathers *(sic)* were generally Protestant, and mid-twentieth-century US social psychology was powerfully influenced by the European Jewish diaspora. Catholic theologians, until recently more likely to be clergy than lay, will traditionally have frequently had little exposure beyond introductions to psychodynamics (see also note 29, in this chapter).

40   S. Oliver (2009), 'Introducing Radical Orthodoxy: From Participation to Late Modernity', in Milbank and Oliver, *The Radical Orthodoxy Reader*, pp. 3–27, for a clear recent introduction. For a more advanced 'state of the art' treatment see Milbank, 'The Grandeur of Reason and the Perversity of Rationalism: Radical Orthodoxy's First Decade', in Milbank and Oliver, *The Radical Orthodoxy Reader*, pp. 367–404.

41   Oliver, 'Introducing Radical Orthodoxy', p. 18.

42   Nicholas of Cusa, *De Docta Ignorantia*, available in J. Hopkins (1986), *Complete Philosophical and Theological Treatises of Nicholas of Cusa*, Vol. 1 (Minneapolis: The Arthur J. Banning Press), p. I, 4.

43   Ibid., p. I, 4.

44   S. Oliver (2009), 'Introduction to part II', in Milbank and Oliver, *The Radical Orthodoxy Reader*, pp. 65–7. See also J. H. Newman (1895), *An Essay in Aid of a Grammar of Assent* (London: Longmans, Green and Co); Pope John Paul II (1998), *Papal Encyclical: Fides et Ratio*; and for a more analytic approach, J. Haldane (2004), *Faithful Reason* (Abingdon: Routledge); J. Haldane (2010), *Reasonable Faith* (Abingdon: Routledge).

45   Oliver, *The Radical Orthodoxy Reader*, pp. 65–8.

46   J. Milbank (2009), 'Truth and Vision', in Milbank and Oliver, *The Radical Orthodoxy Reader*, especially pp. 74–86.

47   Newman, *An Essay in Aid of a Grammar of Assent*, especially pp. 75–88.

48   C. Pickstock (1998), *After Writing: On the Liturgical Consummation of Philosophy* (Oxford: Blackwell), especially pp. 220–52.

49   Pickstock, 'Duns Scotus'.
50   Matthew S. Haar Farris, 'Interdisciplinary Studies as a Spiritual Exercise: or, How Doing Interdisciplinary Studies Can Make Us Better', Presentation delivered at the annual conference for The Association for Integrative Studies, San Diego, CA, 7 October 2010.
51   See as a preliminary Cunningham's extended critique of naturalism and its scientism, Cunningham, *Darwin's Pious Idea*, pp. 265–376, especially p. 361.
52   See Chapter 15, in this volume, by F. Cervantes.
53   N. Lombardo (2011), *The Logic of Desire: Aquinas on Emotion* (Washington, DC: The Catholic University of America Press), pp. 31–40.
54   See, for example, P. J. Hampson and J. Hoff (2010), 'Whose Self? Which Unification? Augustine's Anthropology and the Psychology-Theology Debate', *New Blackfriars*, 91(1035): pp. 546–66.
55   Especially but not only for our understanding of issues such as lifespan development.
56   Mgr R. Strange (2011), 'The Spirituality of Newman', Presentation delivered at John Henry Newman: Theologian or the Church Today Conference, Sarum College, Salisbury, 21 May 2011.
57   See discussion in interview with John Milbank, note 30, in this chapter.
58   I. McGilchrist (2009), *The Master and His Emissary: The Divided Brain and the Making of the Western World* (New Haven: Yale University Press).
59   Retrieved on 1 February 2011 from www.ignis.de/english-abstract.html.
60   See Chapter 1, in this volume, by M. Davies.
61   Milbank, *Theology and Social Theory*, p. 9.

Chapter 9

RELATIONAL SPIRITUALITY, VIRTUE AND PSYCHOTHERAPY

STEVEN J. SANDAGE

(Bethel University, St Paul, MN)

What does it mean to be educated as a Christian practitioner of psychotherapy? And how does university-based psychotherapy research and training contribute to this vocation? These are questions I will briefly explore in this chapter. The questions remind me of my first semester as a PhD student in counseling psychology at a public university in the United States back in 1992 following my theological training at a conservative Protestant seminary. Another Christian graduate student and I wrote a letter to an eminent clinical psychology researcher at one of the top universities after we noticed he had done some collaborative writing with theologians decades earlier before the theme of religion dropped out of his scientific publications. We wondered about his thoughts on the prospect of integrating psychology and theology, and I was initially excited when we received a personal response. My paraphrased recollection of his curt response went something like this: 'Modern biblical scholarship has shown the Gospels to be largely unreliable. Perhaps you will enjoy this philosophical article I wrote on free will and determinism.' The enclosed article was so technical neither my friend nor I could decipher it in any way. Looking back on it now, I believe I was trying to relate to an ideal figure in the field I was entering in the hope of somehow holding on to the sacred beliefs that were starting to feel foreign in this new secular university context. I was disappointed at the time by the lack of validation, but his response helped me in two ways. It awakened me to the reality that I was not in an ecclesial context anymore but one with different intellectual ground rules. And it prompted me to wonder if there was some other way for psychologists to relate to theology beyond the extremes of uncritical dogmatism or abandonment.

During the past 20 years, the fields of psychology and psychotherapy have experienced a profound shift on the topics of religion and spirituality. During most of the twentieth century, the dominant perspectives in North American and European psychology and psychoanalysis employed pejorative, assimilationist or dismissive attitudes toward religion and spirituality. The pejorative view was reflected in the writings of some of the major theorists of psychotherapy such as Sigmund Freud and Albert Ellis, both of whom argued that religiosity was incompatible with mental health. Freud viewed religion as regressive and an illusory defense against facing reality, and Ellis' early work suggested religion is one of many irrational beliefs that contribute to neurotic anxiety and guilt. Both focused on pathological expressions of religion with virtually no consideration of potentially salutary effects. Carl Jung defected from his mentor Freud, in part, due to a more positive and humanistic view of spirituality as part of the quest for meaning and wholeness. However, Jung frequently reinterpreted traditional religious concepts and symbols to assimilate them into his complex psychological theory, which distanced him from some religious scholars and theologians who valued the content of their traditions. While Jung has proved influential among some psychoanalysts, psychologists and spiritual directors, his intriguing symbolic approach to the psychology of religion has not catalyzed a body of empirical research.

Many other psychological and psychotherapy theorists simply neglected or dismissed the topics of religion and spirituality, altogether. For example, behaviorists like B. F. Skinner adopted a logical positivistic approach to science that called for ignoring 'non-observables' in favour of a focus on readily measurable behaviour. This modernistic philosophy of science contributed to the neglect of empirical research on religious or spiritual constructs, which many considered too ambiguous or even impossible to operationalize and measure.

Starting in the 1980s and 1990s, social scientists increased the quantity, quality and breadth of the empirical study of religion, spirituality and health. There is now a significant empirical literature which has found positive relationships between many indices of religion and spirituality and measures of mental and even physical health.[1] The scientific data makes the case that Freud and Ellis were far too pessimistic in their global pathologizing of religion and spirituality, and Ellis even moderated on the topic late in his career. A review of research published in 2009 suggested that most therapists are open to discussing spiritual and religious issues in therapy and that many clients would like to discuss these issues.[2] A growing body of research is forming on various spiritual interventions (e.g. meditation, prayer, forgiveness) in psychotherapy.[3] At the same time, the growing acceptance of religion and spirituality as legitimate topics in the field of psychology does not alleviate certain tensions created by the realities of human diversity. In this chapter, I will outline some contours of a relational approach to spirituality and virtue in psychotherapy as one integrative approach to these questions. I will thematize relationality at the levels of both content and process, or theory and practice, in highlighting some pathways for integrating theology and psychotherapy.

I Relational Spirituality

The growing interesting in spirituality and religion in the field of psychotherapy provides one pathway of integration for Christians and those of other spiritual and religious traditions. An initial challenge is the wide range of definitions of spirituality. Hill and Pargament offered a descriptive and psychological definition of spirituality as the 'search for the sacred' highlighting the active quest of humans to discover the Divine or Ultimate Truth within their developmental contexts.[4] Shults and I adapted this definition to fit an integrative relational framework by defining *relational spirituality* as 'ways of relating to the sacred'.[5] Humans relate to God and the sacred in a variety of ways (e.g. intimacy, distance, fear, surrender, hostility). An emphasis on relational spirituality is useful for several reasons.

First, Shults has chronicled the broader turn to relationality that has had wide-ranging effects on contemporary philosophical and scientific discourse.[6] The move away from a focus on the category of 'substance' and toward an emphasis on the category of 'relation' has significantly impacted recent trends in epistemology, metaphysics and ethics. In theology, Shults has suggested it is more proper to speak of a re-turn to relationality since many of the significant theological proposals in the twentieth century attempted to retrieve resources in the biblical tradition that privileged relational and dynamic categories.

More specifically in Christian traditions, a relational view of spirituality is also consistent with Trinitarian theology and the understanding that God always exists in relationship. God as Trinity exemplifies *differentiated relationality*, that is separate persons existing in intimate and cooperative relationship.[7] This points to the importance of conceptualizing spirituality in relational and differentiated ways rather than viewing spirituality as simply an inner substance or essence of an individual. One point of integrative connection is the construct of *differentiation of self*, which family systems researchers have defined as an ability to balance intimacy and autonomy in relationships.[8] Differentiation of self involves the mature capacity to value both unity and diversity similar to Apostle Paul's teaching in 1 Corinthians 12. High levels of differentiation involve emotional and relational wholeness, which can be likened to the biblical maturity constructs of *Shalom* and *Teleios*.[9] Low levels of differentiation result in the relational extremes of either emotional fusion or cutoff which can severely hinder spiritual development in families and faith communities. A growing body of empirical research has found differentiation of self is positively associated with a variety of measures of well-being, virtue (e.g. forgiveness, gratitude, hope) and intercultural development.[10]

The return to relationality has also greatly impacted contemporary social science. Many models of psychotherapy are emphasizing relationality and contextualization in contrast to a modernistic focus on the de-contextualized individual subject. Social scientists have increasingly construed the self as constituted in and through relationships,[11] and this relational view of selfhood can readily be integrated with communitarian forms of Christian theology. The emerging field of interpersonal neurobiology is mounting evidence that our limbic brains are imprinted with relational templates that move us toward familiar relational patterns, for better and for worse.[12] A wealth of psychological data now confirms the impressions of psychoanalysts that relational experiences, particularly attachment, can shape these templates used in forming God images and theological beliefs.[13] For example, those who had an anxious-ambivalent attachment with their parents are more likely to experience God as inconsistently available compared to those whose parents were consistently warm and responsive. While some continue to view psychotherapy as a technology, a large body of empirical research on the processes and outcomes of psychotherapy supports relational factors (e.g. therapeutic alliance) as effective sources of therapeutic change.[14] All of these developments in social science and psychotherapy can be utilized in conversation with the relational ontology that is central to Christian theology and philosophy.

A relational approach to spirituality can also utilize the lens of human development to consider the range of ways of relating to the sacred: from the immature and even pathological to higher levels of spiritual maturity. Of course, this is a value-laden exercise as the construct of spiritual maturity necessarily involves delineating values or ideals of particular traditions. This may be one reason the groundswell of empirical research on spirituality has largely focused on spiritual well-being rather than spiritual maturity.[15] It may be easier to attempt to define a generic view of a construct like well-being than maturity or virtue. However, definitions of well-being also convey certain implicit values and philosophical assumptions. MacIntyre argued persuasively that virtues cannot be completely de-contextualized from traditions and narratives.[16] Over the past decade, positive psychologists have engaged philosophical discussions of differing views of happiness or well-being, ranging from the hedonic to the eudaimonic.[17] Hedonic approaches emphasize pleasure and feeling satisfied as an individual while eudaimonic views focus on growth, interpersonal virtue and fulfilling one's potential. Some models of psychotherapy tend to hold a more hedonic view of well-being while other models are developmental, relational and more implicitly eudaimonic. Theological and cultural traditions become particularly useful for eudaimonic psychotherapy in explicating the developmental ideals of mature human functioning.

A relational approach to spirituality can also be useful for understanding pathological forms of spiritual development that inhibit growth and maturity. For example, narcissism is a trait that can interfere with the relational virtues of Christian spiritual maturity, such as compassion, humility and forgiveness.[18]

Some who are high in narcissistic ways of relating to the sacred may self-report special revelations and intense levels of closeness with God, however interpersonal measures will often provide a good validity check. Extreme narcissism may lead to encapsulated forms of spirituality that are inconsistent with capacities to connect with others in healthy ways. This can be an important consideration for therapy and ministry training programmes in Christian universities since there is empirical evidence that spiritual grandiosity is negatively correlated with relational health and intercultural competence.[19]

II Relational Integration

Christians have articulated a variety of stances related to psychotherapy. Contemporary Christian approaches to the formal discipline of psychology have been grouped into four primary views which could be extrapolated to psychotherapy.[20] The *Biblical Counseling* tradition views the Bible as sufficient as a source of knowledge for counseling, and the church as the central context for counseling. Theories of psychotherapy are construed as misleading or irrelevant for Christian counseling. More recently, a view formally designated as *Christian Psychology* offers a secondary place for empirical research on therapy but privileges theology and philosophy over psychology in the foundations of knowledge for model-building and therapeutic practice. The *Levels-of-Explanation* view differentiates separate levels or dimensions of reality and heralds the value of the humility of science and rigorous empirical research to complement or even revise theological understandings. This approach can imply that theology and philosophy can somehow be completely bracketed from theories in psychology and psychotherapy. The *Integration* view starts with the understanding that psychology and theology are both hermeneutical or interpretive disciplines that can be mutually enriched by interpenetrating dialogue rather than pre-arranged hierarchy or exclusionary boundaries.

All of the views above have tended to focus on psychology and theology as abstract bodies of knowledge. More recently, some colleagues and I have suggested a *relational integration* approach that moves relational dynamics between psychologists, theologians, therapists and pastors to the foreground.[21] It is actual people who attempt (or resist) the work of cooperative integration. From a theological perspective, the realities of human falleness mean that it is often more natural to mistrust one another and compete across disciplines than it is to collaborate in mutual recognition and respect. Or, there is some initial pseudo-collaboration that occurs until actual differences or conflicts emerge, and then the risks of reactivity, cutoff and estrangement make *differentiated integration* more complicated. By differentiated integration, I mean the capacity to maintain a high level of differentiation in relating to people across disciplinary differences. Differentiation does not mean pretending there are no differences or acquiescing in false agreement (i.e. 'selling out'). Rather, differentiation involves an ability to manage one's own anxiety in relating across differences while continuing to explore the possibilities of collaboration. In some cases, collaborative integration may prove to be impossible without a sacrifice of integrity for one or both parties, but a key question is whether there was premature foreclosure due to formation-based limits in differentiation. When capacities for differentiation are low in any relationship, there can be a pull toward a reliance on hierarchy to privilege one side over the other in an effort to reduce the tension of ambiguity. The quote from the eminent psychologist at the beginning of this chapter is one such example – putting the Bible and theology in a subordinate position to empirical science. Freud's approach to religion is another example of using psychology to 'trump' theology. The hegemony has also gone the other direction with some theologians discounting the fields of psychology and psychotherapy. These non-integrative stances often work from what Ricoeur called a 'hermeneutics of suspicion' that fails to risk mutual recognition or trust of the other as a subject worthy of equal respect and dialogue.[22]

A practical application of this relational approach to integration is to highlight relational factors in the training of psychotherapists. In our marriage and family therapy program at Bethel Seminary, we developed a relational formation approach to training in which we utilize relational sources of gain at multiple levels.[23] Recent graduates help facilitate spiritual formation in small groups (usually four students per group) focused on theological and integrative reflection. The relational goals include fostering differentiated and supportive peer experiences, as well as connection with an early career therapist in something of a mentoring role. We also invite trainees to engage in a self-assessment of their relational strengths and growth areas and utilize feedback from peers, faculty, staff and supervisors in dialogue with students about their personal and professional formation. In our view, a student's interaction style with support staff members can be as important as classroom or practicum behaviour in assessing relational formation.

We also place a strong emphasis on quality relational dynamics in our therapy courses and supervision groups, such as being emotionally present, contributing one's voice and taking an active interest in the views of others. It is hard to envision a trainee repeatedly exhibiting problematic behaviours with colleagues in a way which does not eventually show up in their work with clients. This does not mean we expect relational perfection, but rather a commitment to, authentic growth toward Christian maturity. Since both therapy training and theological education can be sources of personal and ideological deconstruction we also seek to provide opportunities for supportive relationships among faculty, staff and students to facilitate the reconstructive process.

III Relational Hermeneutics

Numerous theorists in the integration tradition have pointed out that both theology and psychology involve interpretation.[24] This means both are hermeneutical and, in fact, all of life is hermeneutical or interpretive. The relational integration approach builds upon the philosophical insights of ontological hermeneutics in viewing interpretation as more than just a methodology. Rather, interpretation is part of being human, and our interpretations in life are shaped by our developmental and embodied personhood. This means that a relational view of spiritual formation is closely aligned with a relational understanding of hermeneutics.[25]

Relational integration also suggests that psychology and theology, broadly defined, are inherent aspects of human experience and spirituality. Everyone makes interpretations, however unconscious or implicit, about human behaviour and about ultimate theological concerns. From this perspective, clients in psychotherapy are typically bringing some psychological and theological assumptions to the therapy process. That is, clients will hold some understandings of both human behaviour and ultimate concern, even if those understandings are not well-formulated or integrated. For example, I worked with an agnostic client who was recovering from a serious drug addiction. During the second year of therapy, she began to verbalize questions such as 'How do people actually change and resist relapse?' and 'What makes me so narcissistic at times?' She was raising these questions, in part, because her own prior 'folk psychology' of human behaviour had not worked and was being stretched in new ways. But these questions and the hard work of the therapy process led to deeper questions, such as 'What is life really about?' and 'Why not just go for the short-term happiness of being high?' The latter are obviously philosophical and even theological questions that empirical science cannot answer. However, I doubt this client would have had the opportunity to reflect on these existential questions with any meaningful level of sobriety without some prior psychotherapeutic and medical intervention. In another clinical case, a client diagnosed with obsessive-compulsive disorder whose hoarding made his house nearly unlivable for his wife and kids explained he saw no need for therapy 'because Jesus is coming back any day now'. These kinds of cases illustrate the reciprocal processes of ontological hermeneutics – our psychological functioning will affect our theological interpretations and vice versa.

As a school of thought, ontological hermeneutics does not necessarily imply the interpretive process is completely subjective or relativistic. Several colleagues joined me in reviewing the influence of differing hermeneutical philosophies on psychology and psychotherapy, and we argued for a dialectical and relational model of hermeneutics drawing on philosophers such as Ricoeur, Gadamer, Habermas and the interdisciplinary work of Don Browning.[26] This dialectical approach to hermeneutical realism suggests that none of us makes interpretations based on a 'blank slate'. We are all shaped and influenced by relationships with our traditions and narrative contexts that provide theological and theoretical frameworks or plausibility structures for interpreting the data of life. This is true of everyone, not just scholars. As Gadamer suggested, we project our interpretive horizons or pre-understandings.[27] Psychoanalysts refer to this as countertransference, and contemporary relational views of countertransference call for responsible self-awareness rather than complete bracketing.[28] From the perspective of relational hermeneutics, psychotherapy is a co-constructive hermeneutical process that engages the interactive interpretive horizons of therapist and client. When the client is a couple or family, the relational and hermeneutical complexity multiplies.

Since we interpret by relating to our traditions, narratives and pre-understandings, I do sympathize with those of the biblical counseling and Christian psychology views that resist the simple formula from some modernistic integrationists that 'all truth is God's truth'. I agree that all truth does belong to God, yet the simple version of this statement can imply a naive minimization of the hermeneutical significance of traditions and interpretive contexts. Human interpretations of special or general revelation cannot attain a purely 'God's eye' view or perfect objectivity and necessarily involve contextual factors. However, methods in both theology and psychology do offer 'moments of distanciation' or distance in the hermeneutical process to see the landscape differently.[29] A partial bracketing of hermeneutical assumptions and pre-understandings is possible through sound methodologies but also requires self-awareness and the formation of mature differentiation.

The hermeneutical process in this dialectical model moves from pre-understandings to distanciation to appropriation or testing the 'fruits' of particular theoretical models of explanation. Empirical tests of appropriation can lead to revising theoretical understandings or the re-forming of theologically integrative models. This is where practical theology and empirical social science offer checks against Gnostic or schizoid forms of cognitive speculation which are not grounded in embodied realities. In my view, a Christian university should be a community that provides formative opportunities for distanciation and constructive reformulation. History has shown that the ideas of both theologians and psychologists can prove to be inaccurate or even immoral, so there is a benefit to ongoing testing of ideas in mutual accountability. Habermas and other post-Holocaust theorists in critical hermeneutics have argued that traditions can also perpetuate distorted and oppressive ideas, such as Christian leaders who have used the Bible to support slavery, Nazism, sexism, Apartheid and other forms of oppression. There is a need for critically testing interpretive traditions with input from outside a particular religious or sociocultural system.

Hermeneutically, theology and psychology can be relationally integrated toward a healthy collaboration that serves the practice of psychotherapy. In general, theology tends to emphasize prescription (i.e. how things should be) and psychology focuses on description (i.e. how things are). This is an oversimplification because theology can also be rooted in history and addresses human realities, and psychotherapy models also imply certain values and ultimate concerns embedded within broader theories.[30] But there are obvious differences of focus and methodology. A Christian approach to psychotherapy should value description as well as prescription in order to empirically test for discrepancies between the ideals and actual human experiences. Kierkegaard called for balancing the relational dialectic of the finite and infinite, which can foster integration of the actual and the ideal.[31] As a therapist, I want my clinical work to maintain fidelity to the Christian traditions, and yet I also work with people who are often facing profound levels of suffering and who have a lot riding on the interventions I choose. These can include clients who are suicidal, too impaired to work, or have their marriage or family relationships on the line. My Christian and my professional integrity require that I seek to relate theological grounding with empirically supported forms of therapy. To date, there is a fairly limited body of empirical research on explicitly Christian therapy interventions compared to the vast literature on secular forms of therapy, so there is much room for future integrative research.[32]

Psychology and psychotherapy can also make valuable contributions to the church and the discipline of theology. For example, psychological research can illuminate hermeneutical understanding of what we 'bring to the text' of scripture and spiritual experience. Personality traits have been found to predict beliefs about Christology or the characteristics of Jesus, and growth in the self-awareness to responsibly manage projections onto scriptural interpretations is central to Christian theology.[33] Empirical studies have also revealed evidence that psychotherapy can contribute to increased spiritual well-being.[34] These hermeneutical contributions highlight further reasons to support a relationally integrative collaboration between psychologists and theologians, therapists and spiritual leaders.

IV Relational Alterity

Another important dimension of a relational approach to integration and psychotherapy training in Christian universities is that of alterity or ways of relating to *otherness*. Globalism and increasing diversity mean that psychotherapy training programmes in all contexts need to consider ways of developing diversity sensitivity and culturally competent practice among their trainees. This is not only a practical reality but an ethical mandate among most major mental health professional associations. Dynamics related to race, ethnicity, gender, religion, social class, sexuality and many other diversity variables can influence the therapy process in multiple ways. A lack of diversity sensitivity and competence can impede the development of a positive therapist–client relationship, lead to misdiagnosis or poorly contextualized interventions or even result in premature termination of therapy. For example, family therapy interventions can require adjustments when moving from African to Korean to Norwegian families even if all are Christians. The dynamics can become even more complex when there are significant racial, cultural or religious differences within the same family system. Therapists who are unaware of their own stereotypes or biases might also side with a certain member of a couple or family system in an unhelpful triangle or, in the worst cases, exhibit hostile or derogatory behaviour toward certain client groups.

Mature relational alterity or diversity competence is also a valuable dimension of Christian spiritual maturity within pluralistic contexts.[35] Christian psychotherapy, influenced by the philosophy of Levinas and the ethics of alterity, involves a willingness to be disrupted by the suffering of the other whose face beckons me to responsibility.[36] Some students at our university, typically Euro-American students, question whether a commitment to diversity competence is an accommodation to political correctness. However, based on Christian theology, I suggest Jesus was an exemplar of diversity competence, demonstrating throughout the Gospels an ability to relate effectively across a variety of social boundaries. Intercultural competence is actually a vital part of missions and contextualized approaches to ministry. People within a given system will not be able to meaningfully accept new input, whether it is a therapy intervention or a religious teaching, unless it is contextualized in a way that makes sense within their system. Moreover, experiences of alterity often generate anxiety related to otherness and difference which can be useful for fostering spiritual formation. Assessment tools like the Intercultural Development Inventory can be used to facilitate student and faculty development, and our initial empirical work on intercultural development suggests significant correlations with spiritual formation factors among our graduate students.[37]

Therapy training programmes at Christian universities can take several constructive steps. First, training partnerships can be cultivated with practicum sites across a variety of social and cultural contexts. In our training programme, students are required to do volunteer work in a social context that is new to them. Such experiential learning needs to be educationally debriefed in supportive settings with attention to spiritual, psychological and intercultural growth. Second, programmes can seek to develop a diverse faculty (residential and adjunct) and set of clinical supervisors. In some cases, it may be necessary for programmes to contract at least temporarily with supervisors or consultants to help support particular students whose ethnic or spiritual background is beyond the expertise of the faculty. Third, all faculty and staff can be encouraged to keep working on their own diversity competence. It becomes problematic if the responsibility of diversity awareness falls on a few faculty and even more so if those faculty are from non-dominant groups. While intrinsic motivation is always ideal, universities can also consider ways that faculty growth in both interdisciplinary integration and diversity competence might be incentivized (e.g. part of tenure and promotion evaluations, supported through faculty resources or competitive awards and grants). This is part of a systemic commitment to social justice and creating a Christian community ethos that values collaboration and diversity.

Mature relational alterity can also be fostered in Christian psychotherapy training programmes by considering cases of those who have suffered from spiritual or religious abuse. These cases can be particularly unsettling for trainees who have previously held idealistic understandings of the Christian faith and its expression in human communities. Such de-idealization can potentially be traumatic if not accompanied by relational supports and instruction that includes hopeful strategies for intervention. Again, there is need to encourage tolerance for ambiguity and realism among therapy trainees, but balancing deconstruction and reconstruction is a key to healthy relational integration.

For Christian psychotherapy trainees, it can also be challenging to manage the transitions between secular clinical settings and their own faith communities. Dueck described this as part of the integrative process with his brilliant metaphor and book title 'between Athens and Jerusalem', with Athens representing cosmopolitan secular contexts and Jerusalem symbolizing faith communities.[38] It is not uncommon for Christian psychotherapy students to begin to feel they do not fit perfectly anywhere. Their clinical training can make them suspect among their church communities or family of origin, and their faith identity can sometimes create prejudice from clinical supervisors in secular settings. This sense of spiritual and cultural homelessness can also be formative toward differentiation when (a) appropriate relational attachments are offered and (b) integrative reflection is facilitated to help students make meaning of this process.

V Relational Virtues

The positive psychology of virtue is another vibrant stream of contemporary research which can be useful for integrating theology, philosophy and psychotherapy. Empirical studies of character strengths and virtues have grown rapidly in the past two decades.[39] Models of psychotherapy always convey certain assumptions, at least implicitly, about 'the good life' and traits of healthy and mature human functioning. This means psychotherapy models can be likened to ancient schools of thought in virtue ethics. The concept of virtue is certainly open to different interpretations, but a common definition is traits of character that contribute to both personal and communal well-being. Virtue traits, such as hope, are obviously relevant to the process of psychotherapy, although differing models may emphasize different strengths or definitions of health and maturity. There is a growing recognition that strengths and virtues can facilitate long-term resilience and healthy functioning. At the same time, many Christian theological traditions highlight the ways in which suffering and periods of diminished well-being can potentially lead to character growth in maturity and virtue. Spiritual maturity is not the same as spiritual well-being or simply 'feeling good' but involves well-developed capacities for coping with suffering. My own preference is for Christian theologies that value community, healthy relationships, social justice, and service to others, all of which involve challenging relational processes that both require and cultivate spiritual maturity and authentic virtue.

While some positive psychologists have tried to extol universal or generic understandings of virtue, others have argued that understandings of virtue are typically embedded in sociocultural contexts and traditions.[40] Often, these virtue traditions include spiritual and theological understandings of health and maturity. A part of healthy relational alterity and diversity competence involves respect for the differences in how various traditions define strengths and virtues. For example, within my own programme of research on interpersonal forgiveness, I have found meaningful differences in understanding of forgiveness across Buddhist, Christian, Animist and Jewish samples. We can find different catalogues of virtue and nuances of meaning even within various religious and theological traditions. This is not to suggest there can be no common ground in definitions of virtue, however I would approach the validation of common ground as an empirical question rather than a philosophical assumption. And the meaningful differences between virtue traditions can be fertile ground for interdisciplinary work across theology, philosophy and the social sciences.

Theology and philosophy are particularly helpful disciplines for deepening the rather 'thin' meaning that psychologists sometimes use in their definitions of virtue. Psychological methods of research can then serve to empirically test models and interventions to promote these virtues. In the context of psychotherapy training in a Christian university, I suggest the overall task is not simply integrating a generic Christian theology with a general psychology of virtue. Rather, the process of integration involves clarifying a particular Christian tradition and a specific psychological or sociological theory in relation to a psychotherapy virtue. For example, Peter Jankowski and I drew upon Miroslav

Volf's sociopolitical theology of 'exclusion and embrace' and Bowenian family systems theory in a study empirically validating differentiation of self as a mediator of the relationship between the virtue of forgiveness and several measures of mental health.[41] In a separate empirical study, Ian Williamson and I switched the theoretical lens to attachment theory and drew upon biblical data and theologian L. Gregory Jones to confirm a model with gratitude mediating the relationship between contemplative prayer and forgiveness.[42] Don Davis and his colleagues have also advanced research on forgiveness and relational spirituality with data showing that those with a secure emotional attachment with God tend to have a more forgiving disposition than those with an insecure emotional attachment with God.[43] In a subsequent study, Davis and colleagues provided a methodological innovation for the study of virtue by developing a measure of a victim's rating of the perceived spiritual humility of their offender which proved to be significantly related to the victims' level of forgiveness.[44] These studies provide just a few recent examples of the fascinating interdisciplinary connections between relational development, theology and virtue.

VI Conclusion

I have argued for an integrative view of psychotherapy as a relational process based on Trinitarian Christian theology and contemporary social science. A relational integration paradigm highlights the possibilities of multiple dimensions of differentiated relationality in psychotherapy research and training. Perhaps the greatest strength of this approach to integration is that embodied relational development and healthy collaboration are made central, and this means movement toward spiritual maturity will also be central.

Notes

This project was supported by a grant from the Fetzer Institute (#2266; www.fetzer.org).

1 P. C. Hill and K. I. Pargament (2008), 'Advances in the Conceptualization and Measurement of Religion and Spirituality: Implications for Physical and Mental Health Research', *Psychology of Religion and Spirituality*, 1(1): pp. 3–17.
2 B. C. Post and N. G. Wade (2009), 'Religion and Spirituality in Psychotherapy: A Practice-Friendly Review of Research', *Journal of Clinical Psychology*, 65(2): pp. 131–46.
3 J. D. Aten, M. R. McMinn and E. L. Worthington, Jr (2011), *Spiritually Oriented Interventions for Counseling and Psychotherapy* (Washington, DC: American Psychological Association).
4 Hill and Pargament, 'Advances in the Conceptualization and Measurement of Religion and Spirituality'.

5   F. L. Shults and S. J. Sandage (2006), *Transforming Spirituality: Integrating Theology and Psychology* (Grand Rapids, MI: Baker Academic); also, see T. W. Hall (2004), 'Christian Spirituality and Mental Health: A Relational Spirituality Paradigm for Empirical Research', *Journal of Psychology and Christianity*, 23(1): pp. 66–81.

6   F. L. Shults (2003), *Reforming Theological Anthropology: After the Philosophical Turn to Relationality* (Grand Rapids, MI: Eerdmans).

7   J. O. Balswick, P. E. King and K. S. Reimer (2005), *The Reciprocating Self: Human Development in Theological Perspective* (Downers Grove, IL: InterVarsity Press).

8   B. Majerus and S. J. Sandage (2010), 'Differentiation of Self and Christian Spiritual Maturity: Social Science and Theological Integration', *Journal of Psychology and Theology*, 38(1): pp. 41–51.

9   S. J. Sandage, M. Jensen and D. Jass (2008), 'Relational Spirituality and Tramsformation: Risking Intimacy and Alterity', *Journal of Spiritual Formation and Soul Care*, 1(2): pp. 182–206.

10 Majerus and Sandage, 'Differentiation of Self and Christian Spiritual Maturity'; S. J. Sandage and P. J. Jankowski (2010), 'Forgiveness, Spiritual Instability, Mental Health Symptoms, and Well-Being: Mediation Effects for Differentiation of Self', *Psychology of Religion and Spirituality*, 2(3): pp. 168–80; S. J. Sandage and M. G. Harden (2011), 'Relational Spirituality, Differentiation of Self, and Virtue as Predictors of Intercultural Development', *Mental Health, Religion, and Culture*, 14(8): pp. 819–38; I. Williamson, S. J. Sandage and R. M. Lee (2007), 'How Social Connectedness Affects Guilt and Shame: Mediated by Hope and Differentiation of Self', *Personality and Individual Differences*, 43(8): pp. 2159–70.

11 S. Chen, H. C. Boucher and M. P. Tapias (2006), 'The Relational Self Revealed: Integrative Conceptualization and Implications for Interpersonal Life', *Psychological Bulletin*, 132(2): pp. 151–79.

12 L. Cozolino (2010), *The Neuroscience of Psychotherapy: Healing the Social Brain*, 2nd edn (New York: W.W. Norton & Co); T. Lewis, F. Amini and R. Lannon (2000), *A General Theory of Love* (New York: Vintage).

13 P. Granqvist, M. Mikulincer and P. R. Shaver (2010), 'Religion as Attachment: Normative Processes and Individual Differences', *Personality and Social Psychology Review*, 14(1): pp. 49–59; Hall, 'Christian Spirituality and Mental Health'.

14 J. C. Norcross (2011), *Psychotherapy Relationships That Work: Evidence-Based Responsiveness*, 2nd edn (New York: Oxford University Press); also see Boston Change Process Study Group (2010), *Change in Psychotherapy: A Unifying Paradigm* (New York: W.W. Norton & Co).

15 Shults and Sandage, *Transforming Spirituality*.

16 MacIntyre (2007), *After Virtue: A Study in Moral Theory*, 3rd edn (South Bend, IN: Notre Dame University Press).

17 For an overview, see Shults and Sandage, *Transforming Spirituality*, pp. 190–5.

18 S. J. Sandage and S. P. Moe (2011), 'Narcissism and Spirituality', in W. K. Campbell and J. Miller (eds), *The Handbook of Narcissism and Narcissistic Personality Disorder: Theoretical Approaches, Empirical Findings, and Treatment* (New York: John Wiley & Sons), pp. 410–20.

19 Sandage and Harden, 'Relational Spirituality, Differentiation of Self, and Virtue'.

20 E. L. Johnson and S. L. Jones (eds) (2000), *Psychology & Christianity: Four Views* (Downers Grove, IL: InterVarsity Press).

21 Shults and Sandage, *Transforming Spirituality*; Also, see J. K. Brown, C. M. Dahl and W. Corbin Reuschling (2011), *Becoming Whole and Holy: An Integrative Conversation about Christian Formation* (Grand Rapids, MI: Brazos); S. J. Sandage and F. L. Shults (2007), 'Relational Spirituality and Transformation: A Relational Integration Model', *Journal of Psychology and Christianity*, 26(3): pp. 261–9; S. J. Sandage and J. K. Brown (2010), 'Monarchy or Democracy in Relational Integration: A Reply to Porter', *Journal of Psychology and Christianity*, 29(1): pp. 20–6.

22 P. Ricoeur (1970), *Freud & Philosophy: An Essay on Interpretation*, (trans. D. Savage) (New Haven, CT: Yale University Press).

23 For some further description of our approach to training, see Sandage et al., 'Relational Spirituality and Tramsformation'.

24 A. Dueck and K. Reimer (2009), *A Peaceable Psychology: Christian Therapy in a World of Many Cultures* (Grand Rapids, MI: Brazos); D. S. Browning and T. D. Cooper (2004), *Religious Thought & the Modern Psychologies*, 2nd edn (Minneapolis, MN: Fortress).

25 M. W. Mangis (1999), 'An Alien Horizon: The Psychoanalytic Contribution to a Christian Hermeneutic of Humility and Confidence', *Christian Scholar's Review*, 28(3): pp. 411–31.

26 S. J. Sandage, K. V. Cook, P. C. Hill, B. D. Strawn and K. S. Reimer (2008), 'Hermeneutics and Psychology: A Review and Dialectical Model', *Review of General Psychology*, 12(4): pp. 344–64.

27 H. G. Gadamer (1989), *Truth and Method*, rev. edn (trans. J. Weinsheimer and D. G. Marshall) (London: Continuum).

28 P. Cooper-White (2004), *Shared Wisdom: Use of Self in Pastoral Care and Counseling* (Minneapolis, MN: Fortress).

29 Sandage et al., 'Hermeneutics and Psychology'. On distanciation, see P. Ricoeur (1981), *Hermeneutics & The Human Sciences* (trans and ed. J. B. Thompson) (Cambridge: Cambridge University Press).

30 Browning and Cooper, *Religious Thought & the Modern Psychologies*.

31 S. Kierkegaard (1849/1980). *The Sickness Unto Death*, Princeton, NJ: Princeton University Press

32 E. L. Worthington, Jr, J. N. Hook, D. E. Davis and M. A. McDaniel (2011), 'Religion and Spirituality', *Journal of Clinical Psychology: In Session*, 67(2): pp. 204–14.

33 R. L. Piedmont, J. E. G. Williams and J. W. Ciarrocchi (1997), 'Personality Correlates of One's Image of Jesus: Historiographic Analysis Using the Five Factor Model of Personality', *Journal of Psychology and Theology*, 25(3): pp. 364–73.

34 See Worthington et al., 'Religion and Spirituality'.

35 Sandage et al., 'Relational Spirituality and Tramsformation'; N. P. Wolterstorff (2002), *Educating for Life: Reflections on Christian Teaching and Learning* (Grand Rapids, MI: Baker Academic).

36 See Dueck and Reimer, (2009), *A Peaceable Psychology*.

37 M. R. Hammer, M. J. Bennett and R. Wiseman (2003), 'Measuring Intercultural Sensitivity: The Intercultural Development Inventory', *International Journal of Intercultural Relations*, 27: pp. 421–43; Sandage and Harden, 'Relational Spirituality, Differentiation of Self, and Virtue'.

38 C. Dueck (1995), *Between Jerusalem & Athens: Ethical Perspectives on Culture, Religion, and Psychotherapy* (Grand Rapids, MI: Baker).

39 Peterson and M. E. P. Seligman (2004), *Character Strengths and Virtues: A Handbook and Classification* (New York: Oxford University Press).
40 S. J. Sandage and P. C. Hill (2001), 'The Virtues of Positive Psychology: The Rapprochement and Challenges of an Affirmative Postmodern Perspective', *Journal for the Theory of Social Behavior*, 31(3): pp. 241–60; Sandage et al., 'Hermeneutics and Psychology'.
41 Sandage and Jankowski, 'Forgiveness, Spiritual Instability, Mental Health Symptoms, and Well-Being'.
42 S. J. Sandage and I. T. Williamson (2010), 'Relational Spirituality and Dispositional Forgiveness: A Structural Equations Model', *Journal of Psychology and Theology*, 38(4): pp. 255–66.
43 D. E. Davis, J. N. Hook, E. L. Worthington, Jr (2008), 'Relational Spirituality and Forgiveness: The Roles of Attachment to God, Religious Coping, and Viewing the Transgression as a Desecration', *Journal of Psychology and Christianity*, 27(4): pp. 293–301.
44 D. E. Davis, J. N. Hook, E. L. Worthington, Jr., D. R. Van Tongeren, A. L. Gartner and D. J. Jennings, II (2010), 'Relational Spirituality and Forgiveness: Development of the Spiritual Humility Scale (SHS)', *Journal of Psychology and Theology* 38(2): pp. 91–100.

Chapter 10

THEOLOGY AND LEGAL EDUCATION

JULIAN RIVERS

(University of Bristol)

If we are to think theologically about the discipline of law as it is pursued in universities, we need primarily a theology of legal education not a theology of law. Our challenge is to think theologically about the proper aspect under which law should be considered and constructed in the context of higher education, and thus about the distinctive contribution that the academic discipline of law can make to law, lawyers and society more generally.

The best way of opening this up is to reflect on the different ways in which the discipline of law has been pursued in universities. Modern legal education reflects all six of these paradigms – therein lies its postmodernity – but in varying measures.

I Six Paradigms of Legal Education

a Traditional

Law was one of the three higher disciplines of the medieval university. Around 1070, Irnerius started to expound Justinian's Digest of Roman law to students at Bologna. Five years later, Pope Gregory VII issued *Dictatus Papae* (1075) with its claim to the supreme jurisdiction of the Roman court over the whole Christian church. In 1140, Gratian produced his *Decretum*: a systematic attempt to collect and render consistent the discordant canons of the church. Thus, soon after its rediscovery, the *corpus iuris civilis* was supplemented with another body of law, the *corpus iuris canonici*. Together they formed a *ius commune*, a common law, based on Roman law, which was studied in law faculties the length and breadth of Europe (Helmholz 2004). Even though medieval universities also engaged in practices which might bring the student closer to real-life problems (*disputationes* and *quaestiones*), what was inculcated was more a mass of concepts and a mode of thought and argument. Education was through immersion in the authoritative texts as well as their subsequent glosses and comments. To modern sensibilities, such an education seems incredibly detailed and un-historical; if historical change is disallowed as an explanation of legal diversity, such diversity has to escape in another direction: the proliferation of distinctions we associate with 'scholasticism'.

b Moral

In 1530, Christopher St German's *Dialogues Between a Doctor and a Student* were published in English (St German 1974). The *Dialogues* are located not in the universities, but in the Inns of Court in London. Their purpose was not simply to introduce readers to the main principles of English law, but to defend the moral legitimacy of the common law courts. Conscience and equity, the doctor insisted, were not the sole preserve of church courts but were equally present in the law of property and contract. Most striking of all was the mode of education. No longer were authoritative texts expounded and distinctions justified. Rather, the doctor and student put problem questions to each other in a joint search for the right answer. It is not difficult to trace the effect of humanist and Reformation thought on this paradigm of legal education. Legal propositions were rooted in the conscience of the newly enfranchised individual, who could argue in moral defence and criticism of the law. Legal texts had become a mere historical expression of the practical moral conscience of the legal community. Accordingly, the faculties of canon law at the universities were suppressed and the Roman-based *ius commune* became increasingly irrelevant.

c Conceptual-Systematic

Formal legal education had collapsed in England by the mid-seventeenth century. It was William Blackstone who sought to re-establish legal education as a university discipline (Hanbury 1958; Prest 2008). In his lectures of 1753 and subsequent commentaries he attempted to provide a systematic exposition of English law. Of course, all legal education must follow some sort of system; the point about Blackstone was that the system he followed was conceptual. His lecture handouts followed the classical logic of definition *per genus et differentiam*. In complete contrast, Jeremy Bentham took the view that English law was such a tangled mass of irreconcilable precedent that one would do much better to sweep Judge & Co away and replace the law with rational codes of legislation according to the felicific calculus (Bentham 1776, 1789). Blackstone provoked his particular ire in part because he was claiming that such radical action was not necessary. English law could already be reconstructed along the rational lines that both agreed was a necessary feature of good law.

d Liberal

The rise of modern legal education can be dated to a House of Commons select committee report of 1846 (House of Commons 1846). The committee found, and deplored the fact, that there was virtually no institutional legal education anywhere in England. University law faculties should be expanded to provide the 'philosophy of the science of law' with new chairs in international, comparative and administrative law. This would form the first stage of legal education, to be supplemented by a new special institution, a 'college of law' to provide professional training. In the event it was the Royal Commissions on Oxford and Cambridge that provided the stimulus for the introduction of BCL (Bachelor of Civil Law) and LLB (Bachelor of Laws) degrees in 1852 and 1855 respectively.

Those who actually provided the new legal education in the universities tended to adopt a liberal view of its purpose. Legal education meant the inculcation of habits of mind and character that would fit young gentlemen for any form of public service. This combined nicely with the interests of the scholar. It is striking, for example, how prominent Islamic and Hindu law were on university curriculums a century ago. This approach could be defended as late as 1948 by Dr William Stallybrass, academic lawyer, vice chancellor of the University of Oxford and president of the Society of Public Teachers of Law. Stallybrass argued that where possible, subjects should be chosen that bore the closest affinity to others studied at university (Stallybrass 1951). The historical and comparative method were extolled; sociology was deprecated as being 'too teleological and subjective'. In practice, legal education for him meant education in Roman law, jurisprudence and international law.

The liberal view came under pressure from two directions. Blackstone's legacy lived on. So, for the conceptually minded, universities still offered the possibility of the systematization of an incoherent common law – a genuine contribution to the law in practice (Dicey 1883). The other direction of pressure came from the more vocationally minded. For them, university legal education was the general part of professional study, the abstract and general precursor on which the student could subsequently graft detailed practical knowledge (Harris undated). Alternatively, the Inns of Court should abandon their unstructured schemes of apprenticeship for a joint School of Law offering structured legal training (Russell 1895). In reality, this is precisely what the new provincial universities started doing from the early decades of the twentieth century.

e Vocational

The way that law is currently taught derives largely from the report of the Lord Chancellor's Committee on Legal Education chaired by Sir Roger Ormrod (Ormrod 1971). This recommended the law degree as the first stage of professional qualification. The committee recommended a core of foundations of legal knowledge, which is still broadly in place today. Students on qualifying law degrees still have to study law for a minimum of two years, of which one-and-a-half years must be given over to English legal system, public law (including constitutional, administrative and human rights law), criminal law, law of contract, tort and restitition, European Union law, law of property and trusts. The other development of note in the same spirit came in 2000 with the issuing of the law benchmark statement covering knowledge, application and problem-solving, sources and research, analysis, synthesis, critical judgement and evaluation, autonomy and ability to learn, communication and literacy and other key skills involving numeracy, IT and teamwork (QAA 2000).

Thus in large part legal education is now vocational in orientation, albeit focused on the articulation and application of substantive legal doctrine rather than processes and remedies.

f Critical

The final paradigm is that of critical legal education. In the context of the United Kingdom, this can be traced back to the 1960s interest in socio-economic dimensions of law. In this respect the United Kingdom was simply starting to tread in the footsteps of its younger cousin across the Atlantic. American legal realism had taken hold in several US law schools in the early decades of the twentieth century (Duxbury 1994). This made a virtue of rejecting 'law in the books', that is the systematic study of legal doctrine, in favour of 'law in action', that is the sociological investigation of legal practice. Two inaugural lectures given in the mid-1960s reflect the change of mood in England (Grodecki 1967; Sheridan 1967). This approach was reflected institutionally in the foundation of Warwick Law School in 1969, but has come to influence significant strands of legal education in all law schools.

Added to this sociological dimension is the rise of Critical Legal Studies (CLS), which can be dated to major conferences in the United States in 1977 (Hunt 1986; Price 1989; Tushnet 1991). In the broadest sense, CLS encompasses marxist and feminist critiques of law, most recently critical race theory, queer theory and other forms of outsider jurisprudence. The obvious institutional bearer of this model of engagement in England is Kent Law School, which prides itself on offering a predominantly critical legal education in the sense defined here. Although one could draw a strict distinction between the socio-legal and critical, in practice sociological analyses of law are often tied to left-wing critiques of the liberal legal establishment, pitting themselves against what are perceived to be more conservative doctrinal scholars.

II The Postmodern Law School

The effect of these six paradigms at the start of the twenty-first century is cumu-lative, producing a multilayered 'postmodern' diversity. This has been facilitated by a number of other elements of the social context of current legal education. The first of these is the enormous expansion of university law schools. The Higher Education Statistics Agency reports that in 2009/10 there were 94,375 law students in higher education in the United Kingdom. Shortly before its demise in 2011, the UK Centre for Legal Education listed 106 law schools, of which 67 had entered the 2008 Research Assessment Exercise. Unit 38 (Law) considered the outputs of 1670.58 research active law staff. Secondly, the pres-sures of research evaluation have shifted the focus of attention of legal scholars away from mere systematic exposition towards novel perspectives.

Coupled with this is the exponential growth of legal materials and the com-plexity of their interrelations. In place of focusing predominantly on the domes-tic law of one legal system, the comparativist H. Patrick Glenn argues for a 'transnational' concept of law, which takes full account of 'suppletive' sources such as the use of persuasive authorities, the modern *ius commune, lex merca-toria*, personal law, community-based norms, transnational contract law and commercial 'best practice' (Glenn 2003). Adopting a term from Ron Bennett (Bennett 2000), John Bell argues that law schools now need to grapple with 'supercomplexity' (Bell 2003), prompting a flight from substance to skills and techniques.

Finally, supercomplexity is made present by modern information technology. All the primary sources of English law, and many foreign and international sources, are now available on any desktop computer. Even ancient legal materi-als are searchable using modern search engines, with a power previously only available to the finest minds. Legal information is accessible as never before, so all the scholarly premium is placed on how it is handled.

As a result, the academic study of law now contains a vast array of subjects, methods and perspectives. And it is not at all easy to organize this diversity. We would probably try to identify core subjects by reference to basic causes of action (private, criminal and public), ancient doctrinal distinctions such as that between obligations and property, or social domains such as family, civil society, commerce and government. Many law modules are specializations within core subjects and increasingly subjects have a European and international dimension as well. Then there are new subjects that pull together relevant law from across the traditional boundaries, such as environmental law, information technology law or entertainment and sports law. There is a tension here between competing organizing principles. It is not always easy to see which of these emerging areas are going to survive and which are simply faddish.

Another group of modules can be identified by reference to their interest in alternative systems of law (Glenn 2010). Some of these alternative systems are simply those of other states, such as French law. These can all be studied at different levels of detail – or they can be studied in connection with their inter-relationship to domestic law as in private international law. Other alternative systems exist at a different level from domestic law, most obviously international law and European Union law. Other alternative systems are culturally different and further removed from domestic law: here one thinks of Roman law, Jewish law, Islamic law, Hindu law and African law.

Then there are different methodologies for the study of law (Cane and Tushnet 2003). Historical, sociological, philosophical, political and economic modes of interaction are used to supplement traditional 'black-letter' doctrinal method. Some of these result in well-established sub-disciplines: legal history, jurisprudence and criminology. The law and economy movement (including economic analysis of law) and the socio-legal studies movements are relative newcomers, but in some places dominant ones. The final complicating factor is an eclectic one, in which modules and approaches can be adopted to represent particular interests and perspectives. Examples that spring to mind here are 'law and literature' and 'law and gender'.

To be fair, self-interest exercises considerable restraint on the postmodern condition of legal education: law schools would not be nearly so popular if they did not collaborate with the professions. As Mary Warnock put it, legal education has become 'vocational, but with strong academic content' (Warnock 1989, p. 12). The major faultline is thus between those who think that university law schools must be closely allied to professional training – whether for reasons of principle or pragmatism, and those who defend a range of alternative approaches in the name of an 'academic' or 'scholarly' interest (Bradney 1992; Twining 1994). In fact, law schools locate themselves strategically between the professions and the academy, playing each off against the other. An excessive focus on processes and professional ethics is resisted in the name of academic integrity on the one hand, while wholesale capitulation to the methods of the humanities is resisted in the name of professional competence on the other.

III *Christian Legal Studies*

It is against the background of this postmodern condition that we must locate the recent rise of Christian Legal Studies. That term embraces several developments within academic legal writing which make some connection between Christianity and law. There are three major components.

First, there is the rediscovery of the roots of the Western legal tradition in Christian thought. Harold Berman argued that Western legal thought is stamped with the imprint of six formative revolutions (Berman 1983, 2003). The first four (Gregorian, Lutheran, Calvinist and Deist) are all powered by a vision of transcendent justice and in some sense a desire to surmount religious authority and religious difference. Berman's work has been continued by several scholars, most notably by John Witte, Jr, at Emory Law School, who has produced several detailed studies of the impact of the magisterial Reformation on legal thought (Witte 2002, 2005, 2007), as well as other works on the history of family law (Witte 1997, 2009) and religious liberty (Witte 2006, 2010).

The second component of Christian Legal Studies is the re-invigoration of the study of canon or ecclesiastical law. This has both historical and contemporary dimensions. As far as history is concerned, the English-speaking field is led by the magisterial work of Richard Helmholz (Helmholz 2001, 2004, 2010). The torch-bearer for the contemporary study of ecclesiastical law in the United Kingdom is Cardiff Law School's Centre for Law and Religion, led by Norman Doe. Both Norman Doe and Mark Hill have published substantial studies of Anglican ecclesiastical law (Doe 1996, 2002; Hill, 2007). Under Mark Hill's editorship, the *Ecclesiastical Law Journal* (*ELJ*) has grown since its inception in 1987 from being a quasi-private venture of a small club of ecclesiastical lawyers to become the major UK law and religion journal. The *ELJ* has recently been joined by the new *Oxford Journal of Law and Religion*. Of course, canon and ecclesiastical law has always had a stronger presence in many states of continental Europe, and academic interaction is fostered by societies such as the European Consortium for Church-State Research.

The third component of Christian Legal Studies is a rather miscellaneous collection of Christian perspectives on law. As far as the United Kingdom is concerned, the revival started with a Lawyers' Christian Fellowship academic conference held in London in 1996, which resulted in a book edited by the instigator, Paul Beaumont. There were in total four of these (Beaumont 1998a and b, 2002; Beaumont and Wotherspoon 2000). At around the same time, Yale University Press brought out 'Christian Perspectives on Legal Thought' (McConnell et al. 2001), a collection of essays by 29 academic lawyers from the United States. Many of the essays had their genesis in conferences of the Law Professors' Christian Fellowship.

The Yale book provides a good example of what goes on under 'Christian Perspectives on Law'. The essays in part I consider various schools of legal thought, such as liberalism, legal realism and critical legal studies, critical race theory, feminism and the law and economics movement. In part II, one of the editors reworks H. Richard Niebuhr's classic fivefold division of Christian responses to culture (Niebuhr 1951) into five models of Christian engagement with law. The essays are then arranged according to this typology. The final part of the book takes aspects of six areas of substantive law and shows how Christian engagement can illuminate the underlying issues. A more recent volume which continues in this vein, albeit with a more historical focus, is *Christianity and Law: An Introduction*, edited by John Witte, Jr, and Frank Alexander (Witte and Alexander 2008).

A possible emerging fourth strand of Christian Legal Studies is a growing interest in 'biblical law', characterized by the application of modern anthropological and semiotic techniques to Old Testament materials (Jackson 2000; Burnside 2003). Although not necessarily Christian, by focusing on the biblical text and distinguishing itself from Jewish law in the rabbinic tradition, biblical law is likely to appeal to Christian scholars (McIlroy 2004; Burnside 2010).

Against the background of the postmodern law school, the rise of Christian Legal Studies is ambiguous. Though it is tempting to read it as a reassertion of a full-blooded Christian commitment on the part of academic lawyers, it is easier and perhaps more honest to see it simply as part of the postmodern landscape. In this view, the recovery of the intellectual history of Western legal thought is nothing more than an exercise in genealogy; canon law is just one more option taking its place as part of a general interest in the legal 'other'. And Christian perspectives are merely the view from here, now that 'here' has become rather more diverse. They make no claim to hegemony, nor do they even seek to transcend difference. They are simply offered to anyone who might happen to take an interest, and indeed can take their place in a wider field of 'law and religion' (O'Dair and Lewis 2001). Coming from a position in which express Christian affiliation has often been seen as inimical to sound scholarship, there is considerable institutional pressure to reduce the claims that might be made by postmodernizing them. Or perhaps with less transparency, to adopt the dominant and highly problematic term 'religion' as a cover for what is essentially an interest in 'Christianity plus'.

IV A Theological Framework

There are several debates within theology and theory of law, which appear to be connected, but not clearly so. Staking out a comprehensive and defensible theology of law is a complex and unfinished task. For the legal theorist, the most obvious interpretative grid is the opposition between natural law theory and legal positivism. Natural law theory must be understood in this context as the thesis that human reason is capable of identifying the first principles of justice and the means of bringing these to bear on the concrete determination of community coordination problems (Finnis 1980). Legal positivism stands for the idea that law is a human creation, a tool for good or evil, and thus for the 'separation of law and morality'.

However, these terms mask different theses. On a methodological interpretation, natural law theory asserts that law necessarily strives for moral value, and that unjust law is defective *as law* (Murphy 2006). Legal positivism, by contrast, stands for the proposition that the study of law should proceed by way of 'descriptive sociology' (Hart 1961: Preface), bracketing off questions of moral evaluation for the purposes of clear analysis and subsequent critique. The debate about whether social science methods can be evaluatively neutral is complex and controversial; the specifically legal twists to this debate are, first, that in the case of law one is considering a social phenomenon which itself claims normativity, and even moral correctness (Alexy 2002), and, secondly, that 'legal positivism' as an intellectual tradition has had an interest in conceptual clarification which sits ill with a rigorous sociological descriptivism (Perry 1998). The theological stakes in this particular methodological debate are not clear.

By contrast, the political interpretation of the natural law/legal positivism divide focuses on the institutional significance of the relationship between law and justice. Natural law theory tends to the view that the capacity to know the proper content of law is not limited to the legislature. This leans in favour of judicial review of legislation and individual rights of freedom of conscience. The human rights movement, both in international and domestic law, is the clearest expression of this tendency. By contrast, early legal positivism (Hobbes, Bentham) was keen to assert the authority of a single human legislator as the only body that can – for practical human purposes – determine the concrete requirements of the natural law for a given human society. Again, the effect is primarily institutional, requiring subordination to the supreme law-maker.

At first sight, it seems as if the natural law theory/legal positivism debate is replicating a familiar, more obviously theological, debate. Discussions of the impact of the noetic effects of sin lead to more or less optimistic (Thomist) and pessimistic (Ockhamist) accounts of the capacity of unaided human reason to know the good. On the Thomist account, law is not merely the artificial creation of human will, but reflects an innate sense of justice. On an Ockhamist account, law is vulnerable to detachment from the contingencies of divine legislation, and thus reappears as a purely human phenomenon. However, the complexities of this mapping immediately become apparent. Defending the capacity of human reason to know the good seems at least as likely to lead to governmental absolutism, as pessimistic accounts of human nature can lead to the separation of powers and protection of individual rights.

Recent reappraisals from both sides of this division may well lead to a more balanced theological concept of human law (Cromartie 1997; Grabill 2006; McIlroy 2009). But regardless of whether this particular debate reaches closure, a theology of law is by itself inadequate grounding for legal education. The debates just alluded to would all properly fall to be considered in a module on 'Christian legal theory' or 'theological jurisprudence'. But the academic study of law requires a theological framework more attuned to the historical contingencies both of the present and of the political community one finds oneself in. It is not sufficient simply to consider what the proper theological location of 'law' is. This posits law as an abstract timeless human phenomenon. But it does not *explain* the detail of the law that has to be mastered in a law school. For that, we need human law to be located within a tension between two theological paradigms of law: fallen law and redeemed law.

The starting-point in thinking theologically about the academic discipline of law is the universal human phenonomen of law which has at its heart the mysterious capacity of human beings to generate rules, rights and obligations and to disagree about what those normative constraints are or should be. That mystery needs relating to a theological account of human nature as both flawed yet still social and norm-creating. The universal phenomenon of law, and its phenomenal diversity, is the distorted echo of a humankind given authority to govern, yet in rebellion against its divine creator.

The end-point is law in its relationship to Christ, and Christ's ultimate victory in bringing the purposes of God to completion. This is the Gospel, and the question is what contribution can law make to the Gospel? What is 'Christian law' – understood not as some sort of bizarre thought-exercise in which Christians take control of government and re-enact an ecclesiocracy or even Inquisition – but understood as all forms of law – whether secular, ecclesiastical, or social – properly designed to fulfil the limited tasks which they have under God in this age and as part of the purposes of God for this age. This is law redeemed, law that lives in the hope of the Resurrection.

The starting-point and the end-point need to be considered not just atemporally and acontextually, that is in general, but also incarnationally, in our own time and place. Contingencies are real and important. So, in thinking about the fallenness and redemption of human law, we need to think about the fallenness and redemption of (e.g.) English contract law in 2011. There is space here for all the messy realities of social power and oppression, Christian or otherwise. A marxist account of law as a tool of economic oppression may be a rather good account of English contract law. But there is also space for the 'and yets' of our own history, of the ways in which contract law has served, and still serves, the purposes of God.

This dialectic between fallen law and redeemed law is not the distinction between legal positivism and natural law theory mentioned above. Fallen law is not simply law as it is; redeemed law is not simply law as it ought to be. No description of law is adequate if it does not place law in its relation to God and human beings as fallen image-bearers of God; nor is it adequate if it does not notice the real impact of the people of God over time on the historical contingencies of the present. No ideal account of what law could be is complete unless it shows law's rightful part in the rule of Christ and his final victory; nor is it adequate if it loses sight of the 'not yet' of the kingdom. Both the starting-point (fallen law) and the end-point (redeemed law) are interpretative accounts that seek to make sense, in general and in particular, of how law has come to be what it is and of how law might come to be something else within the overall narrative of God's purposes for creation.

From such a theological perspective, the rationales for modern legal education seem thin and unappealing. The reconstructive exercise of conceptual exposition (Blackstone, Dicey) lacks ambition, even if in Blackstone's case there was an attempt to connect his construction to natural human rights. The comfortable superiority of a 'liberal' legal education too easily becomes a mere projection of cultural hegemony. Teaching general technical skills alone might earn one a living, but there is an insufficient relation to truth and justice. To be critical in a postmodern age requires one to deny any basis to one's own position, leading ultimately to an unhappy oscillation between frivolity and despair.

V *Towards the Christian Law School?*

This brings us inevitably to the question of the institutional location of such an account of law. If legal education is to be shaped by a theology of law and of legal education, does it not follow that the only institutional context in which that can be fully expressed is the Christian law school?

There are three difficulties. The first is the diversity of views among Christians as to the nature and purpose of law. Apart from the relatively small number of British Christian academic lawyers there is no single Christian position which could form the ideological basis for a coherent curriculum. Even if one could gather a critical mass of like-minded scholars, the boundaries would quickly be challenged and blurred. The interpretative community may simply not be big and cohesive enough.

The second difficulty arises from the practical need to take secular law as the major subject matter of the curriculum. Of course, one can envisage an education programme that does something entirely different. A curriculum made up of biblical studies, theology of law, medieval and modern ecclesiastical law, Jewish and Islamic law and the law of the modern state would be rather fun, but not actually in competition with existing provision. Assuming a law school is to offer a qualifying law degree, or prepare students for a life in legal practice to the extent that modern secular law schools do, the subject matter has to be substantially secular law. Christian critique requires a thorough grasp of its subject matter as well as a critical framework within which to locate it.

There is a third difficulty of principle. It is the assumption that a law school is itself an ecclesiastical location, in other words a place in which the true story of law is told in all its theological fulness. But as well as preserving distance, law schools must also participate in their object of study. Unless they are to be completely isolated from the legal community which they purport to study and serve, they cannot avoid responsibility for modelling legal reasoning for the next generation of lawyers. They must, in some way, be exemplars as well as critics of law and legal reasoning.

The story of law includes the ways in which modern, liberal democratic state law is in part a product of the Gospel of Christ. Modern secular law makes possible the mission of the church without supplanting it and it reflects and sustains a mutating but important Christian moral legacy. But modern secular law also has the role of mediating fairly between people regardless of religious belief. It represents one of the few remaining sources of social cohesion in an age of fracturing worldviews (Habermas 1996, 1999). It relies on sources and modes of reasoning that can command widespread assent regardless of Christian faith. In short, law represents – unavoidably and rightly – a form of public reason in a world of competing rationalities. Legal education can and should be construed as an attempt to inculcate the capacity to be public reasoners in the service of this goal. It has a political as well as a moral and intellectual purpose. The paradox of legal education is that as distant critic the law school must tell the Christian story, lest the law lose the sources of its inspiration, but that as engaged exemplar, it must refrain from telling it.

Thus the very constraints of legal education require forms of parallel commentary and engagement, a spiritual 'voice-over' as the student learns to negotiate the forms of public reason. It is institutional models such as the supplementary reading list, the gap year programme, the summer school and the evening class which offer greater potential here.

VI *Conclusion*

It is not difficult to be concerned about the future of the British academic law school. The incipient privatization of higher education together with the growing demands of technical expertise on the part of professional bodies is resulting in new forms of integrated legal training with degree status. The subtle balance between those tensions which has enabled law schools to flourish in the last half-century may be about to snap apart. But the postmodern condition of legal education makes it hard to articulate any vision beyond that of offering 'a range of perspectives on a range of subject-matters'.

It is tempting to look to Christian higher education as a rational and sustainable alternative. However, this presupposes a theology of law without a theology of legal education. The purpose of Christian legal education must be to tell the law-relevant parts of the story of God's work in the world, and to locate legal phenomena and legal actors (including the student himself or herself) within that story. The real challenge is to develop the intellectual and personal resources to offer the law student supplementary resources which can complement and locate theologically their 'secular' legal studies.

Bibliography

Alexy, Robert (2002), *The Argument from Injustice*, trans. Paulson and Paulson (Oxford: Oxford University Press).

Beaumont, Paul (ed.) (1998a), *Christian Perspectives on Law Reform* (Carlisle: Paternoster Press).

— (ed.) (1998b), *Christian Perspectives on Human Rights and Legal Philosophy* (Carlisle: Paternoster Press).

— (ed.) (2002), *Christian Perspectives on the Limits of the Law* (Carlisle: Paternoster Press).

Beaumont, Paul and Wotherspoon, Keith (2000), *Christian Perspectives on Law and Relationism* (Carlisle: Paternoster Press).

Bell, John (2003), 'Legal Education' in Peter Cane and Mark Tushnet (eds), *The Oxford Handbook of Legal Studies* (Oxford: Oxford University Press).

Bennett, Ron (2000), *Realising the University in an Age of Supercomplexity* (Berkshire: Open University Press).

Bentham, Jeremy (1776, 1988), *A Fragment on Government*, ed. J. H. Burns and H. L. A. Hart, 1977 (Cambridge: Cambridge University Press).

Bentham, Jeremy (1789, 1970), *An Introduction to the Principles of Morals and Legislation*, ed. J. H. Burns and H. L. A. Hart (University of London: The Athlone Press).

Berman, Harold (1983), *Law and Revolution: The Formation of the Western Legal Tradition*, Vol. I (Cambridge, MA: Harvard University Press).

Berman, Harold (2003), *Law and Revolution: The Formation of the Western Legal Tradition*, Vol. II (Cambridge, MA: Harvard University Press).

Bradney, Anthony (1992), 'Ivory Towers and Satanic Mills: Choices for University Law Schools', *Studies in Higher Education*, 17(1):pp: 5–20.

Burnside, Jonathan (2003), *Signs of Sin* (Sheffield: Continuum).

Burnside, Jonathan (2010), *God, Justice and Society: Aspects of Law and Legality in the Bible* (New York: Oxford University Press).

Cane, Peter and Tushnet, Mark (eds) (2003), *The Oxford Handbook of Legal Studies* (Oxford: Oxford University Press).

Cromartie, Michael (ed.) (1997), *A Preserving Grace: Protestants, Catholics and Natural Law* (Grand Rapids: Eerdmans).

Dicey, Albert Venn (1883), *Can English Law Be Taught at the Universities?* (London: Macmillan).

Doe, Norman (1996), *The Legal Framework of the Church of England* (Oxford: Clarendon Press).

Doe, Norman (2002), *The Law of the Church in Wales* (Cardiff: University of Wales Press).

Duxbury, Neil (1994), *Patterns of American Jurisprudence* (Oxford: Clarendon Press).

Finnis, John (1980), *Natural Law and Natural Rights* (Oxford: Clarendon Press).

Glenn, H. Patrick (2003), 'A Transnational Concept of Law' in Peter Cane and Mark Tushnet (eds), *The Oxford Handbook of Legal Studies* (Oxford: Oxford University Press).

Glenn, H. Patrick (2010), *Legal Traditions of the World: Sustainable Diversity in Law*, 4th edn (Oxford: Oxford University Press).

Grabill, Stephen J. (2006), *Rediscovering the Natural Law in Reformed Theological Ethics* (Grand Rapids: Eerdmans).

Grodecki, J. L. (1967), *Legal Education: Dilemmas and Opportunities* (Leicester: Leicester University Press).

Habermas, Jürgen (1996), *Between Facts and Norms: Contributions to a Discourse Theory of Law and Democracy*, trans. William Rehg (Cambridge, MA: MIT Press).

Habermas, Jürgen (1999), 'Between Facts and Norms: An Author's Reflections', *Denver Law Review*, 76: p. 937.

Hanbury, Harold Greville (1958), *The Vinerian Chair and Legal Education* (Oxford: Basil Blackwell).

Harris, Seymour F. (undated), *Universities and Legal Education*.

Hart, H. L. A. (1961), *The Concept of Law* (Oxford: Clarendon Press).

Helmholz, R. H. (2001), *The Ius Commune in England: Four Studies* (Oxford: Oxford University Press).

Helmholz, R. H. (2004), *The Oxford History of the Laws of England, Vol. I, The Canon law and Ecclesiastical Jurisdiction from 597 to the 1640s* (Oxford: Oxford University Press).

Helmholz, R. H. (2010), *The Spirit of Classical Canon Law*, 3rd edn (Georgia: University of Georgia Press).

Hill, Mark (2007), *Ecclesiastical Law*, 3rd edn (Oxford: Oxford University Press).

House of Commons Select Committee Report on Legal Education, 1846. HC 638.

Hunt, Alan (1986), 'The Theory of Critical Legal Studies', *OJLS*, 6(1): pp. 1–45.

Jackson, Bernard S. (2000), *Studies in the Semiotics of Biblical Law* (Sheffield: Sheffield Academic Press).

McConnell, M. W., Cochrane, R. F. and Carmella, A. C. (2001), *Christian Perspectives on Legal Thought* (New Haven: Yale University Press).

McIlroy, David H. (2004), *A Biblical View of Law and Justice* (Carlisle: Paternoster Press).

McIlroy, David H. (2009), *A Trinitarian Theology of Law* (Carlisle: Paternoster Press).

Murphy, Mark (2006), *Natural Law in Jurisprudence and Politics* (Cambridge: Cambridge University Press).

Niebuhr, H. Richard (1951), *Christ and Culture* (New York: Harper & Row).

O'Dair, Richard and Lewis, Andrew (2001), *Law and Religion. Current Legal Issues Vol. IV* (Oxford: Oxford University Press).

Ormrod, Roger (1971), *Report of the Committee on Legal Education*, Cmnd 4595 (London: HMSO).

Perry, Stephen (1998), 'Hart's Methodological Positivism', *Legal Theory*, 4: p. 427.

Prest, Wilfrid (2008), *William Blackstone: Law and Letters in the Eighteenth Century* (Oxford: Oxford University Press).

Price, David Andrew (1989), 'Taking Rights Cynically: A Review of Critical Legal Studies', *CLJ*, 48(2): pp, 271–301.

Quality Assurance Agency (2000), Subject Benchmark Statement: Law. Retrieved on 28 March 2011 from www.qaa.ac.uk/academicinfrastructure/benchmark/honours/law.asp.

Russell of Killowen (1895), *Legal Education An Address* (London: Wyman & Sons).

St German, Christopher (1974), *St. German's Doctor and Student*, ed. T. F. T. Plucknett and J. L. Barton (London: Selden Society).

Sheridan, L. A. (1967), *Legal Education in the Seventies* (Belfast: Queen's University).

Stallybrass, W. T. S. (1951), 'Law in the Universities', *Journal of the Society of Public Teachers of Law (New Series)*, 1: p. 157.

Tushnet, Mark (1991), 'Critical Legal Studies: A Political History', *Yale Law Journal*, 100: p. 1515.

Twining, William (1994), *Blackstone's Tower: The English Law School (The Hamlym Lectures, 46th series)* (London: Stevens & Sons/Sweet & Maxwell).

Twining, William, and Miers, David (2010), *How to Do Things with Rules*, 5th edn (Cambridge: Cambridge University Press).

Warnock, Mary (1989), *Universities: Knowing Our Minds* (London: Chatto & Windus).

Witte, John, Jr (1997), *From Sacrament to Contract: Marriage, Religion and Law in the Western Tradition* (Louisville, KY: Westminster John Knox Press).

Witte, John, Jr. (2002), *Law and Protestantism: The Legal Teachings of the Lutheran Reformation* (Cambridge: Cambridge University Press).

Witte, John, Jr. (2006), *God's Joust, God's Justice. Law and Religion in the Western Tradition* (Grand Rapids: Eerdmans).

Witte, John, Jr. (2007), *The Reformation of Rights: Law, Religion and Human Rights in Early Modern Calvinism* (Cambridge: Cambridge University Press).

Witte, John, Jr. (2009), *Sins of the Fathers: The Law and Theology of Illegitimacy Reconsidered* (Cambridge: Cambridge University Press).

Witte, John, Jr and Kingdon, Robert M. (2005), *Sex, Marriage and Family in Calvin's Geneva* (Grand Rapids: Eerdmans).

Witte, John, Jr and Alexander, Frank S. (2008), *Christianity and Law: An Introduction* (Cambridge: Cambridge University Press).

Witte, John, Jr and Alexander, Frank S. (2010), *Christianity and Human Rights: An Introduction* (Cambridge: Cambridge University Press).

Chapter 11

POLITICS AND INTERNATIONAL RELATIONS

NICHOLAS RENGGER

(University of St Andrews)

For much of the period since the end of the Second World War, the subject areas of Political Science and International Relations[1] have been largely deaf to religious melodies. The dominance – especially in the United States – of so-called positivist methodologies spoke against seeing religion in general or Christianity in particular as anything other than a 'variable', like any other, which could be used to account for certain things (voter alignment perhaps or geopolitical rivalry) but certainly not taken seriously in its own right.

However, over the last few years, religion in general has become much more central to certain areas of work – religion, as some repentant political scientists confessed, was often the 'forgotten dimension' of statecraft – and even Christian theology itself has become increasingly important, in certain contexts. In this chapter, therefore, I want to focus on three areas where what one might call the new political theology raises profound questions for established ways of seeing the political world, domestic, international and global.

I Histories

The first of these areas raises profound questions about the origin of our contemporary political structures. According to a very familiar narrative, the modern world emerges from the Christian one gradually, from the seventeenth to the nineteenth centuries. This process is generally seen as one of 'modernization' and 'secularization' and it has been discussed at length by a number of prominent contemporary social scientists.[2] Recently, however, a number of prominent political theologians have begun to challenge it. It is a central theme, for example, in Oliver O'Donavan's *Desire of the Nations*,[3] plays a role in the influential, though problematic, work of the German Jurist Carl Schmitt[4] and is touched on (as we shall see in a moment) by writers such as Charles Taylor and John Milbank. Perhaps the most complete recent challenge to this general thesis, however, has come from the US based scholar Michael Allen Gillespie.[5] Gillespie's argument essentially is that the modern world – which we deem to be thoroughly secular and which is predicated on a rejection of the religious basis of earlier European society, especially in the medieval period – is in fact erected on a major medieval theological debate and that to fail to see this is to fail to understand just how central theological assumptions still are to this modern 'secular' world. To a very large extent, because we fail to see this we have no understanding of how centrally the theological is still embedded in the modern and thus fail to understand the modern itself.

The crucial debate that Gillespie refers to is the so-called realist-nominalist debate, and to understand its significance a small philosophico-theological detour is necessary. The debate arose out of the medieval discussion of the creation and in particular of the character of so-called universals, itself parasitic on the medieval understanding of ancient Platonism,[6] which held that 'universals' alone are truly real, existing *ante res* – prior to particular things. Thus, for defenders of this view – the so-called realists – particular things are fixed by their participation in the essence of the universally real which is, of course, God's creation. God in essence was, for the realists, the supreme universal. The anti-realist position, however, argued that what were called universals are in fact simply names that appear *post res* – after the existence of particular things – hence the term, 'nominalism'.

It is important to emphasize that this debate was, in the medieval period, a debate *between* Christian theologians. It was not that the nominalists were not Christians, quite the contrary, but they did want to assert – as against the traditional assumptions of the time – that if God was all powerful, He could (if He so chose) change the nature of the universe overnight. In which case, there could be no eternal or universal essences which particular things participated in. To suppose there was, threatened to make God subordinate to aspects of his creation (or so they claimed).

However, the effect of nominalism according to Gillespie was to begin the process of separating out *created* order from *constructed* order and, in the process, opened a space for an increasingly voluntaristic, instrumental conception of human agency which paves the way for modern natural science, and which also introduced distinctions between the 'natural' and the 'supernatural' that had not been present in previous thought.[7] This also produces the notion of order (including political order) as 'immanent' and therefore the creation *of* human reason – rather than the discovery *by* human reason of a pre-given pattern of order – which becomes central to the emerging political ideas of the Renaissance and early modern periods – and which reach a culmination of sorts in Hobbes. It is the origin of the tradition of thought in the West that depended, in Michael Oakeshott's pregnant phrase, on 'will and artifice'.[8]

The rest of Gillespie's book is taken up with detailing the various ways in which essentially nominalist arguments became the central building blocks of modern thought, taking in, along the way, Renaissance humanism – and especially Petrarch's notion of individuality – Descartes, Hobbes and the Enlightenment. But the central point is that most of the things we take for granted in the modern world rest upon, in the last instance, a central medieval and theological distinction.

Although Gillespie does not make very much of this, one of the obvious implications of this story is the extent to which politics in the modern world is effectively a hybrid between a system built on will and artifice yoked together with a rhetoric that effectively assumes the older 'realist' transcendent conception of reality. One can see this in many respects throughout the seventeenth and eighteenth centuries, where the likes of Grotius and Vattel consistently try and emphasize the voluntaristic character of human agency with a sense of transcendent truth. And the whole history of the idea of natural law from the thirteenth century to the present is clearly marked by this dilemma. Hobbes is in this, as in many other things, the most farsighted and the most consistent of his contemporaries in refusing the hybrid and saying point blank that (for example) the Mortal God, the Leviathan, *creates* what is good and what is just, rather than *discovers* what is good and what is just, as the – now intellectually hollowed out – tradition of natural law would suggest.

By the nineteenth and twentieth centuries the hybrid would be even flimsier, yet increasingly central to debate about international relations. What Michael Barnett has recently called the 'humanitarian big bang',[9] essentially the rise of 'compassion' in the late eighteenth century and after, is absolutely saturated with the ambiguities the hybrid creates, and that remains true, I think, of, for example, human rights activism today. Can one have a fully and only constructed and artificial sense of agency and society *and* a belief that anything is universal? I confess, it seems unlikely to me, but at the very least it raises a powerful problematic for those in the contemporary world who wish to hold on to both.

II Secular and Post-Secular

The second theme that I want to discuss, and which flows fairly naturally from this first is, of course, the nature of secularity and its significance for politics in general. There has been much talk in recent years of the 'post secular' character of the age,[10] but perhaps the most far-reaching recent investigation of the character of the secular – and therefore of what the opposition to it, or modification of it, might be – comes from Charles Taylor.[11] As he says, one can understand the claim that we live in a secular age in three distinct ways. One way of saying we live in a secular age, he tells us, is, he says, 'to emphasise that whereas the political organization of all pre-modern societies was in some way connected to, based on, guaranteed by some faith in, or adherence to God, or some notion of ultimate reality, the modern Western state is free from this connection . . . religion or its absence is largely a private matter'. A second way is to see secularity as 'the falling away of religious belief and practice, in people turning away from God'. However, Taylor tells us he is going understand the question in a third way, though it's fairly closely related to the second and not unconnected to the first. He wants to understand secularity as a question about 'the conditions of belief' or as he says 'the change I want to define and trace is one which takes us from a society in which it was virtually impossible not to believe in God, to one in which faith, even for the staunchest believer, is one human possibility among others'.[12] Taylor's exploration of these 'conditions of belief' is then carried out over 874 pages of hugely erudite and often quite stunning virtuoso argumentation, which it would be impossible, as well as invidious, to seek to summarize.

But I do want to highlight one aspect that has, I think, especial relevance to thinking about politics. It will seem, no doubt, an unlikely vehicle for reflecting on international relations; it is the examination Taylor gives of Ivan Illich's reading of the parable of the Good Samaritan.[13] The parable of the Good Samaritan is, of course, one of the best known in Scripture. But, as both Taylor and Illich insist, its very familiarity has to an extent hidden the astonishingly radical claims that constitute it. The parable comes, of course, as the answer Jesus gives to the scribe who asks him 'and who is my neighbour'. A traveller is robbed and beaten and left by the roadside. A priest and Levite – both important figures in local Jewish society, as Taylor reminds us – pass by 'on the other side'. But then a Samaritan, that is a despised outsider, comes and takes up the man, binds his wounds and takes him to an inn to recuperate. Taylor then points to the way in which 'moderns' tend to see this as an answer to the original question:

> Our neighbours, the people we ought to help when they are in this kind of plight, are not just the fellow members of our group, tribe, nation but any human being, regardless of the limits of tribal belonging . . . this story can be seen as one of the original building blocks out of which our modern universalist moral consciousness has been built. . . . So we take in the lesson, but we put it in a certain register, that of moral rules, how we ought to behave. The higher moral rules are the universal ones, those which apply across the whole human species.[14]

But Illich's take on the parable is powerfully different from this. While it is certainly true that the Samaritan breaks the rule of the accepted 'we's' of his own time, he does not do so out of any sense of 'moral rules' but rather as a result of a specific response to an embodied self (the injured Jew). This, for Illich (and for Taylor), represents the real message of the parable. The parable does not point towards universality at all, but rather towards *agape,* properly understood, which comes about, Taylor says, because God became flesh.

> The enfleshment of God extends outward, through such links as the Samaritan makes with the Jews, into a network which we call the Church. But this is a network, not a categorical grouping; that is it is a skein of relations which link particular, enfleshed people to each other rather than a grouping of people together on the grounds of their sharing some important property (as in modern nationalism, we are all Canadians, American . . . or universally we are all rights bearers . . .).[15]

However, Illich's argument does not rest there. The problem comes when such a network is 'normalized', when in order allegedly to prevent falling away from the 'spirit' of the network we seek to institutionalize such relations, introduce rules, divide responsibilities'. Taylor argues that something new emerges out of this:

> [M]odern bureaucracies, based on rationality and rules. Rules prescribe treatment for categories of people, so a tremendously important feature of our lives is that we fit into categories . . . these shape our lives, make us see ourselves in new ways in which category-belonging bulks large.[16]

Taylor (and Illich, on his reading) suggest that these features of the modern world are brought about by the increasingly rule-centered focus of the early church such that, as Taylor puts it, '*corrupted* Christianity gives rise to the modern'.[17] And Taylor adds, echoing here philosophers such as MacIntyre and Bernard Williams – that modern ethics joins in with this 'fetishisim of rules and norms'[18] – and in doing so creates a yet bigger problem he thinks.

> A world ordered by this system of rules, disciplines, organizations can only see contingency as an obstacle, even an enemy and a threat. The ideal is to master it, to extend the web of control so that contingency is reduced to a minimum. By contrast contingency is an *essential* feature of the [Samaritan] story as an answer to the question that prompted it. Who is my neighbour? The one you happen across, stumble across, who is wounded there in the road.[19]

Taylor concludes this discussion by suggesting that while we cannot completely do away with rules and codes we have to be aware of their dangers and recognize that they are not all there is. He tells us:

> Codes, even the best codes are not as innocent as they seem. They take root in us as an answer to some of our deepest metaphysical needs [but] can rapidly become the crutch for our sense of moral superiority ... worse, this moral superiority feeds on the proof offered by the contrast case, the evil, warped, inhuman ones ... we will do battle against axes of evil and networks of terror and then we discover to our surprise and horror that we are reproducing the evil we defined ourselves against.[20]

He acknowledges that 'this message comes out of a certain theology', but adds 'it could be heard with profit by everybody'.[21]

This reading of the parable not only chimes brilliantly with Taylor's more general explanation of the rise of secularity but is full of implications for specific aspects of contemporary politics as well. To begin with it certainly raises a powerful challenge to standard ways of thinking about political ethics – dominated as they tend to be by a broadly cosmopolitan form of ethical universalism. Think of the now burgeoning literature on global distributive justice which inevitably suggests greater international institutionalization and more regulations (hence rules). As does, similarly, the more general literature on global governance or even human rights. Nothing that Taylor says suggests we should not think about such issues, but it does suggest we should think about them in the context of the critique of rule and norm fetishism he draws from Illich's work. And the invocation of the experience of much (at least) of the campaign against al Qaeda in the last ten years is too direct to need much commentary.

III The Sacred

The arguments of scholars such as Gillespie and Taylor represent, then, a very powerful challenge to the familiar, broadly secular understandings of politics and international relations that have largely dominated university departments of politics and international relations since the war. But it is worth adding that they do so, at least in some contexts, from within. Gillespie is a political theorist who holds a joint chair of philosophy and political science; Taylor, of course, is one of the world's most eminent philosophers (though he too once held chairs in politics as well). Taylor is also, of course, a Roman Catholic, a fact which has played a larger and larger role in his work over the last few years, and that brings me to the third major theme I want to explore in this chapter.

This is simply the growing importance and power not simply of religion but of Christian theology in thinking about politics and international relations. Of course, one might see this as a return rather than a completely new chapter. It was not all that long ago that the theological argument was relatively familiar in the general discussion of politics and international relations. In the United States, for example, Rheinold Niebuhr, perhaps the most influential Protestant theologian of the last century, was a noted influence on scholarly and public discussion of politics and international affairs from the 1930s through to the 1960s. In the United Kingdom too, the founders of the British Committee for the theory of international politics,[22] Herbert Butterfield and Martin Wight, were both deeply devout Christians whose work on international relations was often overtly or implicitly underpinned by theological claims. And Wight in particular was also influenced strongly by a third member of the British committee, the theologian Donald Mackinnon, widely regarded as the most original and influential British theologian of the last century.[23] Influential theologians on both sides of the Atlantic would also regularly write about politics and international affairs for a wide audience.[24]

And if one looks beyond the Anglosphere – which, of course, frequently monolingual Anglophone scholars are generally happy not to do – one can see the influence of various different theological positions on debates about international relations. The young Arnold Wolfers was strongly influenced by the Christian socialism of Paul Tillich part of which was a committed internationalism. Further, as I have already suggested, Carl Schmitt was steeped in Catholic political theology. In France, writers as diverse as Charles Maurras, Jacques Maritain and Emmanuel Mournier had important things to say about politics (Mournier strongly influenced the political thought of Paul Ricoeur, still scandalously under-read in Anglophone circles).[25] More recently, liberation theology has an obvious relevance,[26] as does the critical political theology of theologians such as Johann Baptist-Metz,[27] some of the concerns of the *Nouvelle Theologie* in France in the inter-war and immediate post-war period,[28] much of Catholic social thought and so on.

Yet such voices have been relatively rare in recent years, though there have been partial exceptions such as the Cambridge historian and political theorist Maurice Cowling and the philosopher Stephen R. L. Clark.[29] Now, however, they are a much greater presence. In part this is due to the path-breaking work of scholars such as Alasdair Macintyre, whose trilogy of the 1980s so marked moral and political theory in Anglophone countries[30] and whose on-going work has continued to mark out an explicitly theological trajectory (Macintyre became a Catholic convert). But in this essay I want to concentrate on one of the most far-reaching theological voices to discuss politics in recent years – and also one of the most controversial – John Milbank.

It is worth emphasizing at the outset that Milbank is a *Theologian*: one who has consistently said, from his earliest theological essays to the present, that theology must assert its own role as the Queen of the Sciences or fade to nothing. As he puts it in one of the essays in his recent collection *The Future of Love*,

> The first thing which members of a modern theology or religious studies department must face up to is that a large percentage of their . . . colleagues in the academic world would probably consider theology or any other mode of religious reflection as none other than a fantasizing about the void . . . in the face of such doubts there is, in the end, no convincing apologetic ground on which theology and religious studies can stand. In secular terms they should not exist.[31]

But Milbank thinks that there is one good reason for hope.

> This is the possibility that the secular . . . consensus might be challenged. And the grounds for this challenge would be simply that they have got everything the wrong way round. They claim that Theology, alone amongst purported academic disciplines is really 'about nothing'. But theological reason, if it is true to itself, replies to this with a counter claim: all other disciplines, which claim to be about objects, regardless of whether those objects are related to God, are, just for this reason, about nothing whatsoever . . . purely secular disciplines, even if they can show us how, amorally, to more and more seek to possess a realm of illusion . . . are, precisely as secular disciplines . . . . through and through nihilistic. By contrast, theology understands itself as alone studying things as ineliminably real.[32]

Or in other words, as Milbank makes clear both elsewhere in *The Future of Love* and in more detailed compass in his recently delivered Stanton lectures,[33] for Milbank, theology should eschew the nominalizing process that gave birth to modernity and hold fast to the truths of metaphysical realism, the *philosophia perennis* which in his terms bears the name radical orthodoxy. But this should not be seen as a 'going back' for his view is that we still inhabit the nominalizing Middle Ages, as he puts it in his first Stanton lecture:

> [W]e still live within a Franciscan Middle Ages, and this can be shown to be as true of our politics as it is of our philosophy. The question is whether an alternative, Dominican Middle Ages can yet be revived in order to shape, in the 21st Century, an alternative modernity.[34]

The essays in *The Future of Love* are, for the most part, attempts to critique the aspects of the 'Franciscan' Middle Ages that dominate our current modernity or to flesh out what shape a 'Dominican' modernity might take. And in this context the 'international' in many respects takes centre stage. In the preface to the collection as a whole he argues:

> [T]here are now three crucial global forces in the world: capitalist rationality, Islam and Christianity . . . (and) this means that the anomaly pointed out almost a century ago by Hilaire Belloc is likely to pose its cultural contradiction ever more strongly upon the world stage. This is the manifest gap between the teachings of Christianity that still undergird Western morality on the one hand, and the theory and practice of capitalism on the other.[35]

His own position, he tells us, is that only the Church has the theoretical and practical power to challenge the hegemony of capital and to create a viable politico-economic alternative, the alternative he refers to as 'Dominican' in his Stanton lectures, and to which the general arguments apply not only of Milbank but of other theologians associated with radical orthodoxy.[36]

The essays in *The Future of Love* consider many different aspects of politics in the contemporary world and the recent past. Christian socialism is an abiding theme of Milbank's and it is reflected in several essays in this collection – essays on nineteenth-century English and French socialism and on Coleridge, for example – the politics of the Church(es) another – the brilliant essay on the 'management shaped Church' being perhaps the best indication of this. As the above quotation also suggests, Milbank has an ongoing, and growing interest, in international relations. Perhaps the key article in the collection for illustrating how this impacts on international relations is chapter 10, 'Sovereignty, Empire, Capital and Terror'.

This essay is obviously a reflection on the significance of the 9/11 attacks, and Milbank begins by asking why there was outrage on such a gigantic scale, given that, shocking though it clearly was, it was 'only a terrorist attack carried out by a few individuals, unusual only in the extent of the physical damage inflicted and the number of lives lost'.[37] He offers two answers. The first, he suggests, was the threat to sovereign power that was involved. The fact that the attack came from a non-state actor – 'their mode of action threatened the very idea of the state' – he suggests, in that it is only the state that is supposed to be able to kill on this scale.

His second answer is much more significant, however, that in fact the attacks provided an opportunity 'to do things that some in the West had wanted to do for a long time. An assault on so-called rogue states: a continuous "war" against "terrorists" everywhere; a policing of world markets to ensure that free markets exchange processes are not exploited by the enemies of capitalism. But above all', Milbank suggests, 'the attack provided an opportunity to re-inscribe state sovereignty'.[38] Why? Because, says Milbank, 'the modern secular state rests on no substantive values . . . because it exists mainly to uphold the market system, which is an ordering of a substantively anarchic . . . competition between wills to power – the idol of liberty at which we are supposed to worship . . . (and) pure liberty is pure power – whose other name is evil'.[39]

In the anarchic 'states system', a system is, then, itself a system of pure power (and thus evil) made worse by the abandonment of those few restraints on sovereign power which still existed – for example *habeas corpus* rights – which, significantly for Milbank, are essentially early medieval creations. Of course radical Islam is also a challenge to the secular state but, Milbank asserts, it is also much more like a twin to it than is usually supposed. Indeed in certain respects, Milbank argues, the emergent states system of the 'secular' West shares a good deal with its Islamic supposed other.

Milbank argues:

> In the year 1277 the Christian West reached its crisis: certain drastic edicts issued by the archbishops of Paris and Canterbury meant that it decided more or less to outlaw the common Hellenistic legacy of Aristotle fused with Neo-Platonism and blended with allegorical readings of the Bible which it shared Islam, Judaism and Byzantium. A common culture of mystical philosophy and theology, focussed around analogy and ontological participation . . . was rendered impossible. The West and Islam parted along Fideistic lines, since Islam too, inclined in this period to outlaw this perspective. Islam became a doctrinally orthodox, scriptural and legalistic civilization to the exclusion of dialectics and mystical theology (apart from . . . mystical Shi'ite and Sufistic tendencies).[40]

The conventional view, Milbank argues, is that from this point forward, the West became secular and Islam became theocratic, but he demurs:

> Western Christian theology started to look more and more itself like Islamic orthodoxy: it started to read the Bible more like the Quran . . . (and above all in the political domain . . . the sunni linking of the absolute will of the Caliph with the will of Allah, and with the right to fight holy wars, was taken over by Christian thought. As earlier in Islam, so now also in the West, a mere de facto grounding of state sovereignty is absolute right to do what it likes.[41]

The dependence of both on the 'nominalism' that Milbank highlights elsewhere and which he thinks is the constituent of 'Franciscan' modernity (and the analysis of which closely follows Gillespie's) highlights the extent to which 'Islam' and 'capitalist' modernity are two arcs of a single movement. As he puts it towards the end of this essay, which contains many more provocative asides on aspects of contemporary international relations:

> Both empty secular power and arbitrary theocratic power, in their secret complicity, show us no way forward. Neither Enlightenment nor Fundamentalism can assist us in our new plight. Instead, we need to consider again the biblical and Platonic-Aristotelean metaphysical legacy common to Christianity, Judaism and Islam. We should ponder ways in which this legacy may provide us with a certain area of common vision and practice, including economic practice, while at the same time respecting social and cultural spaces for exercised difference. Such a common vision would eschew all idolizations of formal power, whether in the case of individual rights or of absolute state sovereignty. Instead it would trust that human wisdom can intimate, imperfectly but truly, something of an eternal order of justice . . . a shared overarching global polity would embody this intimation in continuously revisable structures dedicated to promoting the common good insofar as this can be agreed upon. It would also embody this imperfection through the maximum possible dispersal and deflection of human power.[42]

It is clear then that, for Milbank, the political and international challenges of our time are insuperable without a fully realized Christian metaphysical realism (most emphatically not to be confused with the Christian realism of a Niebuhr, of which he has been very critical, since in his view it accommodates itself far too closely to the modern state),[43] a view he shares with Stephen Clark and which certainly challenges not only the standard positivism of much political science and international relations literature but also the dominant – critical theoretic, post-structural and post-metaphysical – challenges to it.

Even if I would disagree in certain respects with aspects of the intellectual history on which Milbank rests his case (as I would with Gillespie's version too), it cannot be denied that most of the things we see as determinative of the 'modern' are articulated in ways that indeed look very derivative of nominalism. He puts his finger firmly on the biggest problem, as it seems to me, for much of contemporary work about international relations of many different stripes. This is what I referred to earlier as the 'hybrid' character of modernity – a world that, it is claimed, is constructed, not discovered – coupled with claims relating to the supposedly universal character of certain sorts of (say) rights and obligations.

But the one aspect of this that perhaps Milbank does not dwell on much is the effectively conditional character of the argument. To say that secular power and arbitrary theocratic power offer us no way forward may well be true but the argument that he makes depends (of course) on *faith* in the truth of the alternative he proffers. Some might simply suggest that there *is* no way forward. John Gray, for example, is one contemporary thinker who can be read in this way, I think,[44] and who would add that to think in terms of a 'way forward' is precisely to adopt the linear temporal assumptions that Christianity bequeathed to the 'modern' West and which gave rise to what he would see as the myth of progress.

The point here is not to agree with Gray (I do not) but simply to suggest that Milbank's argument must, in a certain sense, be rhetorical in a strongly Aristotelian sense. Perhaps we might do better to call it 'imaginative': he must try to suggest *why* we should see the world in the way in which he thinks we should and since this is a matter of faith rather than of logic, the form of that suggestion must be imaginative. I think, in fact, Milbank recognizes this – chapter fifteen of his book, entitled '*Faith, Reason and Imagination*', makes these connections explicit – and much of his ongoing project is concerned to yoke the imaginative and the reasonable together, to point out the endless contradictions that the secular modern imagination creates and to offer an alternative vision. Of course, this cannot be *proved*, but only a secular modern would expect it to be.

IV Some Final Reflections

The three themes that I have discussed in this essay have only, of course, scratched the surface of the relevance of Christian theology for politics and international relations – there is much that I left out and much that I have simplified. But before I close I want to reflect on one final issue that I think is especially interesting and important. One of the central questions that has been much debated in politics and international relations over the last couple of decades – as it has, of course in many other disciplines as well – is what usually goes by the name of globalization. This – it is widely assumed – is bringing in its train great changes to at least aspects of the world order – economic organization, global institutions – and confronts many of the most central political challenges of the twenty-first century – climate change, greater degrees of global integration and so on. These concerns are connected to what we might call the 'shape' of the world order.

Political scientists and International Relations scholars are perhaps used to seeing the world order either in terms of states (most commonly) or in terms of individuals (as many in the critical or cosmopolitan turn might do for example). But many of the scholars I have discussed in this chapter would offer both a different analysis and a different prognosis. Milbank, for example, emphatically does not see the world order in either of these ways and several of the essays in *The Future of Love* emphasize, albeit briefly or *en passant*, a conception of world order that is highly diffuse, filled with local, regional, corporate (in the original and not capitalist sense) bodies and where the structure of authority is filtered through the notion of gift. As he puts it,

> [T]he Christian principles of polity stand totally opposed to any idea of the nation-state as the ultimate unit and rather at once favour at once the natural pre given region on the one hand and the universal human cosmopolis on the other. Likewise they oppose the manipulative politics of human rights and propose instead the distribution of specific liberties offices and duties to certain individuals and groups in certain circumstances according to the discernment of what is specifically desirable and has a tendency to cement human solidarity.[45]

This idea is also touched on by Taylor towards the end of *A Secular Age*, where he recalls Jacques Maritain's integral humanism and its concern for disaggregated, locally situated communities as opposed to the states system that Maritain himself knew. Of course, the similarity is perhaps not accidental. Maritain was influenced by the *Nouvelle Theologie* movement in France, which has been strongly influential on Milbank, but in Milbanks'case there is also the influence of eighteenth- and nineteenth-century Christian socialism, especially Ruskin (mentioned many times in *The Future of Love*) together with the influence of what he calls in his preface the 'minority report' of British intellectual history that resists reductive empiricism and utility in the name of what Coleridge called the 'old, spiritual, Platonic England': the England of Hooker, the Cambridge Platonists and indeed Coleridge himself (the first chapter of *The Future of Love* is a reflection on Coleridge). A very similar vision of world order is also found in Clark's *Civil Peace and Sacred Order* and the source is also similar – a Platonizing vision of Christian theology (though Clark also thinks it is similar to the way an 'educated philosophical pagan' would have thought).

The lineaments of the conception of world order found in these worthies and this tradition have not been commented on much in the contemporary literature of politics and international relations and yet they offer a striking challenge to accepted ways of thinking about world order both historically and normatively. It may be that we would want to amend or redevelop such ideas in a distinctive contemporary idiom. It maybe too, that in the multi-cultural plural world, that is the world of the twenty-first century, they would pose as many challenges as they resolve. But it might also be that they help to resolve some as well. After all, as Clark points out, the Platonizing tradition is one 'the West' shares with at least some of 'the rest' (Islam, Judaism) and so that tradition might be key to helping us arrive at a conception of world order that all can accept and live with together. At the very least, such an investigation surely would be worth undertaking. We might finally agree with Clark and Plato that it is the job of 'poets' – a group that includes philosophers and perhaps even political scientists – to give voices to the wind. In doing so perhaps Political Science and International Relations – and even elements of politics and international relations – might be changed out of all recognition.

Notes

I am grateful to the editors for inviting me to contribute to this volume and to many friends for discussions in connection with it. Parts of it draw on an article of mine forthcoming in the journal *International Relations*.

1　In what follows, I follow custom and use Political Science and International Relations (capitalized) to refer to the academic fields in question and politics and international relations (non-capitalized) to refer to their referents.
2　See for example Ernest Gellner (1981), *Plough, Sword and Book: The Structure of Human History*, London: Paladin.
3　Oliver O'Donovan (1996), *The Desire of the Nations*, Cambridge: Cambridge University Press.
4　See for example Carl Schmitt (2007), *The Concept of the Political*, Chicago: University of Chicago Press.
5　Michael Allen Gillespie (2008), *The Theological Origins of Modernity*, Chicago: University of Chicago Press.
6　Largely, in fact, dominated by Neo-Platonic readings of Plato. A good general essay which surveys this is John Rist's excellent chapter, J. Rist (1996), 'Plotinus and Christian Philosophy' in Lloyd Gerson (ed.), *The Cambridge Companion to Plotinus*, Cambridge: Cambridge University Press.
7　A point also made by the French *nouvelle theologie* theologian Henri de Lubac in his crucial and hugely controversial work: H. de Lubac (1946), *Surnaturel*, Paris: Aubier.
8　See Michael Oakeshott (1960), introduction to *Thomas Hobbes, Leviathan*, Oxford: Blackwell.
9　Michael Barnett (2011), *Empire of Humanity: A History of Humanitarianism*, Ithaca: Cornell University Press.
10　Associated with thinkers from radically different perspectives such as Jurgen Habermas, Wilhelm Halbfass and William E. Connolly.
11　Charles Taylor (2007), *A Secular Age*, Cambridge: Harvard University Press.
12　Quotations in this paragraph are from ibid., pp. 1–3.
13　Ibid., pp. 737–44.
14　Ibid., pp. 737–38.

15 Ibid., p. 739.
16 Ibid., p. 739–40.
17 Ibid., p. 740 (emphasis added).
18 Ibid., p. 742.
19 Ibid. (emphasis added).
20 Ibid., p. 743.
21 Ibid.
22 See for the most complete account of this, Brunello Vigezzi (2005), *The British Committee on the Theory of International Politics 1954–1985: The Rediscovery of History*, Milan: Edizioni Unicopli.
23 For the centrality of theological concerns for both Butterfield and Wight, see Michael Bentley's superb monograph, M. Bentley (2011), *The Life and Thought of Herbert Butterfield: History, Science and God*, Cambridge: Cambridge University Press, and Ian Hall's equally superb I. Hall (2006), *The International Thought of Martin Wight*, London: Palgrave Macmillan. Mackinnon lacks a full biography though he has been hugely influential on British theology (the current Archbishop of Canterbury was one of Mackinnon's most brilliant students); his influence on Wight has not received anything like the attention it deserves – another side-effect, I suspect, of the theological tone deafness of most contemporary international relations scholarship. A good essay tracing Mackinnon's central ideas is that by Daniel Hardy in David Ford (ed.) (1989), *The Modern Theologians*, Oxford: Blackwell.
24 I am thinking of figures such as W. R. Inge and from a younger generation, George Bell in Britain and figures such as John Courtney Murray in the United States.
25 Maurras and *Action Francaise* are discussed well in Noel O'Sullivan's superb book: Noel O'Sullivan (1976), *Conservatism*, London: Dent. An excellent study of Maritain in general is William Sweet's essay in the Stanford encyclopaedia of philosophy, retrieved on 19 November 2011 from http://plato.stanford.edu/entries/ maritain/. His political theory is well discussed in Timothy Fuller and John Hittinger (eds) (2001), *Reassessing the Liberal State: Reading Maritain's Man and the State*, Washington, DC: Catholic University Press of America.
26 See, as the *locus classicus*, Gustavo Guttierez (1988), *A Theology of Liberation: History, Politics and Salvation*, Maryknoll, NY: Orbis Books.
27 See for example Johann Baptist-Metz (1977*)*, *Glaube in Geschichte and Gesellschaft*, Mainz: Mathias-Grunewald- Verlag.
28 The main figures in this movement were Marie-Dominique Chenu, Jean Danielou, Hans Urs Von Balthasar and perhaps most importantly Henri De Lubac. It is worth emphasizing that others were connected in a looser way – for example Teilhard de Chardin, Jacques Maritain and Etienne Gilson and that its influence spread beyond France, to figures of the significance of Karl Rahner. It has also become very influential on the last two popes. Pope John Paul II made de Lubac a cardinal; Benedict XVI, as Josef Ratzinger, was associated with the more conservative wing of the movement.
29 See, for Cowling, the Three Volumes of Maurice Cowling (1984, 1986, 2004), *Religion and Public Doctrine in Modern England*, Cambridge: Cambridge University Press; for Clark, the first volume especially of his *Limits and Renewals* Trilogy, Stephen R. L. Clark (1989), *Civil Peace and Sacred Order*, Oxford: The Clarendon Press.

30 See Alasdair Macintyre (1981), *After Virtue: A Study in Moral Theory*, London: Duckworth; Alasdair Macintryre (1988), *Whose Justice, Which Rationality*, London: Duckworth; Alasdair Macintyre (1990), *Three Rival Versions of Moral Inquiry*, London; Duckworth.

31 John Milbank (2007), *The Future of Love: Essays in Political Theology*, London: SCM Press, p. 302.

32 Ibid., pp. 303–4.

33 See the texts of the lectures on the website of *The Centre for the Study of Theology and Philosophy*, which Milbank directs; retrieved on 19 November 2011 from http://theologyphilosophycentre.co.uk/.

34 Retrieved on 19 November 2011 from http://theologyphilosophycentre.co.uk/papers/Milbank_StantonLecture1.pdf.

35 Milbank, *Stanton Lecture 1*, p. xi

36 For example Catherine Pickstock and Graham Ward.

37 Milbank, *The Future of Love*, p. 302.

38 Ibid., p. 224.

39 Ibid., pp. 224–5.

40 Ibid., p. 230.

41 Ibid.

42 Ibid., p. 241.

43 See his essay 'The Poverty of Niebuhriansim' in John Milbank (1997), *The Word Made Strange*, Oxford: Blackwell.

44 See especially John Gray (2002), *Straw Dogs: Thoughts on Human and Other Animals*, London: Granta Books.

45 Milbank, *The Future of Love*, pp. 246–7.

Chapter 12

Orthodoxy and Heresy in Departments of Economics

William T. Cavanaugh

(De Paul University)

In 2003, the economics department at the University of Notre Dame was split into two. Economics and Econometrics – to which seven professors were assigned – was to pursue mainstream economics focused on quantitative analysis. Economics and Policy Studies – to which eighteen professors were assigned – was to carry forward the more heterodox type of economics for which Notre Dame had become known. In this department would huddle the historians of economics, the Marxists, and those who questioned the reigning paradigms in academic economics. At least since the 1970s, Notre Dame's economics department had been known for taking seriously currents in Catholic social thought, and bringing a distinctive emphasis on social justice, labour, and development not found in most economics programmes granting doctoral degrees, where the emphasis was on supposedly value-neutral analysis of economic facts and behaviours. Alas, that department also tended to be ranked in the lowest quartile of doctorate-granting economics departments, in part because leading journals would not publish its work. 'There are some journals that focus on heterodox economics', as the neoclassicist chair of the economics department noted. 'Most of them don't even rank in the top 50, which means that they don't have a great deal of impact'.[1] And so a separate department of econometrics was created with a mandate to publish in more acceptable journals.

Not everyone was pleased. In an open letter, members of the Notre Dame community criticized mainstream economics for giving the false impression that economics is a value-free 'natural science' and avoiding any questioning of such assumptions: 'this perspective ignores the reality that neoclassical theory's starting assumptions and supporting logic carry an embedded ethics and have serious social implications'.[2] Even neoclassical economist Robert Solow of MIT wrote to Notre Dame's president, calling the split a 'cruelly bad idea' and arguing: 'Economics, like any discipline, ought to welcome unorthodox ideas, and deal with them intellectually as best it can. To conduct a purge, as you are doing, sounds like a confession of incapacity.'[3]

The split, it turned out, was temporary. In 2009, Notre Dame announced it was dissolving its Economics and Policy Studies department. Faculty in that department would be dispersed to other departments in the university, most being unwelcome in the triumphant mainstream department. 'In light of the crash of the economy, you would think there would be some humility among economists, some openness to new approaches', commented economics professor emeritus Charles Wilber. 'There's not a lot.'[4]

The borrowing of theological language – 'orthodox' versus 'heterodox' – to characterize this debate ought to tell us something interesting about economics as a discipline. On the one hand, defenders of neoclassical approaches tend to speak in terms of economics as a science because of its reliance on quantitative analysis and its supposed descriptive and predictive power. On the other hand, they dismiss other approaches as 'heterodox', which indicates that *belief*, or *doxa*, is in fact what is at issue, despite the claim of science to have superseded mere belief. Indeed, defenders of a secularist model of the university claim that it is precisely the overcoming of the cramped limitations of orthodoxy that most marks the success of the secular university over the previous faith-based model. Perhaps some would claim that orthodoxy and heterodoxy are just metaphors when used to describe the science of economics. Those on the losing side of the battles for institutional recognition at Notre Dame and other places are unlikely, however, to experience these terms as 'mere' metaphors. They are terms that do real work to mark out what kinds of enquiry are acceptable and what kinds can be safely ignored.

In this essay I explore the ways that economics as a discipline is described and the work those descriptions do in situating economics within a faith-based university. In this essay I will examine three different images Christian economists use to describe economics: economics as science, economics as ethics and economics as theology. I will argue that only by examining the theology implicit in economies and economics can a fully satisfying science of economics emerge.

I *Economics as Science*

'To have influence in the academic discussion, it is important to excel in one's discipline. It takes quality scholarship, as defined by the mainstream, to get a seat at the discussion table.'[5] Thus begins an essay by economist Judith Dean on being a Christian economist. Her approach is probably quite similar to what the administration at Notre Dame had in mind when moving in a more mainstream direction: the goal of a Christian institution is to have influence, to influence society for the good, and one cannot have influence unless one is respected by one's academic peers. When asked by a student 'If I were to take your course in econometrics, would I be able to tell you are a Christian?' Dean's answer is 'no'. But she emphatically denies that she has thereby compromised her Christian faith, any more than C. Everett Koop has compromised his just because the way he does surgery varies not at all from techniques used by non-Christian colleagues.[6] While acknowledging that Christian economists should sometimes play the role of 'philosopher', challenging the philosophical presuppositions of their field, Dean's preferred image for what Christian economists do is that of 'research physician'. She sees her role as that of improving the health of the economy. Just as a research physician must have a solid understanding of the human body, carrying out empirically verifiable experiments on the effectiveness of various treatments, so must an economist apply technical expertise to diagnosing and curing a sick economy.[7]

There will be no difference, according to Dean, between a Christian and a secular economist on the question of 'technical methodology'. The Christian's faith will make a difference, however, in three areas: (1) in the choice of research topics, a 'Christian's choices will reflect God's priorities'; (2) in the formulation of research questions, 'the choice of definitions of terms should be affected by their faith'; and (3) in the way she or he evaluates potential solutions to problems, 'evaluation of potential solutions should use both transcendent and immanent criteria'. What this last indicates is that criteria from both economics, such as efficiency, and Christianity, such as 'ethical treatment of human beings' should have an influence on formulating solutions.[8] As an example, Dean discusses her research on removing non-tariff restrictions on textile exports from developing countries to developed countries. Her faith motivated the choice of research topic because of the issue's effect on the poor, one of God's priorities. Her faith, she says, affected her choice of methods in that she chose criteria that would not underestimate the number of trade barriers that really inhibit trade.[9] Finally, in terms of potential solutions, she was able to give an accurate assessment of whether or not removal of the barriers would be detrimental to poor countries.

It seems clear that her training as an economist has prepared Dean to make a potentially useful contribution to a debate important to poor countries. Her Christian faith has motivated her to do honest analysis and come up with a solution based on what she believes would benefit the poor. What is unclear is whether and how Christianity actually provides content, not just motivation, for her economic analysis. Dean is trying admirably to explain the influence that Christian economists can and should have, but the language of Christian belief – that is what Christians think is true about the world – quickly turns into the language of motivation to do the right thing. What counts as the right thing is generic: being honest and helping disadvantaged people.

The problem with articulating a genuine impact of Christianity on economics comes with the power of the scientific metaphor which Dean uses, and the sharp distinction between descriptive and normative activities that it reinforces. If an economist is to be likened to a research physician, then economics takes on the aura of a 'hard' science, itself a metaphor that indicates the unyielding and given nature of facts. In such a view, economic facts are simply out there, a reality that one bumps into as one bumps into a chair. The economist then must seek to understand those facts, just as a research physician seeks to understand the human body, using the best instruments and techniques at his or her disposal. The task at this stage is purely descriptive. Subsequently, one may or may not apply various values in determining what to do with those facts. But that is another enterprise in which the economist might or might not wish to engage.

The story that mainstream economics likes to tell about itself is one of the progressive separation of the analysis of fact from that of value, and the eventual congealing of the former analysis into a proper science. Roger Backhouse's history of economics, for example, describes the inklings of economics in the medieval scholastic debates over the morality of usury. Though primarily concerned with ethics, ethical questions inevitably required people to think about the way in which economic activities 'actually worked'.[10] This distinction – a basic duality between 'moral questions' and 'what is actually going on in the world and what can be done'[11] – gradually opened up into a full-blown separation of economics from theology first, then from philosophy and politics. Eventually, in the twentieth century, economics emerged emulating science with its own distinct, and thoroughly mathematized, methodology.

Given the prestige of the natural sciences, there are obvious advantages for economists in presenting what they do as scientific. There are reasons to think, nevertheless, that economics is *not* best understood on the model of the natural sciences. There is extensive literature calling this model into question and arguing that economics has made only negligible progress in describing the world and predicting human behaviour. Those calling it into question, however, are those labeled 'heterodox,' who find themselves largely excluded from the privileged circle of influential economists. Economics as science is something of an echo chamber in which the very application of the metaphor of 'hard' science to economics prevents some forms of inquiry that might truly be called scientific from questioning the assumptions on which the discipline often operates.

Sheila Dow's book *Economic Methodology: An Inquiry* finds that 'it is extraordinarily rare for empirical evidence [in economics] to settle a theoretical dispute'.[12] An example of the malleability of empirical data is a 1991 article by David Hendry and Neil Ericsson on econometric analysis of UK money demand, in which the authors used data provided by Milton Friedman and

Anna Schwartz and came up with opposite conclusions to those reached by Friedman and Schwartz.[13] Hendry's earlier article 'Econometrics: Alchemy or Science?' explores some of the same problems.[14] The scientific status of econometrics has been questioned from within and without the field, leading to conclusions like that of Wassily Leontief that 'in no other field of empirical inquiry has so massive and sophisticated a statistical machinery been used with such indifferent results'.[15] Edward Leamer, in an article entitled 'Let's Take the Con out of Econometrics,' has written that 'economists have inherited from the physical sciences the myth that scientific inference is objective, and free of personal prejudice. This is utter nonsense . . . the false idol of objectivity has done great damage to economic science.'[16] The main problem, according to Leamer, is that economists tend to select the set of estimated models that yield 'the most congenial results'.[17]

The search for laws is generally understood as marking a science, but the presence of laws in economics that are the equivalent to the law of gravity in physics is much disputed. *The New Palgrave Dictionary of Economics* claims that 'no scientific law, in the natural scientific sense' has been found in economics, and 'the list of generally accepted economic laws seems to be shrinking'.[18] Laws in economics – 'agents always perform those actions with greatest expected desirability',[19] 'in all capitalist societies, the likelihood of getting out of unemployment falls as the unemployment rate increases'[20] – have been criticized for being vague and self-evidential, or simply the codification of commonsense observation. The fact that bond prices have an inverse relationship to interest rates is an observation that can be made by experience in markets. When the language of 'law' is pressed to conform to the model of law in the natural sciences, the results are inevitably distorting. As Backhouse writes, 'we cannot "see" many economic concepts in the same sense as we can see a polyhedron' and furthermore there is a 'lack of agreement on the basic concepts that economics should be seeking to explain'.[21] Preferences, utility, desires, intentions, motives, class and a host of other terms are not fixed in the same way that independent variables necessary to natural sciences are. Often human economic behaviour is described in terms of preferences, but the preferences are in turn explained by the behaviours. As Alexander Rosenberg comments, 'the crucial explanatory variables are characterized and individuated by the very events whose occurrence they are cited to explain'.[22] Similar observations have led Rosenberg to conclude that rational choice theory has the 'predictive accuracy of common sense'.[23] A slightly more jaundiced view is that of Clive and Cara Beed, who write that in economics '"Theory" is no longer seen as propositions purporting to describe, explain, or predict the real world. It is becoming schemata describing how the real world might look if people behaved in the way the theory suggested.'[24]

This brief compendium of doubt is not meant to constitute a complete argument that economics is not a science, only to indicate that there are serious reasons for having this argument.[25] The problem is that universities – even Christian universities like Notre Dame – tend to be structured to preclude such arguments. The metaphor of economics as science ensures that 'philosophical' arguments about the status of economics as a science cannot take place in economics departments, precisely because they see what they do as an analysis of fact, leaving arguments about deeper 'values' to others.

II *Embedded Ethics*

There are Christian scholars who more directly challenge the idea of a value-neutral economics. According to Lorna Gold, the dominant idea that economics is the dispassionate study of self-interested rational individual actors has helped to create the reality it purportedly describes; the more people are told they act from self-interest, the more they actually do so. What this indicates is that the difference between descriptive and normative is not always as neat as the advocates of economics as science would have it. Gold advocates a Christian business model in which 'An instrumental economic rationale, in a sense, is subdued or "framed" by the communitarian ethic in practice.'[26] According to Gold, the goodness of a business depends on the culture in which it is embedded.[27] The metaphor of embedding comes from Karl Polanyi, who famously described how markets are embedded in culture, but gradually came to be seen as separate and independent of culture, to the point where culture could be described as an epiphenomenon of markets. But, as Gold points out, Polanyi saw the independence of markets as an illusion; they are in fact embedded in and require a certain kind of culture, for better and for worse. The same point is typical of Catholic Social Teaching, especially as articulated by Pope John Paul II. As he writes in *Centesimus Annus*:

> If economic life is absolutized, if the production and consumption of goods become the centre of social life and society's only value, not subject to any other value, the reason is to be found not so much in the economic system itself as in the fact that the entire socio-cultural system, by ignoring the ethical and religious dimension, has been weakened, and ends by limiting itself to the production of goods and services alone.[28]

The metaphor of 'framing', or 'embedding', circumscribes the autonomy of economics. If economics is somehow located 'within' culture, which includes religion and ethics, then Christianity will certainly have an effect on how economics is practiced. If we picture economics and culture in this metaphor as concentric circles, with culture as the larger of the two circles, it remains unclear to what extent the circles interpenetrate; to what extent does Christianity, for example, actually alter what is going on inside the inner circle of economics? There are different ways that this question gets answered, but most commonly the effect on economics is an 'ethical' effect.

I will illustrate this effect with an essay by Rebecca Blank,[29] Dean of the Public Policy school at the University of Michigan. Blank more directly than Dean challenges the value-neutrality of economics, refusing to carve out a 'technical methodology' where Christianity does not penetrate. Blank describes the benefits of the competitive model of markets for predicting behaviour, rewarding creativity, fostering efficiency and doing so without central planning. Nevertheless, Blank questions the assumptions about human behaviour in markets that a typical student would encounter in an introductory economics course. Individuals are assumed to act always to maximize their self-interest. They are assumed to know their own preferences and to have the information they need. The individual is the key actor in this model; aggregate demand is simply the sum of individual decisions, explained by individual preferences. Finally, more is assumed to be better; more goods is better than fewer, more choice is better than less.[30]

Blank says that these assumptions about human behaviour are often accurate; people make decisions at the grocery store based on what they like, what the price is and how much money they can afford to spend. Blank also recognizes that economists are also not blind to situations in which this ideal account of the market does not work. Economists analyse how lack of full information can lead to non-competitive market outcomes, as can externalizing costs and a host of other factors. Nevertheless, the simple competitive market model is the starting point for economic analysis, and it is, as Blank says, a 'public icon'.[31] We find the behaviours it describes as obvious – of course people will buy less of something if the price rises – but, as Blank says, 'this seems obvious only because the economic competitive model is deeply embedded in the culture and experience of those who grow up in market economies. Persons living in non-market economies would not necessarily find these behavioural responses self-evident'.[32]

Writing from a Christian point of view, Blank contrasts the behavioural assumptions of the market model with 'some of the widely held Christian messages about what constitutes "right action"'.[33] 'First, Christian faith calls people into community with each other.'[34] 'Second, the Christian faith calls people to be other-interested as well as self-interested.'[35] The model for this love is the love that people experience from God, as demonstrated in the life and death of Jesus Christ. Third, Christianity affirms the abundance of life in terms of spiritual life not of material goods. Fourth, choices are not morally neutral for

the Christian; some preferences are better than others, and they should be evaluated on whether or not they turn one towards God. Fifth and finally, 'Christian
faith demands that Christians be concerned for the poor and those in need.'[36]
Given these five requirements of Christian faith for economic behaviour, Blank
concludes with some reflections on how Christians can practice other-interest
in the global market. We have no choice whether or not to participate in the
market economy, any more than we can choose whether or not to be human.
We can, however, make better choices in our purchases and become active in
global groups, including the church, that are advocating for better conditions
for all.[37]

Blank's approach is helpful insofar as it makes clear that economic models are not value-neutral. Written into basic presuppositions of the neoclassical
economic model of market behaviour are certain assumptions about human
behaviour that in some cases contradict the Christian ideal of human behaviour.
In neoclassical models there is – as the writers of the Notre Dame open letter
said – an 'embedded ethics', one often directly at odds with Christian ethics.
One cannot withdraw from the market, but a Christian can apply Christian
norms of behaviour to move the market toward more equitable and loving outcomes. Economic activity enjoys only a qualified measure of autonomy from
other spheres of human life. The implication is something like what one finds
in Catholic Social Thought: markets are a qualified good, but they should be
seen as under the watchful eye of a broader culture informed by Christian
norms. Blank never spells out how this approach makes a difference for how
she teaches economics at a secular university. She is probably constrained as to
how Christian norms might be contrasted with market norms, though she could
at least make the students aware that what they are getting in their economic
classes is not norm-free. At a Christian university, one could presumably go
further and supplement the typical economics curriculum with an examination
of Christian norms in the marketplace.

As helpful as this approach could be – and as much of an improvement as
it would be on the approach taken by many Christian universities, where economics courses are indistinguishable from what is on offer at secular universities – I am still not convinced that it gets to the heart of the issue. The fact/value
divide is qualified but remains in place because the confrontation between neoclassical economics and Christianity remains at the level of ethical norms. The
Christian contribution to economics is given in terms of what Christianity says
we ought to do; it does not confront neoclassical models on the question of fact.
Christians are, for example, called to live in community; we are not told that
individualism is in fact a fiction, and a dangerous one at that. In the Christian
view, all humans (not just Christians) are in fact created by a good God in the
image of God, a fact which means we are essentially other-oriented in our very

being. The comparison between Christianity and market models as worldviews should be at the level of fact, not merely values.

III *Economics as Theology*

There is a third type of image for economics that reveals this confrontation more directly: the image of economics as a kind of theology. Here theology is understood not simply as a set of values that generates certain norms of behaviour, but as a comprehensive set of doctrines about how God and the world God made really are. Theology makes claims about God and the world, claims that imply an ethical stance but are not exhausted by that stance. Theology does away with sharp distinctions of fact and value by indicating that how we behave in the world is a function of seeing rightly how the world really is, in light of its creation by a good God.

Robert H. Nelson, a non-Christian economist, has perhaps done more than anyone else to pursue the image of economics as theology. Nelson is not always consistent with his terms: economics is sometimes 'religion', sometimes 'priesthood', and sometimes 'theology' in his writings. It is not entirely clear if economics is theology for a market religion, or if the practice of professional economics is itself a religion. He seems to lean toward the latter; economics, and not the economy, is a type of religion. He states his basic point this way: 'Modern economics offers its own worldview, one that stands in sharp contrast to the Christian worldview.'[38] Nelson came to this realization while working as an economist at the US Department of the Interior. There he realized that economists rarely had influence through analysing facts; they had influence by persuading others to act in accordance with an entire way of seeing the world that amounted to a religion.[39]

> To the extent that any system of economic ideas offers an alternative vision of the 'ultimate values', or 'ultimate reality', that actually shapes the workings of history, economics is offering yet another grand prophesy in the biblical tradition. The Jewish and Christian bibles foretell one outcome of history. If economics foresees another, it is in effect offering a competing religious vision.[40]

Economics does not just suggest other ways of acting in the world, but presents an alternative vision of 'ultimate reality', the forces that are driving history. What this means for Nelson is that Christian attempts to reconcile orthodox economics with Christian theology are doomed to fail. 'There has been a long conflict in the modern era between – as I would put it – secular religion and

Christian religion. It seems to me that scholars have to make a choice. It is one or the other. Otherwise it is like saying that you are a Christian and a Muslim simultaneously.'[41]

It is commonly recognized that academic economics has grown from ecclesiastical roots, from the Reverend Malthus at the beginning of the nineteenth century to social gospeler Richard Ely – founder of the American Economic Association – at the end of century. The usual story told, however, is of the rapid secularization of economics thereafter as it found a home in universities who were busily shedding their denominational identities in the interest of embracing the German model of *wissenschaftlich* higher education.[42] Nelson tells the story differently, as not the secularization of economics but the conversion to a new, progressive, religion. Original sin was replaced by an original competition over scarce goods. The salvation story was that economic progress would save the world. Progressive economists such as John Bates Clark in the late nineteenth century made explicit reference to God guiding the economy toward the good. Eventually Clark simply replaced these references to God with references to 'natural law', which was still part of God's dispensation. Once the shift was made to laws of nature that govern human behaviour, however, the 'scientific' quest to uncover those laws could commence, and reference to God could become purely optional, at best.[43]

Both the old and the new religions were striving for the achievement of heaven on earth. Contrary to the common view that orthodox economics treats people as crassly self-interested, Nelson sees economists as offering a distinct kind of social salvation. It may be that self-interested behaviour can help achieve that goal, but fulfilling self-interest is not the goal itself.[44] If this is true, then the theological import of Adam Smith's idea of the 'invisible hand' of the market is not that there is an ethic of self-interest embedded in neoclassical economics, but rather that such economics serves as a type of theodicy that explains how divine providence turns evil into good. Nelson does not, however, think that economics offers a uniform theological point of view. Nelson identifies a direct parallel between the Catholic/Protestant split and the divide between progressivist and Chicago-school economists. Progressivists are those who have a strong belief both in the perfectability of human society through economic progress and the necessity of a class of scientific managers to guide that progress through the application of rational principles. Nelson uses Paul Samuelson and his influential textbook as an example of progressivism. Despite the textbook's insistence that economics is a hard science, Nelson finds a doctrinaire insistence on change, efficiency and other contestable values that issue from an optimistic anthropology. Progressivists are like Catholic theologians, who both underplay the damage done by original sin and believe in a clerical elite to guide the laity to salvation.[45] The Protestants in this story are the Chicago school, people like

Frank Knight, whose account of original sin casts doubt on the ability of a technocratic elite to act in the public interest. Self-interest is endemic, which is why economic decisions are best left to the individual, not to the government, which can only represent self-interest writ large.[46]

A similar approach to Nelson's can be seen in Philip Goodchild's book *Theology of Money*. But while Nelson uses the language and vocabulary of theology and religion rather loosely to suggest that economics offers an alternative way of seeing the world – a worldview – to that of Christianity, Goodchild's work is more precisely theological, in that it attempts to show that money formally occupies the place that God once occupied in Christian society. It is theological, that is, because it is about God, not simply about anthropology or soteriology. Goodchild also extends the range of his analysis beyond the work of professional economists to the market economy as a whole.

Goodchild begins his theological reflections with the opposition that Jesus posited between God and wealth, or Mammon (Mt. 6.24). What is in question is not simply ethics, but metaphysics; Jesus puts the power of God and the power of money into opposition.[47] It is not so much that people actually worship money or accumulate it for its own sake. It is rather that, in modern society, time, attention and devotion are organized by the social institution of money, in ways that are directly in opposition to God. Money is the one thing that guarantees access to all the benefits, pleasures and goods of modern life. Money is therefore the one thing that unites all the diverse people of the world. Money takes the place that God once held, as the source of the value of values.[48]

It would be a mistake to place money and God on opposing levels of reality, as if God were transcendent and spiritual on the one hand, and money were mundane and material on the other. As Goodchild shows, money is not a tangible thing, but is essentially a system of social obligations based in debt. The modern money system originated in banks creating notes that represented loans and in turn could be used to pay off further obligations. Credit came to occupy the space that coinage alone had previously occupied, and the whole system depended upon confidence and trust. As Goodchild puts it: 'the finitude of currency has been overcome by treating signs of monetary value as themselves valuable, ensuring the value of newly created money by issuing it in the form of loans, attached to debts.'[49] Furthermore, money can be created from speculation. A bank can create money by loaning to a speculator, whose assets can rise in value because of the very activity of speculation. (The rise in real estate values created by speculation before the 2008 crash is an example.) If the speculator can sell the assets while the value is high, he or she can repay the loan and keep the difference. Goodchild refers to this as making money 'out of pure thought'.[50] Money, like God, transcends the merely material.

The value of money is transcendent; no one has ever seen a dollar, only a promise to pay a debt marked by a value called a dollar. Money is the supreme value, since all other social values are realized in its terms. Furthermore,

> The value of assets is determined not by their intrinsic worth but by their expected yield, their anticipated rate of return. The value of assets is determined by speculative projections. Moreover, even if these anticipations prove misguided, at every stage the value of assets is determined by the next wave of anticipations about the future. Thus, the future never ultimately arrives: it is purely ideal. Financial value is essentially a degree of hope, expectation, trust, or credibility. Just as paper currency is never cashed in, so the value of assets is never realized. It is future or transcendent.[51]

The structural parallels between the position that God and money occupy in different types of society, however, do not mean that God and money offer the same things. Indeed, what is on offer provides the sharpest contrast.

> Where God promises eternity, money promises the world. Where God offers a delayed reward, money offers a reward in advance. Where God offers himself as grace, money offers itself as a loan. Where God offers spiritual benefits, money offers tangible benefits. Where God accepts all repentant sinners who truly believe, money may be accepted by all who are willing to trust in its value. Where God requires the conversion of the soul, money empowers the existing desires and plans of the soul.[52]

Because money occupies the place of God, Goodchild uses the term 'religion' to describe the system of social obligations that money puts in motion. 'Being transcendent to material and social reality, yet also being the pivot around which material and social reality is continually reconstructed, financial value is essentially religious.'[53] When money is created as a debt, it holds its value only as long as there is trust in the commitment to repay the debt. The money system is not only a system of inclusion through trust and social obligation, but also a system of exclusion for those without the wealth or willingness to complete such obligations. Goodchild says that debt occupies the position of religion in society,[54] but there is a crucial difference between the financial system and what he calls 'traditional religion'. That difference is the lack of consciousness about the transcendent status of money in the former. We regard God as shrouded in mystery and beyond human manipulation, but we continue to see money as mundane, an object of human control and a mere means to other ends. In fact money has become our end, though we refuse to acknowledge it. 'It is in modern life that alienation is complete and the consciousness of humanity departs entirely from the conditions of its existence. It is in modern life, rather than religious life, where ideology is most fully instantiated.'[55]

The profession of economics is part of that ideological apparatus that keeps us from recognizing the transcendent nature of the money economy. The so-called science of economics is concerned with the effects of money on value, but value is only measured in terms of money. Economics carefully chooses for its object of study only that which is exchangeable, which imposes exchangeability as a value and a form of evaluation.[56] What is needed, according to Goodchild, is the rescue of evaluation from its subordination to the demands of those with access to money. This requires the recognition that a true science of evaluation is necessary, and this science must be consciously theological. Theology, whether Christian or not, has as its most fundamental role the determination of the nature of true wealth. In Christian terms, it is applying the judgement of the God revealed in Jesus Christ to the fundamental question of power in the world, that is, the determination of what is truly of value.[57]

IV Economics and Theology in the University

Of the approaches that I have explored above, the third gets closest to the heart of the matter, not only because it is the most theologically rich, but because it conforms most closely to way that the economy and economics in fact function in the world. It is the model that is most empirically satisfying. In the wake of rolling blackouts that hit California's electricity supply in 2001, the architect of the deregulation that caused them was quoted in the *New York Times* expressing his conviction that 'free' markets always work better than state regulation: 'I believe in that premise as a matter of religious faith.'[58] Jesus – as his comments on God and Mammon indicate – would not have been surprised. One need not immediately jump to charges of idolatry, however. A more sympathetic approach might be a kind of Augustinian awareness that in this temporal existence desire that is actually for God alights on all sorts of inferior objects. It becomes idolatry not when one consciously bows down and worships, but rather when it unconsciously takes the place of the divine in one's life. The role of theology in economics would be to mark when in fact God has been supplanted. But that need not always be the case. There is in fact room in the university for a more modest economics that does not necessarily stand in tension with theological convictions.

As Deirdre McCloskey has pointed out, although the official rhetoric of orthodox economics is positivist, in actual fact orthodox economics relies on metaphor, analogy and appeals to authority in order to persuade.[59] There is no reason to conclude, as does the self-professed naturalist Tony Lawson, that 'the whole project [of economics] is riddled with confusion and incoherence',[60] unless one assumes that economics must conform to the standards of the natural sciences. The problem with orthodox economics is not that it uses metaphor and images, but that it denies that it does. Good economics, as Robert Solow says, is akin to story-telling. The true function of economics is: 'to organize our necessarily incomplete perceptions about the economy, to see connections that the untutored eye would miss, to tell plausible – sometimes even convincing – causal stories with the help of a few central principles, and to make rough quantitative judgments about the consequences of economic policy and other exogenous events.'[61]

Solow still seems to view 'the economy' as an object to be studied; I would want to question how the story that there is a 'the economy' to study gets told and the work that it does. A good economist must do more than apply ethical criteria to 'the economy' as such, and must bring to light the kinds of theological stories that the practice and the study of economics construct. The economist must be a theologian, at least in some rudimentary way. (Theologians should also be economists, in some rudimentary way. The fact that most theologians cannot articulate connections between theology and economics accounts in part for the marginal status of theology in the academy and society.) The economist does not necessarily need to have a thorough grounding in the Nestorian controversies of the fifth century. The economist should, nevertheless, be attuned to the ways in which the *topoi* of economics can function like the *topoi* of theology. This is only to say that all economics supposes a particular articulation of what ultimate reality is like. Economics cannot – and, more to the point, does not – function without one.

That having been said, at the university level there is no question of dissolving the economics department into the theology department. Economists have important work to do, not only in conducting empirical studies of people's behaviour, but in questioning the basic underpinnings of belief motivating that behaviour, and that of the economists themselves. To do so, a more flexible definition of orthodoxy than that institutionalized at Notre Dame will have to prevail. Foundational arguments about what economics is all about should be allowed and encouraged, not avoided or stifled. Debate between 'orthodox' and 'heterodox' economists can reveal the true theological basis of economics.

Notes

1   Robert Jensen, quoted in Gill Donovan, 'Economics Split Divides Notre Dame', *National Catholic Reporter*, 4 April 2004, retrieved from http://natcath.org/NCR_ Online/archives2/2004b/040904/040904c.php.

2   The letter can be retrieved from http://paecon.net/petitions/petition NotreDame.htm.
3   Quoted in Donovan, 'Economics Split'.
4   Charles K. Wilber, quoted in David Glenn, 'Notre Dame to Dissolve the "Heterodox" Side of its Split Economics Department', *Chronicle of Higher Education*, 16 September 2009, retrieved from http://chronicle.com/article/Notre-Dame-to-Dissolve/48460/.
5   Judith M. Dean (2005), 'The Christian Economist as a Mainstream Scholar' in James W. Henderson and John Pisciotta (eds), *Faithful Economics: The Moral Worlds of a Neutral Science* (Waco, TX: Baylor University Press), p. 25.
6   Ibid., pp. 25–6.
7   Ibid., p. 28.
8   Ibid., p. 30.
9   Ibid., p. 32.
10 Roger Backhouse (2004), *The Ordinary Business of Life: A History of Economics from the Ancient World to the Twenty-First Century* (Princeton: Princeton University Press), p. 41.
11 Ibid., p. 65. For example, Backhouse describes the emergence of proper economics in the early modern period this way: 'Instead of disputing the morality of profit, such writers were beginning to take profit-seeking behaviors for granted and attempted to work out its implications', ibid. It is not clear why taking profit-seeking behaviours for granted is not a type of moral judgement.
12 Sheila Dow (2002), *Economic Methodology: An Inquiry* (Oxford: Oxford University Press), p. 36, quoted in Clive Beed and Cara Beed (2006), *Alternatives to Economics: Christian Socio-Economic Perspectives* (Lanham, MD: University Press of America), p. 160.
13 David Hendry and Neil Ericsson (1991), 'An Econometric Analysis of UK Money Demand', in M. Friedman and A. Schwartz, 'Monetary Trends in the United States and the United Kingdom', *American Economic Review*, 81(1): pp. 8–38,
14 David Hendry (1980), 'Econometrics: Alchemy or Science?' *Economica*, 47(188): pp. 387–406.
15 Wassily Leontief (1971), 'Theoretical Assumptions and Nonobserved Facts,' *American Economic Review*, 61: pp. 1–7, quoted in Beed and Beed, *Alternatives to Economics*, p. 205.
16 Edward Leamer (1983), 'Let's Take the Con out of Econometrics', *American Economic Review*, 73(3): p. 36, quoted in Beed and Beed, *Alternatives to Economics*, p. 206.
17 Ibid.
18 Stefano Zamagni (1987), 'Economic Laws'. in John Eatwell, Murray Milgate and Peter Newman (eds), *The New Palgrave Dictionary of Economics* (London: Macmillan), p. 54, quoted in Beed and Beed, *Alternatives to Economics*, p. 231.
19 David Papineau (1978), *For Science in the Social Sciences* (London: Macmillan), p. 81, quoted in Beed and Beed, *Alternatives to Economics*, p. 257.
20 Mario Bunge (1996), *Finding Philosophy in Social Science* (New Haven: Yale University Press), p. 28, quoted in Beed and Beed, *Alternatives to Economics*, p. 257.
21 Roger Backhouse (1997), *Truth and Progress in Economic Knowledge* (Cheltenham: Edward Elgar), pp. 206–7, quoted in Beed and Beed, *Alternatives to Economics*, p. 240.

22	Alexander Rosenberg (1980), *Sociobiology and the Preemption of Social Science* (Baltimore, MD: Johns Hopkins University Press), p. 74, quoted in Beed and Beed, *Alternatives to Economics*, p. 226.

23	Alexander Rosenberg (1992), *Economics: Mathematical Politics or Science of Diminishing Returns?* (Chicago: University of Chicago Press), p. 134, quoted in Beed and Beed, *Alternatives to Economics*, p. 271.

24	Beed and Beed, *Alternatives to Economics*, p. 299.

25	A summary of heterodox critiques of the 'scientific' status of economics is found in Beed and Beed, *Alternatives to Economics*, chapters 7–12, from which the preceding two paragraphs of my chapter is mostly taken.

26	Loma Gold (2010), *New Financial Horizons: The Emergence of an Economy of Communion* (New York: New City Press), p. 77.

27	Ibid., pp. 9–10.

28	Pope John Paul II, *Centesimus Annus* (1991), §39, retrieved from www.vatican.va/holy_father/john_paul_ii/encyclicals/documents/hf_jp-ii_enc_01051991_centesimus-annus_en.html. Avery Dulles thinks the most significant contribution of Catholic Social Thought to economics is the view of economics as embedded in culture; see Avery Dulles S. J. (1999), '*Centesimus Annus* and the Renewal of Culture', *Journal of Markets and Morality*, 2(1 Spring): p. 4.

29	Rebecca M. Blank, 'Market Behavior and Christian Behavior', in Henderson and Pisciotta, *Faithful Economics*, pp. 35–49.

30	Ibid., pp. 37–8.

31	Ibid., p. 39.

32	Ibid., p. 40.

33	Ibid.

34	Ibid.

35	Ibid., p. 42.

36	Ibid., p. 43.

37	Ibid., pp. 43–9.

38	Robert H. Nelson, 'The Theology of Economics', in Henderson and Pisciotta, *Faithful Economics*, p. 89.

39	Robert H. Nelson (2001), *Economics as Religion: From Samuelson to Chicago and Beyond* (University Park, PA: The Pennsylvania State University Press), p. xvi.

40	Ibid., p. 23.

41	Nelson, 'Theology of Economics', p. 90.

42	Nelson, *Economics as Religion*, pp. 41–2.

43	Ibid., pp. 102–3.

44	Nelson, 'Theology of Economics', pp. 93–5.

45	Nelson, *Economics as Religion*, pp. 49–88.

46	Ibid., pp. 119–38.

47	Philip Goodchild (2009), *Theology of Money* (Durham, NC: Duke University Press), pp. 3–4.

48	Ibid., pp. 4–7.

49	Ibid., p. 11.

50	Ibid., p. 16.

51	Ibid., p. 12; also p. 170.

52   Ibid., p. 11. The parallels extend also to the doctrine of creation; according to Goodchild, God presides over a world created good as it is, whereas money constantly seeks to change the world through creative destruction, ibid., p. 211.

53   Ibid., p. 12.

54   Ibid., p. xiv.

55   Ibid., p. xv.

56   Ibid., p. 16.

57   Ibid., pp. 4, 198.

58   Philip Romero (2001), quoted in Alex Berenson, 'Deregulation: A Movement Groping in the Dark', *New York Times*, 4 February 2001: p. 4.6.

59   Deirde McCloskey (1986), *The Rhetoric of Economics* (Brighton: Wheatsheaf).

60   Lawson Lawson (1997), *Economics and Reality* (London: Routledge), p. 14, quoted in Beed and Beed, *Alternatives to Economics*, p. 263.

61   Robert Solow (1985), 'Economic History and Economics', *American Economic Review*, 75(2): p. 330.

PART 3

HUMANITIES

Chapter 13

Theology and Literature:
Reflections on Dante and Shakespeare

Robin Kirkpatrick and Vittorio Montemaggi

(University of Cambridge and University of Notre Dame)

I

The relationship between theology and literature, if sometimes fractious, is intimate and thriving. It always has been, of course, as could be illustrated by even the most rapid survey of ancient cultures, whether Greek or Hindu or Aboriginal, where the hymns of the devout are rarely to be distinguished from the songs, drama and epic narratives that poets have been called upon to offer.

Our concern, however, in this essay is with the ways in which this relationship might be developed within the specific confines of Christian theology and the present-day academy.[1] In particular, we wish to place the work of two writers in a theological perspective. The two writers in question are Shakespeare – whose Christian affiliations are richly oblique, ambiguous or deliberately concealed[2] – and Dante – who is a confessed and highly sophisticated Christian thinker.[3] But before proceeding to any detailed consideration of these writers, it will be as well to explain briefly the general principles that underlie this choice of example, and to consider the particular view of the relationship between theology and literature which these principles – all of them closely interrelated – may be taken to reflect.[4]

The first of these principles asserts a particular competence in theological thinking to explicate complex texts and establish connections between works, at least within the European tradition, which might at first appear to be unconnected. This competence is in part a matter of intellectual history. Christian theology arches over the development of European culture and even writings which do not share its architecture may be brought in mutually illuminating dialogue with it. But the issue is also one of conceptual complexity. Theology,

throughout its long career, has meditated upon questions of the utmost difficulty. It is almost a definition of the science – considering its concern with God,
the Trinity and the meaning, say, of Real Presence – that it should set its mind
upon such questions. And whatever one may think of the conclusions it offers,
the methods it has developed and its conceptual range may well be called upon
to make more precise the issues that arise in the heat of imaginative vision, or
under the pressure of emotional crisis, or even in the context of reflection on the
intellectual implications of scientific discovery. The particular case that arises in
the texts we are considering is that of evil and suffering. But love, forgiveness,
creation, otherness and neighbourliness are topics that might equally benefit
from consideration in a theological perspective.

Yet in making this claim, it should not be thought (and this is the second
principle) that theology necessarily has a sovereign supremacy over all other
disciplines or modes of thought. On the contrary, there is a case for arguing
that a certain humility or admission of failure is intrinsic and constitutive of
all theological practice. After all, the subject of theology is God. And there
are theologians who would argue that the only rational foundation for such a
study is an admission of the limits of rationality.[5] More specifically, theology,
in proper acknowledgement of its own limits, will seek to collaborate rather
than to command when it comes into conversation with other disciplines.[6] In
its relation, specifically, with literary study, theology can undoubtedly bring
to bear its own conceptual sophistication. At the same time, it should also be
prepared to yield sometimes in wonder, sometimes in a willingness to learn,
before the force of a work of art, as identified and expounded by the literary
critic. It is, indeed, theologically fruitful to engage constructively with matters
pertaining to the nuances of literary construction, with genre, with irony, with
dramatic form, with the possibilities and effects of metaphor, or of rhythm
and rhyme.[7]

But if neither theology nor literary study should claim dominion over the
other, their collaboration may also be founded upon a characteristic which
they can share in a marked contra-distinction from many forms of academic
discipline, even in the humanities, and even within the study of theology and
literature themselves. In many academic contexts, priority is given to the establishment of evidence, the accuracy of their results and the rigour of method. And
to be sure, both theology and literature ought properly to cultivate their own
forms of professional rigour. Yet dispassionate neutrality can never be the only
factor in their procedure or the only measure of their success. The fields in which
they operate are fields that have been opened up by particular persons or communities at the fullest reach of their existential, intellectual or imaginative commitment. Studies in this field would be wholly out of keeping with their subject
unless they willingly acknowledge this foundational reality. In both theological

and literary study it would be a contradiction if some conception of academic disinterestedness prevented the scholar from contributing – through witness, rhetoric or simply enthusiasm – to the furtherance of performative possibilities. In this light, the identification of valuable singularities will be as important as any security of general proposition. Responsibility will require (in response to the text and to the need of those who encounter one's arguments) that the scholar is also allowed to contribute directly to conduct, vision or continuing acts of the creative mind.

To argue thus is *not* to lead scholarship into the realm of the incommunicably personal. Rather, in committing oneself to the service of flourishing complexity rather than definitive proof both the theologian and the literary critic commit themselves both to read anew and indeed to *be read* anew. That is we need to return, as practical interpreters, to the details of our texts, to be surprised by these or to be informed by them and to transmit their significance to others. This need not be seen as a resort to a covert activity of private appreciation – or, as sometimes happens, *self*-appreciation. To say we are read by books is to say that we abandon (as many a deconstructionist and many a theologian might agree) any sense that we are here simply to enrich our sensitive egos with exquisitely private pleasures. In reading closely, we enter into, and attempt to develop, the communal language that we practice, and swim in the current of ideas whose source lies way beyond merely bibliographical definition. In that sense literary study and theology are essentially interrogative in character, being as ready themselves to be interrogated by as to interrogate their chosen texts. And arguably the ultimate product of both forms of study will lie in the furtherance of a creative question.

II

In the play that we are primarily concerned with here – Shakespeare's *Macbeth* – many of the above methodological considerations seem to be dramatized.

Thus the play clearly concerns evil, and there is indeed some sense in which it might be said to enter into contemporary debate on that front: King James on witchcraft and Marlowe's Faustus are not far away. Under principle one, we could therefore call on the competence of theology to contribute to discussion in both historical and analytical terms. But then a great deal of the play focuses upon language and in particular upon equivocation:[8] the devil is an equivocator says the Porter; 'Fair is foul and foul is fair' say the witches.[9] The play is full of linguistic and dramaturgical complication, and no account of evil that failed to account for how these refract and define the general question of evil is likely to be adequate; thus inviting consideration under principle two.

But it is principle three – first-person collaboration in the field of cultural critique – that may well produce the richest results. For the play, in its daring concentration on a murderer as its protagonist, raises a question that is current and dangerously alive whenever one hears the commonplace that in literature only villains are interesting. This notion now finds its way into the meanest soap-opera. But justification is often sought and traced to a Shakespearian origin and the fascination supposedly exerted by figures such as Iago, Richard III and Macbeth himself. Drawing upon figures such as these, Milton in depicting Satan conceived a figure who (at least to a certain kind of Romantic eye) was an attractively energetic rebel. And only Milton's literary and theological expertise as exercised in *Paradise Lost* could arguably repel the imputation that the poet was 'of the devil's party without knowing it'. Theologians and literary critics may well need to act in concert if they are to explode the myth in its modern manifestations.

One way of furthering this collaborative effort would be to look at the subsequent history of the problem of evil in its imaginative dimension, discussing say the relation of the play to *Crime and Punishment*, *The Brothers Karamazov* or *The Heart of Darkness*. But if, instead, we turn to Dante's *Commedia*, it is because we here seem to find a theologian and also a poet who, under the same view that favours the figure of Satan to God, seems to prefer his damned souls to his blessed. That view is still to be heard in dissuasions against the *Paradiso*. Yet a more analytical view will not support that prejudice; in Dante's case the imaginative will require a far more nuanced understanding in both literary and theological terms. It should also be said that we do not wish to argue that Shakespeare had read or been directly influenced by Dante; in important respects, however, they can be seen to inhabit the same culture.[10]

III

Evil, for Dante, is utter negation, total deprivation of Good.[11] This is of course at one with a theological understanding of evil defined at least as early as Augustine's *De libero arbitrio* and recently restated, for example, by the theologian John Milbank and a literary critic Terry Eagleton.[12] Satan is rarely mentioned in the *Commedia*, and when he is mentioned Dante emphasizes how meaningless and empty his actions are. In *Paradiso* 19, Lucifer is said to fall from the height of creation through a total failure to comprehend his relation to his Creator: '*per non aspettar lume*' ['he would not wait for light'].[13] No glamourous rebellion but blank impatience and stupidity. So, too, in the one extended appearance of Satan, in *Inferno* 34, the erstwhile Lucifer is no climactically appalling figure but a summation of non-life. He stands gigantic but frozen at the dead centre of the cosmos, his wings flapping merely to refrigerate the lowest circles of Hell, his three ghastly mouths mechanically chewing at three representatives of treachery, according to Dante the most heinous of all sins. The only other function that this figure performs is, passively, to provide Dante and Virgil, now travelling towards Purgatory, with a means by which, climbing over him, they can move towards the stars.

Dante's theology, then, is both assured and orthodox. But to say this is not to diminish the imaginative or poetic force of his text. The final cantos of *Inferno* demand as close a reading as any literary critic can summon up, and in particular an understanding of how the human imagination can itself, self-destructively, conspire with and betray itself into the hands of satanic negation.

So in Canto 33, where Dante passes judgement on all forms of treachery, whether to country, friends, kinspersons or guests, there occurs within the span of 150 lines a profoundly comic and also profoundly tragic view of how negation can erode the relationship on which human identity most radically depends. In grotesquely comic form, at the end of the canto Dante speaks of Branca d'Oria, who notoriously murdered a guest (his father-in-law) whom he had invited to his banquet (lines 133–47). Dante is astonished to find this figure in Hell, since, to his certain knowledge, Branca is still living in Genova where he 'eats, drinks, sleeps and puts his clothes on' (line 140). And so he does. But that is because Branca's soul has now been replaced by a devil.

From a theological point of view, Dante could here be said to be 'betraying' one of the most fundamental principles of his own thought: that the soul by definition is intrinsically (or hylomorphically) at one with the body. It might well be said that, for reasons of imaginative effect, Dante is here flirting with the 'uncanny', where (to invoke Coleridge) 'the nightmare life-in-death' is to be discovered – and many a modern zombie. Yet the case is not so simple.

For one thing, the theological transgression that Dante might here appear to commit is also a concise anticipation, in comic form, of the privation-theory of evil that will be presented in the figure of Satan a canto later: a human life, conjoined in acts of treachery with the satanic betrayal of creative relationship, itself becomes as mechanical as Satan always is. And if Dante's comedy reveals this here, then it is entirely at one with the comedy of the medieval Mystery plays which, in depicting for instance the Harrowing of Hell, regularly depict the devil who stands against Christ as ridiculously impotent.[14]

Furthermore, the first half of *Inferno* 33 establishes (in preparation for a comic undercutting of its pretensions) a tragic version of the canto's comic (and theological) conclusion. The shift of perspective between the tragic and the comic here anticipates a mode of imaginative action that is regularly associated by literary critics with Shakespeare. In *Macbeth*, for instance, the doorway to the castle in which Macbeth has treacherously murdered his guest and sovereign Duncan is guarded by a comically drunken Porter, who invites us to think of this castle as Hell. In Dante and in Shakespeare, rhetorical and generic perspectives, as literary critics now understand very well, are constantly challenged. Theologians too can benefit from such a refusal to be constrained by fixed perspectives.

What we encounter in the first part of the canto is Ugolino, a father whose enemies have had him starved to death, along with his innocent children. This figure could appear as one of the many in Hell with whom Dante is often thought to sympathize, as though questioning the authority of divine judgement: Has not Ugolino suffered enough? Do not his desperation and distress display genuine fatherly affection towards his children? Why should he so tragically be in Hell? Dante does indeed give to Ugolino, as he narrates the agonising demise of his family, a high degree of heroical pathos: '*ahi dura terra, perché non t'apristi?*' ('Hard, cruel earth, why did you not gape wide?')[15] Yet any simple compassion for the suffering individual is immediately complicated when, as literary critics are trained to do, one considers the context and polyphonic subtext of this speech.

For Ugolino is not only the victim of treachery but also a politician deeply implicated in the vengeful affairs of Duecento Pisa and guilty of treachery himself (*Inferno*, 33, 79–87). Accordingly he is confined in the lowest circle of Hell in company with the man who condemned him to starve to death: Archbishop Ruggieri. It is also thought, moreover, that Ugolino, after the death of his children, might have begun to feed on their corpses.

But if these might be Dante's historical foundations, in imagining the scene in Hell he grasps a far greater moral complexity in the situation. Thus Canto 33 opens with the picture of Ugolino gnawing with ghastly relish at the nape of Ruggieri's neck, as though to suck from it the brains that had devised his own tormented death: indeed, Ugolino tells Dante that his primary aim in recounting his story is, vengefully, that of sowing 'the fruit of hate / to slur this traitor' (lines 7–8). In context, the mouth that delivers the tragic, pathetic and fearsome account of the fatal scene is a mouth that drips, cannibalistically, with the blood of his murderer. The literary critic, with an eye to meta-narrative and the interplay of fact and fiction needs to assess the ironies that come into play here – and the unthinkable variations that Dante composes on the theme of anthropophagy. At the same time the critic may well form an alliance here with the theologian.

Throughout, Ugolino is the single, uninterrupted speaker, but his speech is traversed by voices other than his own, those of his dying children. Thus with the purpose of augmenting the heroic pathos of the scene, Ugolino recalls (lines 58–63) how, at a certain point, his children, supposing that their father was in the final throes of hunger, offer him their own bodies as sustenance:

'*Padre, assai ci fia men doglia / se tu mangi di noi*' ('Father, for us the pain would be far less / if you would choose to eat us'). In the crazy innocence of the offer, we have a delirious logic, verging on the comic: '*tu ne vestisti / queste misere carni, e tu le spoglia*' ('You, having dressed us / in this wretched flesh, ought now to strip it off'). But the ear of Christian theology cannot fail to respond here to Eucharistic undertones. And this association with Christ's sacrifice is strengthened when at the moment of death one of Ugolino's sons cries out, in words reflecting Christ's: '*Eli, eli lama sabachtani*', '*Padre mio, ché non m'aiuti?*' ('Why don't you help me, Dad!'). With this, we are alerted to a reference running all through this scene of need and hunger to the Lord's Prayer: 'Give us this day our daily bread.'[16]

The same reference, however, reveals how far from divine the apparently heroic Ugolino is. Not only has he failed to provide daily bread for his offspring but his apparently heroic fortitude, and even his moving compassion for his children, has in the end produced no word at all. Where his children speak, Ugolino says nothing to them at all. For days, he maintains an eerily unbroken silence. In his story, as he tells this story in Hell to Dante, his purpose is stoically high-minded, intending, as he says, not to distress his children further. But critic and theologian alike can assess the implications of that silence.

So, when Ugolino speaks of how 'stony he grew within': '*sì dentro impetrai*' (49), one option is to see a critique of that single-mindedness or pride which inhibits the bonds of language and kinship that relate us, at every moment, each to another. In that sense, Ugolino is not only a political traitor but a traitor against relationships deeper than those expressed in the political bond. And it is the theologian – indeed Dante himself as a theologian – who can best articulate the depths to which Ugolino has sunk. For the voices of his children are the voices of that primal Good which is the foundation of all reality, endlessly parodied as this may be by the satanic nothingness of evil and sin. At the very centre of his poem – *Purgatorio* 16 – Dante speaks of how this Goodness creates the human soul. The picture he gives is of the Creator loving and drawing to herself the '*anima semplicetta*' ('little simple soul'), who responds to the gift of existence as a child responds to life in all the innocence of its tears and laughter. Ugolino has been deaf precisely to any such claim upon him – whether as a father or himself the child of a divine creator. Single-mindedness, egotism (even unwitting egotism), heroism and heroic self-regard prevent him from attending to the polyphony of voices that sound around him – and indeed *in* him. That polyphony is there to be recovered through a close reading of Ugolino's words. And in that recovery we also voice anew the question of the truth our existences live and thrive in, in the context of a mystery which both exceeds and inspires our attempts at verbal or intellectual definition.

The primacy of Good, the role of children as bearers or, better say, sacramental symbols of that Good, evil as privation and negation, pride and self-assertion as the agents of violence and division: these themes are as central in *Macbeth* as they are in *Inferno* 33.

All these themes call for theological discussion. But initially they are all to be observed in both works on a level which might well be considered quite distinct from theology, that of secular politics. Ugolino's story is told explicitly to aggravate the hatred and treachery that had arisen in Pisa between his party and that of Archbishop Ruggieri – whose head he is now cannibalizing. But this voice is pitched against and perverts the innocence embodied in the voices of his children. Correspondingly, Shakespeare, writing at the time of King James's accession to the English throne, looks back to the rivalrous Scottish origins of that sovereign and discerns a difference between Banquo, ancestor of King James, and Macbeth. Following the witches' prophecy, Banquo bides his time and suffers death, in the assurance that his children will eventually become kings. The childless Macbeth is driven increasingly to murder and to murder not only Banquo but also the children of Macduff, all his 'pretty chickens and their dam / at one fell swoop' (4.3.219–20).

So in each work, a contrast – even a tragic conflict – is to be observed between the exercise of secular power with all its consequences, and faith in those generative or re-creative possibilities that are released through abdication and humility, and which are regularly signified in the imagination by reference to 'children'.

In his romances – which are often taken to possess a theological dimension – and most notably in *The Tempest,* Shakespeare explicitly contrasts the claims of violent egotism with the claims of the communal *longue durée*.[17] In *Macbeth*, however, these same contrasts are played out *ex negativo* in the moral imagination and above all the language of Macbeth himself. And in this regard a full account of this will require the expertise of both literary critic and theologian. For Macbeth, especially in the first half of the play, speaks, as does Ugolino, with a double or even polyphonic voice. One voice is that of violent ambition, the other that of primal good, ineluctably articulated by the same mind that resists and violates that good.[18] The primary attraction of Macbeth's imagination is not (*pace* the post-Romantic commonplace) to evil but to a vividly imagined good.

Consider 1.7.21, where Macbeth contemplates the consequences of murdering (in a treacherous act worthy of medieval Pisa) his sacred sovereign and guest, Duncan:

> And pity, like a new-born babe,
> Striding the blast, or heaven's cherubin, horsed

Upon the sightless couriers of the air,
Shall blow the horrid deed in every eye

These lines, if allowed to resonate in the theological ear alongside Dante's *'anima semplicetta'*, carry the sense of innocence and pity (in the sense both of sentiment and compassion) as being part of the creative order against chaotic blasts, and this is precisely that which Macbeth represses and simultaneously, if unknowingly, voices. The task here is to discern the irony, density and strangulated elusiveness of these lines. There are glancing references to the Apocalpyse. But these are oddly deformed, beyond any commonplace interpretation that theological scholarship might provide. The fatal 'horses' are ridden by cherubim and, though carrying the agents of revelation, are themselves 'sightless'. And while 'blow' may evoke the trumpets of the Last Judgement, the effect is less of an authoritative conclusion to all temporal confusion than an infecting mote in the eye of watching humanity. These complexities need to be explored rather than explained. If such lines possess strange beauty, it is the responsibility of literary critic and theologian to identify and communicate this beauty in all its particularity.

A passage, then, such as this (of which there are many in *Macbeth*)[19] leads one back to the importance of collaboration between the literary and theological mind, to a consideration, that is of those complexities and interrogatives which both theology and literature can cultivate. And, considering all too rapidly the play at large, there are two ways in which this consideration leads to those urgent demands on us, *in propria persona*, to which theological and literary criticism may be expected to respond.

In the first place, the play requires that we view the ever-present evidence of evil in a new and challenging light. The play indeed seems deliberately to depart from the model of Marlowe's *Dr Faustus*, where the Devil has a leading role and where Faustus employs a highly charged theological vocabulary to great rhetorical effect ('See where Christ's blood streams in the firmament!'). Shakespeare eschews any such reference to an established theological scheme. Instead, we see evil as inhabiting, and intertwined with, the details of our daily lives and language. 'Light thickens' – the phrase that Macbeth is given when he initiates the murder of Banquo (3.2.51) – compresses in its metaphor two of the primary elements by which we live: the solidity or reliability of matter and the direction that is given by eyesight that enjoys the light – and both of these essential factors in existence are here confused and violated by language.

In a similar and more extended way, *Macbeth* is consistently concerned with the spaces in which we normally live our lives, and with the ways in which these can be perverted.[20] It is true that actions begin on the Blasted Heath and are concluded on the battlefield. But the play also concentrates claustrophobically on bedrooms (where kings are murdered, and out of which a sleepless queen rages in insomniac agony). Or else on doorways (which drunken porters represent as gates of Hell) or on parlours (where Lady Macduff sees the children she has been dandling slaughtered before her eyes). So, too, banquets are perverted out of their normal and productive use by murderous intent and the hauntingly intangible phenomenon of Banquo's ghost: Banquo is exactly where, by any normal rule of placement, he should be, but exactly where he should *not* be since he is now dead and Macbeth's murderous intentions have exactly been fulfilled.

In such respects, Shakespeare's play resembles the final cantos of the *Inferno*. For in those cantos, too, the treachery of Ugolino and Branca d'Oria produce a parody of quotidian life: for the prisoners in the Tower of Hunger, the shutting of a door is a sinister event, the withdrawal of food a minute-by-minute agony; in the darkly comic parallel to this, the mundane realities of Branca d'Oria's existence – sleeping, eating, drinking and slipping on clothes – are, after his betrayal at the banquet, all sustained by the actions of an indwelling demon. Evil here is not dramatic or thrillingly imaginative but rather a banal yet inextricable part of our everyday existence.

Similarities between *Macbeth* and the Christian understanding of evil (and good) outlined above, also reveal themselves if one reflects on the importance of certainty for Macbeth. Faced with the witches, Macbeth is called upon to solve a riddle and is destroyed by a desire for certainty, becoming, as the play proceeds, ever more rigid in his language and actions (as zombie-like as Branca d'Oria, as 'petrified' as Ugolino). This play between certainty and mystery is theologically significant. Unlike other tragic heroes, Macbeth does not, any more than Ugolino does, offend hubristically against the inscrutable but inimical power of destiny. Rather he offends against and betrays (as does Ugolino) the goodness intrinsic in the ordinariness of human existence.[21] Neither Shakespeare nor Dante could ever fully commit to the familiar cry of tragedy: 'better not to have been born'. For each is concerned with the working of that primal good which is expressed in the metaphor, and reality, of the child. That goodness works mysteriously in Macbeth's imagination and in Ugolino's narrative regardless of their own intentions. It is a mystery – the mystery of evil – that they resist it. But this mystery is only secondary to the primal mystery that human life exists at all and can proceed, creatively, to divine and fathom its equivocations.

Invoking principle three, one might conclude that Macbeth is a bad critic and, equally, a bad theologian. He cannot tolerate (still less enjoy) ambiguity, whether in the form of the witches' oracular utterances or in the form of that deep ambiguity revealed in the subtext of his language. Equally, his desire for certainty in matters of good and evil could be seen as a dark version of those forms of theodicy which presume solution rather than submission to the creative mystery of existence.[22] In purely Shakespearian terms, too, Macbeth tragically fails, where Bottom (before him) and Prospero (after him) succeed, the former speaking of relish for a dream that has 'no bottom' in it,[23] the latter abdicating his own magical powers in full acknowledgement that 'we are such stuff / as dreams are made on'.[24]

But in viewing Macbeth's tragic failure, the spectator is also, *in propria persona* – as critical reader and 'interrogative' theologian – directly implicated and driven to witness an ambiguity as great as that which Macbeth faces in confronting the witches: what they are to him, he is to us. Shakespeare has made a murderer his hero, the focus of interest and engagement. So attention must fall on him (rather than, say, the wholly – and designedly – ineffectual Malcolm). And in one sense, this imaginative dependence leads us (as Dante does in constructing his journey through Hell) into the heart of darkness. Yet since 'fair is foul and foul is fair', it is this same dependency that will give us access, in the subtext of Macbeth's language, to his repressed visions of pity, sacrality and judgement. In the face of this, it will not be enough simply to offer some coolly neutral diagnosis, as for instance that Macbeth is a noble individual with a tragic flaw. We need imaginatively to allow ourselves to be implicated in the same mystery as implicates Macbeth but keep – as he does not but critics and theologians should – the questions that he raises vitally alive.

But here, in the manner of our implication, certain differences as well as similarities begin to emerge between Dante's mode of Christian operation and Shakespeare's. For while Dante's narrative does indeed embrace the impulsion of doubt, and embody an unending series of questions (and surprises),[25] this is all part not merely of a highly systematic poem but also of a poem that depicts a quest, a narrative moving from point to point, always seeking resolution. Shakespeare's dramaturgy – at least in *Macbeth* – freezes its audience in confrontation with a spectacle – a monster which is also a *monstrum* or even monstrance – and as the play ends so too, *per impossibilem*, do the natural sequences of time. There is indeed a contextual narrative here – possessing some validity in historical perspective – of kings and dynastic successions. But, concentrated on the figure of Macbeth, we are increasingly compressed into a moment where our only option seems to be the lethal paralysis of judgemental certitude. Shakespeare, in the theological theatre of *Macbeth*, demands that we directly re-enact the intellectual and imaginative drama that its protagonist has himself experienced.

This may be illustrated by considering the speech Macbeth delivers at the end of the play on hearing of Lady Macbeth's demise:

Tomorrow, and tomorrow, and tomorrow,
Creeps in this petty pace from day to day

> To the last syllable of recorded time,
> And all our yesterdays have lighted fools
> The way to dusty death. Out, out brief candle.
> Life's but a walking shadow, a poor player
> That struts and frets his hour upon the stage,
> And then is heard no more. It is a tale
> Told by an idiot, full of sound and fury,
> Signifying nothing. (5.5.18–27)

Here, rhythmically, all narrative progress ceases and yields to the repetitions in which even the conjunction 'and' speaks of and exemplifies monotony. There is indeed certainty here but it is a certainty that embraces the extinction of all complicating utterance, to the very last syllable. There is demonstrably nothing here of that depth of resonance or subtext encountered in the 'Pity' speech explored above. And in this respect, the lines resemble those in which Ugolino records the death of his sons:

> *Quivi morì; e come tu mi vedi,*
> *vid'io cascar li tre ad uno ad uno*
> *tra 'l quinto dì e 'l sesto; ond'io mi diedi,*
> *già cieco, a brancolar sovra ciascuno* (33, 70–3)[26]

Here number – mechanically registered – governs Ugolino's words. And indeed the rhythms of Dante's interlinked *terzine* – which are normally so effective in promoting both narrative and argument – fracture into disjointed enjambments and caesurae. Yet number, for Dante, always carries with it an ulterior theological significance. So if the three-faced Satan is a parodic figure for the Trinity, here we are presented with a parodic act of un-creating as the *three* sons dissolve into incommunicable 'ones', leaving the blind singularity of the father to scrabble pointlessly over the bodies that he refused to embrace while they were living. Equally the process here is parodic of the liturgy, where number and rhythm are themselves charged and re-charged with significance: the desperate attempt at Eucharistic communion that Ugolino's sons had made is here contrasted with merely material computation. But there is a perspective of possibilities here which will be revealed when number, realizing once again its profound significance, is celebrated in, for instance, the liquid rhythms displayed by Dante in the *Paradiso* in praising the ultimate mystery of the Trinity:

> *Quell'uno e due e tre che sempre vive*
> *e regna sempre in tre e 'n due e 'n uno,*
> *non circunscritto e tutto circonscrive* (14, 28–30)[27]

But in *Macbeth* no such perspective suggests itself. To be sure, in his romances Shakespeare will use theatre in ways that include ritual, symbolic and even quasi-liturgical elements.[28] But in *Macbeth* we are required to know what it means to live without these resources. Indeed, the resources of theatre itself are here derided and employed, scathingly, in derision of life. Life is 'a poor player' who merely 'struts and frets'. Language itself is nothing but bluster, signifying nothing. In other plays (notably *A Midsummer Night's Dream* and *The Tempest*) fiction and life are seen to intertwine, and in doing so to grow so that theatre and metatheatre (or dream) become a vivifying entry into the depths of mystery. But here Macbeth himself offers us only the anti-theatre of stasis. All that is left for us to behold is the severed head of a figure who has already in this speech become as much an instrument of the devil as Branca d'Oria. Of course, if we were good Jacobeans, we might rejoice in the triumph of King James's ancestors. Yet the play, concentrated as it has been on Macbeth, hardly encourages that reaction. What it does allow is the exercise of a theological and literary interrogative. Whether present or absent, dead or alive, Macbeth haunts our imagination as Banquo haunted his host at the celebratory dinner-party, insisting on a question which can lead us, unless we insist upon impossible certitudes of interpretation (that things are necessarily as dark as Macbeth would seem to make them, or alternatively that *we* have a neat explanation at our disposal telling us unambiguously why this is not the case), to participate in the ultimate mystery of goodness, of which evil is the parodic face.

V

A familiar demand in literary study is that we should 'willingly suspend our disbelief'. One might equally suggest that in the conjunction of literary study and theology, we should willingly surrender belief itself in the interests of refreshing both our own responses and the living reputation of the texts we have jointly set ourselves to read – with this proviso: that we should not thereby surrender our capacity for believing. It is thus crucial, in reflecting on the possible significance of the study of 'theology and literature' in the modern academy, that we keep alive and constantly refine our ability to appreciate the generative value of the singularity and significance that the work before us possesses, regardless of any ideological inflection. Readers of any text – scriptural, theological or literary – can be invited by the act of close reading to abandon preconception in the interests of propagating a continuing inquiry – or of engaging with a mystery. The spirit in which this inquiry ought to proceed is not one of anxiety but of imaginative animation, impelled always by admiration, or even by wonder, as words and patterns reveal themselves under analysis in new and unexpected configurations.

Notes

1   In this respect, and in the context of the present collection, we should note that the present reflections are tied, on an institutional level, to our work carried out in and across the universities of Cambridge and Notre Dame; thus, on an institutional level, they are tied to work developed in and across *both* a secular and a religious university. For a broader spectrum of possibilities for configuring an understanding of the wider field of 'Religion and Literature', see Susannah Monta (ed.) (2009), *Religion and Literature* 41(2 Summer); dedicated entirely to the exploration of this question from a set of richly varied methodological and religious perspectives. For recent, prominent examples of the fertile crossover between theological and literary reflection, see Rowan Williams (2005), *Grace and Necessity: Reflections on Art and Love* (London: Continuum), and Nicholas Boyle (2004), *Sacred and Secular Scriptures: A Catholic Approach to Literature* (London: Darton, Longman & Todd). For the question of the relationship between theology and literary theory, see Graham Ward (2000), *Theology and Contemporary Critical Theory*, 2nd edn (New York: St Martin's Press).

2   See Piero Boitani (2009), *Il vangelo secondo Shakespeare* (Bologna: Il Mulino); A. D. Nuttall (2007), *Shakespeare the Thinker* (New Haven and London: Yale University Press).

3   See Vittorio Montemaggi and Mathew Treherne (eds) (2010), *Dante's 'Commedia': Theology as Poetry* (Notre Dame: University of Notre Dame Press).

4   On Dante and Shakespeare, and the question of the relationship between litera-ture and Christian theology see also Nicholas Boyle (1998), 'The Idea of Christian Poetry', in *Who Are We Now?: Christian Humanism and the Global Market from Hegel to Heaney* (Edinburgh: T&T Clark).

5   See, for example, Denys Turner (2004), *Faith, Reason and the Existence of God* (Cambridge: Cambridge University Press).

6   See also George Pattison (1997), *The End of Theology – And the Task of Thinking About God* (London: SCM).

7   See, for example, Ben Quash (2005), *Theology and the Drama of History* (Cambridge: Cambridge University Press); Janet Martin Soskice (2007), *The Kindness of God: Metaphor. Gender and Religious Language* (Oxford: Oxford University Press).

8   See Harald William Fawkner (1990), *Deconstructing Macbeth: The Hyperontological View* (Cranbury, NJ: London; Mississauga, Ontario: Associated University Presses).

9   And, indeed, at the end of the play Macbeth begins: 'To doubt th'equivocation of the fiend, / That lies like truth' (5.5.41–2). The text of *Macbeth* is taken from *The Oxford Shakespeare: The Complete Works*, ed. Stanley Wells, Gary Taylor et al. (2005), 2nd edn (Oxford: Oxford University Press).

10 See Robin Kirkpatrick (1995), *English and Italian Literature from Dante to Shakespeare: A Study of Source, Analogue and Divergence* (London: Longman).

11 For a detailed account of Dante's metaphysics see Christian Moevs (2005), *The Metaphysics of Dante's 'Comedy'* (New York: Oxford University Press/AAR).

12 John Milbank (2003), *Being Reconciled: Ontology and Pardon* (London: Routledge); Terry Eagleton (2010), *On Evil* (New Haven and London: Yale University Press).

13 Dante's text is cited from *La Commedia secondo l'antica vulgata*, ed. Giorgo Petrocchi (1994), 2nd edn, 4 vols (Florence: Le Lettere). Translations are from

Dante, *The Divine Comedy*, ed. and trans. Robin Kirkpatrick (2006–7), 3 vols (London: Penguin).

14 For how this aspect of the medieval imagination might be related to Shakespeare, see Helen Cooper (2006), *Shakespeare and the Middle Ages: Inaugural Lecture Delivered 29 April 2005* (Cambridge: Cambridge University Press).

15 Compare Macbeth's 'Thou sure and firm-set earth, / Hear not my steps which way they walk, for fear / Thy very stones prate of my whereabout, / And take the present horror from the time, / Which now suits with it' (2.1.56–60); and 'I 'gin to be aweary of the sun, / And wish th'estate o'th' world were now undone' (5.5.47–8).

16 See Piero Boitani (1981), '*Inferno* XXXIII', in Kenelm Foster and Patrick Boyde (eds), *Cambridge Readings in Dante's 'Comedy'* (Cambridge: Cambridge University Press); Vittorio Montemaggi '"Padre mio, ché non m'aiuti": Ugolino and the Poetics of the *Commedia*', in Claire Honess (ed.), *Dante and the Ethical Use of Poetry*, supplement to *The Italianist* (forthcoming). For the broader question of Dante's relationship to Scripture, see Peter S. Hawkins (1999), *Dante's Testaments: Essays in Scriptural Imagination* (Stanford: Stanford University Press).

17 See, for example, G. Wilson Knight's influential readings in G. Wilson Knight (1947), *The Crown of Life: Essays in the Interpretation of Shakespeare's Final Plays* (London: Oxford University Press). See also G. Wilson Knight (1967), *Shakespeare and Religion: Essays of Forty Years* (New York: Barnes & Noble).

18 A fuller analysis of the play would, of course, have to consider how this might be compared to the words and actions of Lady Macbeth.

19 Compare Nicholas Brookes' (1990) introduction to *Macbeth* (Oxford and New York: Oxford University Press).

20 See also Julia Reinhard Lupton (2011), *Thinking with Shakespeare: Essays on Politics and Life* (Chicago: University of Chicago Press).

21 John Bayley identifies Shakespeare's concern with heroic 'ordinariness' in John Bayley (1981), *Shakespeare and Tragedy* (London: Routledge & Kegan Paul).

22 For theological reflection on the importance of mystery in addressing the 'problem of evil', see David Burrell (2007), *Deconstructing Theodicy: Why Job Has Nothing to Say to the Puzzle of Suffering* (Grand Rapids: Brazos Press); Denys Turner (2011), *Julian of Norwich, Theologian* (New Haven and London: Yale University Press).

23 *A Midsummer Night's Dream*, 4.1.198ff.

24 *The Tempest*, 4.1.156–7.

25 See *Paradiso* IV, 124–33.

26 'And there he died. You see me here. So I saw them, / the three remaining, falling one by one / between the next days – five and six – then let / myself, now blind, feel over them, calling . . .'

27 'The one and two and three who always lives / and always reign in three and two and one, / uncircumscribed and circumscribing all.'

28 Witness the 'baptismal' aspects of *The Tempest* or the dirge in *Cymbeline*.

Chapter 14

ENGLISH LITERATURE IN THE UNIVERSITY

LUCY BECKETT

(Formerly of Ampleforth College)

The story of English Literature as a university degree subject is short and contentious. In the middle of the nineteenth century it had not yet been invented. In 1854 Newman inaugurated in Dublin the School of Philosophy and Letters in the grandly named but for years inadequately staffed and funded Catholic University of Ireland. In his address for the occasion, 'Christianity and Letters', he defended the study of Greek and Latin literature as an 'instrument of education' central to the future of what was then uncontroversially called Civilization. He stressed the close historical connexions between classical learning and Christianity, asserting that the study of classical texts, essential to 'the cultivation of the mind', should never be replaced by what he called 'the Baconian method', training in empirical science. This, he said, despite 'its inestimable services and inexhaustible applications in the interests of our material well-being', 'is proved to us as yet by no experience whatever' to have a similar educational effect.[1]

Newman was up against Mr Gradgrind: *Hard Times* was published in that year. But 'What I want is facts', as the overriding demand on education, long predates Newman and Dickens. Cato the Censor, who died in about 150 BC, famously regarded the philosophy and poetry of the Greeks as a bad influence on practical republican Rome. In an earlier lecture in *The Idea of a University* Newman said of him: 'He despised the refinement or enlargement of mind of which he had no experience',[2] as one might now say of Richard Dawkins and all those who, in George Santayana's words, writted in 1905, 'are proud of how much they have rejected, as if a great wit were required to do so'.[3]

The issue is not religious or metaphysical contempt for the sciences. Orthodox theologians of a philosophical bent, from Augustine to Alasdair MacIntyre, have always held that no truth cancels any other, and that verified scientific facts are to be respected as such. Newman's faith was not shaken by Darwin. The issue, rather, is the distinction between acknowledgement, required by facts, and the humility and faith, the personal commitment, demanded by truth. According to an instructive legend, when Galileo was accused by his students of cowardice for abandoning, under pressure from the Church, his assertion that the earth revolves round the sun, his defence was that one does not die for a fact that someone sooner or later would establish in any case. In the middle of the seventeenth century, Pascal, a brilliant mathematician and physicist with professional respect for the facts revealed by scientific method, wrote: 'Knowledge of external things will not console me for ignorance of the good in times of affliction, but knowledge of how to live will always console me for ignorance of physical science.'[4] More than a century later Dr Johnson defended the educational value of the humanities when criticizing Milton's recommendation of a 'modern', Baconian system of scientific education:

> The first requisite is the religious and moral knowledge of right and wrong ... We are perpetually moralists, but we are geometricians only by chance. If I have Milton against me, I have Socrates on my side. It was his labour to turn philosophy from the study of nature to speculations upon life, but the innovators whom I oppose are turning off attention from life to nature.[5]

What is at issue in the defence of truth, not in opposition to but in distinction from proved facts, is the education, the progress, of the soul, the heart and the mind – not as separable as we sometimes assume – of the person. When Newman said: 'Religious truths, unlike scientific truths, cannot take care of themselves'[6], he was making Galileo's point: the commitment to truth is to be found in people one by one or not at all. 'Science', he said in his lecture on 'Literature' in the Catholic University in 1858, 'has to do with things, literature with thoughts; science is universal, literature is personal'.[7] This lecture has a magnificent peroration, a single ten-line sentence, the gist of which is: 'If great authors are . . . the spokesmen and prophets of the human family, it will not answer to make light of Literature or to neglect its study.'[8]

In 1854 Newman had said: 'Even to this day Shakespeare and Milton are not studied in our course of education.'[9] In 1856 he appointed as professor of English Literature a high-profile but erratic Catholic convert, Thomas Arnold, son of his old opponent, Arnold of Rugby, and younger brother of the poet Matthew Arnold. In the Catholic University this was more a schoolmaster's job than an Oxford Chair. However, the long-established Trinity College, Dublin, followed suit with a professorial appointment in modern, that is English literature, in 1867. And in that same year Henry Sidgwick, the heavyweight Cambridge philosopher, in *Essays on a Liberal Education*, edited by F. W. Farrar, made a serious case for the study of English literature for the many intelligent students who had never progressed in the classics beyond what he called 'unmeaning linguistic exercises'. Sidgwick (not mentioning girls though he was a firm supporter of women's education) pleaded that:

> [A]ll boys, whatever their special bent and destination, be really taught literature – so that, as far as possible, they may learn to enjoy intelligently poetry and eloquence, . . . that some comprehension of the various development of human nature may ever after abide with them, the source and essence of a truly humanizing culture.[10]

'Culture': a century would elapse before the word would lose its connotation of high quality. Meanwhile it was the word of the moment, especially in Germany. And in England the man of the moment was Thomas Arnold's more famous brother Matthew, whose influential essay 'Culture and Anarchy' appeared in 1869. Arnold had been Professor of Poetry at Oxford from 1857 to 1867, the first who was not a clergyman, and the first to lecture in English. The study of literature was central to his project for civilizing philistine – his word in this connexion – England. In a late lecture, 'Literature and Science', delivered in America in 1884, he defended, against T. H. Huxley, the great Victorian explainer of Darwin and coiner of the word 'agnostic', the merits of a literary education. 'The ability and pugnacity of the partisans of natural science make them formidable persons to contradict', he said. Undaunted, he maintained that the result of a purely scientific curriculum would be:

> [K]nowledge, knowledge not put for us into relation with our sense for conduct, our sense for beauty, and touched with emotion by being so put; not thus put for us, and therefore, to the majority of mankind, after a certain while, unsatisfying, wearying.[11]

He could not say outright that we will cultivate the soul as well as the mind if we love goodness and beauty as well as truth: he knew enough about Plato to know where these words lead. If the soul, then God. But Arnold was no less an agnostic than Huxley, and in this same lecture said that the Christian faith which underpinned the medieval universities was anchored in 'supposed knowledge', what is not, and therefore was not ever, true.[12]

Arnold's agenda was very different from Newman's. Newman saw the Christian and literary traditions as inseparable. Arnold, though equally keen to protect the humanities from utilitarian priorities and the encroachments of science, wanted quite specifically to replace Christianity with literary culture as the path to salvation. He thought it no longer possible for an educated person to take Christian dogma seriously. Praising the vague transcendentalism of Wordsworth and Emerson in a lecture in America in 1883, he remembered the

Anglican Newman of his own Oxford youth and added, of Newman's conversion to Catholicism: 'His genius and his style are still things of power, but he has adopted, for the doubts and difficulties which beset men's minds to-day, a solution which, to speak frankly, is impossible.'[13] Starvation of the soul there might be: in 1869 Arnold had written that 'the British nation has searched all anchorages for the spirit, and has finally anchored itself, in the fullness of perfected knowledge, on Benthamism'.[14] But food for the soul was not to be looked for in Christian truth, because in Christianity there was moral uplift and a dash of helpful emotion, but certainly no truth.

Literature, graded by criticism, which he defined in 1865 as 'a disinterested endeavour to learn and propagate the best that is known and thought in the world',[15] must fill this void. Arnold actually envied the French their stifling Académie française, founded by Richelieu in 1630, because England had 'no sovereign organ of the highest literary opinion', to tell people which authors to approve of.[16] He made a start himself in 'The Study of Poetry' in 1880. Homer, Dante, Shakespeare and Milton are the poets of 'high seriousness . . . which gives to our spirits what they can rest upon'.[17] Poets are sure to become, beyond Shelley's assertion, the *acknowledged* legislators of the world: 'The future of poetry is immense, because in poetry, where it is worthy of its high destinies, our race, as time goes on, will find an ever surer and surer stay.'[18]

In the generation after Arnold's death, gentlemanly lovers of poetry, Sir Walter Raleigh at Oxford from 1904, and Sir Arthur Quiller-Couch at Cambridge from 1912, the first holders of newly founded Chairs in English Literature and English respectively, showed no inclination to take up Arnold's challenge. A similar figure, Sir Henry Newbolt, however, reporting to the government's Board of Education in 1921 on *Teaching English in England*, regarded the study of the country's literature as vital: 'the nation that rejects this means of grace, and which despises this great spiritual influence, must assuredly be heading for disaster'.[19] (Hindsight may detect an unpleasant proto-Fascist tinge to these words.)

Arnold's conscious heir, tougher and with more intellectual grip than Arnold, never mind Raleigh, Quiller-Couch and Newbolt, was born in 1895, only seven years after Arnold's death, and lived, taught and wrote in Cambridge, his home town, until he died in 1978. F. R. Leavis was never the Cambridge professor, was regarded with suspicion or scorn by many in the academic and literary worlds and always thought himself unjustly persecuted or ignored. But his influence, through his teaching of generations of students, through his books and his 20-year editorship of *Scrutiny*, on the development of English literature as a school and university subject was of unparallelled importance for at least half a century.

Leavis collected from Arnold an overwhelming sense of responsibility for the continuity of English literary culture in the absence of any other living tradition, by which he meant Christianity and the rooted life of organic communities. In 1933 he wrote: 'The fact that the other traditional continuities have . . . so completely disintegrated, makes the literary tradition correspondingly more important.'[20] Thirty years later he wrote proudly, quoting Arnold, that *Scrutiny* had been the result of his own 'effort to maintain in Cambridge a community of critical intelligence which would make it possible for people widely separated in space and interests to discover "the best that is known and thought in the world"'.[21]

For decades the English syllabus at schools and universities owed much to Leavis. He expected a student beginning a university English course to have 'come to intelligent critical terms with, and made himself, with personal conviction, intelligently articulate about, two or three of the great Shakespeare plays, two or three major novels, and some poems of diverse kind by great poets'.[22] Hence the poems of Donne, Blake, Hopkins, late Hardy and T. S. Eliot, *Hard Times* and *Great Expectations*, the best novels of George Eliot, Conrad, James and Lawrence, were studied at A level along with whole tales of Chaucer, two books of *Paradise Lost* or a bunch of other works by Milton, and at least two Shakespeare plays which had to be known in depth and detail. (In the last 25 years the A level syllabus, not to mention GCSE as compared to the O level, has thinned and softened almost beyond recognition.)

All this was Arnold's aspiration become reality: '*great* plays, *major* novels, *great* poets'. At the same time 'personal conviction' was at the heart of the enterprise. We are here in Keats's 'vale of soul-making', for belief in the absolute value of the person was central to Leavis's approach to literature: '[O]nly in living individuals is life there, and individual lives cannot be aggregated or equated or dealt with quantitatively in any way.'[23] These words come from Leavis's 1962 'Two Cultures?' lecture, his ferocious attack on C. P. Snow as a 'portent' of trivialization and the gathering opinion that education in the sciences is the key to the future. The lecture's subtext is Leavis's warning against the threat of Marxist utopian materialism, which had much impressed Snow. In it Leavis almost explicity defended the study of English as a substitute for religious belief:

> [F]or the sake of our humanity – our humanness, for the sake of a human future, we must do, with intelligent resolution and with faith, all we can to maintain the full life in the present – and life is growth – of our transmitted culture.

A university must be 'more than a collocation of specialist departments'. It must be 'a centre of human consciousness, perception, knowledge, judgement and responsibility', and the centre of a university will therefore be in 'a vital English school . . . a centre of consciousness (and conscience) for our civilization'.[24] A Christian is bound to ask: 'Faith' in what? 'Responsibility' to what? 'Conscience' the voice of what? But just as Leavis was no more able than Arnold to acknowledge that belief in the absolute value of the person depends on belief in God, so it was as impossible for him as for Arnold to connect his sense of the value of great writing to the absolutes of goodness, beauty and truth united in God. Neither would have agreed with, but both would have been hard put to it to refute, Nietzsche's note printed in *The Will to Power*:

> For a philosopher to say 'the good and the beautiful are one' is infamy; if he goes on to add 'also the true', one ought to thrash him. Truth is ugly. We possess art lest we perish of the truth.[25]

Leavis repeated his call to arms for English in the university to the end. But years before his death cracks had begun to open in what many had regarded as his sufficient model of English as an academic subject. In 1965, in Cambridge itself, Lionel Trilling's lecture 'The Two Environments: Reflections on the Study of English' referred to Leavis's 'Two Cultures?' but not to continue the attack on Snow. Rather, Trilling defined, with striking prescience, a fresh distinction, that between a dreary academic closedness familiar to Sidgwick and Arnold, 'Philistine and dull, satisfied with its unexamined unpromising beliefs',[26] and a new environment which is an exhilarating but intellectually lazy development of what Arnold had hoped for and Leavis had established. This new environment 'identifies itself . . . by its adherence to the imagination of fullness, freedom, and potency of life'.[27] Trilling referred to a recent *Times Literary Supplement* editorial lamenting that students of English no longer had the intellectual stamina for the English classics and wanted to study only modern literature, and quoted Graham Hough who, in *The Dream and the Task* (1963), had deplored the requirement that 'English' should 'provide the foundations of feeling, conduct and belief for those who have no other source of supply', a literary religion 'without a system, without an ethic, without a creed'.[28] Hough's attack, not so much on Leavis as on what had already become of his teaching, was reinforced by Trilling's amplification: this religion did have an ethic, and its ethic was selfishness. The new priorities were freedom, choice, fulfilment, 'life' and 'style', that is self-construction for public display, as far from the vale of soul-making as could be conceived. This now prevailing environment, Trilling said, 'still finds it to its purpose to call upon a pathos which is no longer appropriate to its size and strength' and teachers of English were aware that in 'the very structure' of this environment 'there exists a trivializing force'.[29]

Leavis's enterprise, in other words, had been the victim of its own success, or, more accurately, Leavis's rigorous standards of judgement, having no firmer philosophical or theological backing than his own vision of 'life' and 'self-responsibility', had degenerated into a truth-free, value-free competition for attention, in which no person, text or kind of behaviour was to be regarded as 'better' than any other. Lawrence was perhaps more to blame for this development than Leavis himself, but to understand how badly Leavis needed Lawrence as his great exemplar of post-Christian literature is itself a criticism of Leavis's unanchored aspirations.

Leavis died in 1978. In an obituary essay Terry Eagleton, educated in the Cambridge English of the 1960s, described the current state of the subject. There are various ways, he said, of making a university course in English more than 'spending three years reading a lot of poems, plays and novels that you might well have read anyway'.

> One way is to make the whole enterprise as boring and futile as possible, so that it at least acquires the trappings of academic respectability. If your students arrive from the sixth form flushed with enthusiasm about the Spirit of Man and the Creative Imagination, you can beat them slowly into the ground by setting them to study watermarks, Elizabethan handwriting, textual revisions and Victorian book-binding. . . Alternatively, you can encourage the handling of large, slippery abstractions like the Creative Imagination and fool yourself that what you are up to is some sort of displaced theology.

Thus a Marxist brought up as a Catholic. 'Or again', he added, 'you can try to turn the whole enterprise into a science, viewing literature as a logical system powered by its own laws'.[30] Eagleton was writing this in the early years of the triumph of Theory with a capital T as Civilization once had a capital C.

Anthony Julius, who studied English at Cambridge at just this time, the late 1970s, recently recalled the subject rancorously divided between Leavisite 'conservatives', all for the canon and for the 'redemptive' power of literature, and the 'radicals', dismissive of both as 'utterly untheorized', in their enthusiasm for German, French, Marxist, Freudian, American theory in any combination and however remote from any actual poem, play or novel.[31] A few years later, in 1983, Geoffrey Strickland in his own tribute to Leavis, gave a description of the subject most people would still recognize:

> 'English' is the name given to an educational programme which was almost unheard of in England a hundred years ago, which has enjoyed enormous prestige since then and which was once advocated in fairly unanimous

terms. It now, of course, holds by sheer right of occupation a prominent place in the school and university syllabus, though it can no longer claim to be justified by any view of its purpose which is shared by all or even a majority of those who teach it.[32]

Is this cause for discouragement, or even despair, among those who teach, those who learn, those who want to learn, English literature in a university? Certainly not. Good work is being done in university English departments by teachers, scholars and students who know that enthusiasm for reading more deeply, for understanding more exactly and more intelligently what is going on when a good writer uses words to attract, to interest, to move a reader, need not be quenched by fashionable scepticism. If a teacher wants to recommend that a student pressed for time should read – to take some obvious examples – *Under Western Eyes*, *The Rainbow* or *A Passage to India* and leave for later lesser novels by their authors, he or she should not be shamed into silence either by realizing that a value judgement is involved or by the extraneous priority of some political agenda. This sounds like Leavis because it is like Leavis.

But, as we have seen, there is more at stake than mere personal confidence that statements as to the comparative worth of texts have actual meaning. A teacher needs to be able to explain to a student why it is worth spending time and trouble on a major text when a minor one might repay much less effort with an adequate examination mark. If a text has the attractiveness, the seriousness, and the capacity to move a reader that make it, in I. A. Richards's useful phrase, 'inexhaustible to meditation', the teacher needs to be able to confirm coherently the student's own awe at its quality. Some of these words are heavier than they might appear. 'Personal confidence' in value that is real is faith. 'Attractiveness, seriousness and the capacity to move' describe imperfectly the beauty, truth and goodness that in any human work are always partial, always relative, but not relative to nothing.

In other words, the value both Arnold and Leavis recognized in great writing cannot become, as they hoped, a substitute for the Christianity they thought discredited, but can be properly, that is rationally, understood only in relation to it, or, at least, in relation to a sense of God as the source and guarantee of all beauty, truth and goodness. Arnold, whose sense of truth was indistinct, thought that the approach to goodness and beauty through literature was much easier than the approach through Christianity. Literature will without trouble produce 'the judgement which forms itself insensibly in a fair mind along with fresh knowledge'. 'The good of letters is, that they require no extraordinary acuteness such as is required to handle . . . the doctrine of the Godhead of the Eternal Son',[33] he wrote, having failed to see that Christianity, as was observed long ago, is a sea in which a child can paddle and a wise man swim. Leavis knew that his rigorous programme for the preservation of the literary tradition in the absence of any other was for the clever and perceptive few. Both would have been horrified by the confusion of differing objectives and priorities which has overcome the hope, and in Leavis's case the lifelong effort, each of them invested in literature as the saving alternative to religion 'in the face', in Leavis's words, 'of the euphoric regardlessness of technological progress' which masks 'desperate human need'.[34]

There is no doubt that the hope was noble, nor that it was founded on the instinct for what in great writing is of real value to any receptive reader. Is there anything now, in the present fragmented and uncertain condition of English in the university, that can be reconnected to the grandeur of what Arnold and Leavis thought to be the possible power and weight of literary study?

Perhaps there is. Let us consider a figure whose influence on him Newman denied and about whom both Arnold and Leavis were loftily dismissive. Coleridge's Christian faith, both shaken and confirmed by the sufferings of his disorderly life and by the German philosophy he worked hard to understand and then left to one side, set him apart from the other Romantic poets and also from the other nineteenth-century English sages, of whom he was the first. He started some uncatchable hares in *Biographia Literaria*, but his definition of the imagination became one of them only because most people discussing it found its anchorage in God imposssible to acknowledge.

> The primary IMAGINATION I hold to be the living Power and prime Agent of all human Perception, and as a repetition in the finite mind of the eternal act of creation in the infinite I AM. The secondary I consider as an echo of the former, co-existing with the conscious will.[35]

Properly understood, this is a tentative but brilliantly illuminating attempt to connect the creative perceptiveness of the poet to that of any human being, and both to the eternal creativeness of God. As a suggestion of why great writing moves us and why our sense of its value to us may be regarded as secure, it has not been improved on. A few years later, in one of the essays in *The Friend*, Coleridge wrote that 'the living and substantial faith' of the soul in God 'affords the sole sure anchorage in the storm, and at the same time the substantiating principle of all true wisdom . . . This alone belongs to and speaks intelligibly to all alike, the learned and the ignorant, if but the *heart* listens.'[36]

If the sense persists in university English teaching that there is real value in great literature, value, that is, anchored in something reliable, it is likely to be reinforced by the truth, beauty and goodness to be found in Shakespeare, the greatest of all our writers. Teachers, scholars, students and schoolchildren continue to respond to Shakespeare with fascination, love, a recognition of enrichment that no other English writer delivers so often or at such depth. There are, of course, innumerable scholarly, historical, critical, theoretical ways of approaching Shakespeare. All begin, or should begin, however, from the initial response to the poet's words that Coleridge described as the response of the primary imagination, 'the prime agent of all human perception', to something produced by Shakespeare's superlative secondary imagination. If the Arnold-Leavis project of replacing religion with literature had not been doomed by its fundamental mistake, the decision to regard literature as absolute and religion as relative, Shakespeare might have been its central and exemplary figure. But perhaps he can be the central and exemplary figure of a different project: the relocation of literature, of the study of English literature in particular, in relation to Christian truth.

It has been the almost universal critical consensus of the last two and a half centuries that Shakespeare's work is free of theology, free of philosophy, free of ethical bias. Dr Johnson, a counter-cultural Christian in Enlightenment times, thought this so and deplored it. Shakespeare, he wrote,

> sacrifices virtue to convenience, and is so much more careful to please than to instruct, that he seems to write without any moral purpose . . . He makes no just distribution of good or evil . . .; he carries his persons indifferently through right and wrong, and at the close dismisses them without further care.[37]

Hazlitt, 50 years later in the newly libertarian nineteenth century, rejoiced in what Johnson had deplored, the quality George Steiner in the twentieth century, in agreement with Harold Bloom and many other critics, summed up as Shakespeare's 'concrete universality . . . his observant neutrality in the face of the extant'.[38]

The most notable exception to this consensus is Coleridge, who firmly and straightforwardly said that Shakespeare 'never rendered that amiable which religion and reason taught us to detest; he never clothed vice in the garb of virtue'.[39] Five years later he wrote that in all his lectures at the Royal Institution it had been his 'Object to prove that . . . the Judgement of Shakespear is commensurate with his Genius – nay, that his Genius reveals itself in his Judgement, in its most exalted Form'.[40] I would suggest that the security of Shakespeare's judgement, missed by Dr Johnson, who was thinking in terms of rewards and punishments visible in this life, is a central element in his lasting appeal to people of different times and places, different levels of intelligence and learning and even different languages. In many of the plays, the judgement Shakespeare presents to, and evokes in, his audience or his reader, is complex, apparently open, suspended, but never absent. We may watch or read a play with our sympathies painfully divided between characters juxtaposed and contrasted in ways that Shakespeare does not resolve by bringing us finally to one side or the other. Whereas good or bad characters have much in common with each other – there is no bad character anywhere in Shakespeare who might not say, with Richard, Duke of York, as early as *Henry VI, Part III*, 'I am myself alone'[41] – many plays present us with pairs of characters whose motives and actions are mixed beyond any simple decision between good and bad. Richard II and Bolingbroke, Portia and Shylock, Falstaff and Hal, Brutus and Cassius, Antony and Octavius, Prospero and Caliban: we may not be given, or come to, a moral judgement at the end of these plays, but we are never left with the sense that therefore moral judgement is a meaningless concept. In other words, Shakespeare's sense that the final, the last, judgement belongs to God is never absent from the penumbra of each play.

In the four great tragedies, widely though the heroes differ from each other in character, age, intelligence and depth of personal responsibility for the sin which drives the play, the horizon of divine judgement, divine justice, behind the action is most clearly felt. In the secular, Nietzschean view, that tragedy is essentially unChristian in the death-devoted vitality of its Dionysiac abandonment, there is, of course, no divine horizon. Adrian Poole, in his *Tragedy* (1987), is here representative when he writes of *King Lear*: 'Tragedy affirms the ruthless truth that hearts must break, that the cords that bind people to each other and that hold the heart together must all in time fail.'[42] In this view tragedy conveys only paradoxically exhilarating despair. But if death does not cancel all goodness, truth and love, then *Lear* and Shakespeare's other tragedies return to intelligibility. Hamlet's calm resignation of himself to the will of God; the acknowledgement of truth in the face of death that is reached by Othello and even Macbeth; and the loving forgiveness – demanding not even penitence, let alone punishment – between Cordelia and Lear, Kent and Lear, Edgar and Gloucester: all are felt by the audience to have an eternal value which death cannot annul. The tragedies, and in fact almost all the other plays, even, by implication, the darkest, *Troilus and Cressida* and *Measure for Measure*, evoke in audience or reader assent to the propositions that loyalty, trust, forgiveness, truthfulness, respect for the autonomy of others are good; and that betrayal of trust, lies, exploitation of others and conscienceless pursuit of power are evil. These propositions are theologically founded in God, whether those who regard them as sound know it or not. As Hans Urs von Balthasar wrote about Shakespeare in the first volume of his *Theo-Drama*: 'He knows the dimensions of the realm of evil. For he has an infallible grasp of what constitutes right action . . . [and] can translate the ethical into a sphere where, behind the moral squalor, the good heart shines through.'[43]

So, on the one hand, it is possible to read and to teach Shakespeare's plays, or any other literary text, whether or not written by a Christian, against an absolute horizon that is the guarantee of its meaning. Or, on the other hand, literature has to be taught in the context of secular orthodoxy, in which truth, in

Rorty's chilling phrase, is no more than 'what your contemporaries will let you get away with'.[44] There are no other alternatives, certainly not the substitution for religion of literature, the value of which, however great, will always be relative. 'Straw', St Thomas Aquinas at the end of his life called all his incomparable work. Balthasar, in a theological discussion of freedom in the first volume of his *Theo-Logic,* puts the issue like this:

> The creature, by God's liberality, acquires a share in God's truth, and God reveals his truth precisely by granting participation in this way. God thus equips the creature to be a relative centre of truth . . . A kind of plenitude . . . can descend upon the creature, and when it does, it gives the creature its greatest fascination. But it is so delicate, it requires such careful handling, that one has to have a completely ordered relation to God in order not to succumb to the temptation of divinizing the creature.[45]

This, though not intended as such, is an admirable description of any great writer, and most particularly of Shakespeare, a grammar school boy probably brought up as a Catholic, who kept his adult beliefs to himself, perhaps because they were dangerous. There are certainly passages in the plays that cannot be understood outside a Catholic context. Henry V's conversation with his soldiers during the night before battle depends for its point – 'Every subject's duty is the King's, but every subject's soul is his own'[46] – on a Catholic conception of the sacrament of penance, the sacrament abused by the manipulative Duke in *Measure for Measure.* Hamlet's murdered father is an unabsolved soul in Purgatory, while Hamlet himself, for all his Wittenberg education, is a Catholic prince at whose death Horatio echoes the ancient Latin prayer of the Requiem Mass: 'chorus angelorum te suscipiat'. The sacrament of penance, belief in Purgatory and praying for the dead had all been outlawed by Queen Elizabeth's Thirty-Nine Articles establishing the Church of England two years before Shakespeare was born.

At a deeper level than the sectarian, there is a Christian assumption everywhere in Shakespeare that the truth of a human life lies between the soul and God. Each of his kings who is capable of penitence, from Richard II to Lear, comes down from whatever heights of arrogance, folly and *libido dominandi,* to a recognition of his common humanity in the uniqueness of his soul before God. And at a still deeper level, Shakespeare is only the greatest we have of all the writers in English, whether they are or are not themselves Christians, whose imaginative openness to the structure of being reveals to us through their words our given direction towards the goodness, truth and beauty, ultimately of God, which is so often hampered by our pride, selfishness and greed.

At present the university study of the humanities, not just English, needs reforming as perhaps never before. In a recent review of Martha C. Nussbaum's *Not for Profit*, which argues a secular case for the humanities as essential to democracy, Barton Swain says that governments cannot be blamed for losing confidence in them:

> University departments in the humanities have disgraced themselves . . . Bogus sub-disciplines spawn like bacteria. Academics spend their time and energy writing unreadable monographs on pointless subjects. Revered works of art and literature are treated with disdain even as the productions of nonentities receive the lavish attention of graduate seminars.[47]

In her challenging 2010 book, *Absence of Mind*, Marilynne Robinson pleads for the sustaining of trust, in the mind in relation to experience, in the value of the past in relation to the present, and in the soul, the person, in relation to God.

> The degree to which debunking is pursued as if it were an urgent crusade, at whatever cost to the wealth of insight into human nature that might come from attending to the record humankind has left . . . may well be the most remarkable feature of the modern period in intellectual history.[48]

Most weightily, Alasdair MacIntyre's latest book, *God, Philosophy, Universities*, makes a closely reasoned case for a Catholic context, theologically Augustinian, philosophically Thomist, within which coherence, the very coherence Leavis hoped in vain an English department could create, might return to all university studies. At present, subjects and disciplines, including philosophy and theology, and of course English, are self-contained, often mutually incomprehensible, full of internal disagreement and unwilling to consider the unity in truth of different kinds of knowledge or the nature and destination of the person. 'All adequate understanding', MacIntyre says, 'is in the end a theological understanding', because '[i]n directing ourselves towards truth we direct ourselves towards God'.[49]

If MacIntyre's aspiration towards a new, Catholic framework for all university study were to be realized – and of its prospects he says only that 'there is always more to hope for than we can reasonably expect'[50] – English would find within it a clear and defensible place. The qualities of beauty, truth and goodness in great writing would be allowed their appropriate value, and no one would be embarrassed by the effort to find and more firmly to grasp them. Without MacIntyre's framework, much along these lines could nevertheless be achieved by academics in English departments brave enough to think through and declare why they do what they do. Disinterested personal commitment is the key to fruitful study in either context, although the Christian teacher of literature would obviously find his or her own intellectual development, and that of his or her students, easier to come by with the support and collective responsibility (to God) of a Christian institution.

Here are a few instructive quotations. Trilling concluded his 1965 Cambridge lecture with a plea for university teachers of English to question whether preparing their students for the mere free-for-all of choice and opinion is enough. He quoted a sentence from a letter of Keats which, he said, 'should make the earth shake, although it does not; which should haunt our minds, although it does not'.[51] Keats wrote that poetry, for all its energy and grace, 'is not so fine a thing as philosophy – for the same reason that an eagle is not so fine a thing as a truth'.[52] Coleridge a few years earlier wrote in *The Friend*:

> Truth considered in itself and in the effects natural to it, may be conceived as a gentle spring or water-source, warm from the genial earth, and breathing up into the snow drift, that is piled over and around its outlet. It turns the obstacle into its own form and character, and as it makes its way increases its stream. And should it be arrested in its course by a chilling season, it suffers delay, not loss, and waits only for a change in the wind to awaken and again roll onwards.[53]

And Saul Bellow had his unhappy academic Moses Herzog write:

> The people who come to evening classes are only ostensibly after culture. Their great need, their hunger, is for good sense, clarity, truth – even an atom of it. People are dying – it is no metaphor – for lack of something real to carry home when the day is done.[54]

Notes

1   J. H. Newman (1891), *The Idea of a University* (London: Longmans), p. 263.
2   Ibid., p. 106.
3   G. Santayana (1905), *The Life of Reason*, Vol. I (London: Constable), p. 9.
4   B. Pascal (1954), *Oeuvres Complètes* (Paris: Gallimard), p. 1137.
5   S. Johnson (1793), *Lives of the English Poets*, Vol. I (London: Buckland, Bathurst & Davies), pp. 83–4.
6   I. Ker (1988), *John Henry Newman* (Oxford: Oxford University Press), p. 677.
7   Newman, *The Idea of a University*, p. 275.
8   Ibid., pp. 293–4.
9   Ibid., p. 260.
10   L. Trilling (1967), *Beyond Culture* (Harmondsworth: Penguin), p. 184.

11   M. Arnold (1963), *The Portable Matthew Arnold*, ed. L. Trilling (New York: Viking), p. 415.
12   Ibid., p. 419.
13   M. Arnold (1903), *Essays in Criticism, Second Series* (London: Macmillan), p. 349.
14   Arnold, *The Portable Matthew Arnold*, p. 231.
15   Ibid., p. 264.
16   Ibid., p. 298.
17   Ibid., p. 317.
18   Ibid., p. 299.
19   A. Julius (2010), *Trials of the Diaspora* (Oxford: Oxford University Press), p. xxii.
20   F. R. Leavis (1967), '*Anna Karenina*' *and Other Essays* (London: Chatto & Windus), p. 223.
21   F. R. Leavis (1963), *Two Cultures?* Biographical note, clearly by F. R. L. (New York: Random House), p. 10.
22   F. R. Leavis (1969), *English Literature in Our Time and the University* (London: Chatto & Windus), p. 5.
23   Leavis, *Two Cultures?* p. 40.
24   Ibid., pp. 49–50.
25   F. Nietzsche (1967), *The Will to Power*, trans. Walter Kaufmann and R. J. Hollingdale (New York: Random House), no. 822.
26   Trilling, *Beyond Culture*, p. 197.
27   Ibid.
28   Ibid., p. 191.
29   Ibid., pp. 198–9.
30   T. Eagleton (1978), 'The Importance of Leavis', *The Tablet*, 13 May, pp. 457–61.
31   Julius, *Trials of the Diaspora*, pp. xxii–xxiii.
32   G. Strickland (1983), *New Pelican Guide to English Literature*, Vol. 8, ed. Boris Ford (Harmondsworth: Penguin), p. 176.
33   M. Arnold (1903), *Literature and Dogma* (London: Macmillan), pp. 7–8.
34   F. R. Leavis, *English Literature*, p. 9.
35   S. T. Coleridge (1983), *Biographia Literaria*, Vol. I, ed. James Engell and W. Jackson Bate (Princeton: Princeton University Press), p. 304.
36   S. T. Coleridge (1969), *The Friend*, Vol. I, ed. Barbara E. Rooke (Princeton: Princeton University Press), p. 524.
37   S. Johnson (1968), *Selected Writings*, ed. P. Cruttwell (Harmondsworth: Penguin), p. 270.
38   G. Steiner (2001), *Grammars of Creation* (London: Faber & Faber), p. 68.
39   S. T. Coleridge (1987), *Lectures 1808–1819 On Literature*, Vol. II, ed. R. A. Foakes (Princeton: Princeton University Press), pp. 263–4.
40   Ibid., Vol. I, p. 520.
41   Shakespeare, *Henry VI, Part III*, V. vi. 83.
42   A. Poole (1987), *Tragedy: Shakespeare and the Greek Example* (Oxford: Blackwell), p. 230.
43   H.-U. von Balthasar (1988), *Theo-Drama*, Vol. I, trans. Graham Harrison (San Francisco: Ignatius Press), p. 478.
44   S. Blackburn (2003), 'Richard Rorty', *Prospect*, April, p. 58.
45   Balthasar, H.-U. von (2000), *Theo-Logic*, trans. Adrian J. Walker (San Francisco: Ignatius Press), pp. 232, 236.

46 Shakespeare, *Henry V*, IV. i. 85–290.
47 B. Swain (2010), 'Martha C. Nussbaum: *Not for Profit*', *Times Literary Supplement*, 19 November p. 27.
48 M. Robinson (2010), *Absence of Mind* (New Haven: Yale University Press), p. 29.
49 A. MacIntyre (2009), *God, Philosophy, Universities* (Lanham: Rowan & Littlefield), pp. 142, 167.
50 Ibid., p. 180.
51 Trilling, *Beyond Culture*, p. 202.
52 J. Keats (1952), *The Letters of John Keats*, ed. Maurice Buxton Forman, 4th edn (Oxford: Oxford University Press), p. 316.
53 S. T. Coleridge, *The Friend*, Vol. I, p. 65.
54 S. Bellow (1965), *Herzog* (Harmondsworth: Penguin), p. 28.

Chapter 15

Philosophy, Theology and Historical Knowledge

Fernando Cervantes

(University of Bristol)

In philosophical climates that claim to be able to explain reality in purely mechanistic terms, historians inevitably face a problem. The obvious way for them to operate in such contexts is to concentrate on 'objective' facts and to accumulate masses of detail without heeding their wider significance. There is no room for religion in this schema, and certainly no place for the traditional role of history as the handmaiden of theology. In the past, the Christian Church's vocation as the New Israel was not something distinct from her history. It was only as the New Israel, as a people with a specific historical destiny, that the Church could stand as a mystery and a sign of God's love for humanity. Like the Hebrews before her, the Church was never a community that merely happened to have a 'special' knowledge of the divine mysteries: her beliefs were themselves an interpretation of her own history. This vision has subsided in proportion as modern source criticism has questioned the claims of sacred scripture to be based on historical fact. Religious considerations are now best left to the subjective, interior sphere, where they might still have value for some, but from where they cannot be allowed to interfere with the scientific aims of professional historians.

In recent decades these assumptions have themselves been called into question. The growing realization that historians cannot help being *agents* in the reconstruction of the past, even when they claim to analyze it theoretically, has turned any attempt to achieve total reflexive clarity into an illusion based on untenable notions generated by the attempt to organize the world according to the dictates of instrumental reason.[1] This illusion sinks deep roots into the early modern period, which saw the rise of what Charles Taylor has recently called a 'representationalist epistemology'. Taylor sees this process neatly encapsulated in a claim of René Descartes to be absolutely certain that he cannot have any knowledge of anything that is outside himself other that through the 'mediation' (*'l'entremise'*) of ideas inside himself.[2] Based on this comment, Taylor calls this picture 'mediational', in the sense that knowledge involves some kind of contact with outer reality but that it is only possible to get this contact *through* some inner states.

It would seem to be precisely this kind of epistemology that historians now generally find wanting, often claiming that 'representationalism' was convincingly subverted by Kant. As Taylor shows, however, Kant's solution did not do away with the 'mediational' picture first evoked by Descartes. The 'mediational' structure not only remains in Kant but, in some respects, it also becomes even more inescapable. Kant's *Vorstellung* is the same thing as empirical reality. This can only come about because human intuition is shaped by the categories which the human mind produces. 'It is only through the shaping of the categories', writes Taylor, 'that our intuitions furnish objects for us, that there is experience and knowledge. Without the concepts which *we* provide, intuition would be "blind". "Inner", "outer" and "only through" all take on new meanings . . . But the basic structure survives'.[3]

The same trend can be observed in all the other attempts in the history of modern philosophy to escape from Cartesian dualism. Willard Quine's famous attempt to 'naturalize' epistemology, for example, was based upon his denial of one of Descartes's terms: 'mental substance'. Yet Quine insisted that our knowledge comes *through* 'surface irritations' – the points where the various stimuli from the environment impinge upon our receptors. Although 'inner' is clearly material here, the 'mediational' structure remains, and this materialist epistemology is in turn at the basis of all the popular and learned conjectures about imaginary brains in vats which might be fooled into thinking that they are really embodied agents so long as they get the right 'input'.[4]

Even the so-called 'linguistic turn' is immersed in the same 'mediational' structure. Despite its persuasive questioning of any attempt to explain the contents of the mind on the basis of the 'mediation' of ideas, the linguistic turn invariably enthrones 'beliefs' in the place of 'ideas'. Admittedly explained in more scientific or linguistic terms, 'beliefs' are understood as sentences which are held true by the agent. Nevertheless, the fact that the perceived truth of the sentences in the minds of individual speakers very often remains unspoken is, again, a symptom that the 'mediational' structure has not been removed: reality is outside; perceived truths are inside.

Historians influenced by the linguistic turn are now in the majority, and they commonly deny that there are any remnants of Cartesianism in their approach. An intriguing question at the heart of Hayden White's influential study *Metahistory*, first published in 1973, is 'What is it that makes a work of history, history?' Is, for example, *The Anglo Saxon Chronicle* a work of history? Does history not need a narrative, a story? And once this is done, is it not evident that this story still needs to be made intelligible *as* history? And in order to do this, is it not inevitable that historians have to make their histories conform to their preferences?

As we might expect, these suggestions were not very well received by historians in the 1970s. They were, after all, being told that objectivity would not get them much further than what mere chroniclers did; and perhaps not even that far, for the mere fact that certain 'facts' had been preserved but not others at once raised very disturbing questions about the alleged objectivity of 'facts'. Science was definitely not a model for historians. As the Greeks had rightly insisted, history was a Muse. This was not, of course, an original idea. Just this very argument had been eloquently put forward in a classic essay with the evocative title 'Clio: A Muse' by George Macaulay Trevelyan, first published in 1930.[5] But White gave the idea quite a radical spin by proposing that the 'preferences' from which no historian could escape came under three headings: 'ideology', 'argument or explanation', and 'emplotment'. These in turn were related to the 'formist', 'organicist', 'mechanicist' and 'contextualist' modes and their various correspondences with 'Romance', 'Comedy', 'Tragedy' and 'Satire'. From this White reached the somewhat alarming conclusion that all historical writing defined itself by reference to these categories.

White's argument carried the inescapable implication that there could be no 'correct' way of writing history. As he provocatively put it, historians are 'indentured to a choice'. Everyone has a theory, even (perhaps especially) those who think they do not have one. Every history is a 'metahistory', and it either states or it implies a general view of the nature of history. The way in which the 'historical field' takes shape in the historian's mind is ultimately determined at a deep level where each person's mind is biased towards a certain way of making links between data.[6] White's decision to borrow terms from rhetoric to describe this process – his famous 'tropes': metaphor, metonymy, synecdoche and irony – turned out to be both a strength and a weakness. Nancy S. Struever accused White of reducing rhetoric to poetics: 'to reduce rhetoric to a consideration of "style,"' she wrote, 'and then to reduce the consideration of style to a scheme of tropes, is particularly dysfunctional'.[7] This was because history could in no satisfactory way be explained as the study of isolated texts. History was not about such things but about *argument*. Therefore, what was needed was a 'discourse' not of 'tropes' but of 'topics' which Struever described as having the function of specifying 'our common humanity not as a set of absolute presuppositions of value and goal' but as 'very complex, open-ended list of approaches, responses, which use relations.'[8]

Struever's argument echoed some isolated voices that had begun to call for a revision of the naively positivistic claims in historical writing well before White ignited the wider debate. As early as 1966, for instance, Quentin Skinner already seemed to take it for granted that he was in the middle of a clear trend away from positivism. Skinner had clear targets in mind; at this time the bulk of Cambridge historians was still quite smug about Skinner's chosen field of specialization, intellectual history, which was widely regarded as not sufficiently scientific because it was not based on empirical 'hard' facts.[9] Although Skinner was confident that positivism was definitely on the wane, he also stated that none of its opponents had so far produced a satisfactory alternative to it. Most of them tended to fall back on a vague 'common sense' which was at best ambiguous. Consequently, if it seemed imperative for historians to abandon the obsession with positivist empiricism, it was no less urgent for them to find a convincing alternative to it. Here, unfortunately, Skinner had similarly inconclusive suggestions to make about what he called 'a more descriptive, more inclusive, perhaps even much more metaphorical language for the whole business of trying to provide explanations of the past'.[10]

Despite its relative tentativeness, Skinner's very reference to language already pointed to a radically different perspective. His suggestion that the language used by historians needed to be 'even much more metaphorical' suggests an awareness of the importance of intuition and poetry in human understanding that modern neuroscience is increasingly emphasising. 'If it is true', writes Iain McGilchrist in his recent study of the structure of the brain,

> that most syntax and vocabulary, the nitty-gritty of language, are in most subjects housed in the left hemisphere, it is nonetheless the right hemisphere which subserves higher linguistic functions, such as understanding the meaning of a whole phrase or sentence in context, its tone, its emotional significance, along with use of humour, irony, metaphor, and so on.[11]

This insistence on metaphor as 'the crucial aspect of language whereby it retains its connectedness with the world'[12] in turn points to the importance of understanding history as a 'traditional' discipline – I use the word, not in the sense of 'old-fashioned' or 'opposed to change', but in the sense of the need to work within a *tradition* of thinking. In this context, despite Struever's criticisms, the importance of White's work is hardly in need of elucidation. In an equally unsympathetic piece published in 1987, for instance, Donald R. Kelley acknowledged the need to engage with White's arguments because of the way they had popularized widespread philosophical perspectives that had persuasively subverted any attempt to get inside the minds of past authors.[13] This was an especially disturbing notion from the perspective of the tradition that Kelley was setting out to defend. As the editor of the *Journal of the History of Ideas*, he must have been aware of the explicit conviction that the founder of that prestigious journal had once expressed: good intellectual history consists in knowing what the author of a given work *intended* to say.[14] In sharp contrast, White's work had alerted historians to a host of recent philosophical trends that seemed to be doing to language what Copernicus had done astronomy, Darwin to biology and Freud to psychology. This, according to Kelley, unhinged the notion of intention in a way that constituted both 'a limitation and a challenge'. 'Language can and must', Kelley recognized, 'accommodate a meaningful dialogue with the past'.[15]

In a memorable paragraph, Kelley reminded his readers that recent historiography had shifted its attention not only from thought to 'discourse' but also from the conscious to the unconscious, from creation to imitation, from intention to meaning, from authorship to readership, from the history of ideas to the 'social history of ideas', from science to the occult, from tradition to 'canon formation', and from the sociology of knowledge to the 'anthropology of knowledge'. The issue, then, was 'how to reconcile efforts of purely historical reconstruction with current "projects" of philosophy, literature, criticism, and the human and natural sciences'.[16]

Skinner's original intuition about the need for a more 'metaphorical language' is not far away from all this, and Kelly takes the fascinating step of reminding his readers of the neglected medieval 'levels of meaning'. These are: (1) the *literal*, involving a historical reconstruction which pays due respect to authorial intention; (2) the *allegorical*, which places texts in a longer intellectual continuum, through the common language and 'prejudices' which allow for an historical understanding of changing meanings; (3) the *moral*, which takes into account the 'ideological' dimensions of discourse; and (4) the *anagogical*, which turns its attention towards the future and to questions of more general 'significance'.[17]

From this perspective Kelley concluded that what historians needed was 'not a rigid *theoria* but a flexible *phronêsis*'.[18] This invocation of *phronêsis* is, like Streuver's, an undisguised appeal to Aristotle. At first sight this might appear unashamedly defensive, but it would be an unforgivable simplification to see here a mere traditionalist or reactionary attitude. In the context of what has happened in much contemporary thought to the assumptions that underpin the 'mediational' structure, appeals to Aristotle might actually appear groundbreaking. The notion of 'intention' exemplified in Arthur Lovejoy's belief that the truth of a text can be established by determining what the author of that text *intended* in writing it, presupposes that human beings are self-sufficient and autonomous individuals with readily recognizable intentions derived from a kind of private language. This still widely-persuasive notion is increasingly revealing itself to be a nonsensical myth. It was Ludwig Wittgenstein who provided the most thorough and devastating criticism of the possibility of a private language. Language, Wittgenstein convincingly argued, is not an abstraction from life but an extension of life: 'to imagine a language means to imagine a form of life'.[19] As we have seen, it is now widely accepted that human beings characteristically reach their beliefs in the context of a tradition, and this means that historical meanings derive much more directly from the linguistic structures present in society than from the mental activity of particular self-sufficient and autonomous individuals.

It is not difficult to understand why such a development should have become a source of some nagging anxieties. The relative ease with which it seems to leave the door open to extreme forms of subjective relativism has in great measure been confirmed by the influential claim of the post-modern sceptics who pronounce the whole of history to be a chimera. There are no fixed or stable meanings, they argue, so texts are open-ended and their readers are free to do whatever they like with them. The reason for this, as Jacques Derrida once argued in a truly remarkable passage, is that 'signification' presupposes that 'each so-called "present" element . . . is related to something other than itself, thereby keeping within itself the mark of the past element, and already letting itself be vitiated by the mark of its relation to the future element'.[20] What this amounts to is that we cannot have knowledge of intentions because we cannot have knowledge of anything outside language; but the reason for this – and this is where all reactionary comments seem justified – is that language does not refer to reality! If language does not refer to reality then history can only aim to be a lower form of fiction. It should not be too hard to identify the resilient survival of Taylor's 'mediational' structure in all this. Language does not refer to reality because the 'mediational' structure has proved defective. Yet, it has not been removed. Indeed, it still seems somehow necessary, but we simply do not have it. To pretend that we do is to deceive ourselves, and to pretend to write history is the biggest deception of all.

There seems to be no way for historians to defend themselves against this unpalatable state of affairs unless they can find a way out of the 'mediational' trap. Modern thought, as we have seen, provides little solace here. But Aristotle's notion of 'actualized knowledge' (*epistemê*) as he explains it in his *de Anima*, does provide a potentially fruitful analysis of the way in which the human mind is capable of attaining unmediated knowledge of the object known. As Charles Taylor puts it,

> just as the real object is what it is because it is shaped by the Form (*eidos*) appropriate to its kind, so the intellect (*nous*) in its own very different way can come to be shaped by different *eidê*. In correct knowledge of an object, the *nous* comes to be shaped by the same *eidos* as forms the object. There is no question here of a copy or a depiction; there is one and only one *eidos* of any kind. When I see this animal and know it is a sheep, mind

and object are one because they come together in being formed by the same *eidos*. That is why it is *actualized* knowledge which forms one with its object. . . . [W]e can think of the Form as a kind of rhythm giving shape to both objects and intellects. Where there is knowledge, the self-same rhythm joins both mind and thing. They become one in this single movement. There is unmediated contact.[21]

It is only in the context of such an unmediated epistemology that Kelley's invocation of *phronêsis* can make proper sense. *Phronêsis* came to be called *prudentia* in the medieval Latin West, so it is commonly translated as 'prudence', one of the four cardinal virtues alongside justice, courage (or fortitude) and temperance. Unfortunately, the modern connotations of the word could not be further removed from the meaning of the term in its classical and medieval settings. Interestingly, the way in which this strange development came about is itself inseparable from the 'mediational' structure; for the emergence of this structure in the early modern period coincided with the eclipse of the tradition of the virtues brought about by the confluence of Cartesianism with the effects that the Reformation had upon Christian ethical thought on either side of the confessional divide.

John Bossy has suggestively traced the origins of this development to the late middle ages. In the course of the fourteenth and fifteenth centuries, there was a detectable shift in Christian moral teaching from a broadly 'communal' approach that gave pride of place to the Seven Deadly Sins, to a more 'individualist' perspective in which the Decalogue became increasingly prominent.[22] This is a complex and controversial topic, but it is clear that the movement was linked to a tradition of thought that sat rather uncomfortably with the attempt to incorporate the writings of Aristotle into Christian theology, an attempt associated particularly with the work of the great thirteenth-century Dominican St Thomas Aquinas. Many theologians saw St Thomas's use of Aristotle, especially the way in which it sought to defend the autonomy of the natural law, as a dangerous and ultimately unacceptable affront upon the absolute sovereignty of the will of God – an influential theological trend known as 'voluntarism'. The historical circumstances were, moreover, particularly propitious for the development of this comparatively defensive attitude. The Black Death and the horrendous suffering it had caused, the Great Schism and the nagging doubts it had engendered, gave rise to a comparatively introverted and defensive spirituality in which men and women felt increasingly compelled to identify more closely with the passion and sufferings of Christ.

There was little room in this climate for any moral teaching based on the life-affirming virtues of the classical, pagan world. The stress was now on the duties and obligations prescribed in the scriptures, and especially in the

Commandments. Pious Christians needed guidelines, directives, rules, 'ways of perfection'.[23] Moreover, the trauma of the Reformation reaffirmed this trend and helped to entrench a persistent rigour in Christian moral teaching that has been with us ever since.

It is true that the challenge of Protestantism led to a reassessment of the thought of St Thomas in Catholic circles: the Catechism of the Council of Trent reiterated the authority of the great Dominican and confirmed his interpretation of the natural law as a reflection of the divine law. Nevertheless, nowhere was this re-evaluation accompanied by a corresponding reassessment of the role of the virtues in the moral life of Christians. The climate was now one of dogmatic re-definition on both sides of the confessional divide and it all went hand in hand with a corresponding need to redefine the obligations and duties that men and women needed to observe in order to make 'progress' in the spiritual life.

It is clear why the virtues did not fit easily into this schema. But, additionally, any attempt to highlight their importance was further hindered by the inescapable impact of the 'mediational' structure. What is quite startling to realize is that, in their apologetic efforts to defend the Christian God against the increasingly intractable problem of evil in the voluntaristic climate that characterized the seventeenth and eighteenth centuries, Christian theologians themselves too often sank deeper and deeper into the very 'mediational' bog that they should have been the first to expose.[24] Descartes's radical separation of mind and body, with its inevitable denigration of the senses and the passions, ironically proved an inescapable temptation for Christian thinkers immersed in a tradition marked by an increasing distrust of the body and a morality of rules and guidelines, duties and obligations. This was just the kind of Christianity that proved so distasteful to some of the greatest minds of the nineteenth century, most notably Friedrich Nietzsche who once memorably remarked that he would be prepared to think more carefully about the alleged truths of the Christian religion if only Christians took the trouble to 'look more redeemed'.[25] Despite the relative improvement on this front since the Second Vatican Council, the legacy of Descartes has entrenched itself so deeply in modern thought that, as Fergus Kerr has convincingly shown, it shows itself worryingly often in most strands of Christian theology.[26]

The term 'prudence' simply does not help in all this. The closest modern equivalent is perhaps Jane Austen's 'good sense', as she used the term in *Sense and Sensibility*, a novel which, in his fifth, posthumous book, Herbert McCabe refers to as 'arguably the best treatise on *prudentia* in English.'[27] According to St Thomas, 'good sense', Aristotle's *phronêsis*, is right practical reason.[28] As McCabe explains, this is the 'disposition of the mind to do well the job of deciding what to do about achieving some good end that we desire'.[29] There is nothing 'mediational' about it. *Phronêsis* is an intellectual virtue, of course, but this in no way prevents it from getting involved in a sensitive evaluation of experience. Indeed, as St Thomas explains it, the role of *phronêsis* necessarily involves a grasp of concrete individual situations such as is impossible to the human intellect alone.[30] Yet, this involvement of the senses goes far beyond the mere mechanical reception of so-called sense data that the 'meditational' structure has so insistently accustomed us to expect.[31] This is why St Thomas insists that besides the 'external' senses, *phronêsis* requires the involvement of a set of 'internal' senses which alone can provide the input of external sense-data with the necessary structure to make them meaningful to human bodily life. These internal senses are: (1) the *sensus communis,* which plays a co-ordinating role; (2) the *imagination*, which in St Thomas's schema plays the role of retaining what it was like to experience something, thus forming a 'storehouse of forms received through the senses'; (3) the *sensus aestimativus*, an 'evaluating' sense through which we grasp the sensual significance of our various individual experiences; and (4) the sense-memory which stores what it was like to have such significant experiences.[32]

It is clear that St Thomas would have readily agreed with the linguistic turn's assumption that whatever has meaning necessarily has a role as part of a structure. But for St Thomas the implications can go much further because they are not vitiated by any form of 'mediation'. He would have been utterly bewildered by the idea that a purely intellectual skill might be capable of finding meaning within a given structure. Instead, he thought that whenever human beings need to refer to individuals as such they have to make direct use *not* of their intellectual faculties but of the kind of interpretation of reality provided by bodily sensation. Admittedly this involved a disposition of the internal senses, but the way in which he understood and explained their operation still attributed much of what became the job of the 'conscious' or 'disengaged' mind in the 'mediational' schema to the sensibility that humans share with other animals.[33]

This unmediated epistemology is what makes it possible for *phronêsis* to be the linchpin of the virtues. It understands the *bodily* interpretation of the world as a fundamental requirement for humans to know anything at all, which, in turn, necessarily involves what modern science has explained as the genetically-received structure of the nervous system. This new scientific outlook has little to do with 'objective' and 'subjective' points of view. As Iain McGilchrist has demonstrated, these are concepts which 'are themselves a product of, and already reflect a "view" of the world'. They are not 'different ways of *thinking about* the world: they are different ways of *being in* the world'.[34]

In an exceptionally suggestive reading of Shakespeare's *Hamlet*, Alasdair MacIntyre points to precisely these mechanisms. What he calls Hamlet's 'epistemological crisis' could only be resolved after Hamlet had laboriously constructed a new narrative that made sense of his previous deception and, in turn, made him aware that what he had now was not the 'right' account but only the best account so far, and that it could still change in unpredictable ways.[35] To see this as a symptom of Shakespearian scepticism entirely misses the point. The point is not that there is no such thing as truth, but that the human quest for truth is progressive and that it can only advance through the construction and re-construction of more adequate *narratives*. After all, we all begin from myths, and if we are not told the right myths at the right age we sooner or later struggle to make sense of reality. All this suggests, in MacIntyre's words, that 'to raise the question of truth need not entail rejecting myth or story as the appropriate and perhaps the only appropriate form in which certain truths can be told'.[36]

Here, at last, we have a solid and persuasive way to undermine the claims of the 'mediational' trap. There can be no such thing as a 'clear and distinct idea' in our mind simply because there cannot be anything in our minds that has not come through the senses.[37] This is what Descartes did not recognise, leading to what MacIntyre calls his 'complex failure'; that is, his going directly against everything he was trying to do by making himself understood through the writing of a dramatic narrative, a personal history, which was itself intrinsically dependent upon the cultural norms and values that he had inherited, the languages in which he wrote, and the very powerful intellectual traditions which influenced him, of which the most conspicuous is none other than the thought of St Augustine.

What is truly staggering is that despite the clear contradiction in Descartes's 'complex failure', the 'mediational' structure should have become so difficult to escape. Take, for example, what most of us think of Galileo. We are quite happy to say that he appealed to the *facts* against the *myths* of Ptolemy and Aristotle. In other words, we argue that Galileo got it right because he got the facts right, and that Ptolemy and Aristotle got it wrong because they got the facts wrong and therefore gave us myths instead. In a deliciously ironic phrase, MacIntyre refers to this as the 'old mythological empiricist view of Galileo'.[38] What Galileo actually did was to give a new *account* of what an appeal to the facts had to be: 'We are apt to suppose', he continues,

> that because Galileo was a peculiarly great scientist, therefore he has his own peculiar place in the history of science. I am suggesting instead that it is because of his peculiarly important place in the history of science that he is accounted a peculiarly great scientist. The criterion of a successful theory is that it enables us to understand its predecessors in a newly intelligible way. . . . It recasts the *narrative* which constitutes the continuous reconstruction of the . . . *tradition*.[39]

Dramatic narrative, MacIntyre reiterates, 'is the crucial form for the understanding of human action'. Natural science, therefore, can only be rational if the writing of a true narrative can be rational. This means that scientific reason has to be subordinate to historical reason, for it can only become intelligible in terms of historical reason. 'And if this is true of the natural sciences', MacIntyre concludes, 'as fortiori it will be true of the social sciences.'[40]

Far from being a lower form of fiction, history emerges from this as a fundamental epistemological tool. It would seem that the only way to establish the superiority of one scientific theory over another is to have a prior understanding of the superiority of one historical narrative over another. In sharp contrast to what the 'mediational' structure so resiliently forces upon us, any theory of scientific rationality has necessarily to be embedded in a philosophy of history. For it is only through the construction of historical narratives that can be rationally compared with one another that it is possible rationally to compare any other theory.[41]

Only when theories are located in history, in other words, is it possible to overcome the 'mediational' trap and its two unpalatable alternatives: dogmatism on the one hand and capitulation to scepticism on the other. Once this is achieved, the door is again wide open to the important role that religion has always played in historical knowledge. Despite their meditational assumptions, historians have never behaved in accordance with the assumptions of scientific objectivity. Whether they like it or not, they are all heirs to the nineteenth-century reaction against the rationalism of the Enlightenment which ushered in the Romantic movement. The ideal of knowledge espoused by Romanticism was not rationalist empiricism but imaginative vision. Where the Enlightenment had defined a people as a mass of separate individuals united artificially, nineteenth-century historians tended generally to evoke a spiritual unity. It was this characteristic that constituted the chief difference between history and antiquarianism, for it was only when history entered into relations with philosophy and produced the new type of philosophical historians – like Hume and Gibbon (who anticipated the trend), and Tocqueville and Michelet, and Burckhardt and Ranke and Marx – that it became one of the great formative elements of modern thought. It was this peculiarity that gave the European historiographical tradition that distinctive ability not merely to preserve the past but also to re-create it and to enter with imaginative sympathy into the lives and thinking processes of past ages and different cultures.

The Romantic movement found its best representatives in Germany, notably in the literature of Schiller and Goethe, in the music of Beethoven, Schumann and Brahms, and in the philosophy of Kant, Fichte, Schelling and Hegel. Although its original inspiration came from the French Enlightenment, the spirit which animated it could not have been further removed from the French cult of 'clear and distinct ideas'. As Christopher Dawson once put it, the Romantic ideal of knowledge was 'that direct intuition of reality by imaginative vision which unites the mind with its object in a kind of vital communion'. By virtually abolishing the rationalist opposition between matter and spirit, together with its dualism of the outer and the inner worlds, the Romantic theory of knowledge made it possible to conceive of the unity of existence as 'a kind of vital rhythm which reconciles opposite and apparently irreconcilable realities into an ultimate harmony'.[42]

It seems fitting to conclude with the most significant thinker whose influence Descartes failed to recognize but who has as good a claim as any to be regarded as the founder of the philosophy of history. St Augustine of Hippo's most ambitious work, *The City of God*, managed to unite in a coherent system two distinct and, up until then, irreconcilable intellectual traditions. The first was Hellenism, which possessed a theory of society and a political philosophy from which St Augustine derived his realization of a universal reasonable order which bound all nature together and governed the course of the stars and the rise and fall of kingdoms alike.[43] The second tradition was, of course, Christianity, which had no philosophy or theories of society or politics but had something that the Greco-Roman world had never developed: a theory of history. There were, of course, plenty of historians in Classical Antiquity, but their aim was overwhelmingly cosmological rather than historical. Time had little significance for them; it was an unintelligible element that intruded as a result of the impermanence and instability of things and became intelligible only insofar as it was regular, recurrent and cyclical. Its only value was in the examples that it gave of moral virtue or political wisdom. Even Thucydides or Polybius saw history as governed by an external necessity, Nemesis or Tyche.

The Hellenic theory of cyclic recurrence seemed to St Augustine to be a natural consequence of the belief in the eternity of the world. But once the doctrine of Creation was accepted, there could be no return. The mystery of time could only be understood in its relationship to the mystery of created being. From this perspective, the identification of time with the movement of the starts became a naïve objectivism which could not explain the grasping of past and future. Since the past had ceased to exist and the future did not yet exist, all that remained was the present of the passing moment. From this St Augustine intuited that the measure of time could not be found in things: it was a spiritual extension.

This new theory of time made possible a new conception of history which itself became a creative process. It no longer repeated itself meaninglessly but grew into an organic unity with the growth of human experience. The past did not die: it became incorporated into humanity. And hence progress became possible, for the life of society and of humanity itself possessed continuity and the capacity for spiritual growth no less than the life of the individual. This vision is much closer to the Romantic ideal of knowledge as inspired by an imaginative vision which unites the mind with the object of knowledge than to the positivist ideal which searches in vain for an objective truth in empirical facts. To evoke St Augustine and the fundamental role that the Christian tradition has played in the development of the West's historical sense should not be seen as an attempt to minimize the tremendous importance of the modern techniques of historical criticism that have contributed so much to our knowledge of the past and will continue to do so. Rather, it should be seen as a salutary reminder that the mastery of these techniques will never produce great history, any more than the mastery of metrical technique can produce great poetry. However uncomfortable historians might feel about it, there can be little doubt that the true sources of their creative power will always lie much closer to a transcendent vision, more akin to the nature of religious contemplation than of empirical verification. History's debt to religion can only be ignored at the cost of doing away with history itself and with the great historiographical heritage that the Judaeo-Christian tradition has bequeathed the modern world.

Notes

1   See, for example, Charles Taylor (1995, 1997), 'Overcoming Epistemology', in *Philosophical Arguments* (Cambridge, MA and London: Harvard University Press), pp. 1–19.

2   See Charles Taylor's reply to Fernando Cervantes (2010), '*Phronêsis* vs Scepticism: An Early Modernist Perspective', *New Blackfriars*, 91: p. 1036; 'Symposium on Charles Taylor with his responses', Kieran Flanagan and Peter C. Jupp (eds) (November, 2010): p. 694.

3   Ibid,. pp. 696–7 (my emphasis).

4   Ibid., pp. 695–6.

5   George Macauley Trevelyan (1930), *Clio, a Muse: and Other Essays* (London: Longmans).

6   Hayden White, *Metahistory: The Historical Imagination in Nineteenth-Century Europe* (Baltimore: The Johns Hopkins University Press, 1973), pp. 1–41.

7   Nancy S. Struever (1980), 'Topics in History', *History and Theory*, 19(4) (December): pp. 66–79 at 66.

8   Ibid., p. 69.

9   The most influential of these in Cambridge was Geoffrey Elton, whose views were put together in Geoffrey Elton (1969), *The Practice of History* (London: Fontana, 1969). It is tempting to imagine Skinner writing with Elton in mind.

10 Skinner (1966), 'The Limits of Historical Explanation', *Philosophy*, 41(157) (July): pp. 199–215 at 215.

11 Iain McGilchrist (2010), *The Master and His Emissary: The Divided Brain and the Making of the Western World* (New Haven and London: Yale University Press, p. 99). 'Metaphor', writes McGilchrist, 'comes *before* denotation'. The 'understanding of language at the highest level . . . the making sense of an utterance in its context, taking into account whatever else is going on, including the tone, irony, sense of humour, use of metaphor, and so on, belong . . . to the right hemisphere'; ibid., pp. 118, 125. See also George Lakoff and Mark Johnson (1999), *Philosophy in the Flesh: The Embodied Mind and Its Challenge to Western Thought* (New York: Basic Books), pp. 123, 129.

12   McGilchrist, *The Master and His Emissary*, p. 125.

13   Donald R. Kelley (1987), 'Horizons of Intellectual History: Retrospect, Circumspect, Prospect', *Journal of the History of Ideas*, 48(1) (January-March): 143–69 at 156.

14   Arthur O. Lovejoy (1938), 'The Historiography of Ideas', *Proceedings of the American Philosophical Society*, 78(4) (March): pp. 529–43.

15   Kelley, 'Horizons', p. 156.

16   Ibid., p. 160.

17   Ibid., p. 166.

18   Ibid., p. 168.

19   Ludwig Wittgenstein (1967), *Philosophical Investigations*, ed. G. E. M. Anscombe and R. Rhees, 3rd edn (Blackwell: Oxford), part 1, §19, p. 8. See also Ludwig Wittgenstein (1969), *On Certainty* (Oxford: Blackwell). On 'intention' see Anscombe's classic study, G. E. M. Anscombe (1963), *Intention*, 2nd edn (Oxford: Blackwell).

20   'Difference', in Jacques Derrida (1982), *Margins of Philosophy*, trans. A. Bass (Brighton: Harvester Press), pp. 1–27.

21   Taylor, reply to Cervantes, pp. 697–8. Taylor is citing *De Anima*, Book 3, 430a20 and 431a1: *'to d' auto estin hê kat' energeian epistêmê tôi pragmati'*. 'Later', explains Taylor in footnote 42, 'Aristotle says that "knowledge is the knowable and sensation is the sensible". This doesn't mean that the sensible and cognitive faculties are identical with the object as a material entity; "for the stone doesn't exist in the soul, but only the form of a stone" (431b22, 432a1). It is in the *eidos* that the mind and object come together.'

22   John Bossy (1985), *Christianity in the West, 1400–1700* (Oxford: Clarendon Press), pp. 35–8, 138–9.

23   The phrase is borrowed from the title of St Teresa's *Camino de Perfección*, which is among the most influential treatises on spirituality in the post-Tridentine age. For a sympathetic counterbalance see Simon Tugwell (1984), *Ways of Imperfection: An Exploration of Christian Spirituality* (London: Darton, Longman and Todd). On St Teresa, one of the most perceptive recent studies in English is Rowan Williams (2004), *Teresa of Avila* (London: Continuum).

24   On this see Michael J. Buckley (1987), *At the Origins of Modern Atheism* (New Haven and London: Yale University Press), pp. 145–85 and passim.

25   Cited in Paul Murray (2006), *The New Wine of Dominican Spirituality* (London: Continuum), p. 46.

26   See especially, Fergus Kerr (1986), *Theology after Wittgenstein* (Oxford: Blackwell), pp. 7–21, and Fergus Kerr (2002), *After Aquinas: Versions of Thomism* (Oxford: Blackwell), pp. 17–34.

27   Herbert McCabe (2008), *On Aquinas*, ed. Brian Davies (London: Continuum), p. 104.

28   St Thomas Aquinas, *Summa Theologiae*, IIa-IIae, 47.1. ad 3.

29   *On Aquinas*, p. 134.

30   *Summa Theologiae*, IIa-IIae, 47.3. ad 2: '. . . *quia infinitas singularium non potest ratione humana comprehendi, inde est quod sunt **incertae providentiae nostrae**, ut dicitur Sap* [*Wisdom* 9, 14]. *Tamen per experientiam singularia infinita reducuntur ad aliqua finita quae ut in pluribus accidunt, quorum cognitio sufficit ad prudentiam humanam*' (St Thomas's emphasis).

31 Even as perceptive and sympathetic a philosopher as Anthony Kenny is misled by a 'mediational' understanding of the senses as mere faculties for understanding the world of sensible experience into dismissing St Thomas's notion of internal senses as 'contradictory'. See McCabe, *On Aquinas*, p. 111.

32 *Summa Theologiae* I, 78.4, resp.

33 St Thomas seems in agreement with the findings of modern neuroscience and cognitive psychology. '. . . abstract reason', write Lakoff and Johnson, 'builds on and makes use of forms of perceptual and motor inference present in "lower" animals . . . Reason is thus not an essence that separates us from other animals; rather, it places us on a continuum with them'; *Philosophy in the Flesh*, p. 4.

34 *The Master and His Emissary*, p. 31 (McGilchrist's emphasis). McGilchrist refers to the Japanese word *kansatsu*, used by Japanese scientists and often translated as 'observe' but in fact closer to our word 'gaze' 'which', writes McGilchrist, 'we use only when we are in a state of rapt attention in which we lose ourselves, and feel connected to the other'. When Japanese scientists observe an object, in other words, they come to feel a 'one-body-ness' with it; ibid., p. 168.

35 'Epistemological crises, dramatic narrative, and the philosophy of science', in Alasdair MacIntyre (2006), *The Tasks of Philosophy*, Selected Essays, Vol. I (Cambridge: Cambridge University Press), pp. 4–6.

36 Ibid., p. 8.

37 *Nihil est in intellectu nisi prius fuerit in sensu*. This is the famous Aristotelian-Thomist dictum that was so often repeated in a derisory spirit by Descartes and his followers.

38 'Epistemological crises', p. 10.

39 Ibid., p. 11 (my emphasis). Iain McGilchrist makes a very similar point when considering the importance of metaphor in our understanding of Galileo; *The Master and His Emissary*, p. 186.

40 Ibid., p. 15 (my emphasis).

41 Ibid., pp. 22–3.

42 Christopher Dawson (1929), *Progress and Religion: An Historical Enquiry* (London: Sheed and Ward), pp. 26, 28. Dawson cites Goethe's memorable phrase: 'My thought is inseparable from its objects – my intuition is itself a thought and my thought an intuition.' In this connection, McGilchrist comments: 'That we take part in a changing world and that the world evokes faculties, dimensions, and characteristics in us, just as we bring aspects of the world into existence, is perhaps the most profound perception of Romanticism', *The Master and Its Emissary*, p. 360.

43 See *De Civitate Dei*, V.11. This is the work of St Augustine the avid reader of Plotinus and Cicero. It was marked by a sense of the aesthetic beauty of order and universal harmony.

Chapter 16

THEOLOGY AND CLASSICS

RICHARD FINN
(Blackfriars Hall, Oxford)

The truth, as St Augustine concedes to Alypius in one of his *Cassiciacum* dialogues, is all too well represented by the figure of Proteus. As often as not, when someone thinks to have truth within grasp, it slips away.[1] The comparison, commonplace in classical literature, now found a new use as Augustine tried his hand at a distinctively Christian philosophy or philosophical theology.[2] Though the figure came with polished ease, he would indeed have to think harder and for much longer about how his classical education related to his vocation as a theologian. There is no reason to think we are absolved from a like labour in reflecting on the relationship between Christianity and Classics.

The relations are in fact so many and complex that they cannot all be encompassed in a single essay, and so the focus here will be on the academic disciplines of Classics and Theology. Certainly, even to discuss the relationship of Theology to Classics is to discuss two protean disciplines whose histories both inside the academy and more widely have long been deeply interwoven, but whose internal coherence, fundamental nature and resultant boundaries have been the subject of much scholarly dispute over the last 150 years. It will be argued in this essay that while Classics generally has gained in coherence, Theology has fragmented and lost its coherent identity in the secular university as a single discipline, but that Theology potentially offers both valuable assistance in correcting distorted perspectives within Classics, and a crucial grounding for Classics, the coherence of which may at the same time be an educational insufficiency.

It was not always a story of disputed changes. Within the English-speaking world of the eighteenth and early-nineteenth centuries, Classics, as that study of a Greek and Latin canon inherited from the Late Roman elites which focused on literary style and fluent command of the languages, served a stable role in the formation of the cultured governing classes. This role was indeed similar to that which such study had once performed when the young St Augustine was initiated into the values and social networks of the empire in Late Antiquity, although in theory (if not always in practice) the virtues involved had been

transposed and integrated into a distinctively Christian ethic (a change in which
Augustine had himself played a role). More narrowly, the Classics taught from
a young age to public schoolboys and perfected in the colleges of Oxford and
Cambridge was closely allied to Theology. The latter was understood primarily
as that study of the Bible, Church Fathers and later divines which prepared
scholars to teach the creed and defining articles of the Protestant Church of
England. This alliance held good from North America where the 'original nine
colonial colleges were founded to provide training for colonial clergy [and] . . .
taught classics and theology', to Africa, where in Sierra Leone, for example,
what became the University College was in the mid-nineteenth century a seminary likewise teaching Classics and Theology.[3]

This relationship between the disciplines was also in large measure paralleled
by that which existed between Classics and Theology within the Catholic world,
its colleges, seminaries and universities in continental Europe and beyond. The
confidence of the sixteenth-century Jesuits in this sequential education was
neatly captured by the inscription which hung from 1551 over the door at the
Collegio Romano describing it as the '*Schola di Grammatica, d'Humanità e
Dottrina Christiana, gratis*'.[4] Jesuit schools, however, were at first distinctive
in the Catholic world for the place given to Greek as well as Latin, and to
the attention paid to the Classical orators, whose rhetorical skills were now to
serve a Christian catechetical and polemical purpose.[5] Catholic theology as the
systematic study and comprehension of *sacra doctrina* necessarily involved a
different understanding of the range and interplay of authorities which oper-
ated to shape its account of Christian orthodoxy, but this did not alter the basic
relationship between the disciplines nor the conviction of their mutual benefit.

In each case, Classics was ancillary to Theology, and its propaedeutic role
was largely to equip the scholar to read or write Christian texts in the classical
languages, as well as to sharpen his (and not her) reasoning skills though the
study of classical philosophy, especially Aristotelian logic, although the metaphysics and ethics of Plato and Aristotle also played varying preparatory roles.
In each case, Theology was properly what in modern parlance would be termed
both a 'dogmatic' and 'systematic' Christian theology, though in practice it
might amount to little more than apologetics.[6] In this old alliance, the historical
study of the early Church belonged within the theological disciplines of either
New Testament studies or Patristics, the dominant interest of which lay in doctrine perceived as a stable body of mutually supporting beliefs, and in the con-
comitant attack on heresies or on other religions external to Christianity. Where
Protestants and Catholics disputed doctrine and church order, study of the early
Church served to quarry support for a presumed uniformity and continuity of
belief on the part of the orthodox party. Protestants focussed in particular on
'the fathers of the first two centuries, who, in their view, remained closer to the

revealed truth of the Bible'.[7] Church history was rarely contextualized within the cultural history of a wider Graeco-Roman world.

Since the mid-nineteenth century, however, these parallels, the underlying relationships between the academic disciplines and the agreed boundaries between them have increasingly broken down. Each academic discipline has undergone significant change in the Anglophone world. The nature of each no longer commands such assent as was formerly shared at least within the churches which once controlled the schools and universities where these disciplines were either introduced or pursued to the highest level. An account of the respective changes forms a necessary preface to consideration of present relations between the disciplines, the territories to which they lay claim and how scholars may best negotiate this terrain.

With respect to Classics as an undergraduate course of study, one widespread change over the long term was the declining importance of Greek and Latin composition. This was determined partly by the changing use to which linguistic competence was to be put, and partly by a lowering of the linguistic competence of many entrants who no longer began both languages at an early age. Composition would be retained either as an optional specialization or on a small scale as a preparatory heuristic exercise within an expanding proportion of the syllabus devoted to language teaching. This resulted at Oxford in the 1850 reform of the *Literae Humaniores* whereby Honour moderations, with the emphasis on language and literature, preceded a Greats course devoted to history and philosophy.[8] This shift is not in itself evidence that the discipline itself was differently conceived beforehand and afterwards, but it could reasonably be asked, for example, whether the place of modern philosophy within the syllabus of Greats at Oxford for much of the period since 1830 (when reference to modern authors was first permitted), unparalleled in Cambridge, indicates a different conception of the discipline in each university.[9] The development at Oxford caused deep concern among those who saw it as tending to an intellectual and moral education severed from a Christian theological context and controls.[10] For a time this development opened up the prospect favoured by the Cambridge don Augustus Vansittart of two schools – 'Oxford classics (philosophical) and Cambridge classics (philological).'[11] It certainly resulted in a discipline at Oxford which refused to this extent the apparent academic closure or self-containment of Classics as an essentially historical study.

Cambridge, however, did not adopt Vansittart's vision. Instead it did much to promote the historically bounded yet multidisciplinary conception of the discipline favoured by many modern scholars whereby the discipline is understood as 'the study of the extended Mediterranean world within a certain timeframe'.[12] This was significantly advanced in Cambridge through its early (if optional) inclusion in the late-nineteenth-century syllabus of archaeology, the history of art and the comparative study of myth and ritual.[13] This gave Classics an ability to contextualize early Christianity, and so to elucidate better the meanings of its texts and practices, but also the potential to reduce the truth claims of Christianity to data in a study of religion. The apparent closure of Classics from modern philosophy might then also shield historians from critical reflection on the presuppositions of the new social sciences, their sometimes thin description of religious practices with an 'in-built secular bias'.[14]

Other changes were also afoot with implications for the relationship of Classics to Theology. The inherited canon of Greek and Roman classics had long given pride of place to what W. R. Connor, in discussing the teaching of Classics in North American universities before the 1960s, identified as 'power, the individuals who wielded that power, the principles that ought to govern the use of power and the effects of power on society'.[15] In the process this canon also gave more detailed attention to some people, times and places than to others: adult male citizens or senatorial elites; cities rather than their rural hinterlands; in particular, Athens of the late fifth and early fourth centuries BC; and Rome from the late Republic to the early Empire. While something of the canon still remains in place, because of its centrality to the high culture of the Graeco-Roman world, and the influence of that culture on the extent and nature of extant artefacts, Classics also changed during the latter half of the twentieth century partly as the multidisciplinary approach opened up exploration of the countryside through land surveys or popular religion through study of myth, religion and finds at shrine sites. It further changed, however, as the 'new humanities' in social science opened up questions concerning the negotiation of power through cultural productions and performances, and as social change raised questions about the role of women and slaves. Thus, 'Roman historical studies have moved, as E. J. Champlin remarked, "downward, outward, and later" – downward, to the study of those excluded from the political power, especially slaves and women; outward, to the boundaries of the classical world; and later, to the world of late antiquity and to the rich interior landscape it offers.'[16] For much the same reasons, the canon of texts to be studied at university widened to give new prominence to the ancient novel and lyric poetry.[17] This shift had the potential to direct the attention of theologians away from the Fathers' writings, their abstract doctrines, to how ordinary Christians lived and worshipped, and to the relationship between elite discourse and popular piety.

What, then, of changes in the discipline of Theology? In David Lodge's novel *Deaf Sentence* its chief protagonist, a retired professor of English, observes in his diary that 'academic theologians these days tend to be a rather sceptical lot, and profess something called Religious Studies rather than Christianity or any other faith'.[18] In describing the academic as 'professing' Religious Studies, Lodge's bemused diarist allows us to hear a comic dissonance between teaching as a 'professor' in the secular academy and the traditional Christian's 'profession of faith'. Even where the scholar is herself or himself a practising Christian, Theology in such a setting within the English-speaking world is often held to be a properly non-confessional discipline. The very notion that Christian discourse about God should lay claim to the title and field of 'Theology' *tout court* appears implausible and morally suspect from the perspective of post-holocaust, multicultural Western societies. How has Theology developed to reach this point, and where have these developments left the relationship of Theology to Classics?

In arriving at an answer, changes within Oxford and Cambridge over the last century and a half may again prove helpful as indicative of Theology as it has emerged from strictly confessional settings. A key element in both universities was clearly the challenge posed to orthodox Anglicanism, as it was understood and defended by the late eighteenth century, both from a Darwinian theory of evolution and from the rise in German scholarship of form criticism as this touched upon the composition history of the Pentateuch and of the New Testament. It should be noted, however, that this was not at first a problem about the coherence or goal of an academic discipline in the sense of a subject taught as an interrelated set of studies at school and university. The Cambridge fellow Herbert Marsh could write in his 1792 *An Essay on the Usefulness and Necessity of Theological Learning to Those Who Are Designed for Holy Orders* that 'theological learning forms no necessary part of our academical education'.[19]

At Cambridge 'there was no systematic undergraduate teaching in Theology until the 1870's'.[20] Rather, individual theologians (often classical scholars by training) who held university chairs or college fellowships came to hold differing positions in taking up the challenges of German biblical scholarship in particular, and their differences in relation to the once-defining articles of the Anglican church no longer cost them tenure of their posts nor, in some cases at least, ecclesiastical advancement. Thus, Brooke Foss Westcott, Regius Professor of Divinity at Cambridge from 1870 until his elevation to the see of Durham in 1890, could assert with some vehemence how he objected to the thirty-nine articles '*altogether*, and not to any particular doctrines: I have at times fancied that it is presumptuous in us to attempt to define, and to determine what Scripture has not defined; to limit when Scripture has placed no boundary; to exact what the Apostles did not require; to preach explicitly what they applied practically. The whole tenor of Scripture seems to me opposed to all dogmatism, and full of all application; to furnish us with rules of life, and not food for reason.'[21] Julius Hare and F. D. Maurice came to hold differing views on subscription to the thirty-nine articles and on baptism.[22] At the same time, what united these theologians was a conviction that theology had to engage with the questions raised by German scholarship or changing accounts of natural history derived geology or evolutionary biology. Joseph Barber Lightfoot, elected Hulsean Professor of Divinity in 1861, made Lady Margaret's Professor in 1875, and appointed Bishop of Durham from 1879, had declared in 1855 that 'the timidity which shrinks from the application of modern science or criticism to the interpretation of the Holy Scriptures evinces a very unworthy view of its character . . . It is against the wrong application of such principles . . . that we must protest . . . From the full light of science and criticism we have nothing to fear.'[23] The advent of an undergraduate Theology course saw such critical engagement included within a syllabus of subjects shaped by Anglican theological tradition, but which did not itself require that answers to one set of theological questions be integrated with those to other such questions. Such integration as existed was probably in large measure the product of the student's prior confessional background, and the influence of individual tutors, more than an outcome of the syllabus itself.

At Oxford, there was likewise no Theology honours school before 1872. While the year before had seen the abolition of any test to determine religious orthodoxy as prerequisite for graduation as a Master of Arts, the history of the Oxford Movement exerted different pressures upon Oxford Theologians. The new degree was theoretically open to non-Anglicans but was clearly vocational with Anglican ordination as its goal, and its subject matter necessarily reflected this: 'The emphasis was on knowledge of the *subject-matter* of all the Pauline epistles as well as the four Gospels and Acts and of four books of the Old Testament. The other subjects were dogmatics (in 1873 the texts were the catechetical lectures of Cyril of Jerusalem, Irenaeus *Adversus Haereses*, III, the Articles, and the first two books of the seventeenth-century Bishop Bull's *Defensio Fidei Nicaenae*); the history of the early Church; apologetics (Butler's *Analogy*, Tertullian's *Apologia*, and Book I of Hooker); liturgy (including the Book of Common Prayer as well as the ancient liturgies); and textual criticism.'[24] Examiners had to be Anglican clergymen, and this vocational matrix was not seriously questioned until the early twentieth century. The fact that teaching was overwhelming provided by tutors who were also Anglican college chaplains long secured some significant if varied dogmatic coherence for the subject.[25] Even in this context, however, the only detailed study of the Oxford Theology Faculty in the period from 1850 until 1932 acknowledges that it was characterized by 'methodological pluralism' and observes that 'it is impossible to discern any satisfactory consensus among Oxford theologians as to how to talk about God'.[26]

Already by 1911, the Regius Professor Henry Scott Holland was privately proposing that 'the religious phenomena of humanity should be studied in a University, not in relation to any dogmatic position, but simply as a body of fact and experience which can be defined, classified, examined, compared and discussed according to the intellectual standards of historical and philosophical criticism'.[27] What in fact developed at Oxford after the First World War was effectively a school of liberal Protestant Theology determined in part by the eventual inclusion within the Theology faculty of experts within the constituent sub-disciplines of theology who were not Anglican ministers. Senior members of the Congregationalist and Unitarian colleges, Mansfield and Manchester college respectively, though institutionally independent of the university, became able to join the faculty. W. B. Selbie, Principal of Mansfield, was co-opted onto the Faculty Board in 1913 and repeatedly re-elected. His fellow nonconformist, George Gray, an outstanding Old Testament scholar, was appointed Grinfield Lecturer in the Septuagint in 1919 and was likewise a Faculty Board member.[28] In 1914, lectures by teachers at Mansfield and Manchester appeared on the faculty lecture lists, and in 1920 a university statute recognized the BD and DD as being in Christian Theology rather than specifically the doctrine of the Anglican church.[29] The restriction on examiners being Anglican clerics was lifted in 1922, and two years later Selbie became the first Free Church examiner in the theology schools.[30] It was likewise a Mansfield nonconformist, C. H. Dodd who became University Lecturer in New Testament in 1926, and Grinfield Lecturer in 1929.[31] When Henry Wheeler Robinson, a leading scholar in Old Testament studies, arrived as Principal of Regent's Park College in 1927 he was swiftly made a university examiner, lecturer and tutor. In 1937 he became the first nonconformist to chair the Faculty of Theology.[32]

This meant that a broadly liberal Protestant school did not share a wholly unified theological vision, but that the coherence of the discipline as taught might in some cases be (variously) assured through the nonconformist and Anglican ministerial training colleges which provided their students with supplementary courses, and which in time became Permanent Private Halls (Mansfield, 1955; Regent's Park, 1957; Manchester, 1990–6; Wycliffe, 1996; St Stephen's House, 2003). In the aftermath of the Second Vatican Council the faculty would be further altered by the inclusion of Catholics, and the variety of ways in which the coherence of the discipline might optionally be assured for individual students increased to include that offered by Catholicism, with supplementary courses delivered at Blackfriars, a Permanent Private Hall from 1994.

The Oxford syllabus expanded in the later twentieth century to include papers which studied non-Christian religions from religiously neutral or otherwise non-Christian perspectives. By the beginning of the present century, the Oxford BA syllabus retained only ghostly echoes of the degree's vocational origin (the compulsory focus on Scripture and the development of doctrine to 451, the required discussion of such doctrine in the light of German scholarship, and the relative inattention to ecclesiology and the sacraments of the Church) amid a number of 'tracks' or pathways through the degree and a plethora of optional papers. Whether the current Oxford BA is one of Christian Theology as a coherent, systematic discipline or of Religious Studies (of one of several kinds) is in large part what the student makes of it. The faculty in which he or she studies does not so much share a common academic discipline as offer a common home for academics of varied religious beliefs or none who are expert in different aspects, broadly historical or doctrinal, of the world's major religions. Here, too, there are ghosts from the past, key professorships which remained tied to Anglican orders and cathedral canonries.

On the other hand, the Permanent Private Halls, Anglican, Baptist and Catholic, continue to offer varied contexts in which more or less coherent syntheses of Christian doctrine can be constructed either through ministerial training courses or, if desired by the student, through guided pathways within the Theology BA supplemented by additional courses. The Cambridge Theological Federation offers similar possibilities. It has been argued that 'theology itself as an academic discipline has tended to fragment into a variety of discrete activities' mastered by professionals who are rarely if at all required to synthesize the fruits of these multiple labours.[33] The histories of Oxford and Cambridge theology at least partly bear out this verdict. The secular faculty comprises academics whose particular theological expertise is not essentially directed by that department towards a coherent overview of its discipline, but only provides those who desire such a good with the skills and knowledge that may function as building blocks in a structure the architecture of which is not the faculty's responsibility.

What has been the upshot of the changes within these university disciplines? Within ancient history, they have led to the ready embrace within its bounds of Early Church history, and of approaches to doctrinal controversy strongly informed by wider reflection on social history and the negotiation of power and social standing. As Averil Cameron has written: '[I]t has been one of the major changes of the last generation that people who would once have considered themselves "ancient historians" now see Christian and other religious material as forming a central part of their concerns, indeed in some cases *the* central part.'[34] In the process, the object of study has come to be differently perceived and construed: 'The organization of academia and the rapid growth of religious studies programmes are . . . significant institutional factors in the shift to "early Christian studies"'.[35] Severed from the theological interest in identifying and defending continuity in belief and practice, historical study has shifted from thinking about the Early Church as a single developing entity to the identification and interrelation of early 'Christianities.'

Much good has been claimed for this development which should not be denied. Early Christian studies are sensitive to the role of classical culture within Christianity as well as to the porous boundaries between Christianity and other religions, or religious practices and beliefs. Peter Brown's *The Body and Society*, for example, set sexual renunciation by Late Antique Christians within a medical and philosophical context in which its symbolic significance is more clearly recognized. Christian theology which has widely come to accept the significance of tradition in arriving at normative belief (rather than reliance on *sola scriptura*) is well served by studies that prevent anachronistic readings of the past and which allow past Christians to make their voices better heard in their complexity and variety.[36] Thus, Paul Bradshaw has challenged the simplistic assumption of once uniform rites common to the churches of the first few centuries prior to later liturgical development.[37] Theology can only welcome the broader concern within modern Classics to question the portrayals and social articulation of power that for so long shaped the classical canon. St Augustine, in the *City of God*, insisted on adopting a historical and theological perspective that stripped the Roman empire of a false glory: 'Why this hiding behind talk of praise and of victory? Once the hindrances of a crazy imagination have been cleared away, let the unvarnished deeds be recognized; let them be weighed unvarnished, judged in their unvarnished state.'[38] Likewise, early Christian studies have benefitted from the Classicists' movement of interest 'downward, outward, and later' noted earlier. This is reflected in work on the social teaching of the Early Church and its impact on Late Antique society.[39]

However, both theology as Religious Studies, and theology as the confessional discipline of faith seeking understanding may also have pertinent criticisms to make, and be able to supply a necessary corrective to the new Classics. It will be suggested in this final part of the essay that both give rise to doubts about current readings of motive in early Christian studies, while Christian theology poses valuable questions about the place of Classics in a wider scheme of education. In the first case, a recurrent temptation or strategy in the new Classics, under the influence of its long interest in power and more recent hermeneutic suspicions about power, has been a reductionist account of motivation in the history of theological dispute. Raymond van Dam offers a suitable recent instance of this tendency: 'Just as earlier arguments over orthodoxy and heresy had been disputes over identity and authority, so these new [Christological] controversies should be interpreted as idioms for articulating the ecclesiastical roles of emperors and the relative power of bishops. Through a discourse over Christology, people tried to imagine the contours of a distinctively eastern empire.' We are to contrast what was apparently at stake with the real underlying dynamic of political competition for status: 'Cyril of Alexandria engineered the deposition of Bishop Nestorius of Constantinople, ostensibly over disagreements about Christological doctrines.'[40] The question is why we should accept this reductionist interpretation.

It is not necessarily a simple question of good versus poor scholarship. This can be seen by contrasting the characterization of Augustine's ambition arrived at by two undoubtedly fine scholars, James O'Donnell, Professor of Classics at Georgetown, and the late Professor Henry Chadwick, whose home was long within the theology faculties of Oxford and Cambridge. Neither of their biographies depends for its viewpoint on material unknown to the other. Both recognize the powerful drive that Augustine saw in himself, but each moves towards a tonally and substantially distinct presentation of their subject's moral character: O'Donnell perceives an unceasing self-regard: 'What Augustine shared with the more flamboyant of his ascetic contemporaries was the instinct, not to say the deliberate purpose, of self-promotion and self-presentation.'[41] What does the qualifier 'not to say' effect here? It intimates a negative judgement with which the author does not quite wish to identify himself. A little later, however, the judgement is explicitly asserted: '[F]or all the time we can hear his voice, he lived at the centre of this expanding pool of fame, and he worked very hard to make it grow.'[42] Chadwick understands an earlier and proud self-regard as subverted from within by the author of the *Confessions* who uses 'his mastery of language not to evoke admiration but for a religious end. The religious content of the book is never the means to achieve the end of an exquisite style or the applause of his readers.'[43] For O'Donnell, means and end are reversed: 'When writing about his first book in the *Confessions*, he reproached himself for his worldly ambition, even as, with the *Confessions*, he was carrying out an ecclesiastical version of the same social climbing.'[44] O'Donnell, it appears, does not allow the good which Augustine is explicitly focussed upon to be the good which in fact motivates him. There is a form of disbelief about the hold of such a good upon Augustine's mind. It is hard to see how such disbelief can be substantiated except by a meta-narrative or anthropology external to the evidence of the text, something akin to Nietzsche's claims that apparently Christian beliefs were (in Alasdair MacIntyre's words) 'unrecognized expressions of and masks concealing a resentful will to power'.[45]

A similar contrast recurs when we compare the two biographers in their approach to Augustine's adherence to Manichaeanism. In O'Donnell's judgement: 'Manichaeism was . . . the one truly impassioned religious experience of [Augustine's] life.'[46] It is again far from clear what account of the passions this could depend upon. Chadwick is more circumspect: 'being by his own account a very zealous member . . . He did not think of Manichee adherence as a break with Christ, but only with the Church of which he was highly critical . . . After his conversion to Christianity a Manichee reader of the Confessions named Secundinus told him he had never really assimilated the great truths; and probably his mind always had mental reservations about some of the mythological clap-trap.'[47] It is hard to avoid the conclusion that the scholars concerned approach their subject with opposing sympathies.

Alongside, and possibly behind, the shifts in characterization lie more diffuse attitudes towards religion in general and Christianity in particular. O'Donnell describes the absence of many North African Christians from frequent church attendance by relating that 'the bulk of the Christian population made do without the weekly inoculation of ritual'.[48] Whose perspective is being given by the metaphor of inoculation? From the beneficial reminder of the complexity and pluriformity of early Christianities mentioned above, the Classics professor now makes the further claim that Augustine 'and the other visionary leaders of that time, many of whom have been long acclaimed as "Fathers of the Church" more appositely than their admirers knew, were indeed the people who invented the belief system we call Christianity'.[49] It would of course not be wholly impossible to mount an argument for so sweeping a conclusion, and early Christian studies would provide necessary evidence of diversity in belief and practice; but this would remain a highly tendentious conclusion and a *theological* conclusion at that rather than a simple historical fact. Paul Ricoeur has written that 'the purpose of all interpretation is to conquer a remoteness, a distance between the past cultural epoch to which the text belongs and the interpreter himself'.[50] Christian theology, then, has at least the minimal task with respect to those Classicists who engage in early Christian studies of reminding them that this distance exists in the first place. Christian concern for doctrine, worship and discipleship may be motivated in some part by reasoning and desires now alien to the thought world of these scholars. Peter Brown has written of how a new narrative was generated by St Augustine and other Christians in the late fourth and fifth centuries by virtue of which the believer was 'poised . . . between two cultures', Catholic and profane.[51] Classicists need to recollect the distance as well as the overlap between these two cultures, and to attend to the ways in which such distances were constructed and negotiated.

Finally, can theology invite the Classicist to integrate her or his understanding of the Ancient World within a larger philosophical, ethical and theological formation? Classicists, like other scholars in the humanities are often reluctant to contextualize their studies in any broader account of education. An old 'English University tradition in which the university is assumed to be the place where the moral character of students is determined' and where the humanities were regarded as central to that formative task, has passed into history.[52] With the demise of this unifying goal, intellectual as well as moral virtues may be impaired. Alasdair MacIntyre has noted that modern research universities suffer first from the lack of 'any large sense of and concern for enquiry into the relationships between the disciplines and, second, any connection of the disciplines as each contributing to a single shared enterprise' which forms 'a certain kind of shared understanding'.[53] This concern echoes that of Stanley Hauerwas that 'too often university curriculums make it impossible for anyone, Christian and non-Christian alike', to make sense of the world in which we find ourselves.[54] MacIntyre clearly doubts whether such integration can occur in universities where 'by restricting reference to God to departments of theology, such universities render their secular curriculum Godless', a condition which he understands to involve not just 'the subtraction of God from the range of objects studied, but also and quite as much the absence of any integrated and overall view of things'.[55] Reflection on the academic history of Classics and Theology at Oxbridge bears out MacIntyre's conviction to the extent that even these Theology faculties do not in themselves teach an agreed, coherent account of Theology as a discipline. MacIntyre judges such disconnection between disciplines to be of grave concern for our wider polity. Yet, it is also clear that academic Theology when synthesized within a number of confessional perspectives continues to hold out the promise of an integrated Christian vision and formation. The challenge is to find better and affordable ways for those students, Classicists as well as Theologians, who so desire it to be formed in such a vision while gaining the specialized knowledge and skills taught in the secular faculties.

Notes

1   Augustine, *Contra Academicos*, III, 6, 13.
2   Eugene TeSelle (1970), *Augustine the Theologian* (London: Burns and Oates), pp. 83–4.
3   Joanne R. Euster (1995), 'The Academic Library: Its Place and Role in the Institution', in Gerard B. McCabe and Ruth J. Person (eds.), *Academic Libraries: Their Rationale and Role in American Higher Education* (Westport, CT and London: Greenwood Press), p. 1; Gerald T. Rimmington (1965), 'The Development of Universities in Africa', in *Comparative Education*, 1(2): pp. 105–12, at p. 105.
4   John W. O'Malley (1995), *The First Jesuits* (Cambridge MA: Harvard University Press), p. 205.
5   Ibid., p. 215.
6   For a discussion of these terms, see John Webster (2007), 'Introduction: Systematic Theology', in John Webster, Kathryn Tanner and Ian Torrance (eds), *The Oxford Handbook of Systematic Theology* (Oxford: Oxford University Press), p. 1.
7   Elizabeth A. Clark (2008), 'From Patristics to Early Christian Studies', in Susan Ashbrook Harvey and David G. Hunter (eds), *The Oxford Handbook of Early Christian Studies* (Oxford: Oxford University Press), pp. 7–41, at p. 9.
8   W. H. Walsh (2000), 'The Zenith of Greats', in M. G. Brock and M. C. Curthoys (eds), *The History of the University of Oxford*, Vol. VII, 'Nineteenth-Century Oxford, Part 2' (Oxford: Clarendon Press), pp. 311–26, at p. 313.
9   Ibid., p. 312.
10 M. G. Brock (2000), 'A "Plastic Structure"', in Brock and Curthoys, *The History of the University of Oxford*, pp. 1–66, at pp. 25–6 and p. 31.

11 Christopher Stray (1999), 'The First Century of the Classical Tripos (1822–1922): High Culture and the Politics of Curriculum', in Stray (ed.), *Classics in 19th and 20th Century Cambridge: Curriculum, Culture and Community* (Cambridge: The Cambridge Philological Society), pp. 1–14, at p. 6.

12 Amy Richlin (1989), '"Is Classics Dead?" The 1988 Women's Classical Caucus Report', in Phyllis Culham and Lowell Edmunds (eds), *Classics, A Discipline and Profession in Crisis?* (Lanham, MD, New York and London: University Press of America), pp. 51–65, at p. 64.

13 Mary Beard (1999), 'The Invention (and Re-Invention) of "Group D": An Archaeology of the Classical Tripos, 1879–1984', in Stray, *Classics in 19th and 20th Century Cambridge*, pp. 95–134, at p. 104 and pp. 122–3.

14 John Milbank (2006), *Theology and Social Theory: Beyond Secular Reason*, 2nd edn (Oxford: Blackwell Publishing), p. xii.

15 W. R. Connor (1989), 'The New Classical Humanities and the Old', in Culham and Edmunds, *Classics, A Discipline and Profession in Crisis?* pp. 27–38, at p. 28.

16 Connor, 'The New Classical Humanities and the Old', p. 32.

17 Ibid., p. 29.

18 David Lodge (2008), *Deaf Sentence* (London: Penguin), p. 113.

19 David M. Thompson (2008), *Cambridge Theology in the Nineteenth Century: Enquiry, Controversy and Truth* (Aldershot: Ashgate), p. 31.

20 Ibid., p. 7.

21 Ibid., p. 100.

22 Ibid., pp. 91–2.

23 Ibid., p. 107.

24 Peter Hinchliff, 'Religious Issues, 1870–1914', in Brock and Curthoys, *The History of the University of Oxford*, pp. 97–112, at p. 98.

25 It was only in the 1960s that Maurice Wiles succeeded in securing three faculty lectureships independent of the colleges. F. M. Turner (1994), 'Religion' in Brian Harrison (ed.), *The History of the University of Oxford*, Vol. VIII, *The Twentieth Century* (Oxford: Clarendon Press), pp. 293–316, at p. 305.

26 Daniel Inman 'God in the Academy: The Reform of the University of Oxford and the Practice of Theology, 1850–1932', Unpublished D.Phil. thesis, p. 25. I am most grateful to the Rev. Dr Inman for permission to cite this invaluable and detailed study.

27 Cited in Inman, 'God in the Academy', p. 197.

28 Elaine Kaye (1996), *Mansfield College, Oxford: Its Origin, History, and Significance* (Oxford: Oxford University Press), p. 157.

29 Kaye, *Mansfield*, p. 154; Turner, 'Religion', p. 296 and 305–6; Inman 'God in the Academy', p. 239.

30 Inman, 'God in the Academy', p. 239; Kaye, *Mansfield*, p. 154, n. 27.

31 Kaye, *Mansfield*, p. 175.

32 Turner, 'Religion', p. 297.

33 Stephen F. Fowl (1997), 'Introduction' in *The Theological Interpretation of Scripture: Classic and Contemporary Readings* (Oxford: Blackwell Publishing), pp. xii–xxx, at p. xiv.

34 Averil Cameron (2006), 'New Themes and Styles in Greek Literature, a Title Revisited', in Scott Johnson (ed.), *Greek Literature in Late Antiquity: Dynamism, Didacticism, Classicism* (Aldershot: Ashgate), pp. 11–28, at p. 17.

35 Elizabeth A. Clark, 'From Patristics to Early Christian Studies', p. 15.
36 For the 'quiet acceptance' of tradition as a 'theological norm', see Anna Williams, 'Tradition', in *The Oxford Handbook of Systematic Theology*, pp. 362–77, at p. 375.
37 Cf. Paul F. Bradshaw (1992), *The Search for the Origins of Early Christian Worship* (London: SPCK).
38 Augustine, *City of God*, III, 14: *Quid mihi obtenditur nomen laudis nomenque victoria? Remotis obstaculis insanae opinionis facinora nuda cernantur, nuda pensantur, nuda iudicentur.*
39 Cf. Susan Holman (2001), *The Hungry Are Dying: Beggars and Bishops in Roman Cappadocia* (Oxford: Oxford University Press); Richard Finn OP (2006), *Almsgiving in the Later Roman Empire, Christian Promotion and Practice* (Oxford: Oxford University Press), pp. 313–450; Pauline Allen, Wendy Mayer and Bronwen Neil (2009), *Preaching Poverty in Late Antiquity: Perceptions and Realities* (Leipzig: Evangelische Verlagsanstalt).
40 Raymond Van Dam (2008), 'The East (1): Greece and Asia Minor', *The Oxford Handbook of Early Christian Studies*, pp. 323–41, at p. 334.
41 James O'Donnell (2005), *Augustine, Sinner and Saint: A New Biography* (London: Profile), p. 88.
42 Ibid., p. 89.
43 Henry Chadwick (2009), *Augustine of Hippo, A Life* (Oxford: Oxford University Press), p. 95.
44 O'Donnell, *Augustine*, p. 138.
45 Alasdair MacIntyre (2009), *God, Philosophy, Universities: A Selective History of the Catholic Philosophical Tradition* (Lanham, MD and Plymouth: Rowman and Littlefield), p. 177.
46 O'Donnell, *Augustine*, p. 47.
47 Chadwick, *Augustine*, pp. 14–15.
48 O'Donnell, *Augustine*, p. 32.
49 Ibid., p. 194.
50 Paul Ricoeur (2008), p. 16, cited Niketas Siniossoglou, *Plato and Theodoret: The Christian Appropriation of Platonic Philosophy and the Hellenic Intellectual Resistance* (Cambridge: Cambridge University Press), p. 15.
51 Peter Brown (1995), *Authority and the Sacred: Aspects of the Christianization of the Roman World* (Cambridge: Cambridge University Press), p. 24.
52 Stanley Hauerwas (2007), *The State of the University: Academic Knowledges and the Knowledge of God* (Oxford: Blackwell Publishing), p. 6.
53 MacIntyre, *God, Philosophy, Universities*, p. 174.
54 Hauerwas, *The State of the University*, p. 2.
55 MacIntyre, *God, Philosophy, Universities*, p. 17.

Chapter 17

Liturgy, Music and Theology in the English Choral Tradition

John Harper
(Bangor University)

In an influential lecture about the nature of liturgy delivered in 1981, Aidan Kavanagh stated: 'A liturgical act is a theological act of the most all-encompassing, integral, and foundational kind' (Kavanagh 1984, p. 89). His own thinking extended from Alexander Schmemann's earlier observation that liturgy 'is the ontological condition of theology, of the proper understanding of *kerygma*, of the Word of God' (Schmemann 1963, p. 175). Kavanagh set this *theologia prima* against the more familiar *theologia secunda*, a theology which 'since the high Middle Ages with the advent of the university and of scientific method . . . is something done in academies out of books by elites with degrees producing theologies of this and that' (Kavanagh 1984, p. 74).

In a number of late medieval and early modern institutions in which the pursuit of Kavanagh's *theologia secunda* prospered, worship enhanced by music was also a high priority. The statutes of Magdalen College, Oxford (1480), are typical in setting forth these two priorities: scholarship and liturgical prayer. The scholarly function was led by the 40 fellows of the college, together with 30 undergraduates (demies); the intercessory function was principally delegated to the four chaplains, eight clerks and sixteen boy choristers – though all the fellows were expected to be competent in singing plainsong. However, '[i]t was assumed that most of the Fellows . . . would immediately begin to study theology' (Harriss 2008, pp. 30–2).

Unlike collegiate churches (including secular cathedrals) and monasteries, where study had to take its place within the constant round of services of the daily Office and Mass, the new university colleges made stronger delineation between scholarship and teaching on the one hand and the conduct of the daily round of the liturgy on the other. That liturgy included considerable musical embellishment, notably polyphony intended for the extended range of the later-fifteenth-century choral ensemble that made full use of boys as skilled singers. The majority of extant polyphonic music of the period was intended for Mass, Vespers and the evening Antiphon. Much of it was composed by the new breed of choir-masters who emerged in the second half of the fifteenth century. These were skilled men, not necessarily ordained, who were recruited to oversee the musical training and direction of the boy choristers in particular and the choral music in general in the colleges, as well as in some household chapels (notably the Chapel Royal) and in monastic and cathedral Lady Chapels (Bowers 1999).

Such persons include the earliest recipients of university music degrees in Britain: Henry Abyndon (d. 1497), the first recorded supplicant, was admitted to the degree of Bachelor of Music at Cambridge in 1464, and to a doctorate a year later, during his tenure of the post of master of the choristers at the Chapel Royal (Bowers 2001). Knowledge of the science and practice of music was expected of those supplicating for a degree in music, but no period of residence for study was required: the submission took the form of musical composition in which the necessary knowledge of the science and practice of music was expected to be displayed.

Music was, however, part of the university curriculum; not the practice of music, but the conceptual study of music based on number in the work of Pythagoras, and on the philosophy of Plato. It was most often studied through the neo-Platonic writing of Boethius in *De institutione musicae*, a work which retained its place in the university statutes at Oxford as late as the mid-nineteenth century (Caldwell 1986, p. 201). However, among the Church Fathers, it was Augustine who made the strongest case first for the study of the worldly subjects of the liberal arts (including music) 'as integral to the proper formation of the Christian', and second for the recognition of music as 'one of the disciplines that enabled the mind to transcend sensual reality and rise to a knowledge of rational truth, to a knowledge of the divine' (Bower 2002, p. 141).

The survival of these late medieval choral foundations in both cathedrals and university colleges is a remarkable and particular British phenomenon. They have persisted, notwithstanding the upheaval of the sixteenth-century Reformation, their dissolution in the seventeenth-century Commonwealth, and the financial demands and social and religious changes of the twentieth century; indeed their cultural profile is currently not only high but international. The carol service broadcast from King's College Chapel, Cambridge, each Christmas Eve, is a worldwide event with almost as many listeners as the total population of England. Not only have the medieval foundations been sustained, but newer nineteenth- and twentieth-century cathedrals have used them as models for their own choral provision (within their financial resources). Furthermore, in the nineteenth century, King's College, London, and Royal Holloway College included choral provision from their initial foundation, and both continue to sustain significant choral activity in their chapel services today. Similarly, most of the colleges of Durham University have also been furnished with chapels in the manner of Oxford and Cambridge, and a number have organ scholars, while choral scholarships are offered in the cathedral. In the same way, a number of other cathedrals in university cities offer organ and choral scholarships for undergraduate and graduate students.

To some extent Oxford and Cambridge college choirs are more closely integrated with the academy than at their inception. The organ and choral scholars are usually students of the college. Since most Oxford and Cambridge colleges began to admit both male and female undergraduates in the last quarter of the twentieth century, there has been a rapid blossoming of mixed chapel choirs, some of which match or even surpass the standards of the ancient choral foundations with boy choristers. An increasing number of colleges now engage a professional musician to direct or at least oversee the chapel music. Not all the directors are engaged in university teaching; similarly, not all organ scholars and only a minority of choral scholars are reading music for their degree. Nevertheless academic study and choral worship are joint endeavours for a significant number of students. However, there is rarely a direct relationship between chapel worship and academic study, either for musical director or music students; the same disconnection may be observed with regard to liturgy and theology with regard to both chapel clergy and student of theology. These musical and theological disconnections are rooted in history.

Aidan Kavanagh, in the first of his lectures published in *On Liturgical Theology*, laments the early separation of the pastoral from the academy. In considering three problems facing the discourse between Church and World, he observes: 'The pastoral quality faded rapidly in the West as theology focused in medieval universities under the scholastics, who were academics and almost never pastors. Theology began to withdraw from pulpits and the liturgy into the classroom and study' (Kavanagh 1984, p. 18). His other concerns are objectivity, and the theological curriculum. The last is pertinent here.

> In most schools of theology, the curriculum assigns highest priority to the studies of Bible and systematic theology about equally, perhaps with an edge given to biblical exegesis. History gets shorter shrift; cultural concerns such as anthropology and the arts, when they are taught at all, are most often electives; and the various pastoral crafts . . . remain at a distance from biblical and theological disciplines and tend to follow recent methodologies worked out in clinic and classroom. (Ibid., pp. 19–20).

As he sets out the case for the inseparable relationship of liturgy and theology, he turns to an earlier statement made by Massey Shepherd in 1978:

> If we believe that worship is the experiential foundation for theological reflection, that the practice of worship is the source of rubrical and canonical legislation, and that the ministry of clergy and laity is exhibited most clearly in liturgical assemblies, then it is incumbent on our Academy [i.e. the North American Academy of Liturgy] to work for this recognition. It is the unfortunate way of our Western tradition to compartmentalize particular concerns in separate consultations and commissions that need to be coordinated. (Shepherd 1978, pp. 312–13, quoted by Kavanagh 1984, pp. 78–9).

More than 30 years on, the nature of religious studies has diversified and changed in emphasis, certainly in Britain. Biblical studies – indeed Christian studies in general – are rarely pre-eminent, though better informed by hermeneutics; anthropology and sociology of religion often have higher profiles.

Like liturgical studies, musicology is rooted in German-language scholarship of the later nineteenth century, and was stimulated in the English language by émigré scholars in the 1930s and 1940s. In Britain it began to blossom only after the 1939–45 war; but the emphasis was placed on critical editing – especially of British music – a trend marked by the establishment of the scholarly series *Musica Britannica*. However, in the later twentieth century, English-language musicology has proliferated. The parameters of research in music as a whole have also expanded. Musical composition, for which the earliest English music degrees had been awarded, became recognized as a valid research activity by at least the 1960s; performance only attained that status in the later 1990s in Britain, in a process shaped by the government-driven periodic assessment and evaluation of research activity. Not only did this redefine the place of the music conservatoires by enlarging the scope of the academy, it also raised the research profile of those university musicians engaged in performance in choral foundations: broadcasts, recordings and concerts of new or rare music, often informed by research into performance practice, rightly gained some of these music directors a place in the top echelons of research through performance.

Among the new fields of music research is critical musicology, which established itself rapidly as part of 'the new musicology' in the last two decades of the twentieth century. It had an unexpected outcome in a particular approach to research into theology and music in the work of Jeremy Begbie. Within a larger movement of exploring theology through the arts, based initially at Cambridge and then at St Andrews, Begbie's writings on theology and music have been strongly influenced by the progress of research in critical musicology.

This change can be observed, for instance, by comparing the key texts from critical musicology he draws on from his earlier writings (e.g. Begbie 1989, 1991) up until his major study, *Theology, Music and Time* (2000). The importance of Begbie's stimulation of the dialogue between theology and the arts in general, and with music in particular, should not be underestimated. However, he is inclined to steer his subject matter and his discussion away from music in worship.[1] In a student-directed, introductory book, *Resounding Truth* (2007), he makes this absolutely plain: 'to limit the theology-music dialogue to a discussion of music in worship' is one of a series of pitfalls. He continues,

> although the rejuvenation of worship music is certainly an urgent priority for the church, I am increasingly convinced that many of the dilemmas and difficulties currently plaguing music in worship will begin to be alleviated only when we stand back a little and address broader issues about what kind of medium we are dealing with, how it functions in different settings, and how it links up with God's wider intentions for the world. (2007, pp. 23–4).

Begbie's approach to the discussion of music and theology, using critical musicology as an important resource in his work, ensures that music is treated as music, and that its theological import is drawn from the musical content and its sound in performance. Much of his material is taken from the instrumental and orchestral repertory, drawing a clear line between his work and the theology that relates to the musical setting of sacred text. His writing is a valuable foil to a range of publications intended as practical guides to the use of music in worship. Many of these have appeared in the wake of the liturgical changes effected in the later decades of the twentieth century. The most influential have been intended for music in the Roman Catholic liturgy; however, some of these have been based on selective reading and interpretation of the official documents on liturgy and sacred music emanating from the Second Vatican Council. The driving theological force behind much of the writing about music in worship has been practical, pastoral theology. It has tended, often over simply, to treat music as functional commodity, as vehicle for the building of community, as handmaid of the text. The starting point has usually been the parish community gathered for worship. The principal agendum has been the building of assembly, often informed by the need for mission and in some cases evangelization.

In addressing pastoral priorities and engaging the assembly in active participation, there has been an uneasy process of attempting to reconcile the inherited culture of the Church with the contemporary culture of God's people gathered for worship. In the case of the Roman Catholic Church, moving with unanticipated speed and decisiveness in the 1960s from Latin to the vernacular, this has often led to the total abandonment of the inherited musical culture of the Church, in part because it set what had become a redundant language, but also because it was so remote from the contemporary cultural experience of the people. This has been a cause of considerable unease for Joseph Ratzinger, now Pope Benedict XVI. A man steeped in Western culture, including music, and the brother of a one-time director of music at Regensburg Cathedral with its fine choral tradition, he has been troubled by the cultural gulfs effected unintentionally by the liturgical changes that flowed from Vatican II, in whose preparation he participated. He has expressed himself on matters of music at some length (e.g. Ratzinger 1986, 1996 and 2000). In fact, though the new vernacular liturgy hastened the process of abandonment, the nineteenth-century revival and promulgation of both Gregorian chant and Renaissance polyphony had lost much of its momentum well before Vatican II, just as the Anglican choral revival of the same period was weakened in part by new pastoral emphasis but also by changes in social patterns which affected regular church attendance and by new musical opportunities offered to both teachers and pupils through the promulgation of instrumental tuition and orchestral playing.

In an article reflecting on the burgeoning of liturgical study in the twentieth century, Robert Taft noted: 'Serious, scientific, university-level liturgical studies, for all practical purposes a non-existent academic field . . . seventy-five years ago, has burgeoned into a scholarly discipline of enormous breadth, with a huge number of practitioners' (2001, p. 46). Some of the best of that scholarship has been historical, including that of Robert Taft himself. However, if those interested in the discourse between theology and music have steered clear of liturgy and liturgical music for the most part, liturgical scholars have focused most of their attention on the early Christian centuries and the present time. At least in western Europe the great majority of the extant culture of the Church dates from the eighth to the eighteenth century; nineteenth-century Britain drew much of its inspiration from the high and late Middle Ages. Few current liturgical scholars have an interest in high or late medieval liturgy, and therefore those scholars of architecture, art and music who wish to understand this cultural inheritance are rarely adequately equipped to engage with either the liturgy or the theology of the time. Furthermore, there has so far been little attempt to engage in the study of the practice and experience of worship either in our own time or through practical, historically informed investigation. There have been historical re-enactments of past liturgies, sometimes in the space for which they were originally devised, but in general the re-enactment is the end of the process, rather than an intermediate stage that leads to reflection on the experience per se, and to theological reflection. The resources to undertake this work are available in British choral foundations. Indeed, research in this field might assist these choral foundations better to understand their purpose, meaning and potential, both within a historical context and in their regular patterns of worship.

One current research project is endeavouring to address some of these matters, and may serve as a pilot for future investigation. *The Experience of Worship in Late Medieval Cathedral and Parish Church* is a three-year project (2009–12) within the larger *Religion and Society* research programme jointly funded by the Arts and Humanities and the Economic and Social Research Councils.[2] The project is based at Bangor University, but the practice-led research is being conducted at Salisbury Cathedral and at the small medieval parish church of St Teilo now relocated in St Fagans: National History Museum Wales, outside Cardiff. The investigation includes the enactment of a small group of liturgies following the order and ritual customs of Salisbury Cathedral as they may have been celebrated in the first half of the sixteenth century. Such research raises a host of practical and interpretative questions, and invites the engagement of a whole raft of disciplines and methodologies from musicology, theology, history, anthropology, sociology, performance and cultural studies, and a number of their respective sub-disciplines. Here, I simply want to address some of the issues in relation to music that have been raised at Salisbury Cathedral, working with the cathedral clergy, servers, choir and musicians and engaging with some members of the cathedral congregation. Although these enacted liturgies are exceptional in their language, form, musical repertory and idiom, ritual, theology and spirituality by comparison with the regular daily round, they have raised questions and revealed issues that relate directly to contemporary worship in the cathedral. The exceptional nature of these liturgies, and their distance from regular practice, have sharpened awareness of these matters and enabled discussion and discernment that might have been less clear in observations of the normal pattern of services.

The Latin liturgies conducted at Salisbury Cathedral consist of two contrasting Masses, a festal procession and (from a separate initiative in 2008) Vespers, Compline and the Antiphon of the Blessed Virgin Mary. All of the liturgy that is heard is sung throughout,[3] and there are therefore only two basic states of aural experience – music and silence: the spoken word has no place in the liturgy. The experience of the aural is inseparable from the spatial. The spatial experience is both physical and aural, dependent on the nature of the space and the configuration of the people within it; on where the singing takes place, who sings (a single voice, a small group, or the whole choral body) and where it is heard.[4] In the Middle Ages, when the whole cathedral clerical community from boys to dean would sing in quire, there was additionally the contrast between the voicing of music as singer, and the reception of the music as listener, according to one's allocated duties on a particular day.[5] There are distinctions between chants sung by the whole choral body, chants sung in dialogue between those on one side of the quire and those on the other (e.g. psalms and canticles), chants sung in dialogue between an officiant and the choral body (e.g. the liturgical greeting) and those sung by one or more soloists.

These experiences of sound and silence have a theological dimension in the way an individual and a gathered body encounters a sacred text. The spatial dimension can take on added theological significance in relation to posture. There is an obvious distinction between what is sung or heard when standing, sitting or kneeling; but the direction in which either ministers or the choral body are required to face is even stronger in its theological implications. Medieval cathedral and monastic quires and college chapels consist of a single, relatively long rectangular space set east to west, with two banks of stalls (generally in two or three rows) facing one another on the longer north and south sides, with a central aisle and an eastern altar. The natural configuration of the gathered body is in two groups facing one another, emphasizing the dialogue between the two sides in the singing of psalms and canticles which dominated the eight services of the medieval daily Office. Such a configuration tends towards visual engagement with the group on the opposite side, not with the altar at the east. However, the medieval customs required that prayer and praise to God was directed eastwards. When the officiant sang 'Oremus' (Let us pray), all turned east and faced the altar; at the end of each of the 150 Jewish psalms sung on a weekly cycle, all turned east to sing the Christian doxology Gloria Patri (Glory be to the Father); so too in specific phrases of praise and adoration in the 'Gloria in excelsis Deo' (Glory to God in the highest) and the Nicene Creed at the Mass; and from the Sanctus to the end of the Mass all faced east, either kneeling on ordinary days or standing on festal days.[6] At the Mass the celebrating priest normally faced the altar, away from the gathered body; therefore, the few occasions when he turned to sing towards the people for the liturgical greeting 'Dominus vobiscum' – The Lord be with you) and the greeting of peace had aural as well as visual impact. These aural encounters are inseparable from theological understanding of the encounter with and address to the divine.

The manner in which a sung text is articulated inevitably has theological bearing. In the Middle Ages, on a specific feast day, or in a specific liturgical season, the same text might be articulated in a number of different ways: sung on a monotone with simple inflection in the dialogue of a versicle and response; as a verse within a regularly recited psalm sung to a repeated formula by one side of the gathered body to the other; as an antiphon to a psalm or canticle sung by all to a relatively simple melody; or set to an elaborate, melismatic melody in the Proper of the Mass or a responsory at Matins, with certain sections allocated to soloists. In each case, the relationship of text and musical treatment, as well as the singers, has theological implications for its significance and meaning. The provision of polyphony for certain sung items of the liturgy takes this one stage further. Not only is the liturgical or Scriptural text now clothed with harmonic, contrapuntal, rhythmic and textural richness, it is most often allocated to a specific body of specialist singers, in some places (e.g. monastic Lady Chapels) separately constituted and additional to the main choral body gathered for regular worship.

It is this situation that most often represents cathedral or collegiate worship today. Most of the music is allocated to and undertaken by a specialist group, often singing at very high standards. Many of those present at worship – including the gathered body of cathedral clergy or college members as well as any others within the gathered congregation – would never aspire to such musical excellence. The implicit divide between the musically gifted, to whom most of the sung liturgy is delegated, and the rest raises significant challenges about the nature of public worship (and especially worship of the gathered community), its pastoral nature and its consequent theology. These are challenges which are germane in the choral foundations within the Church of England, and have not been adequately addressed or resolved.

The new alternative liturgical orders that appeared in the Church of England from the mid-1960s onwards were principally drafted and shaped for parish worship, as was also the case in the Roman Catholic Church. However, unlike the documents of Vatican II, there has been no official guidance from the Church of England to support these new orders. Nevertheless, there has been increasing awareness of the pastoral needs that these new orders addressed, and the pastoral opportunities they afford. There is a body of literature related to these issues, but most has been intended for parish use, and has less direct bearing on choral worship.[7]

In the new liturgical climate, cathedrals and colleges with choral foundations have by stages turned to the new orders of the Eucharist, though some opt for traditional rather than contemporary language. By contrast, the form of Evensong in choral foundations is almost invariably based on the form and language of the 1662 Book of Common Prayer: scarcely any institutions have explored the opportunities offered by the new orders of the Office services in public choral services, though they are often the norm at said Morning or Evening Prayer.[8] At the sung Eucharist, there has been pragmatic resolution of the tensions between the musical (or rather the choral) and the pastoral, and in a number of instances a nave altar and nave choir stalls have been introduced. The modern form of the Eucharist is focused on the assembly gathered around the altar with a priest as president: this assembly is expressed spatially and theologically. It is a liturgy whose structure and language are readily grasped, which flows from one text or action to another. However, at a choral Eucharist, the choir may sing a Latin setting of the Ordinary of the Mass composed in the sixteenth, seventeenth or eighteenth century. The language, style and scale of the music can appear to run counter to the spirit of the rest of the liturgy; the singing of an extended Sanctus and Benedictus in particular can bring the flow of the Eucharistic Prayer to a standstill. In other words, notwithstanding the extensive theological thinking about the nature of worship, the liturgy and the people of God, choral foundations have either opted for the status quo of the Book of Common Prayer at Evensong or for an uneasy compromise in the new order of the Eucharist.

Robert Taft observes that '[l]iturgy, like music, is shared by performers and theorists'. He goes on to state his opposition 'to overdoing the distinction between the "pastoral" and the "historical" or "theoretic" dimensions of any theological discipline, and especially of liturgy' since 'origins, meaning, practice go hand in hand' (2001, pp. 55–6). Such integration can be hard to achieve. We have already observed the absence of connection between practice and scholarship in relation to the practice and study of liturgy and music in university choral foundations and those cathedrals with university connections. The low priority given to liturgy and music in most institutions and courses engaged in the training of clergy and leaders of worship in Britain is notable, as is the absence of education and formation in liturgy and theology for those who are or intend to be engaged in liturgical music. University departments of theology or religious studies appear to have little interest in liturgical studies, and some of the best British liturgists or writers on theology and worship are engaged by American universities (e.g. Jonathan Begbie and Geoffrey Wainwright at Duke, Paul Bradshaw at Notre Dame). There is little common ground between clergy and musicians, or between theologians and musicologists. There is no tradition of dialogue, and no established training or formation to provide the basis for such inter-disciplinary investigation. However, both the situation and the resources are uniquely present in Britain. Over half of the Anglican cathedrals share a city with at least one university, yet two attempts in the past decade to establish a chair in sacred music linking cathedral and university got no further than conversations. Even more pertinently, there are the long-established statutory choral foundations of five colleges in Oxford and Cambridge, together with the new tradition of mixed choirs of high standing in at least another ten colleges. Within a single institution there is both the scholarship and the musical resource, and above all the regular pattern of choral liturgy in the chapel, to take such an investigation forward.

Choral foundations represent a remarkably small part in the larger context of the Church, its mission and its worship. Yet, in the West at least, they offer a particular opportunity to address the question of our response to the inheritance of Christian traditions, culture, art, buildings and music from previous centuries. At a choral service in an Anglican cathedral or college chapel, one most often encounters a space built in the Middle Ages or configured in a medieval manner;

a form of service whose texts are drawn from Scripture written down by the second century CE at the latest, translated in the sixteenth century (or in some cases later); prayers ranging from the early and translated to the extempore; versicles and responses codified in the first millennium but polyphonically clothed in the festal manner of the late medieval and early modern; psalms in a form of chanting established in the first millennium, but with harmonized chants whose origins also derive from late medieval and early modern practice; canticles and anthem whose stylistic idiom is closely related to the art music of the time of their composition – generally between the sixteenth century and the present day. That this is a contemporary event is indubitable: liturgy and music only exist when they are enacted or performed – and they can only exist in the present. However, such a liturgy also embodies at least two millennia of Christian (and to an extent Jewish) culture and religion; its connection is not only with the historical time of Jesus but with the continuity of Christian practice and witness thereafter. The theology of that continuity as well as the theologies embodied in the form and presentation of text and music today deserve our attention.

There are questions to be asked about the aesthetic status of music within the context of liturgy, not least because of the tension that can exist between function and art, especially since the artwork (as self-contained and self-expressing) can appear to be at odds with its use in worship. Recent research in theology and the arts has enhanced engagement and understanding of these issues; but, as we have already observed, consideration of liturgical music has received less attention. There is a gulf, therefore, between practical advice about the function, choice and use of music in worship, and the emotive responses that choral services can sometimes evoke, positively and negatively, both in relation to specific liturgies or repertory, or in general. It is a gulf that serious theological engagement can help to bridge.

There are historical precedents. The monastic pattern and the medieval cathedral pattern placed scholarship alongside sung liturgy. The remarkable library built up in the early decades by the early generations of cathedral canons at Old Sarum, still largely extant in the library of the later cathedral at Salisbury, is testament to serious and up-to-date theological study (Webber 1992). The same body of canons shaped the liturgical pattern at Salisbury in the twelfth century, a pattern that was adopted by thousands of churches in substantial parts of the British Isles (and selectively, further afield); its chant, texts and ritual customs were widely circulated. The complexity of the late medieval cathedral meant that much of the day-to-day conduct of the liturgy and its music were devolved from the canons to vicars choral, and a division between scholarship and practice was inevitable. In the new university colleges that burgeoned from the fourteenth century onwards, the division between the academy and the liturgy was formalized in the foundation statutes, as we observed early in this essay.

As someone who has directed the music of both a Roman Catholic Cathedral and a collegiate choral foundation, has taught in universities, has worked both with religious communities and with the Church of England Liturgical Commission in preparing music for the liturgy and who has endeavoured to help parish clergy and musicians to gain better understanding through the work of the Royal School of Church Music and the International Centre for Sacred Music Studies at Bangor University, I have some experience of identifying and facing the challenges. I also recognize my inadequacies to address them: one person cannot embrace the range of academic disciplines and methodologies – let alone the theology – that can be purposefully engaged in such an endeavour. Any ongoing investigation has to be collaborative. I am, however, convinced by our initial findings in *The Experience of Worship* project that such investigation can be purposefully taken forward through the process of practice-led research, and that observations of the enactment of past liturgy can inform such enquiries.

As we have observed, medieval liturgy in cathedrals and collegiate foundations was primarily sung; and that singing engaged the whole gathered body of the community. Modern worship in cathedrals and collegiate foundations makes sharper distinctions between the sung and the spoken; what is sung does not involve the whole gathered body – indeed at the Eucharist the gathered body may be excluded from song that liturgical teaching would regard as belonging to whole assembly: the Gloria in excelsis, the Sanctus and Benedictus above all, and the Agnus Dei. Such song as is open for all to join in is often not strictly liturgical (e.g. hymnody). Similarly, at Evensong, the people's response to Scripture in the canticles, Magnificat and Nunc dimittis, is delegated to the choir, as is their response to much of the prayer. At some places and on some occasions a liturgically placed hymn for the Office may be sung, but more often hymnody is appended, before or after the Office.

Whatever theological reflection may assist in tackling these challenges, there may be other reflections which can contribute. While modern liturgy may not be sung throughout, as in medieval times, it does not prevent us from reflecting on the whole of a liturgy as a musical experience. The avant-garde composers of the post-1945 generation, especially Karlheinz Stockhausen and John Cage, extended the parameters of music per se, and music and the numinous. Above all, Cage's *4′ 33″* forced us to consider a much wider definition of music as the shaping of sound and silence within time and space. The whole of a liturgy can be considered as shaped sound and silence within time and space, and many of the other parameters found in music – including structure, texture, rhythm and dynamic – are part of that shaping.[9] Additional parameters of movement and gesture may contribute, as well as sensory and emotional stimuli.[10] It is not just a matter of the style and presentation of the liturgy, but of its theological import.

> The liturgy, the dwelling place of present and remembered encounter with the living God, itself begins to think and speak for the assembly and turns wholly into music, not in the sense of outward, audible sounds, but by virtue of the power and momentum of the inward flow. Then, like the current of a mighty river polishing stones and turning wheels by the very movement, the flow of liturgical worship creates in passing, and by the force of its own laws, cadences and rhythm and countless other forms and formations still more important and until now undiscovered, unconsidered, and unnamed. (Kavanagh 1984, pp. 87–8)

The experience of medieval Mass in Salisbury Cathedral in the twenty-first century meant that there was coherence of ritual, chant and space – for what was enacted and sung was contemporaneous with the visual, physical and cultural identity of the space (notwithstanding later alterations and additions). It displayed musical qualities of polyphony in their interaction, and of harmony in their cohesion. There is a far greater ritual, musical and cultural range in a modern choral liturgy in such a building. Each has not only its own style and identity, but also its own underlying theology. A work written or made in any specific century or context needs to be understood on its own merits if it is also to be located in the broader context of a culturally more diverse and stylistically more eclectic choral liturgy. For instance, Boyce's choice and treatment of the text from Job 28, 'O where shall wisdom be found' (published in 1769) may need to be read within the context of the eighteenth-century challenges of Science and Reason; S. S. Wesley's setting of 'The wilderness and the solitary place' Isaiah 35, may helpfully be placed in the context of the early-nineteenth-century response to Nature. Musical styles and identity will remain distinct, and contrasts and juxtapositions can prove very revealing; but by becoming aware of theological emphases and distinctions we may be in a position to identify an underpinning core which can resolve and bring into harmony what appears on the surface to be irreconcilable, and to achieve a far more profound liturgical coherence.

While there may be understanding and intellectual resolution that enable those planning and leading choral liturgies to recognize the coherence, there remains the question of engagement and participation of all present. Somewhat contrarily, it may be the parish experience of medieval worship that may prove helpful here. The laity in the nave of a medieval parish church neither expected to participate in the liturgical action hidden away in chancel and sanctuary, nor to understand (nor necessarily hear) the texts that were recited. Yet this was an age of strong lay prayer and devotion. As we discovered in our celebration of the same group of medieval liturgies in the tiny parish church of St Teilo, this form of liturgy did provide a framework for the devotion of those gathered; it also enabled each individual to engage at their own level, either directly with the liturgy (particularly those who were educated and literate) or within its ambience, using a far greater range of visual and aural stimulus that was not text-dependent. Our post-Reformation expectation of a single sequence of text and event engaging all present whatever their spiritual maturity leaves less freedom for the individual within the larger gathered assembly. The current popularity and growth of attendance at choral worship may perhaps reflect a search for a more flexible engagement with worship. There may be an opportunity to develop a more flexible liturgical theology that takes account of this, and theological materials to support individual engagement within the context of the assembly, and to offer means of engagement in worship that can be free of text.

These initial reflections suggest that there is an opportunity to take the tradition and resources of the choral foundations, and to explore through practice the complex relationship of liturgy, music and theology in relation to the architectural space and its liturgical configuration, and the cultural complexity that is engendered by the combination of texts, music, ritual, ritual objects, sacred art and architecture that may be part of the rich experience of choral worship. As multi-disciplinary research expands, such practice-led investigation may reap rich rewards well beyond present expectation.

Notes

1 Music and Worship represented one of the strands in the Music and Theology Colloquium chaired by Jeremy Begbie in 2002, and five essays on this theme have now been published (Begbie and Guthrie 2011).

2 Further details of the project and its outcomes can be found at www.experienceof-worship.org.uk.

3 Significant portions of the Mass are recited *privatim* by the priest, and cannot even be heard by the other ministers standing or kneeling behind him.

4 From a significantly different standpoint, Deborah Howard and Laura Moretti, working with the choir of St John's College, Cambridge, investigated the relationship of sound and space in Renaissance churches in Venice (Howard and Moretti 2009).

5 The ritual requirements at Salisbury Cathedral are set out in the Old and New Customaries. These are available in Latin in Frere (1898), and also in new transcriptions with translations prepared as part of *The Experience of Worship* research project, at www.sarumcustomary.org.uk.

6 The need to turn east goes someway to explain the use of misericords whose lifting seats did not simply provide a resting point during the recitation of long passages of psalmody but freed space to stand or kneel when facing eastwards. Indeed, the raised position of a misericord must have the norm, since there were so few occasions when one sat in the liturgy – e.g. only during the readings at Matins, and during the Epistle, Gradual and Alleluia at Mass.

7   A listing here would be long and largely irrelevant, but one notable, thoughtful example is Deiss 1996, intended for the Roman Catholic liturgy.

8   In 1982, Magdalen College, Oxford, introduced an alternative form of Evening Prayer on weekdays with a single canticle. This drew heavily on the evidence presented in Paul Bradshaw's study of *Daily Prayer in the Early Church*. It addressed pastoral issues in its placing of the intercessions after the canticle; widened the repertory of music to include chant, medieval polyphony and Continental Latin canticle settings – much of it coincidentally relevant to the academic music history syllabus; and served to distinguish ordinary days from Sundays (which represented the weekly liturgical highpoint in an institution that was not resident to celebrate the seasonal highpoints of Christmas, Holy Week and Easter). A revised form of this service is still used occasionally. Other choral foundations on occasion use the form of Evening Prayer found in Common Worship, particularly on days when either boy or girl choristers sing without the adults.

9   These thoughts are based on my own teaching and writing over the past 15 years or more, but some of the same issues are addressed in Kathleen Harmon's study of a theology of liturgical music (Harmon 2008).

10   In our modern consideration of the shaping of sound and silence and its impact on the listener, particular consideration may need to be given to the amplification or reinforcement of the spoken voice, its relationship to the space and liturgy as a whole and to what is sung: the spoken intimacy and informality made possible through amplification in a large, formal building may be at odds with the space and the choral music.

Bibliography

Begbie, J. S. (1989), *Music in God's Purposes* (Edinburgh: Handsel Press).

Begbie, J. S. (1991), *Voicing Creation's Praise: Towards a Theology of the Arts* (Edinburgh: T. & T. Clark).

Begbie, J. S. (2000), *Theology, Music and Time* (Cambridge: Cambridge University Press).

Begbie, J. S. (2007), *Resounding Truth* (Grand Rapids: Baker Academic, and London: SPCK).

Begbie, J. S. and Guthrie, S. R. (eds) (2011), *Resonant Witness: Conversations between Music and Theology* (Grand Rapids and Cambridge: William B. Eerdmans).

Bower, C. M. (2002), 'The Transmission of Ancient Music Theory into the Middle Ages', in T. Christensen (ed.), *The Cambridge History of Western Music Theory* (Cambridge: Cambridge University Press), pp. 136–67.

Bowers, R. (1999), *English Church Polyphony: Singers and Sources from the 14th to the 17th Century* (Aldershot: Ashgate).

Bowers, R. (2001), 'Abyndon, Henry', in S. Sadie (ed.), *The New Grove Dictionary of Music and Musicians*, Vol. 1 (London: Macmillan), p. 40.

Bradshaw, P. (1981), *Daily Prayer in the Early Church* (London: Alcuin Club/SPCK).

Caldwell, J. (1986), 'Music in the Faculty of Arts', in J. McConica, *The History of the University of Oxford*, Vol. 3 (Oxford: Clarendon Press), pp. 201–12.

Deiss, L. (1996), *Visions of Liturgy and Music for a New Century* (Collegeville: Liturgical Press).

Frere, W. H. (1898), *The Use of Sarum: I. The Sarum Customs* (Cambridge: Cambridge University Press).

Harmon, K. (2008), *The Mystery We Celebrate, the Song We Sing: A Theology of Liturgical Music* (Collegeville: Pueblo/Liturgical Press).

Harriss, G. (2008), 'William Waynflete and the Foundation of the College, 1448–1486', in L. W. B. Brockliss (ed.), *Magdalen College: A History* (Oxford: Magdalen College), pp. 1–43.

Howard, D. and Moretti, L. (2009), *Sound Space in Renaissance Venice* (New Haven and London: Yale University Press).

Kavanagh, A. (1984), *On Liturgical Theology* (Collegeville, MN: Pueblo/Liturgical Press).

Ratzinger, J. (1986), 'On the Theological Basis of Church Music', in *Feast of Faith: Approaches to a Theology of the Liturgy* (San Francisco: Ignatius Press), pp. 97–126.

Ratzinger, J. (1996), *A New Song for the Lord: Faith in Christ and Liturgy Today* (New York: The Crossroad Publishing Company).

Ratzinger, J. (2000), 'Music and Liturgy', in *The Spirit of the Liturgy* (San Francisco: Ignatius Press), pp. 136–56.

Schmemann, A. (1963), 'Theology and Liturgical Tradition', in M. H. Shepherd (ed.), *Worship in Scripture and Tradition* (Oxford: Oxford University Press), pp. 165–78.

Shepherd, M. H. (1978), 'The Berakah Award: Response', *Worship*, 52: pp. 299–313.

Taft, R. (2001), 'A Generation of Liturgy in the Academy', *Worship*, 75: pp. 46–58.

Webber, T. (1992), *Scribes and Scholars at Salisbury Cathedral c. 1075–c. 1125* (Oxford: Clarendon Press).

INDEX